REPRODUCING ANTIQUE FURNITURE

Chippendale Partner's Desk. PROPERTY OF MERLE M. MILLER, M.D., GERMANTOWN, PENNSYLVANIA.

REPRODUCING ANTIQUE FURNITURE

Franklin H. Gottshall

Crown Publishers, Inc. NEW YORK

© 1971 by Franklin H. Gottshall

Library of Congress Catalog Number: 76–147339

Printed in the United States of America
Published simultaneously in Canada by General Publishing Company Limited

This book is affectionately dedicated to my wife, Agnes

Contents

Acknowledgments

THE author wishes to express thanks to the following for material help in the preparation of this book.

To his son Bruce H. Gottshall who has done the greater part of the photographic work in this book.

To Mr. Robert Treate Hogg, cabinetmaker of Oxford, Pennsylvania, for permission to take measurements, make working drawings, and take photographs of many of the fine reproductions built in his workshop. Mr. Hogg also has been most generous in giving of his time and technical advice in the preparation of this book, for which the author is extremely grateful.

To Mr. William Ball of Ball and Ball, reproducers of antique hardware for fine period furniture, for permission to photograph and reproduce much of the hardware shown on the plates in the chapter on hardware.

To The Modern Technical Tools and Supply Co., 211 Nevada Street, Hicksville, New York, for information regarding their clock movements and supplies.

To Mason and Sullivan of 39 Blossom Avenue, Osterville, Massachusetts, for information regarding clock movements and supplies.

To McKinney Manufacturing Company, Scranton, Pennsylvania, for permission to photograph wrought-iron hardware manufactured by them and shown on Plate 2 in the chapter on hardware.

To Mr. Lewis Hamrick for help in getting photographs of chairs made by the author's students at Berry College.

To Berry College, Mt. Berry, Georgia, for permission to photograph furniture built in classes conducted by the author and to use them in the preparation of this book.

To Mr. Richard L. Malmberg, proprietor of Malmberg Antique Shop, Boyertown, Pennsylvania, for permission to photograph the Queen Anne highboy, and the grandfather clock in his collection and to make drawings of these for this book.

To Mr. John Renninger of Renninger Studios, Boyertown, Pennsylvania, for photographing the Queen Anne highboy.

To Mr. Daniel Bush, upholsterer, of Boyertown, Pennsylvania, whose help and advice in working up and checking data for upholstered furniture in the book is greatly appreciated.

Foreword

"ANTIQUES" has come to be a magic word. One trouble with terms of this kind, originally coined to designate a very definite thing, product, or condition, is that with the passing of time it degenerates into misuse, or is abused to the extent that its original connotation is no longer valid. So it is with the term "antiques," which today is greatly maligned to include all manner of junk in hope that the prestige attached to the term will make it salable.

While age does make antiques of items originally in common use, but now often outmoded, many more things besides the age of an item must be considered before one can make a decision as to its worthiness. Good design, suitability for the purpose for which it was originally intended, rarity and scarcity of an item, have a lot to do with the value ascribed to it. Sentimental and nostalgic considerations, and demand, also play a big part in determining the value placed upon items that have come down to us from the past.

There is in most people, we think, a desire to possess things upon which a high monetary value has been placed, and this is quite apt to be especially true if ownership tends to enhance prestige. The fact that the item is in scarce supply seems to augment rather than deter the desire to possess it, and this is especially applicable to the avid collector with wealth, or those who are in a position to supply his wants. Since there is no way of increasing the supply of the genuine article except

by fakery, it is not surprising that good antiques whose origin it is possible to authenticate have increased in value by leaps and bounds in recent years, and all the more so because they have proved to be good investments in a time of great affluence. The chances are they will continue to increase in value for some time to come, for as one connoisseur has aptly put it, "The number of such items will never grow larger."

Anyone who can afford to collect good antiques may deem himself lucky. Good antiques may still be bought and are constantly changing hands, but more and more are finding permanent homes in museums and great private collections where they are apt to remain for long periods of time. Even the wealthiest collector of antiques and fine old furniture is limited by what is available, with all its defects and shortcomings as well as its sterling qualities being part of the package.

Relative to this aspect of antique collecting we think it important to point out that the one who "reproduces" or "designs" has an advantage over one who collects antiques, for in doing this he is afforded the opportunity of improving on the original model, providing he has the capability. Those who insist upon strict adherence to every detail of the original model from which a design is copied are denied this opportunity, but for those of us who have the conviction that improvements can and should be made if we have the proper training and ability to do so, this is a very big dividend to be used to advantage. The author has upon many occasions availed himself of this opportunity, though he freely admits having been criticized for doing so. Being a designer whose work in the field has won him a degree of recognition, and taking into consideration some of the ludicrous results of work foisted upon the public by present-day designers of furniture with less talent than they are given credit for, he makes no excuses for the shortcomings of which he has been accused. If justification is forthcoming it will come with the passage of time. If not, he will at least have had the satisfaction of trying.

The title of this book suggests that genuine antiques are represented here, but in all fairness to those for whom the book has been written, and by this we mean those who plan to build one or more of the pieces shown therein, it should be said that many if not most of the designs and drawings shown deviate in some respects from the original pieces of furniture from which the pieces shown, or drawings of them, were made.

In closing this introduction, the author freely acknowledges that the good things he hopes to pass on to his readers, he has received through the years from his peers, while the mistakes and shortcomings, of which there must be some, are his own.

Franklin H. Gottshall

Boyertown, Pennsylvania

REPRODUCING ANTIQUE FURNITURE

ONE

Some Useful Fundamentals of Cabinet Making

WOOD, being the prime material with which the cabinetmaker should concern himself, we feel that anyone using this book needs to know a great deal, not only about characteristics of this most versatile raw material, but about methods of choosing the proper kind for the use to which it is to be put, shaping it, and getting it ready to use in whatever worthwhile project he may decide on. Much ought to be known about how to prepare various pieces in order to have them ready to assemble, and the best ways of putting them together once this preliminary work has been done. Therefore this chapter will explain a few principles of woodworking to help those whose knowledge of such principles may be limited or nonexistent.

CUTTING STOCK TO SIZE AND SQUARING IT

It has been the author's experience that the essential first step in teaching woodwork to beginners is to teach them how to cut, square, and plane lumber to predetermined sizes, using hand tools only. Insistence at the beginning on the use of hand tools only is important because if handwork in wood is properly mastered by beginners, they will have relatively little difficulty in mastering the essentials of working with laborsaving electric-powered machinery later on. It is not necessary to use large pieces of wood to practice these essential operations. Small pieces of wood have some advantages over larger pieces in the beginning, such as greater ease of manipulation, less surface to cover, and consequently less effort required to accomplish the ends sought.

Start with a piece of yellow poplar, mahogany, red gum, or some other wood similar to these in texture, which is neither too soft nor too hard. Generally speaking, soft-textured cabinet woods, like the ones we have mentioned, require sharp tools to work them, but are not so hard or tough that they will make the job needlessly difficult for the beginner. Practice blocks should be free of knots. While learning to deal with knots is something every beginner will have to cope with later, forcing him to deal with this additional handicap at this time would only slow the learning process and might impede progress rather than help it.

Choose a piece of unplaned stock measuring roughly 1 inch thick, 3½ inches wide, and 7½ inches long. As a first step number the sides, using an ordinary lead pencil. The better wide side or face is #1; the better edge is #2; the better end is #3. The opposite side of 3 is 4; the opposite of 2 is 5; the opposite of 1 is 6. Note: the sum of opposite pairs of sides always equals seven. (See Fig. 1.)

Before starting work on the block, be sure the plane is sharp and properly set. The best plane to

FIG. 1

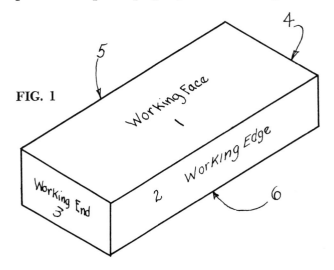

Fig. 2. *Grinding the plane blade. Note carefully how the blade is held.*

Fig. 3. *Whetting the plane blade. Note the angle of the blade resting with bevel flat upon oilstone. Whet blade with a circular motion covering entire stone to keep stone as flat as possible.*

use for the purpose in hand is a jack plane. To sharpen a plane or chisel proceed as follows: grind the plane iron by holding the blade as shown in Fig. 2, with the bevel on a grindstone or emery wheel. The bevel should be considerably wider than the thickness of the blade, straight, and at right angles to the side of the blade. Move the blade sideways, back and forth over the stone, until a smooth, slightly concave bevel has been formed. Keep from burning the cutting edge by dipping the blade into water frequently or by using light pressure when holding it on the stone.

After a plane blade has been ground to shape on an emery wheel or grindstone, it must be whetted to make it sharp. To do this, hold it as shown in Fig. 3, with the bevel flat on the oilstone. Use machine oil thinned with kerosene on the oilstone as a lubricant and to keep the surface of the stone from glazing. Whet the plane iron by moving it over the entire surface of the oilstone with a

circular motion. Exert considerable downward pressure on the blade while whetting. Remove the wire edge formed by whetting by reversing the blade and laying it flat on the stone with the bevel on top and then moving it back and forth over the stone several times. Repeat these processes as often as necessary until the wire edge has been entirely eliminated and the edge is keen and sharp.

Decide the direction to plane by determining which way the grain of the wood runs. Grain lines on the edge of a board are in most cases clearly enough defined to show which way the grain runs on top or bottom, though this is not true in every case. If they are, plane side #1 in the direction the grain lines on the edge of the block go uphill. (Figs. 4 and 5.) If the grain lines are not clearly defined, then try planing in both directions to find

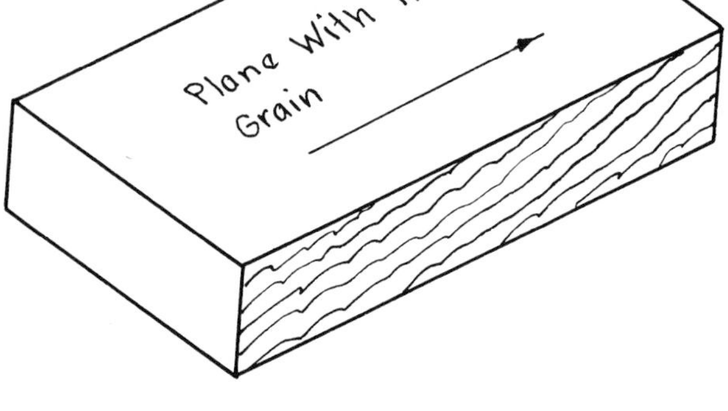

Fig. 3A. *Correct method of laying plane on bench when not in use.*

FIG. 4

Plane With The Grain

Fig. 5. Unless the stock is badly warped, keep the plane parallel to the edges. This helps to keep the surface flat.

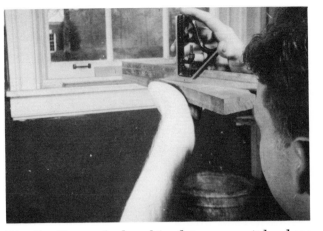

Fig. 7. To test the board for flatness once it has been planed, look toward the source of light testing with the try square across the grain, with the grain, and diagonally.

which way the grain runs. In almost every instance, the grain on the opposite side of the block, or piece of wood, will run in the opposite direction.

Fasten the block in a vise, and plane. Begin planing the side at the edge closest to you. Test the side for flatness (Figs. 6 and 7). Do no sanding.

Plane edge #2 next. To do this, place the block in a vise as nearly level as possible, with edge #2 on top. Keeping the plane in line with the piece of wood you are planing (not angled), and holding it as level as possible, plane the edge (Fig. 8).* Test the edge for squareness with side 1, and for flatness (Fig. 9).

Plane end #3. Place the block in a vise as nearly

* Not all pieces of wood used to illustrate all figures and the procedures they show were alike.

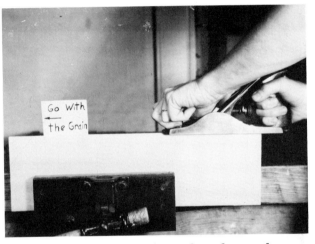

Fig. 8. Shows how plane is used to plane and square up edge #2.

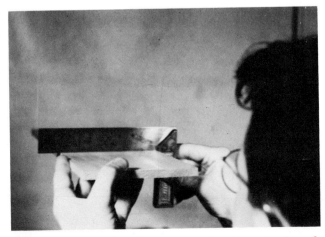

Fig. 6. Testing for flatness on the sides of a board.

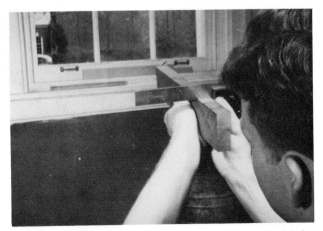

Fig. 9. To test the edge to see if it is square, hold the try square handle tightly against the squared face and see if any light can be seen under the blade. Look toward the source of light.

level as possible and, with one edge turned toward you and the other toward the bench, clamp the block low so that the end is just above the vise. Check the plane for sharpness, then set the blade to cut a fine shaving. Grasp the plane firmly, keeping the wrists fairly stiff. Plane only a little over halfway across the end several times; then reverse the edges and plane in the opposite direction. Repeat this process until the end is smooth, flat, and square with the first two sides. Note: if you were to plane all the way across the end, splinters of wood would be broken off on the far edge. (Figs. 10 and 11.)

Now measure and mark off the length to which you want to plane your block. Saw and plane the block to this line. Place the ruler on the block, as shown in Fig. 12, and mark the length, which should be 7 inches. With a try square held tightly

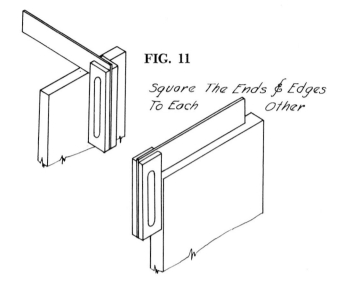

Square The Ends & Edges To The Working Face

FIG. 11

Square The Ends & Edges To Each Other

against the squared edge of the block, draw a fine pencil line or make a knife line at the 7-inch mark. Continue squaring it clear around the sides and edges of the block as shown in Fig. 13. Then clamp the block in the vise with side #1 on top, and with end #4 extended just enough to saw off most of the waste; then saw off the waste, being careful not to split off a piece of the end when the saw cut is completed. Then plane end #4 to this line, going through the same steps as you did when you planed end #3.

Mark the block for width and plane it to this line. Set the marking gauge to the 3-inch mark. Place the hand with which you push the gauge so that the index finger is on one side of the gauge

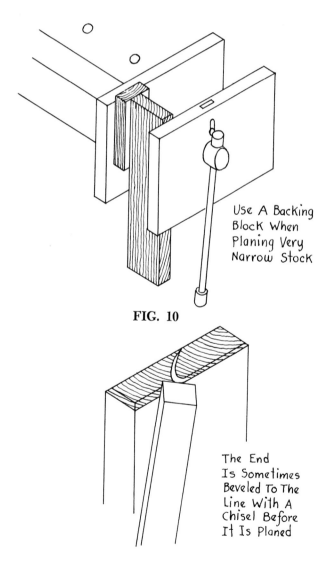

Use A Backing Block When Planing Very Narrow Stock

FIG. 10

The End Is Sometimes Beveled To The Line With A Chisel Before It Is Planed

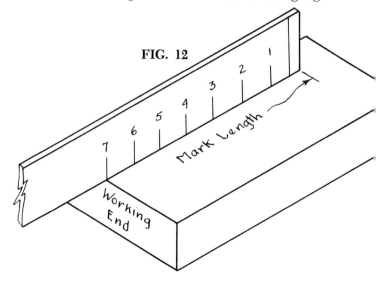

FIG. 12

Mark Length

Working End

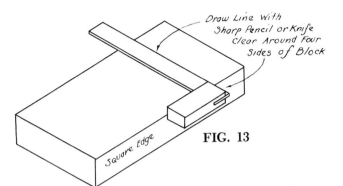

Draw Line With
Sharp Pencil or Knife
Clear Around Four
Sides of Block

Square Edge **FIG. 13**

Hold The Guage As Shown
Push It Away From You

Fig. 14

Fig. 13

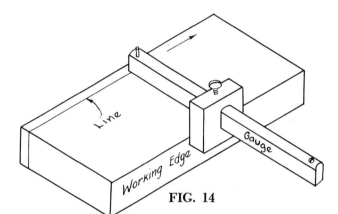

Line

Working Edge

Gauge

FIG. 14

block and the middle finger is on the other side. With the thumb on the beam, push the gauge away from you to mark the width of the block (Fig. 14). If you have a lot of waste left to take off, saw nearly to the line with a ripsaw; then plane to the line.

Mark the block for thickness and plane it to this line. Set the marking gauge to ¾ inch. Tilt the gauge slightly forward and, holding it as before, gauge a line around the block as shown in Fig. 15. Plane to this line until the line disappears, and test for flatness and to see if all sides are square to each other.

While this is a small block of wood you have just planed, squared, and cut to size, large pieces of wood are done the same way, so that what you have learned when doing the small block will apply to doing boards or glued-up stock of much greater size. Instead of using the gauge and try

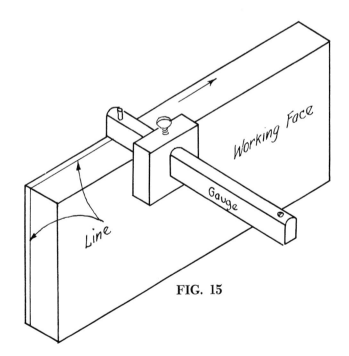

Working Face

Gauge

Line

FIG. 15

square you may have to lay off some of the lines with a framing square and a straightedge on larger pieces of wood, but except for these variations the steps and procedures are the same.

A number of other operations that a beginning woodworker will have to know how to perform may now be tried out on this block of wood. Some very useful ones for the beginner to try are shown in Fig. 16.

Draw all lines and layouts for cutting the mortise, rabbet, gain, and so on, that appear on the block. Use a try square and a sharp pencil or knife for all lines across the grain. Use a gauge for marking all lines going with the grain. Use a compass or dividers for all curved lines. Use a try-and-miter square (shown in Fig. 7) for laying out the 45-degree angle.

To cut the mortise, bore two ⅝-inch holes through the block. Bore only halfway through from each face. Chisel the hole. To do this pare away the wood a little at a time, using a slicing cut. Check the walls of the mortise for squareness.

To cut the gain, drive the chisel, lightly, straight down all around, about ⅟₁₆ inch in on the waste

sides of the lines. The flat side of the chisel should be next to the lines when doing this. Use a wooden mallet to hammer the chisel. Trim out the waste by hammering the chisel from the center of the gain toward the first cuts made, holding the chisel with the beveled side down. Repeat this until the proper depth has been attained. Complete chiseling the gain by trimming with the flat side of the chisel.

To cut the rabbet, saw on the waste side of the line with a backsaw, sawing across the face side of the block. Do not saw entirely to the bottom of the rabbet, but allow a little wood to remain for trimming. Chisel out the waste. Begin near the surface and work down gradually to the line. Finish the rabbet by chiseling across the grain. Turn the bevel of the chisel up when doing this.

To cut the dado on the edge of the block, saw from the edge of the block nearly to the line opposite the edge. Stay on the waste side of the lines going across the grain. Chisel out the waste,

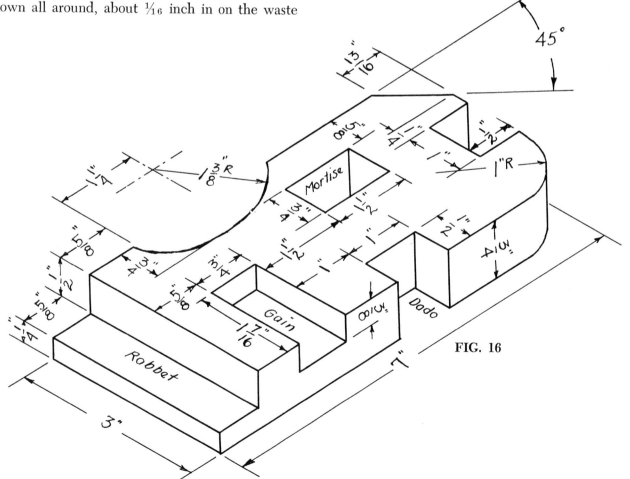

FIG. 16

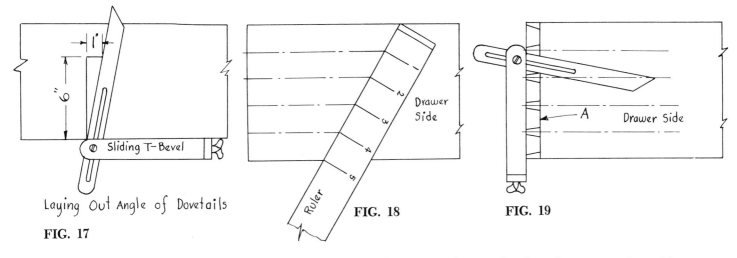

Laying Out Angle of Dovetails

FIG. 17

Drawer Side

FIG. 18

Drawer Side

FIG. 19

cutting from the middle toward both ends of the block. Trim the edges with slicing chisel cuts.

To cut the dado on the end of the block, saw from the end nearly to the line going across the grain. Chisel out the waste, a little at a time, cutting from both faces of the block toward the center of the end. Trim the edges. Some of the waste may be sawed off with a coping saw before it is chiseled, to do the job more quickly.

To cut the miter, saw off on the waste side of the line. Trim to the line with a plane or chisel.

To cut the outside curve, saw on the waste side with a coping saw. When using a coping saw the teeth of the coping-saw blade should be pointed toward the handle of the saw. To hold the saw properly, take the handle in the right hand and place the left hand over the right if you are right-handed. Keep the blade level while you are sawing. Trim to the line with the chisel, using the flat side of the chisel.

To cut the inside curve, saw on the waste side with a coping saw. Trim to the line with a chisel, using the beveled side of the chisel.

LAYING OUT AND MAKING DOVETAIL JOINTS

Many of the pieces of furniture in this book and others like it have dovetail joints to fasten drawer sides to fronts and backs. Dovetail joints are also used to join other members together wherever fine cabinetwork is done.

Dovetail joints, on work where appearance counts, and especially on antique furniture or good custom-made reproductions, are always made with the tail members wider than the pin members. Machine-made dovetail joints may be a little stronger because the tails and pins are made alike in width, but they are not nearly as neat in appearance. To lay out good dovetail joints proceed as follows: set the sliding T bevel to an angle of 10 degrees. If you do not have a protractor to do this, square a line across a board, and on this line measure off a distance of 6 inches. Then at right angles to the 6-inch mark lay off a distance of 1 inch, and set the sliding T bevel to this angle, as shown in Fig. 17. This will give you an approximate 10-degree angle to use in laying out dovetails.

Lay out the tail members of the dovetail joint. On drawers, these will be found on the drawer sides. Decide how many tails you need in the joint and divide the end of the drawer side into that number of equal spaces.

Let us assume you have a drawer side on which you wish to put five tails, with six spaces for the pins to which the tails are to be joined. But you find the width of the drawer side to be such that it is not easily divided into five equal parts with a ruler. To divide the distance quickly and easily, lay the ruler across the drawer side at an angle which spans its width from the 0 to the 5-inch mark, since this distance may then easily be divided into five equal parts, as shown in Fig. 18. Then at distances 1 inch apart on the ruler, draw lines to the end of the board. This will divide the board into five equal parts across its width. Using the division lines as center lines for the pins, tails and pins may be laid out with the sliding T bevel as shown in Fig. 19.

Measure off the distance from the end of the

board for the length of the tails, and with a try square draw this line around all four sides of the board as shown at A in Fig. 19.

If only hand tools are to be used, saw on the waste side of each tail, and then chisel the waste pieces of the tail members by cutting away half the waste from each side of the board, as shown in Fig. 20.

If machinery is used, several methods of cutting out the waste on the tail members of dovetail joints may be used. One of these is to cut them out on the band saw and then flatten the back end of the hole with a sharp chisel. Another method is to saw out the middle of the hole between the tails on the table saw, using one or more dado-head blades, with the board fastened upright to the crosscut fence, and then trimming to the angle with a chisel. Still another, and this one is probably the best method, is to grind the cutting edge of a spacer blade used in a dado head, to the proper angle, and then, tilting the saw arbor to 10 degrees and clamping the board upright against the front of the crosscut fence, cut out the waste right to the line.

Tails are laid out on both ends of a drawer side if the drawer back is to be joined to the drawer sides with dovetail joints.

Now lay out the pin members of the dovetail joint. In putting drawers together, these would be laid out on the ends of the drawer front and drawer back. To do this, clamp the drawer front in the vise with the end on top. Gauge line A across the end for the length of the pins, as shown in Fig. 21. Then lay the tail member, which in this case is

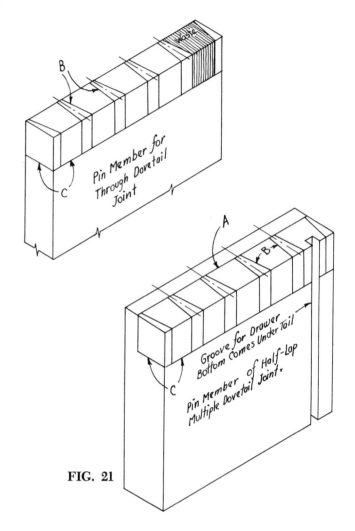

FIG. 21

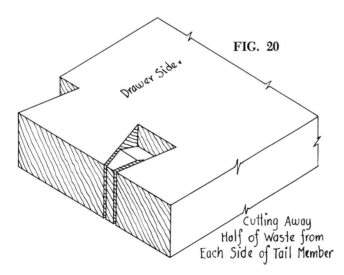

FIG. 20

the drawer side, on top of the end, with its end lined up with line A. Using a knife blade, sharp pencil, or scriber, trace the outlines of the tails on the ends of the drawer front. Having done so you now have the pin members laid out on the ends of the drawer front, as shown by lines B in Fig. 21.

Determine which parts you must keep for the pins, and saw on the waste side of each line with a dovetail saw, or a fine-tooth backsaw. If the dovetail joint goes entirely across the end of this board, this type being known as a through dovetail joint, then most of this waste may be cut out on the band saw to line C, and the rest of it may be removed very easily with a coping saw, if you have first cut to lines B and C with the dovetail saw.

All of the waste between the pins, on through dovetail joints, may be removed on the table saw by setting the crosscut fence to the 10-degree angle, and using a stopblock on the fence to regulate the cuts and remove the waste.

If you are not making a through dovetail joint, but are making a dovetail joint on which the dovetailing does not show on the outside of the drawer front, then the sawing must be done with the dovetail saw held at an angle of 45 degrees when making the cut, which goes all the way to line C, but only about two-thirds of the way across the end of the drawer front as shown in Fig. 22. Such a dovetail joint is known as a half-lap multiple dovetail joint. The waste between the pins must be chiseled out. To do this, use a narrow paring chisel on which not only the cutting edge is beveled, but the sides of the blade as well. With this type of chisel it is easier to get into corners that are almost inaccessible to the ordinary socket-firmer chisel. (See Fig. 23.) In Fig. 24 we show a lowboy with beautifully made half-lap multiple dovetail joints on the drawers.

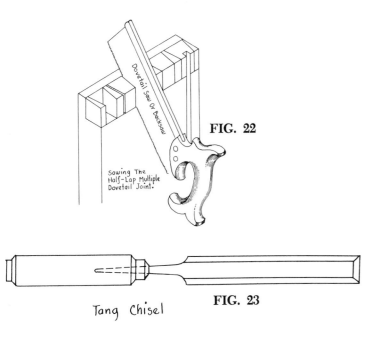

FIG. 22

FIG. 23

Tang Chisel

MAKING MORTISE-AND-TENON JOINTS

Mortise-and-tenon joints rank high as the strongest, best, and longest-lasting method of joining together two members of a frame in high-grade cabinetwork. These joints have probably been used to join framed members to each other as long as

Fig. 24

joinery in wood has been established as a craft, and they may even predate written records of history. The time may be approaching when superior methods of fastening two pieces of wood together, either at right angles or otherwise, may replace this time-tried method. Modern glues and adhesives have been, and are being, developed that may give us joints even stronger than the mortise-and-tenon joint, and that can be made without fitting one member into the other, and do the joining with much less trouble. At the present time, however, the mortise-and-tenon joint is still one of the best and most practical means of fastening and holding together two or more pieces of wooden framework. For this reason the cabinetmaker needs to know how to make and fit mortise-and-tenon joints.

Back in the days when originals of the pieces shown in this book were made, all such joints were made with hand tools, since laborsaving machinery

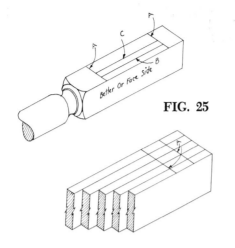

FIG. 25

of the kind we now have had not been produced. The author himself has made countless numbers of mortise-and-tenon joints with hand tools, and has taught hundreds in his woodworking classes to make them this way and to use them in projects of lasting worth. Despite the fact that shops in which he has worked, or taught, were equipped with power tools and laborsaving machinery, many occasions have arisen when he found it to be a skill of great practical value. The cabinetmaker who has acquired the knowledge and mastered the skills required to do high-grade joinery with hand tools is, in most cases, a craftsman superior to the one who is skilled in doing such work by machinery only.

In almost all cases where this joint is to be used, the mortise is made before the tenon. The reason for this is that it is easier to fit the tenon into the mortise than the other way around.

To lay out a mortise on a leg, a rail, or some similar piece of wood the width of which is not too great, make the measurement to the mortise from the end of the wood closest to it, and square lines across the grain on this piece of wood. In most instances this is done with a try square, as shown at A in Fig. 25. If more than one mortise is to be laid out on the same piece of wood, make lines across the wood locating all of them. If mortises that are alike in size are to be located at the same place on a number of pieces that are alike, time in marking where they go can be saved by clamping several together, and then drawing the lines across all of them at once. Now determine how far from the adjacent side or edge of the wood the mortise is

to be located, and set the wooden marking gauge for this distance. Then with the spur of the gauge, scribe a line from one end of the mortise to the other, as shown at B in Fig. 25. Do this for all mortises before resetting the gauge to scribe line C, which gives you the width of the mortise. Keep the block of the gauge against the same side of the stock to scribe lines B and C, and this, in most cases, is the better of the two opposite sides.

With a brace and a bit, which is about $\frac{1}{16}$ inch smaller in diameter than the width of the mortise, bore a series of holes as close to each other as possible and as deep as you want the mortise to go. A bit gauge fastened to the bit may be used to indicate when this depth has been reached. Fig. 26, in which a bit gauge is being used, shows a hole being bored for a wooden peg to hold a mortise-and-tenon joint more securely together. The same setup is used to bore holes for mortises.

When all holes have been bored, use a chisel with a blade slightly narrower than the width of

Fig. 26

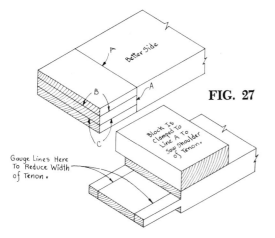

Gauge Lines Here
To Reduce Width
of Tenon.

FIG. 27

the mortise, and with it begin chopping out the wood remaining in the mortise after the holes have been bored. To avoid splitting the wood, cut only across the grain at first, and avoid trying to drive the chisel too deeply into the wood all at once. Only when most of the waste has been removed in this way should the sides of the mortise be trimmed to the line with a wider chisel.

When the mortise has been completely cut out, you are ready to lay out the tenon, and cut it to fit the mortise. Lines are first drawn around all four sides of the piece of wood at the correct distance from the end where the shoulder of the tenon goes. This is done with a try square, this line being marked A in Fig. 27. Set a marking gauge so the block of the gauge rests against the face side of the piece of wood on which the tenon is to be cut. Then with the spur on one end of the gauge set at the proper distance from the face side, scribe the lines marked B around the edges and end of the piece of wood, as shown in Fig. 27. Resetting the gauge, scribe a second line, marked C in Fig. 27, which determines the thickness of the tenon.

When lines A, B, and C have all been drawn, lay the piece of wood on top of the workbench and, clamping a small block of wood with its straightest edge lined up with line A, saw the shoulder to line B with a fine-toothed backsaw. Then turning the piece of wood on its other side, saw the shoulder of the second side in the same way. Remove the block of wood to chisel the waste off both sides of the tenon. If careful, you may save time by sawing the cheek cuts nearly to lines B and C with the back-

saw or with a sharp ripsaw, after which you can trim to lines B and C with a chisel. Then fit the tenon to the mortise, making it just a loose enough fit so the tenon will slide into the mortise without having to be pushed too hard. Sometimes the tenon has shoulders on three or four sides, and if this is the case the third and fourth shoulder cuts will have to be made after lines determining the width of the tenon have been scribed on both cheeks of the tenon. When shoulder cuts have been sawed, the remaining waste should be sawed and chiseled off.

To make mortise-and-tenon joints using machinery to do the work, proceed as follows:

Make the layout for the mortise on the wood, using the same procedure to do this that we gave for making the mortise with hand tools. Complete layouts for all mortises must be made on the wood to mark their exact location. To make tenons this is not necessary, for if there are many tenons to make, and all of them are alike in size, you will need mark off only the first one, and then set up your machine to cut all of them from the marking on the first one. But with mortises this is not so easily done, so it is best to draw all lines for each mortise distinctly marking the place where it is to go.

Fig. 28 shows a setup on a floor-type drill press for doing mortising. Regular mortising machines are set up much the same way and use exactly the same hollow chisel and bit, the only difference being that mortising machines have a carriage with a clamping device to which the piece to be mortised may be fastened, and the bit can be advanced to each succeding cut by merely turning a wheel instead of by hand, as must be done with the setup we show. For the home workshop the drill press, equipped with attachments for mortising, is a practical and less expensive piece of equipment and will do the job well.

In Figs. 29 and 30, we show setups for cutting tenons by using a dado head on the table saw. When cutting tenons, it is extremely important that the pieces of wood on which you are going to make tenons be perfectly square on all sides, and if more than one tenon of the same size is to be made with the same machine setup, every piece of

Fig. 28

Fig. 29

wood, besides being square, must also be alike in width and thickness. Otherwise the tenons may not have square shoulders, nor will they be alike in size after they have been made. The dado-head setup may be made to cut to a width of from ¼ inch to ½ inch for every cut made in an operation such as the one we show here. After the shoulder cut has been made on one side of the board, the operator keeps on pulling the piece of wood away from the rip fence or stop, which regulates its length—a distance about equal to the width of the cut made by the dado head—until the cutting on that side has been completed from the shoulder to the end. The piece of wood is then turned over to make the cut on the opposite side. To cut the tenon to size on the remaining two sides, the dado head may have to be raised or lowered to get the proper width or thickness. Cheek cuts, like the one being

made in Fig. 30, usually are made first, and the edges trimmed off afterward.

HOW TO CUT GROOVES

Fig. 31 shows how grooves may be cut across the grain by hand with a router plane. Such a plane may also be used to cut grooves going with the grain on a board. Grooves like this must often be cut into ends or partitions on cabinets to hold shelves, as on the upper section of the Dutch Cupboard, or on chests of drawers to help hold frames that support drawers, as shown in Fig. 8 in the drawings of the Spice Cabinet.

To make such grooves by hand with a router plane, first draw lines across the board with a try square or a framing square to mark the exact place where the groove is to be cut. Often these grooves

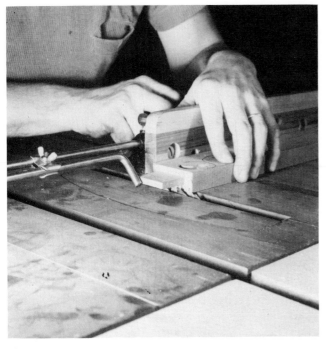

Fig. 30

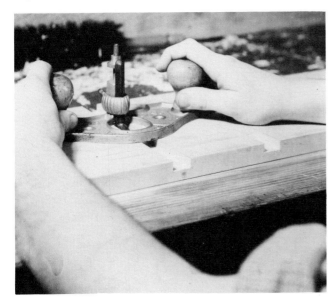

Fig. 31

do not go clear across the board, but are stopped before they reach the front edge, this being the case in Fig. 8 on the Spice Cabinet. Before using the router plane, clamp a straightedge to the line on one side of the groove, and with a sharp sloyd knife score a line deep into the wood. Then do the same to the line on the other side of the groove. This will keep the plane bit from tearing away wood on both sides of the groove, which would otherwise happen, especially when the plane first starts cutting into the surface. Adjust the knife in the plane to make only very shallow cuts, especially at first. Deeper cuts may be made once the plane bit is extended well below the surface of the board. The best results are obtained by planing away the wood rather than being in a hurry and making cuts so deep that the bit tears it out. Keep scoring the sides of the groove with a knife at frequent intervals to prevent tearing out wood at the sides as the groove goes deeper. The cutting edge of the router-plane bit may be either pushed away from you or pulled toward you as you plane out the groove.

To make such grooves by machinery, several methods may be used: Fig. 32 shows how it may be done on the table saw, especially if the board on which grooves are to be made is not very wide. In this setup both the crosscut fence and the rip fence may be used if the piece being done is not too long. For longer pieces, the face of the crosscut fence should have a long face board fastened to its front side with wood screws. To this, stopblocks may be clamped at both ends of the board, to regulate the width of each groove. In the setup shown in Fig. 32, the board is pushed across the

Fig. 32

dado head with the crosscut fence, while the rip fence serves as the stop to regulate the width of the cut being made.

Still another method, and one that is better to use when grooves are to be cut across wide boards or glued-up stock, is the one shown in Fig. 33, where an electric hand router is being used. Here, guide strips to regulate the width of the groove have been clamped to the board on both sides of the hand router. This may be done on boards of any width and using router bits of almost any diameter. Good grooving may be done quickly and efficiently with these machines for they run at very high speeds and cut clean, either across the grain or with the grain.

TO ROUGH OUT BRACKET FEET ON THE TABLE SAW

Fig. 34 shows how molding to make bracket feet, such as are found on the Salem Chest of Drawers

Fig. 33

Fig. 34

and on the Blockfront Chest-on-Chest, is roughed out on the table saw. The shape of the molding is first drawn on both ends of the long piece of stock from which all parts of the feet are to be cut. A series of saw cuts like those shown, with the saw set at various heights as you proceed with the cuts, will shape the front of the feet to almost the exact shape you want. Only light trimming with gouges, chisel, and scraper blade is needed to finish the shaping, after which the surface may be smoothed with sandpaper.

HOW TO USE A CURVE-BOTTOM PLANE TO SHAPE CURVED CHAIR LEGS AND CURVED CHAIR SPLATS OR RAILS

Fig. 35 shows how curved surfaces, and especially curved surfaces on the concave sides of legs or other curved members of chairs, may be planed. All three Chippendale chairs described in this book have members like this, and a curve-bottom plane like the one shown is an exceedingly useful tool to have to help shape such members. Curved members like those used to build such chairs are first band sawed to shape as shown in Fig. 36. Outside or convex surfaces may be planed with ordinary hand planes, but inside curves or concave surfaces cannot be made smooth with planes having a straight bed. A curve-bottom plane, like the one shown in Fig. 35, has a flexible steel bed, the curve of which can be regulated by turning the large adjusting screw on top. For planing curved members on all kinds of cabinetwork, and for chairmaking in particular, such a plane is almost indispensable. Figs. 37 and 38 show how a splat, similar to the one on the Chippendale Pierced Splat-back Chair,

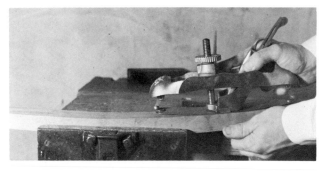

Fig. 35

may be sawed to shape on the power jigsaw and
the saw marks filed smooth afterward.

GLUES AND GLUING

Gluing up stock is a very essential operation in
all cabinetwork. Many new kinds of glue have been
developed recently, which were not available to
cabinetmakers even as late as the end of World
War II. Good animal glue, made from hides and
bones of animals killed in slaughterhouses, was the

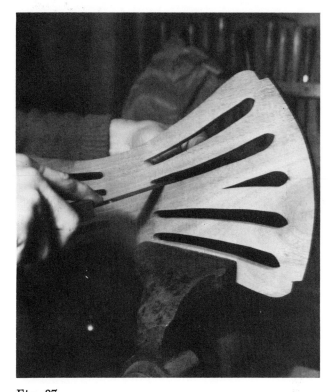

Fig. 37

Fig. 36

Fig. 38

glue almost universally used in cabinetmaking until very recently. The better hide glues are still good to use. They are slow setting and not waterproof. They usually come in flake, sheet, or powder form. Cold water is added to soften the glue to a jellylike consistency, after which it must be heated in a glue pot to a temperature not exceeding 150 degrees. Excessive heating, and repeated heatings, weaken the adhesive quality of animal glue. When using it the room temperature should be 70 degrees or higher, and the wood to be glued should be warm so as not to chill the glue too quickly.

Animal glue is usually heated in an electrically heated glue pot in which a thermostat keeps the temperature within the limits necessary for its proper use. Water must be added to the glue from time to time to replace that lost by evaporation and to keep the glue at a consistency that may be brushed on easily. Since animal glue is not water resistant, it should not be used where joints will be subjected to excessive moisture over a period of time.

Casein glue, made from milk curd and several other ingredients, comes in powder form and is mixed with cold water just prior to its being used. About fifteen minutes after adding the water, the glue is ready to use. Casein glue is water resistant, and since no glue pot is required to heat it, it is a satisfactory product for the woodworker having limited facilities and equipment, and for one whose need for large amounts of glue at any one time is limited. It will adhere to oily woods, like teak or cedar, but will stain some woods, such as oak or maple. Casein glue is usually mixed with water in the ratio of two parts of glue to one of water by volume. Only enough glue should be mixed for the job in hand, since what is left over will soon harden and cannot be reconditioned for later use.

Polyvinyl resin emulsion glue comes in plastic squeeze bottles having a narrow spout, and by merely pressing the sides of the container it is easily applied to surfaces to be joined together. From such a container the glue can be easily injected into small openings, such as drilled or bored holes, small mortises, and so on. For anyone who does not use glue in large quantities, but who needs to use it at frequent intervals, this is a very practical and use-

ful type of glue. It is not a waterproof glue. One advantage this glue has over others is that it does not harden to the extent that it becomes brittle and so is a good adhesive to use where shrinkage or expansion of glued members tends to take place. Clamps may be removed as early as thirty minutes after gluing, but several hours or even a whole day of additional drying time should be allowed for it to harden before resuming work on the glued-up stock.

Contact cement is a useful adhesive where it is essential to make a quick-setting joint and where applying clamps is often difficult or impossible. Surfaces on which this glue is applied bond instantly on contact and so must be aligned properly before they touch each other. Once contact has been established, the alignment cannot be adjusted. The cement is applied to both surfaces—sometimes twice—and left to dry until a piece of paper will not stick to the film. The surfaces are then pressed together with enough pressure so that bonding takes place immediately. This glue may be used to apply thin veneer to the edges of stock, even plywood, and to weld plastic laminates like Formica to tabletops.

Epoxy resin glue is perhaps the strongest of all glues yet developed. Its strength and adhesive qualities are attested by the fact it is used in place of rivets in airplane assemblies. Since it will bond porous to nonporous material, it may be used to join metal to metal, metal to wood, wood to wood, and will even make a waterproof, heat-proof joint on glass or porcelain. It comes in two components, one being the adhesive and the other the catalyst that makes it set up. These are mixed together in equal amounts just prior to using it.

Still other useful glues and adhesives are available to the woodworker, but the above list will serve most of the cabinetmaker's needs.

Proper equipment for making good glue joints should be at hand in even the most modestly equipped shop. This should include bar clamps in various lengths from 2 to 8 feet, metal C-clamps, and wooden adjustable hand screws. A good woodworker's vise on the workbench is essential for use in gluing up stock at times, as well as for other activities engaged in by the woodworker in preparing surfaces for gluing. For the small shop, doing only a limited amount of gluing, a pair of wooden sawhorses is essential equipment to hold stock while glue and clamps are being applied, unless an even better gluing rack is available to take their place.

To glue two or more boards edge to edge, first make sure the edges to be glued are perfectly straight and that they are squared to other sides of the boards. This may be done by hand with a jack plane, with the board held in a woodworker's vise. When doing this, the plane should be kept in line with the edge being planed. For very long boards, a jointer plane having a long bed may be used, but the jack plane whose bottom is about 14 inches long is the most versatile plane for nearly every kind of hand-planing job the cabinetmaker will come across, and if properly used it will serve the purpose like no other plane.

An easier way to joint edges of boards to make them straight and square is with the jointer. On this the fence keeps the edges of the board square with the sides, and, if the machine is properly set up, edges can be straightened very quickly for gluing. Boards that are warped should be ripped into narrower widths. When gluing two of these back together it is best to turn one of the two pieces end for end, so its bottom surface will be on top. This tends to prevent warping in the future, especially when many boards are glued together to make wide pieces, like a tabletop. If the bottom of every alternate board is turned up the stresses of the wood fibers will be exerted in opposite directions, thus tending to neutralize each other and keep the board flat.

Fig. 39 shows the jointer being used to straighten one side of a piece of stock. Note that the forward hand doing the pushing is held well back from the end of the stock as a safety precaution. Jointers are notoriously dangerous machines when used without guards, and the guard on the machine shown in Fig. 39 was removed only for the purpose of taking the picture. Most jointers come equipped with very efficient guards, and these should be used at all times when working on this machine.

Before applying glue to boards for edge-to-edge gluing, the boards should be laid on the sawhorses

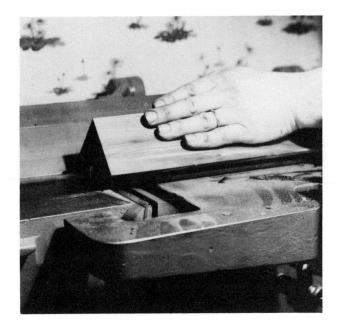

Fig. 39

so they join each other in proper sequence, and lines should then be drawn across the joints to identify mating pairs after glue has been put on the joint. Clamps should be adjusted before putting glue on any joint, to avoid delay after the glue has been put on, when speed in handling often makes the difference between good or poor joints. For edge-to-edge gluing, it is best to put every alternate clamp on opposite sides of the boards, which helps prevent buckling when pressure is applied. The sooner pressure can be applied after glue has been put on surfaces to be joined together, the better. So it will help if boards are stacked on the sawhorses in such a way that glue may be applied to all, or nearly all, joints simultaneously. By piling boards on top of each other as shown in Fig. 40, this may be done. After glue has been brushed on, the boards may be rearranged in their former sequence very quickly, and clamps applied before the glue has time to chill or set.

When applying clamps, first place a bar clamp in the middle or near the middle. Turn up the screw only enough to pull joints together and so that it is still possible to align the boards properly, should this be necessary. Then place clamps at both ends, tightening the screws, but not too tightly. If the stock you are gluing up is comprised of short boards, three clamps may be enough. In this case place the second and third clamp on the opposite

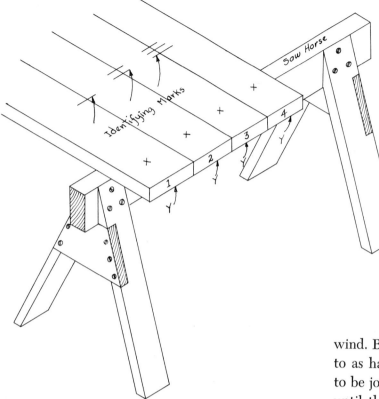

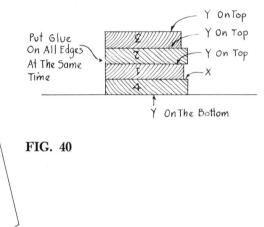

FIG. 40

side from where the first one was put. Then tighten all clamp screws, each one a little at a time, until joints have been pulled tightly together. If the boards are longer, five or more clamps may be needed to pull the joints as tightly together as needed. If this is the case, put the first three clamps on one side, making the screws only tight enough so the boards may be turned over on their other side on the sawhorses without buckling. Holding the bar clamps to the boards on both ends with wooden hand-screw clamps will help prevent buckling when the boards are being turned over. Then place two or more clamps across the second side and tighten all clamp screws a little at a time, until the joints are tight.

Gluing boards side to side to make stock thicker is usually accomplished with **C**-clamps or wooden hand screws. A veneer press, consisting of frames made of heavy timbers, to the top of which screws have been fastened so that pressure can be applied to stacks of boards piled up below them, is also sometimes used to glue boards side to side.

When getting boards ready to glue side to side, it is essential the pieces be flat and free of warp or

wind. Boards having a twisted surface are referred to as having "wind" (rhymes with mind). Boards to be joined together in this way should be planed until they are perfectly flat on both sides before gluing. And then, when clamps are applied to the stack after the glue has been put on, enough clamps should be used so that a sufficient amount of pressure may be applied to pull all joints tightly together. As a general rule, clamps should be put on the middle of the stack first, followed by more clamps next to them, and so on to the very ends. Keep on applying additional clamps until all joints are drawn tightly together.

Gluing frames of various kinds together poses no great difficulties. The gluing up of frames composed of many members necessitates advance planning, so all parts are in place when the frame has been put together. Unless this is done, it is possible to miss getting one or more members in place at the proper time, and much or all of the work will have to be done over. Sides of pieces in a frame should, in almost every case, line up with sides of all other pieces in the frame, but need not necessarily be on the same level. The face of a panel is lined up with the sides of the door stiles and rails, but may be on a level below or above them. Members of a frame supposed to be at right angles to each other should remain so after gluing.

Fig. 41 shows a frame the members of which are

Fig. 41

not square to each other. This frame and three others like it for a wastebasket were made to hold raised panels shaped like them, one of which is shown being raised by tilting the saw on a table saw, in Fig. 42. Fig. 43 shows a simple jig used so mortises can be cut at the proper angle into edges of the stiles.

WOOD TURNING

Turning wood on the lathe is almost a trade in itself and a skill impossible to describe in all its aspects in the space we can give to it here. So we shall try to explain briefly how to do it, and recommend that if the user of this book wants to learn more about it he get a book dealing more thoroughly with the subject, or endeavor to get instruction from a person who has already attained these skills.

Wood turning falls into two categories: one of these is spindle turning, which consists of turning such things as legs for tables or chairs, columns, finials, and other similar objects. The other is faceplate turning, into which category fall such things

as bowls, wide bases for spindle-turned objects like the bases of candlesticks, lamps, and so forth.

Most spindle turning is done between a spur center, mounted near the motor of the lathe, and a cup center mounted in the tailstock at the opposite end of the lathe. By hammering it in with a wooden mallet, the spur center is driven into one end of the stock to be turned; when the motor turns, it rotates the piece of wood. The cup center does not turn, but merely supports the other end of the wood while it is being turned. Very short spindles must sometimes be mounted in a chuck to turn them.

Spindles, before they are turned, are usually square, or nearly so, and are referred to as turning squares. (See Fig. 44.) Both spur and cup centers have tapered shafts, and these are inserted into tapered sockets in the headstock and tailstock of the lathe and held there by friction.

When the spindle has been mounted in the lathe

Fig. 42

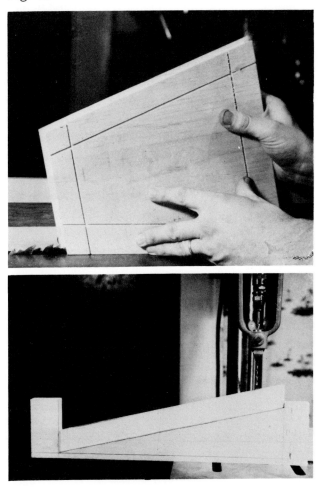

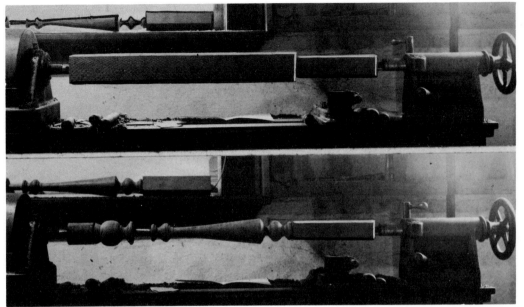

Fig. 44

and turned by hand to see if it will revolve freely, the tool rest is put in place in front of the spindle. This tool rest is mounted so its upper edge falls somewhat below the center of the horizontal spindle. A large gouge is then used to remove the square corners from the turning square. The long handle of the gouge is held at an angle lower than the cutting end of the tool, and the gouge is drawn forward and backward along the spindle to make it round. Average-sized spindles are rotated at a speed of around 1,800 rpm to turn them after they are round. To prevent vibration and as a safety precaution, slower speeds are used before corners have been cut off from turning squares.

After the spindle, or those parts of it which have to be turned, has been rounded, layouts for beads, coves, fillets, or shaped areas are made, distances for these being measured off with a foot rule, and the lines drawn clear around the spindle by spinning the lathe by hand. Convex turnings, known as beads, are made with straight chisels, sharpened on a skew or angle, as shown in Fig. 45. In Fig. 46 the skew chisel is shown being used to smooth the straight shaft of a spindle. Beads are sometimes formed on a spindle with a flat chisel sharpened to a diamond point, but doing it this way requires that the woodturner scrape off the waste instead of cutting it off, which is what he should do if the skew chisel is properly used to cut the bead.

Highly skilled craftsmen always make this cut with the skew chisel, except close to a section of the turning which must be kept square, here a diamond point must sometimes be used.

Coves, concave areas, and areas of greater length but similar to these are shaped with gouges. To turn narrow coves, the gouge is first held so the edge doing the cutting is almost vertical; the cutting edge of the chisel is then rolled to a horizontal position, but all this with the handle of the tool well below the cutting end of the chisel. In Fig. 47 the gouge is shown being used to cut a cove.

In most cases spindle turning is started by cutting fillets first, using a parting tool. The parting tool is a chisel whose blade is thinner at both edges

Fig. 45

than in the middle and whose cutting edge is as wide as the thickest part of the blade. To use a parting tool, one edge of the blade rests upon the tool rest. The shape of the blade reduces friction to a minimum when the tool digs into the wood to form a square shoulder on both sides of the cut. Fillets are the narrow flat areas, and on turnings they are located between a cove and a bead more often than not. Fillets are cut to the proper diameter, and calipers are held in one hand to gauge their diameter, while the parting tool is held in the other hand to do the cutting. As soon as the fillet has reached its proper diameter, the parting tool is withdrawn.

While most spindle work, if done by a skilled

Fig. 46

screws. The screws are driven into the side of the stock where holes will not show after the opposite side has been turned, or where they can be filled with wooden plugs so they will not show enough to matter. If pieces turned on a faceplate must be free of screw holes altogether, a wooden chuck must first be turned after mounting it on a faceplate. The center of this chuck is hollowed out just enough to hold the work by friction. One side of the turning may then be turned by screwing it to the faceplate, and the side where the screws have been taken out may then be turned by placing it in the wooden chuck, which holds it while the side with the screw holes is being turned. Fig. 48 shows faceplate turning being done on the lathe.

Fig. 47

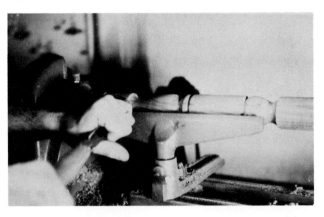

Fig. 48

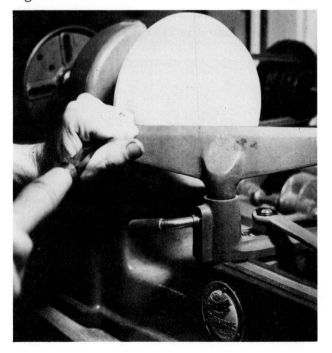

craftsman, is accomplished with the skew, gouge, and parting tool, and the waste is actually cut rather than scraped off, faceplate work is done entirely with scraping tools. The greater diameter of most turnings made on a faceplate makes use of cutting tools like the gouge and skew too dangerous, because of the likelihood of hooking the tool into the wood on this kind of turning. A lot of this is due to the sudden changes of direction in the grain of the wood as the stock spins around and to the high speed at the periphery of the turning. Only diamond points, roundnoses, or straight chisels are used. Diamond points are flat chisels, the cutting edges of which are ground at an angle from both sides to a point in the center; the cutting edges are ground to a half-moon shape on roundnoses and straight across on straight chisels.

Work is mounted on metal faceplates with wood

WOOD CARVING

Since wood carving is used to decorate many of the pieces of furniture we have included in this book, and since this entails skills not generally required of the average cabinetmaker, some instruction for doing it is included here. Wood carving is an art more widely practiced at the present time than most people realize, and many amateurs do highly commendable work in this craft. Wood carving requires not only manipulative skill, but some knowledge and proficiency in the fine art of drawing and modeling, for it is a form of sculpture.

Turned woodwork is often carved while mounted in the lathe, as shown in Fig. 49, where a table leg is being carved. Carving on flat surfaces is not as difficult as some suppose it to be, but reasonable proficiency must be attained before one can tackle carving such as is found on Chippendale furniture, or even on pieces where simpler forms of carving

Fig. 49

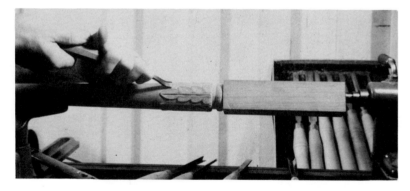

Fig. 50

Fig. 51

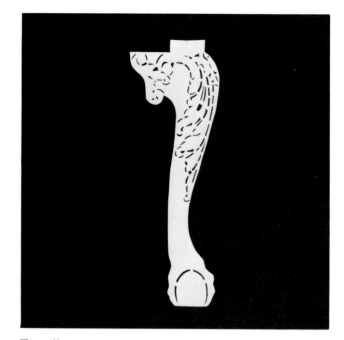

Fig. 52

appear. Contrary to the general belief of those unacquainted with the craft, very few tools are needed to do most of the work. The wood-carver's mallet, shown in Fig. 50, is nothing more than a wooden potato masher turned on the lathe; it makes an excellent hammer to drive wood-carving chisels along through the wood. A small set of chisels, like the set shown in Fig. 51, has enough different shapes to do most, if not all, of the carving on all the pieces of furniture found in this book.

Patterns for carving to be done on furniture are usually made like stencils, as shown in Fig. 52. The cutting out is done with a sharp knife or carving chisels, to make room for the pencil lines traced from the stencil directly upon the surface to be carved. The advantage of such a pattern is that it may be used over again and again when duplicate carvings have to be made.

Any number of different kinds of carving are required in furniture work. Fig. 53 shows how moldings may be shaped by using carving chisels, after some preliminary shaping on the table saw. Moldings like those on top of the Blockfront Chest-on-Chest are carved almost entirely by hand, and most straight moldings may be carved by hand if power shapers are not available.

Furniture in the Jacobean style in England, or early Colonial furniture in America, was often

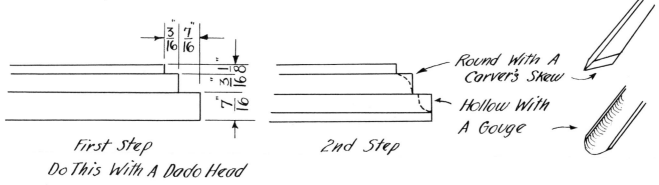

First Step
Do This With A Dado Head   2nd Step

FIG. 53

decorated with simple scratch carving, which was nothing more than lines cut into the wood, often with crude homemade chisels, knives, or other tools. A far more interesting type of carving found on furniture of this early era is known as flat work and strapwork, in which the background around the design was lowered to depths of 1/16 inch or more, bringing the design into relief against the background. This type of carving, in which the surface of the design remains level with the surface of the wood on which it is carved, requires no high degree of skill to execute and is a good type of carving on which to begin.

Another simple form of carving, which can be very interesting and quite effective if carefully done, is chip carving, in which the pattern is achieved by removing triangular-shaped slivers of wood to make the design. In this type of carving,

Fig. 54

Fig. 55

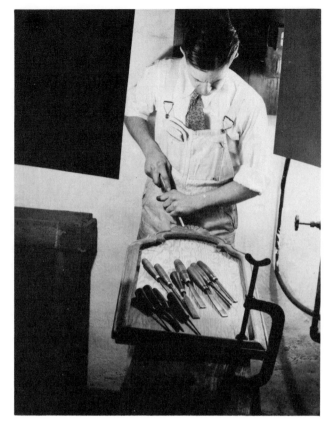

Fig. 56

all or most of the work may be done with sharp, thin-bladed knives, though skew chisel and shallow gouges are also used at times. Chip carving was frequently used to decorate early Spanish furniture.

Most carving on furniture is done in low relief, with elements of the design, such as leaves and flowers, modeled to resemble, to some degree at least, the shape of the objects which inspired the design. Figs. 54 and 55 show how some of this carving is being done. Speaking in general terms, once the design has been drawn, it is outlined either by hammering chisels straight down into the

wood on the waste side near the line, as shown in Fig. 54; by hammering a V tool or very narrow gouge around waste sides of the line as shown in Fig. 55; or by simply pushing the tool into and through the wood as shown in Figs. 56 and 57. Once parts of a design have been outlined, backgrounds around the design may be lowered by removal of waste wood, and then modeling of the design itself can be done very easily. With practice comes skill, and early mistakes may be corrected on work undertaken later.

The most difficult type of carving is a form of sculpture really. It is known as carving in the round. In furniture making most of such work is now limited to carving fairly simple objects, like finials, quarter columns, and feet like the claw-and-ball on our Chippendale wing chair. Once the person who has learned to carve is able to do fairly good modeling in low relief, it is an easy step to carving these simple objects in the round. Some instruction on how to do these has been included in the chapters where such work is found.

Fig. 57

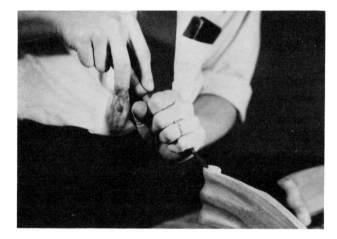

TWO

Furniture Finishing

EVERY bit as important as good design and good construction is the finish put on a piece of furniture after it has been built. The type of finish to be put on a piece of furniture depends to some extent upon the kind of wood that has been used. Wood used to build furniture falls into two general classifications: hardwood, which comes from broadleaf trees like oak, maple, walnut, and mahogany; and softwood, which comes from the cone-bearing trees such as pine and cedar.

The softwoods and some of the semihard woods such as birch and gum are nonporous, or so slightly porous that they need no filling during the finishing process. With the hardwoods, however, it is a different story, for many of them, like oak, walnut, or mahogany, are decidedly porous and will in most cases require a filler.

Regardless of the type of wood used, the completed piece of furniture should be inspected very carefully for blemishes, such as scratches, dents, and plane, machine, or file marks. The finest piece of furniture you can build from plans in this book will look no better than its finish, and the beauty or quality of the finish depends largely upon how thoroughly the blemishes are removed. A very thorough job of sanding and preparing the surface is required to get it ready for a high-quality finish. While many of these blemishes can be removed by planing, scraping, and machine sanding, some hand sanding is also required in most cases.

Sanding is done with abrasive papers. There are several kinds, the most commonly used and least expensive being flint paper. Flint papers are off-white in color. Other abrasive papers now in common use are garnet paper, reddish brown in color; carborundum paper, almost black; aluminum-oxide papers, brown in color; and emery cloth, which is black. All of these may be purchased in various grades. Not only do they run from very coarse to very fine grits, but they come on paper or cloth backings that vary in weight and stiffness. Some are "open-coat" papers, which means that only from 50 percent to 70 percent of their surface is covered with the abrasive material. This helps keep the paper from clogging while it is being used, especially on the softer woods. Open-coat papers are also more pliable as a general rule and therefore more readily adaptable for use on curved or carved surfaces. On "closed-coat" papers the abrasive material entirely covers the surface, and these are the kinds most commonly used. Cabinet papers marked on the back with a "C" or a "D" are medium-weight papers and have medium grits ranging from around 50 to 80 grits to the square inch. These are used for general sanding operations on furniture, with #1 the coarsest having 50 grits, and #1/0 or 0 having 80. The finer finishing papers used by most cabinetmakers range in numbers from 2/0 having 100 grits per square inch to 5/0 having 180 grits per square inch. Even finer grits are obtainable, going as low as 10/0 or finer, but these are used mostly for very fine polishing. Coarser papers than cabinet grade are seldom used on furniture and need not be considered here.

In addition to the papers we have mentioned are wet-or-dry papers. These have a waterproof backing and are used with oil or water for the final rub-down on furniture after the final finishing coats have been applied, and in some cases they are used between coats.

Flint papers, while cheap in price, break down easily under usage and are not highly recommended. They should be used only if the better papers are not obtainable. Garnet papers are of a much better quality, the grits being harder and sharper; they are probably the kind most commonly used by makers of fine furniture. Aluminum-oxide papers are coated with even tougher and more durable cutting agents, but cost a little more and are not as readily obtainable.

In sanding a piece of furniture, it is sometimes necessary to sand parts of a joint across the grain. All final sanding operations should be done parallel to the grain, for as the saying goes: "Sand it twenty times with the grain to remove a scratch made by sanding once across the grain."

Minor blemishes or scratches often go undetected until after some of the finish has been applied, and so it is important that surfaces be inspected closely before starting to put on a finish. Examine surfaces from various angles, tilting and turning them so the light is reflected from them in different directions. Only by doing this can all blemishes be detected.

One of the better tools developed to do finish sanding is the vibrating electric hand sander. When in motion these machines vibrate the sandpaper at high speed, not only backward and forward, but from side to side as well, so that the surface gets a thorough going-over. The vibrating sander is a finish sander and is not designed to do rough sanding. For rough work the portable belt sander is better. Hand sanding may be done by folding the piece of sandpaper over a block of wood, or by fastening it into a rubber sanding block made to hold it. A large proportion of hand sanding must be done with finger pressure only, in which case the sandpaper is held in the hand—the best possible way to do the work.

After all surfaces have been thoroughly prepared and inspected, choose the method of finishing that in your opinion will be most appropriate. Some notes on finishing have been included in several chapters in this book, for example, the method suggested for getting a most interesting color on mahogany on the Sheraton Dressing Table by using quicklime. This is especially good on pieces of furniture on which inlays or marquetry are used, since it colors the mahogany without affecting the woods used in the inlay. A method of finishing used in Colonial days, which has not been greatly improved upon even to this day, will now be described briefly.

To do it well will involve a great deal of time and hard work, and therefore it should not be attempted without a willingness to spend hours of time and effort. The finish one gets with this process has been called an oil finish, a hard oil finish, or an oil and wax finish. The process consists of applying a considerable number of applications of boiled linseed oil, and then rubbing vigorously to build up a rich glossy surface. This type of finish is not recommended for softwoods, on which the more conventional modern finishes will give better results. It is, however, an excellent finish for mahogany, walnut, cherry, or oak. It will darken the wood on which it is used. Stains to color the wood are seldom used or needed when this method of finishing is employed.

After the wood has been prepared for finishing, mix boiled linseed oil with an equal amount of turpentine and warm the mixture in a double boiler or over steam pipes to a temperature of about 80 degrees. Warm oil will soak into the wood much more readily than cold. The work also should be done in a warm room. Apply this mixture often, two or three times a day, until after a twenty-four-hour period the wood will absorb no more of it. Do no rubbing until this point has been reached; then sprinkle fine pumice powder over the surface to be rubbed and, using a burlap pad,* rub the surface vigorously. A burlap pad is recommended since it does not form ridges as a soft cloth would. Repeat the application of pumice and oil and the rubbing for four to five days. Be sure to clean off all residue after each rubbing, or what is left will cause scoring of the wood when the next rubbing is begun. At about the third application of pumice with the oil, use clear linseed oil without adding any turpentine. The final rubbing should be done with rottenstone and oil to get a higher gloss. Finally, finish the job with an application of a prepared carnauba wax polish, which can be purchased from a paint supply house. To keep the surface in good condition, renew it once every two years with an application of oil, well rubbed in, and wax polish.

The conventional methods of finishing usually

---

* Immediately dispose of all rags soaked with finishing materials, since they could easily start a spontaneous-combustion fire.

begin with staining, to get the desired color and to bring out the full rich beauty of the grain. Many of the fine cabinet woods used for furniture in this book are as beautiful without stain as with it. Grain markings and figure in the grain of fine cabinet woods like mahogany, walnut, cherry, curly or bird's-eye maple, and even white pine and poplar impart character and beauty that is often spoiled rather than helped by staining. This is more likely to happen if one who is unskilled in the art of wood finishing does the work. To those with little experience in such matters our advice is to try out the finish you intend to use on small pieces of wood prior to using it on the furniture itself. If stains are to be used, we recommend two kinds to choose from. They are water stain and oil stain.

Water stains are cheaper, are quite transparent, and permit a wide choice of colors. These stains are aniline dyes and dissolve in hot water; they are the most commonly used stains for mass production in factories. Some of these stains are reduced first with a little hot water, and then special solvents supplied by the manufacturer are added to make them "nongrain-raising." Some disadvantages for an amateur in using them are: for best results they should be sprayed rather than brushed on; they have a tendency to raise the grain, which requires the wood to be resanded after water stains have dried; and they should be mixed in rather large amounts and must be stored in glass bottles until used. Also they are not as easily obtainable in paint stores as the ready-mixed oil stains. Resanding the wood after staining with water stains does not alter the color to any great degree, if properly done, because the stains penetrate deeply—this being one of the prime qualities of this kind of stain. Sometimes, before it is stained, the surface is wet down with a sponge, using clear water, and resanded after drying. This reduces the amount of sanding required after the piece has been stained and dried, but does not eliminate the necessity for resanding after the stain has dried.

Some manufacturers of finishing materials offer concentrated water stains which must be greatly diluted before they can be used. Water stains can be brushed on if equipment for spraying them on is not available. An important advantage of water

stain is that almost any desired color may be mixed or matched by combining two or more of the more commonly used colors: oak, running from yellowish to brownish yellow; maple, running from brownish yellow to reddish brown; mahogany, running from reddish brown to brownish red; and walnut, running from brown to blackish brown.

To mix water stain, heat water to just below the boiling point, in any vessel except one made of aluminum. Stir the water as you pour the powder slowly into it. Allow this mixture to cool and store it in a glass bottle. Use about four ounces of powder to a gallon of water. Then when you are ready to use the stain, dilute it to the color or tint desired. If a brush is used, choose a soft bristle brush about 2 inches wide, and as you stain the surface wipe off all excess stain with a soft cotton cloth until the color is as even as it is possible to make it.

Oil stains, unlike water stains, do not raise the grain of the wood and offer an equally wide range of colors. They are somewhat less troublesome for an amateur to use, but are more expensive. Oil stains also are not as transparent as water stains, and the pigments in them will leave a slightly opaque film upon the surface.

Oil stains come in two kinds: the pigmented type, which remains largely on the surface, and the penetrating type, which sinks more deeply into the surface of the wood.

Pigmented oil stains are made of coloring matter mixed with linseed oil as a vehicle and Japan drier to hasten the drying process. The coloring matter is usually the same kind as that used in tinting color for paint. Colors used in these stains usually settle to the bottom of the can and must be stirred before using. On open-grained woods the pores often absorb more coloring matter than the harder surface surrounding them, resulting in dark spots against the lighter background. This is especially true of very coarse-grained wood like oak, rosewood, and others like them, but it is not so noticeable on woods like walnut, mahogany, or cherry.

In penetrating oil stains the coloring matter is transparent, or nearly so, and is more like a dye than a pigment. Penetrating oil stains are more expensive as a rule, but if available, they penetrate the surface to a greater depth than the pigmented types, and this results in rich colors without obscuring the beauty of the grain.

Oil stains are easily mixed to get the colors most needed. These are brownish yellow, usually used as a maple stain; reddish brown for mahogany; and the true brown commonly associated with walnut. High-grade oil stains going under the names of maple, mahogany, and walnut stains may thus readily be intermixed to get the tint desired. They may be thinned with turpentine to make them lighter or the color more transparent. Colors ground in oil, used to color paint, may be substituted for ready-mixed oil stains, and these if thinned with turpentine often make very good stains. Japan drier may be added to make them dry more quickly.

Oil stains can be brushed on in any direction. After the stain has soaked well into the wood, the wood is wiped clean with soft cotton rags.

Sometimes a "wash coat" is used on a wood surface before stain is applied. A wash coat is very thin shellac, the purpose of which is to seal the surface of the wood on which it is put to prevent the surface from absorbing too much stain or coloring matter. We do not advocate using a sealing coat under stain unless the wood is so dried out from age or other factors that the use of a sealer will help preserve the surface on which it is used. For sealers to be used for this purpose, the proportion of shellac should be about one to eight of alcohol, so good absorption will result. A wash coat of this kind should be used only under oil stains and not prior to putting on water stain.

A coat of sealer is often applied to a surface after staining. To get a really smooth finish it is also needed before applying the paste filler. Most wood finishers cannot agree as to the best kind of undercoat to use beneath succeeding coats, but most finishing experts seem to have come to the conclusion that it should be a thin coat of the same material used for the final finishing coats. The purpose of using a sealer over stain or filler is to tie them down so they will not "bleed" into subsequent finishing applications. So, if the final finishing coats are to be shellac, then the sealer should be four-pound cut shellac thinned with eight parts or more of denatured alcohol. If the final coats are to be varnish, then mix the varnish with an equal amount of turpentine to make the sealer.

Lacquer must never be put on over varnish, since the solvents are of an entirely different nature and the two have no affinity for each other.

After the sealer has been put on over a stained surface and has thoroughly dried, the surface should be rubbed down with #0 or 00 steel wool to smooth the surface for what comes next. Any dust that remains on the surface as a result of this must be carefully removed before another coat of finish is put on.

If the furniture is made of mahogany, walnut, oak, or some other wood with large open pores, then a paste filler will be called for in order to make the wood smooth enough so that the final coats may be rubbed down to a glasslike finish. While all liquid materials used in putting on a good finish seal the pores to some extent, none of them with the exception of filler does the job thoroughly enough to avoid a pitted surface on all succeeding coats, and anyone taking pride in his work would find this very objectionable. Paste filler, known as "silex" filler, is made of crushed rock, ground very fine. It has a glasslike transparency, and once it has been thoroughly rubbed into the pores of wood and hardens, all parts of such surfaces level out to a smoothness that makes it possible to rub all subsequent coats equally smooth.

On soft woods like white pine, poplar, and other nonporous woods, filler will not be needed. On furniture made with such woods, the sealer coat may be followed by succeeding finishing coats as soon as the sealer which has been put on over the stain has dried thoroughly. If filler is called for, proceed in the following manner when applying it to the surfaces to be covered.

Most paste fillers come in a neutral gray shade, though colored fillers may also be bought. Most are of a thick, almost puttylike consistency and must be thinned down before they can be used. With a putty knife, transfer some of the paste to a vessel or can large enough to stir the mixture with ease; then add the thinner, composed of about 1 part turpentine to 2 parts of white gasoline. Stir the mixture to a thick souplike brushing consistency. If the piece of furniture on which the filler is to be used has been stained, the filler should be colored with stain dark enough so the colors will match after the filler has hardened. Colors in oil, or colors in Japan of the kind used to tint paint, may be thinned in turpentine and added to the thinned filler to get the color desired. Since both filler and coloring matter mixed with turpentine have a tendency to lighten after drying, it may be necessary to make the coloring matter somewhat darker than the stain had been. Whenever finishing on a piece of furniture is done, it is best to prepare test samples on small pieces of wood first to make sure the colors will turn out as desired.

Before putting on filler, have on hand a plentiful supply of clean burlap and clean rags. Filler, once it begins to set up, does so very quickly, and what residue is left upon the surface must then be removed with great dispatch. For this reason, it should be applied to relatively small areas at a time. To do this, use an old bristle brush on which the bristles are clean, but have been worn short from use. Brush the filler over the part to be filled until it is completely covered; allow this to dry until it loses its shine, which may take anywhere from five to ten minutes. With clean burlap rub the filler well into the pores of the wood, rubbing across the grain or with a circular motion. Filler will gather on the pad surface and with this kind of rubbing will be packed into the open pores to fill them level with other parts of the surface. As soon as you are satisfied the pores have been completely filled, rub off all residue across the grain with clean burlap and rags until none remains upon the surface, so as to avoid the cloudy effect residue would leave. Carvings or moldings may be done by brushing on the filler with a stiffer bristle brush, then wiping off with small pieces of burlap and rags, and cleaning out corners and edges with short wooden sticks the ends of which have been sharpened to a point.

When all surfaces and areas of the furniture have been filled and the surface has had plenty of time to dry, put on a coat of sealer using the same material to be used for the clear final coats of finish. Then sand the sealer coat, after it has dried for not less than twenty-four hours, with 8/0 abrasive paper, 2/0 steel wool, or both, to smooth it down for the succeeding finishing coats. Clean the surface thoroughly with a soft bristle brush and clean rags which are free of lint. The cloth may have to be dampened with a small amount of sealer to remove the last traces of lint or dust from the surface.

The sealer which has been put on over the filler is followed with two or more coats of transparent finishing material, depending upon the type of finish being applied and the quality of finish desired. Lacquer should never be used over a varnish sealer, though sometimes it is used over a shellac sealer. Varnish can be used over a shellac sealer, though some wood-finishing authorities frown upon it. The author, over a period of many years, has obtained good and long-lasting results by using tough floor varnishes over sealing coats of thin shellac, and he has yet to experience a failure as a result of this practice.

The two most suitable finishes for antique furniture, or antique reproductions, are a shellac-and-wax finish, or a hand-rubbed varnish finish. Lacquer finishes, which will be discussed later in the chapter, are not recommended for use on antique furniture either by professional refinishers or by dealers in antiques. While lacquer finishes are good if properly applied, they are mostly used by manufacturers of new, factory-made furniture, because they lend themselves well to assembly-line, high-speed production methods, and they are durable. The objections to the use of lacquer are that a lot of special equipment and facilities are required to use it properly, and that it does not provide the unique, soft, satiny gloss often referred to as "patina," which the older, time-tried methods of finishing seem to provide.

In the Wallace Nutting Studio, when the author worked there, the shellac-and-wax finish was used exclusively, and so far as the author is aware, this is the only kind of finish ever used on reproductions manufactured by Wallace Nutting. The finish seems to hold up well, for the author owns two Windsor chairs on which the finish is as well preserved as it was when the chairs were bought more than forty years ago. A shellac-and-wax finish is easy to apply, but disadvantages of its use are that more coats are required to get results comparable to a good varnish finish and that the finish will not stand up well when subjected to heat, moisture, or alcoholic beverages spilled on it. For these reasons it is a better finish to use on chairs, benches, mirror frames, clocks, and other pieces of like nature, than on tables, desks, chests of drawers, and so on, which are subject to the above-mentioned hazards.

Shellac finishes may be used on almost any kind of wood, but are especially effective on pine or maple, especially if used on wood which has been left unstained. There are two kinds of shellac—orange and white—and these may be mixed to change the color if so desired. When thinned to the proper consistency (see below) with alcohol, a shellac finish is easily put on. Poor jobs usually result from trying to hurry the job by putting on fewer coats of thick shellac than a greater number of thin coats as should be done. Another cause of failure is using shellac which has been kept too long, especially if part of the contents of the can has been used and the remaining contents allowed to remain in a partly filled can. Dirty brushes and containers always result in poor work, as do unsatisfactory heating or ventilating conditions and excessive moisture in the finishing room.

Most shellacking on furniture may be done with a high-grade China bristle brush about 2 inches wide and an equally good #4 sash brush. Brushes should be cleaned with denatured alcohol immediately after use and then hung up to dry in a clean place. The author prefers doing this to keeping the brush hung in a covered container filled so that the bristles are immersed with shellac. This may be done, however, if shellac is constantly being used. Unless this is the case, the author prefers to keep his brushes always clean.

A standard shellac and alcohol mixture is 4 pounds of shellac to 1 gallon of alcohol, known as a 4-pound cut. This should be thinned still more before using by adding more alcohol so the proportion is somewhere near 60 percent of the 4-pound cut shellac to 40 percent alcohol. Brush the shellac on the surface going with the grain as much as possible. A good rule to follow is to do those parts of the work first which are most inaccessible, and finish with those parts easiest to get to. This is also a good rule to follow when doing all other finishing operations. Brush the shellac only enough to get uniform coverage over the entire surface. To avoid drip, wipe the brush over a "strike" wire fastened near the top of one edge of the container. A good shellac finish requires at least four coats, to build up a surface that can be rubbed down on the final coat to a good glossy smoothness and still give a good protective covering.

When thoroughly dry, every coat must be rubbed down with 6/0 or 8/0 abrasive paper, and #0 or #00 steel wool to prepare the surface for the coat to follow. Careful dusting and cleaning after this has been done is essential, and dust must not be left floating in the air in the finishing room when finish of any kind is being put on. Six coats of shellac were put on every piece of furniture produced in the Wallace Nutting Studio, and every coat was carefully rubbed down and cleaned before the next one was put on. The final coat of shellac was then rubbed down by hand with "FFF" powdered pumice stone and water.

After carefully washing off all of the pumice powder that remains after rubbing, the piece of furniture on which a shellac finish has been put should be waxed. Use only a good grade of paste wax to do this, folding some of it into a small piece of soft clean cotton cloth and rubbing it over the entire surface. Allow this to dry for a time, then polish vigorously with a soft cotton cloth until a satisfactory gloss is achieved over the entire surface. Standard paste waxes bought in grocery, hardware, or paint stores will do, but some may be bought that contain small proportions of carnauba wax, a harder, tougher variety often found in car waxes. Furniture waxes containing large proportions of carnauba wax must be put on over only small areas at a time and rubbed before they have dried too long, since otherwise it may become impossible to spread them properly. In the Nutting Studios only beeswax was used. This was prepared by melting beeswax in a double boiler and, when it had slightly cooled, adding a mixture of spirits of turpentine and boiled linseed oil in about equal parts to the melted wax. The proportion of 1 quart of the turpentine and oil mixture to 1 pound of wax will be about right.

The finish the author recommends most highly for furniture made from plans in this book is the hand-rubbed varnish finish. Use only the best grades of 4-hour floor varnish, which is highly resistant to moisture, heat, and alcohol. If necessary this varnish may be thinned with turpentine. High-grade spar varnishes may be substituted, but they dry more slowly and are more expensive. Spar varnishes are more water resistant than floor varnishes as a general rule. Avoid rubbing varnishes, or those labeled "interior" varnishes, because they are mostly of inferior quality.

As few as two coats of good floor varnish will give a good finish, but the use of three and even four is highly recommended for a really first-class job. Longer periods for drying should be allowed between coats of varnish than for shellac, since varnish dries more slowly. The varnishing should be done in a room as nearly dust free as possible, and room temperature and the temperature of the varnish should not be lower than 70 degrees while the work is being done, and until the varnish is dry. The rule we gave for doing the most inaccessible areas first and the most easily reached areas last will apply here as it did when putting on the shellac finish. Varnish will not dry completely in four hours, as the label on a 4-hour can may cause you to believe. This merely implies that under favorable conditions the surface should be dust free in that space of time. As many as seventy-two hours should be allowed between coats, and even longer periods of time of up to two weeks are desirable.

On horizontal surfaces the varnish may be brushed on in even strokes by first brushing across the grain, then smoothing it out by going with the grain, and finally tipping it off with the brush held almost vertically to smooth out the bubbles. Work from the unfinished toward the finished portions as much as possible, and be sure every part of an area is covered before going to the next. You can ascertain if this has been done by looking over the varnished surface toward the light.

When doing vertical surfaces, care must be taken to avoid sags, where the varnish will run before it has dried, especially if too much is brushed on at a time. Brush on the varnish with short strokes from every direction, using only enough varnish on the brush to cover the surface fully and brushing from the outside to the center of each small area as you do it. Varnish dries very slowly, and unless considerable care is exercised in the brushing process, the varnish will run and sag for quite some time, leaving soft and high spots, which you will have trouble getting rid of.

When completely dry, the first coats may be gone over with fine abrasive papers and steel wool, to prepare them for additional coats of varnish. A "tack rag," made by taking a piece of finely woven cheesecloth first soaked in warm water, then wrung out and moistened with turpentine and freely sprinkled with varnish until the cloth turns yellow, is a useful tool for cleaning off dust and particles of dirt that remain after dusting off with steel wool, or dust left from sanding between coats.*

A final coat of varnish may be rubbed down with FFF powdered pumice stone and oil, or powdered pumice stone and water, until perfectly smooth and leveled out. In small shops this rubbing is done by using specially made felt pads about ⅜ inch thick and cut to the size of a rectangle about 3 inches by 4 inches or larger. Where more of this work is being done, vibrating rubbing machines similar in many respects to the vibrating electric sander are used to do most of the work. Paraffin oil, readily purchased in paint stores, is the kind used to rub down furniture with pumice stone. A higher polish may be obtained on a rubbed surface by using rottenstone and oil to rub the surface after the pumice rubbing, but this higher polish is not recommended for antiques or antique reproductions, since such polishing is not in the true tradition of such furniture. Polishing with wax is better and will help preserve the finish, once it has dried hard. Allow some time before waxing, as wax over a newly finished surface tends to soften the finish until some seasoning has ensued.

Lacquer finishes are now almost universally used in furniture factories. The high price of labor, materials, and manufacturing costs makes the use of synthetic materials, which are well adapted to fast production methods and techniques, almost mandatory to hold down costs. Lacquer dries very quickly, much faster than any of the materials we have so far discussed. Once special equipment for using it has been installed, good finishes can be applied almost in a matter of hours instead of days or weeks as is the case with older and more conventional methods of finishing. Lacquer finishes are hard enough and durable enough to satisfy

---

* A tack rag may be kept moist in a closed glass jar. Keep it moist while in use by sprinkling it with water and turpentine, then wring it out and refold it. Varnish in tack rags must not be allowed to harden.

most demands placed upon products on which it is used, and the savings in time and cost of labor passed on to the consumer make the difference between his being able to afford it or having to do without it. At Wallace Nutting Studio the cost of finishing a piece of furniture was calculated to be anywhere from a third to half the cost of manufacturing it, and with present high prices and labor costs, this is a factor to be carefully considered.

While brushing lacquers are on the market, they are not as good as spraying lacquers, but some of them are good enough to be used by amateurs lacking the more sophisticated equipment needed to put on a first-class lacquer finish.

Special fillers must be used under lacquer, since those having an oil base would not bond with the lacquer, and any lacquer put over it would not hold up. Stains if used at all must be either water or acid stains. Recommendation of the manufacturer of the kind of lacquer being used should be followed when choosing stains and filler, to make sure all ingredients used are compatible and will hold up when one is put next to the other.

Two coats of lacquer may be applied in one day, and if the work is kept free of dust no rubbing between coats is required. Some lacquers dry to a satin finish and therefore need no rubbing even on the final coat. Others dry to a gloss finish; if a satin finish is desired when these are used, the final coat must be rubbed down with very fine steel wool, or with pumice stone and water, and then waxed. For a still higher sheen the pumice stone rub should be followed by rubbing down with rottenstone and water.

The foregoing covers most of the operations to be followed in producing high-grade finishes on pieces of furniture. Other phases of furniture finishing such as glazing, shading, bleaching, and preparation for refinishing have not been discussed since this chapter is intentionally on only the minimum essentials.

However, we would like to add a word on bleaching. For a bleaching process which is practical for the amateur to employ, the Sherwin-Williams Company gave the author permission in an earlier book * to refer to their brochure F-501, in which the following procedure was recommended. We would like to repeat here:

Based upon experiments, an ideal bleaching system would be as follows: hydrogen peroxide is applied to the wood first and the piece is then placed in a closet or confined space in the presence of ammonia vapors. This bleaches deeply, and the wood can be sanded well without danger of cutting through to the unbleached wood.

Wood bleached by this method has a natural appearance. The grain stands out and is clear . . . there are no salts or residual bleaching materials remaining on the wood to affect further finishing. This method is economical since only a double coat of hydrogen peroxide is applied and no caustic is needed. Also, no neutralizer is needed after bleaching. The closet or confined space should be air-tight, and the size would depend upon the size and number of pieces to be bleached at one time. This system may be used on unassembled wood or on the completed piece.

The enclosed area confines the ammonia vapors, preventing their escape because of the very volatile nature of the ammonia. The vapors then remain longer in contact with the wood and do a more complete job of bleaching. A pan partially filled with household ammonia is placed somewhere in the confined room. The wood is given a coat of hydrogen peroxide by applying either with a rag or a sponge. A few minutes should be allowed for the solution to soak into the wood. Another coat is then applied and the pieces immediately placed in the presence of the ammonia fumes.

Several hours may be required for the bleaching operation to become complete. As soon as the panel or piece of furniture is dry, it can be sanded and finished. No neutralizer or cleaning agent is necessary.

* *Heirloom Furniture.*

THREE

Hardware

GOOD hardware is such an important item on furniture of good quality that it deserves special attention in a book of this kind. Only the finest hardware obtainable should be used on the pieces presented here, and while the items needed may appear to be a bit high in price when purchased, the quality of workmanship entailed in producing them, and the research and know-how required to ensure authenticity in their design, justify the small difference in cost between items of mediocre quality and these which are the very best obtainable.

Some handwork is involved in the production of many of the items shown on Plates 1 and 2, and the finish and careful attention to detail involved in the production of the brass hardware in particular are of the very highest order. Castings for handles are solid brass, and plates, which in all cases are carefully made reproductions of antique originals, are of heavy metal, with edges carefully beveled like those of the handmade ones. These are finished in a special old color, very closely resembling the aging from natural causes on the originals from which the designs were copied.

Designs on plates like those on the pull shown in No. 1, Plate 1, are hand stamped. This is a pull suitable for use on the Queen Anne Lowboy. Nos. 2 and 3 are examples of very early pulls for Chippendale furniture and may be used on pieces like the Salem Chest of Drawers. Bail plates with fancy scrolled edges, of the kinds shown in Nos. 5, 11, 14,

and 17, and their matching escutcheon plates like the one shown in No. 8, came a bit later, but all are authentic and proper for the finest Chippendale pieces or pieces of that era, like the Blockfront Chest-on-chest.

Pulls like those shown in Nos. 6, 9, and 12 are used on Sheraton and Hepplewhite furniture and on American adaptations of these styles.

Nos. 10 and 16 show pulls used on cupboard doors like those of the Queen Anne Corner Cupboard. They may be fitted with turn fingers for use as door latches, as shown in Nos. 10, 13, and 16.

Many other examples of special hardware items are shown, like the spring catch used on the Snakefoot Tilt-top Table in No. 7. Other special items are the small sliding bolt, No. 18, used on the Spice Cabinet doors; the elbow catch, No. 19, used on the inside of cupboard doors like the left-hand doors on the Dutch Cupboard. The brass keepers, shown in No. 24, are used to hold sections of the Duncan Phyfe Dining Table together. The heavy casters with the brass sheath are used on the same table; and the cover plate for bolts which hold beds together is shown in No. 21. Some bed-bolt covers have round plates, like the one shown in the chapter on the Hepplewhite Bed.

The H hinge shown in No. 20 is brass, and these are also made in the H-L shape like the one made of iron in No. 30. No. 23 shows a hinge which may be used on the door of a grandfather clock.

No. 27 shows a bed bolt like those used to fasten the rails to head- and footposts. The head on these bolts is specially formed so it is possible to tighten the bolt with either a screwdriver or a socket wrench, even though the head of the bolt is recessed in a counterbored hole.

No. 28 shows a table hinge of the kind used on rule joints of a drop-leaf table. No. 29 is a wrought-iron rattail hinge, a very early type of hinge sometimes used on cupboard doors on furniture like the Dutch Cupboard or the Carved Shell-top Corner Cupboard. Although it is possible to buy rattail hinges of brass, these belong to furniture of an earlier era when such hinges were made of wrought iron.

The wrought-iron hardware shown in Nos. 26,

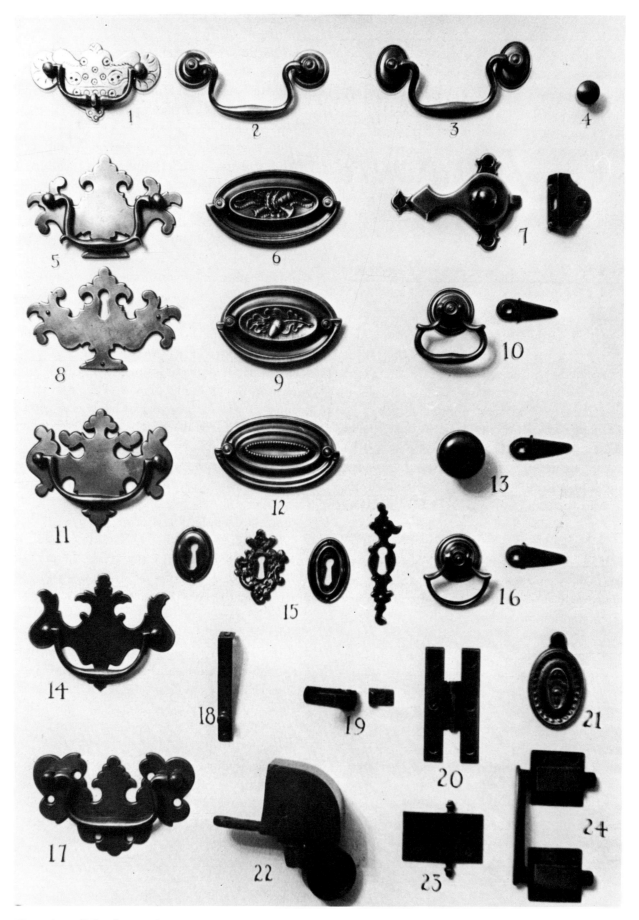

Plate 1. All hardware shown here is manufactured by Ball and Ball, Exton, Pennsylvania.

30, and 31 is of excellent quality and is manufactured in considerable quantities. It is sold throughout the country in hardware stores.

The telescoping drawer supports, No. 25, are relatively modern items in the hardware field and are now being widely used on kitchen cabinets and other pieces of furniture where easy sliding drawers are essential. Ordinarily such modern innovations would be frowned upon for furniture of the kind shown in this book, but in this particular instance they are justifiable and necessary for a drawer like the one shown in the Bachelor's Chest, which holds and hides a telephone, another modern invention.

A few more examples of hardware are shown throughout the book, but the ones shown here describe most of those needed to build the pieces illustrated.

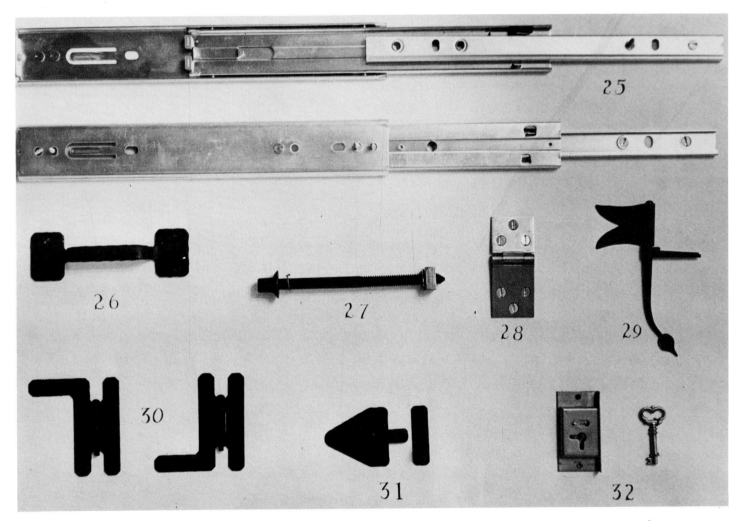

Plate 2. Examples of Ball and Ball hardware except as follows: No. 25, telescoping supports for drawers, manufactured by Grant Pulley and Hardware Company, West Nyack, New York; Nos. 26, 30, and 31 manufactured by McKinney Hardware, Scranton, Pennsylvania.

FOUR

Nested Tables: Set of Four

WHENEVER anyone has a number of guests to entertain at a party, a set of nested tables will be very useful. Another very obvious advantage of owning such a set of tables is the small amount of room they occupy. They may be used for so many different purposes that one need hardly go to the bother of enumerating them, and so we will not attempt doing it here. The scale and proportions of the tables are very good, either stacked or when used individually.

To build the set of tables, get out all sixteen legs at once. Square all sixteen to the 1⅛-inch size given in the Bill of Material. The legs of each table are made ⅞ inch longer than they are on the one below it, but all are tapered from the same point to the floor, as shown on the left in Fig. 3.

The three larger tables are built exactly alike except for size. Mortise-and-tenon joints are used to fasten ends and backs to the legs, but because of the exceedingly slender legs, the tenons are mitered at the ends, where they meet each other on the back legs, so they may be made longer. Such a joint, when glued up, also helps keep the leg stronger if the joint is carefully made and put together.

To make a track in which to slide the table fitting into another, the tops of the legs must be cut away, and a rabbet must be cut on the upper inside edge of each end. The amount of clearance, shown in the drawing at the ends of the tabletops in Fig. 7,

will suffice to ensure easy sliding back and forth and at the same time allow enough to keep the top well into the track, sufficiently to hold it.

Tops are fastened to the table frames with small steel plates, mortised into the tops so the bottom of the plate is level with the underside of the top. The steel plates must first be screwed to the upper edges of the rails and then to the top when putting on the top. Small steel mending plates may be used for this purpose so long as neither they nor the wood screws used to fasten them to the top protrude to scratch the surface of the top below it.

Fig. 1. *Nested Tables, Set of Four.* A ROBERT TREATE HOGG REPRODUCTION.

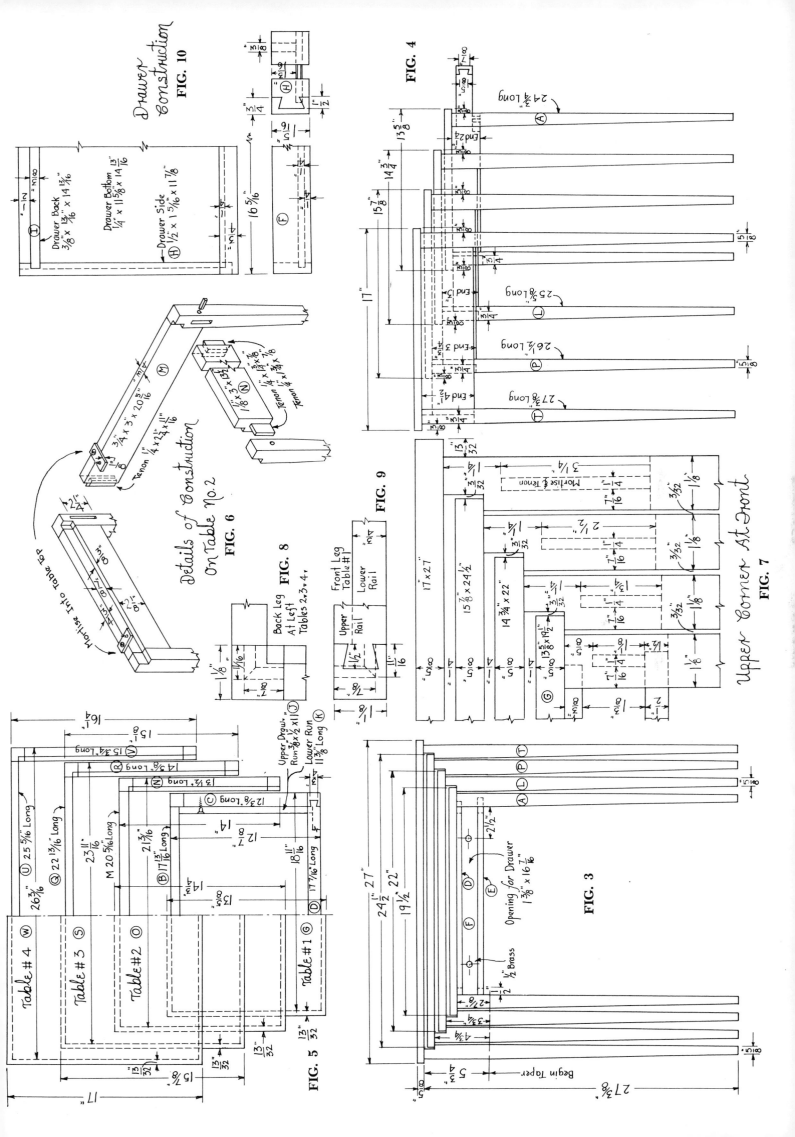

Only the smallest table differs in construction from the other three. This is made necessary by the addition of the shallow drawer. Two rails are joined to the front, above and below the drawer. When assembling this table, glue the ends to the legs first. Then glue the back and rail (E) to the legs. The upper rail (D) may be glued to the legs after the frame has been assembled, provided the dovetail mortises have been cut into the tops of

these two legs before the frame is glued together. Trial assemblies, prior to gluing, are always advisable, to make sure everything fits together properly.

Drawer construction details are shown in Fig. 10, and no difficulty should be experienced here if dimensions given in the drawing are adhered to. Small brass knobs are screwed to the drawer front to open it. No. 4 at the top of Plate 1 on hardware shows one of these.

Fig. 2. Showing the Tables Telescoped Open.

BILL OF MATERIAL

TABLE #1

Mahogany

4 Legs (A) $1\frac{1}{8}$" x $1\frac{1}{8}$" x $24\frac{3}{4}$"
1 Back (B) $\frac{3}{4}$" x $2\frac{1}{4}$" x $17\frac{13}{16}$"
2 Ends (C) $1\frac{1}{8}$" x $2\frac{1}{4}$" x $12\frac{3}{8}$"
1 Rail above drawer (D) $\frac{3}{8}$" x $1\frac{1}{8}$" x $17\frac{7}{16}$"
1 Rail below drawer (E) $\frac{1}{2}$" x $\frac{3}{4}$" x $17\frac{15}{16}$"
1 Drawer front (F) $\frac{3}{4}$" x $1\frac{5}{16}$" x $16\frac{5}{16}$"
1 Top (G) $\frac{5}{8}$" x $13\frac{5}{8}$" x $19\frac{1}{2}$"

Poplar

2 Drawer sides (H) $\frac{1}{2}$" x $1\frac{5}{16}$" x $11\frac{7}{8}$"
1 Drawer back (I) $\frac{3}{8}$" x $1\frac{3}{16}$" x $14\frac{13}{16}$"
2 Drawer runs (upper) (J) $\frac{3}{8}$" x $\frac{1}{2}$" x 11"
2 Drawer runs (lower) (K) $\frac{1}{2}$" x $\frac{1}{2}$" x $11\frac{3}{8}$"

Plywood

1 Drawer bottom $\frac{1}{4}$" x $11\frac{5}{8}$" x $14\frac{13}{16}$"

TABLE #2

4 Legs (L) $1\frac{1}{8}$" x $1\frac{1}{8}$" x $25\frac{5}{8}$"
1 Back (M) $\frac{3}{4}$" x 3" x $20\frac{5}{16}$"
2 Ends (N) $1\frac{1}{8}$" x 3" x $13\frac{1}{2}$"
1 Top (O) $\frac{5}{8}$" x $14\frac{3}{4}$" x 22"

TABLE #3

4 Legs (P) $1\frac{1}{8}$" x $1\frac{1}{8}$" x $26\frac{1}{2}$"
1 Back (Q) $\frac{3}{4}$" x $3\frac{3}{4}$" x $22\frac{13}{16}$"
2 Ends (R) $1\frac{1}{8}$" x $3\frac{3}{4}$" x $14\frac{5}{8}$"
1 Top (S) $\frac{5}{8}$" x $15\frac{7}{8}$" x $24\frac{1}{2}$"

TABLE #4

4 Legs (T) $1\frac{1}{8}$" x $1\frac{1}{8}$" x $27\frac{3}{8}$"
1 Back (U) $\frac{3}{4}$" x $4\frac{1}{2}$" x $25\frac{5}{16}$"
2 Ends (V) $1\frac{1}{8}$" x $4\frac{1}{2}$" x $15\frac{3}{4}$"
1 Top (W) $\frac{5}{8}$" x 17" x 27"

Fig. 1. Nested Tables, Set of Two. A ROBERT TREATE HOGG REPRODUCTION.

FIVE

Nested Tables: Set of Two

THIS set of nested tables is constructed in the same way as the nested tables described in Chapter 4. The only difference in the sets being the sizes, the number of tables comprising each set, and the manner of fitting the drawer into the side of the small table in the set of four and into the end of the table in the set of two. A nice feature of this set is the size of the drawer, which is unusually long for a table so small.

All of the above being quite evident from even the most cursory examination of the drawings, we feel it unnecessary to give additional directions on how to construct the tables in this set and direct your attention instead to the instructions given for the construction of the tables in the set of four.

BILL OF MATERIAL

TABLE #1

Walnut or Teak *

4 Legs (A) 1¼" x 1¼" x 27⅜"
2 Sides (B) 1¼" x 4½" x 26½"
1 Back (C) 1¼" x 4½" x 14½"
1 Top (D) ⅝" x 16" x 28"

TABLE #2

4 Legs (E) 1¼" x 1¼" x 26½"
2 Sides (F) 1¼" x 3¾" x 24¾"
1 Back (G) 1¼" x 3¾" x 11¾"
1 Top (H) ⅝" x 13¼" x 26¼"
1 Drawer front (I) ¾" x 2⁷⁄₁₆" x 9⅝"
1 Rail above drawer (J) ½" x 1¼" x 10¾"
1 Rail below drawer (K) ¾" x ¾" x 11¾"

Poplar

2 Drawer sides (L) ½" x 2⁷⁄₁₆" x 23¾"

1 Drawer back (M) ⅜" x 1¹⁵⁄₁₆" x 9⅛"
2 Drawer runs (N) ½" x ¾" x 22¾"
2 Drawer runs (O) ¾" x ¾" x 23¼"

Plywood

1 Drawer bottom ¼" x 9⅛" x 23½"

* The set of tables shown in Fig. 1 was made of teak, a wood that does not warp easily but is somewhat difficult for the person having a small shop and limited facilities to work with. The reason for this is that teak, when the tree grows, pulls grit and sand into the large wood pores, and this gritty substance dulls ordinary tools very rapidly. Where teak is worked regularly, specially treated blades, such as carbide-tipped saw blades, must be used. These are not affected by the abrasive substance in the structure of teak nearly as much as ordinary saws.

The reason for using teak on the table shown in Fig. 1 is that the grain can be run going in the same direction as the length of the table. Tops made of other kinds of wood would have a great tendency to warp if they were used and this were done. If other woods than teak are used for these tables, we suggest the grain be run to go across the tables instead of lengthwise, to prevent the contingency of trouble from warping.

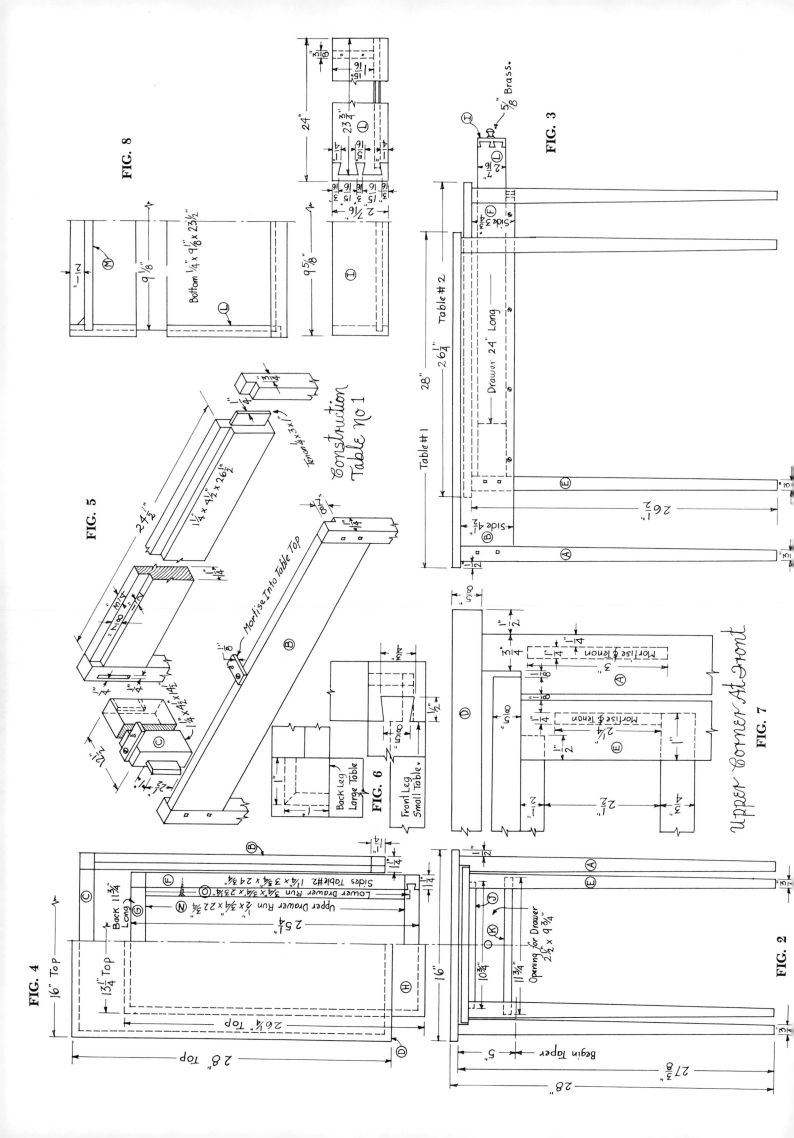

SIX

Queen Anne Tea Table

THE delicately scaled, beautifully proportioned Queen Anne walnut tea table, shown in Figs. 1 and 2, like so many old handcrafted Queen Anne pieces has many unusual features to recommend it. All parts are gracefully formed, and the legs and shaped aprons, running clear around the table, especially so. The tastefully designed and handsomely executed shells carved on the knees, and the hand-carved webbed feet, are accents worthy of note.

Queen Anne pieces having the more sophisticated design features, such as the webbed feet in this one, were often made of mahogany, especially those made after 1720. These webbed feet were also sometimes known as trifid feet, so called because there were three toes separated by deeply cut grooves; they are among the more distinctive features found on late Queen Anne and Early Georgian chairs and tables.

The legs on this table are exceedingly well formed, unfolding in a graceful elongated S curve, instead of having the main part of the leg in the middle straight, as in so many of the earlier and cruder examples of this style of furniture.

To build the table, get out stock for the four legs. Make a full-sized pattern from the drawing of the leg, shown in Fig. 8. Draw this shape on two opposite sides of each leg and saw the legs to the shape of the pattern. Save the waste and tack it back on the leg, being sure the brads used to do

this go into the waste parts to be sawed from the legs on the sides still to be sawed off. Again transfer the pattern outline to the legs, then finish sawing the legs to shape.

Be sure the upper part of the leg is carefully squared and smoothed on all four sides, then lay out mortises to fasten both the rails and shaped aprons. The sizes and location of these may be gotten from Figs. 4 and 7.

When mortises have been cut into all legs, draw the shell on each knee; then carve it. These shell carvings are not raised very high above the surface, not much more than ⅛ inch, in fact. Notice in carving the feet that the webs on the ankles above the foot are carved to a convex shape, while the part immediately below them is concave to make the grooves between the toes. On most such legs, the web on the ankle is hollowed out too.

Make the side and end rails. Cut tenons on the ends of these and fit them to the mortises in the legs. Also cut grooves for the tabletop fasteners, one of which is shown in Fig. 7. Cut out openings

Fig. 1. Queen Anne Tea Table. A ROBERT TREATE HOGG REPRODUCTION.

Fig. 2. A Side View of the Table.

for the sliding candleholders. Make these openings ⅛ inch longer, and at least ¹⁄₁₆ inch wider than the width and thickness of the sliding candleholder board, to allow for easy movement. The same clearance should be allowed when making the sliding candleholder track-rail grooves.

Now make and shape the aprons with the scrolled bottom edges. Tenons should be cut on both ends of these before cutting them to the shape shown in the cross-section view in Fig. 3, and before cutting the scrollwork on the lower edges. Fit these tenons to the mortises in the legs; then, after sawing the aprons to shape on the bot-

toms and smoothing them up with a file and sandpaper, glue the shaped aprons to the bottom edges of the rails. Then glue up the table frame consisting of legs, rails, and aprons.

Make the sliding candleholder rails (I), and groove them to hold the sliding boards. Before fastening these to the frame make the sliding boards and be sure they slide easily in the tracks. There should be enough clearance when these have been fastened to the table frame to permit them to be easily drawn back and forth even after the finishing coats have all been put on. Make fronts for these sliding boards and join them to the slides with tongue-and-groove joints.

Now make the top. The top may be made of a plank 1⅝ inches thick, as we show it in the cross-section view in Fig. 10. However, it is permissible and simpler to glue the molding strips to the upper surface, either after shaping it, or before doing so if the molding is hand carved.* The molding on both ends of the tabletop should, however, be cross grained, so it will swell and shrink about the same as the top itself. If the grain of the molding on the ends of the tabletop went in a different direction, it would cause the top to warp or split, and quite probably both. Even so, to help guard against this possibility this top has saw kerfs cut lengthwise through it underneath, almost from one end to the other, to release tensions and strains in order to prevent warping or splitting. When the top has been made, sanded, and cleaned up, it may be fastened to the table frame by means of the metal tabletop fasteners.

To put on a suitable finish, consult the chapter on wood finishing for directions.

BILL OF MATERIAL

Black Walnut or Mahogany

4 Legs (A) 2¼″ x 2¼″ x 24⅜″
2 Side rails (B) ¾″ x 3″ x 24¾″
2 End rails (C) ¾″ x 3″ x 14½″
2 Side aprons (D) 1¾″ x 2¼″ x 24¼″
2 End aprons (E) 1¾″ x 2¼″ x 14″
2 Sliding candleholders (F) ½″ x 7″ x 13″
2 Fronts for sliding candleholders (G) ⅝″ x 1″ x 7½″
1 Tabletop (H) 1⅝″ x 18½″ x 28¾″

2 Sliding candleholder track rails (I) 1½″ x 2″ x 24¾″
4 Strips to hold sliding candleholder track rails (J) ¾″ x ¾″ x 2″
2 Dowels to stop sliding candleholders (K) ½″ diameter x 1½″

* If the molding is made separately and is to be glued to the ⅝-inch top, spline joints should be made where the pieces are joined at each corner, to strengthen these joints. The tabletop shown in Figs. 1 and 2 is made from a single piece of wood 1⅝ inch thick.

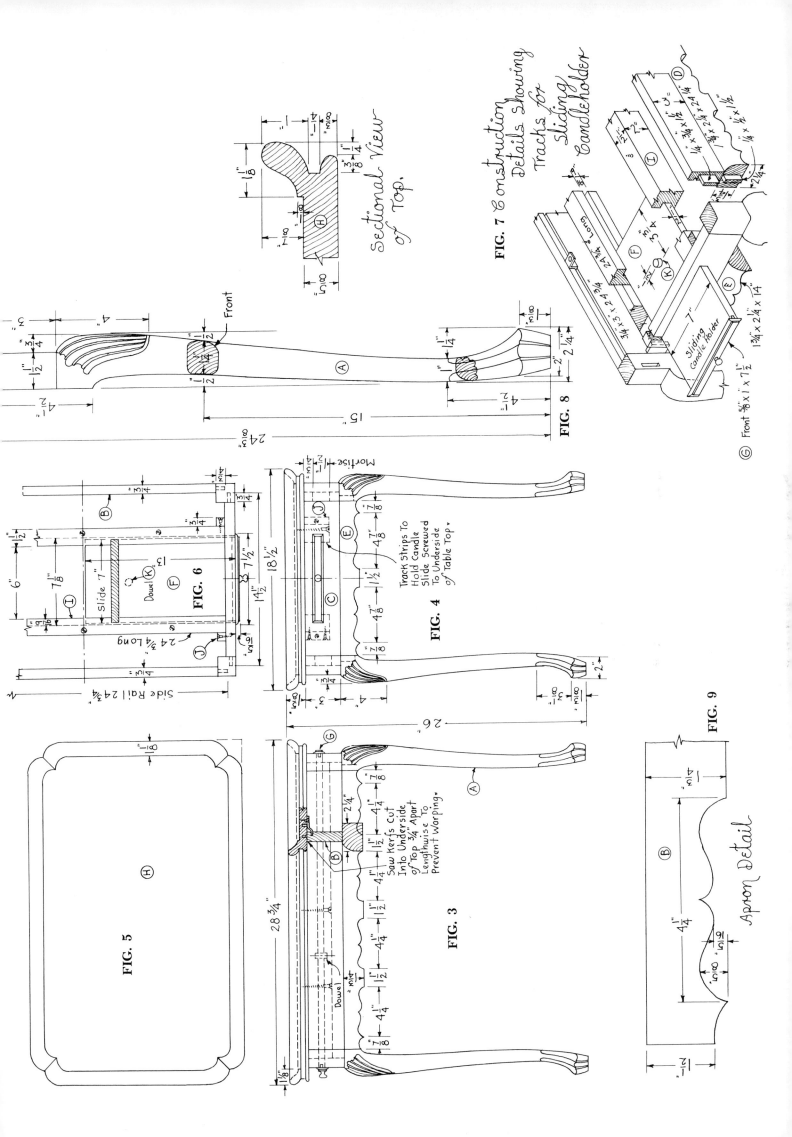

Sectional View of Top.

FIG. 7 Construction Details Showing Tracks for Sliding Candleholder

FIG. 8

Front

FIG. 4

Track Strips To Hold Candle Slide Screwed To Underside of Table Top.

FIG. 9

Apron Detail

FIG. 6

Slide 7″ Dowel (K) 13

Side Rail 24¾ 24¾ Long

FIG. 5

FIG. 3

Saw Kerfs Cut Into Underside of Top ¾″ Apart Lengthwise To Prevent Warping.

Mortise

G Front ⅝ x 1 x 7½″

SEVEN

Queen Anne Pembroke Table

SMALL drop-leaf tables like the Queen Anne table shown in Fig. 1 came to be known as "Pembroke" tables because Thomas Sheraton once indicated that a Lady Pembroke had such a table built to her rather precise specifications. Such tables, which seldom exceed 3½ feet in length when leaves are extended, became quite popular during the second half of the eighteenth century; they were built in every major style of furniture in vogue following the time when Lady Pembroke commissioned her cabinetmaker to build the first one. Most tables in this category are distinguished by having simple, attractively designed members, such as the beautifully shaped legs and feet found on this particular example. Small tables like this will be found to be very useful, and the purposes they serve are many and varied.

To build the table, first get out stock for the legs, which require solid pieces measuring 2½" x 2½" x 25". Before cutting these legs to shape, lay out and cut the mortises on two adjacent sides. Dovetail mortises, for joining rail (H) to the tops of the front legs, may be laid out while making a trial assembly of the table frame. Then they may be cut before the frame is glued together.

Draw a full-sized pattern of the leg from the drawing shown in Fig. 6 and transfer this shape to two opposite sides of each leg. Cut two sides to shape on the band saw, saving the waste pieces so they can be bradded back on the leg to cut the other two sides to shape.

Blocks (B) are not part of the 2½-inch-square stock, but are glued to the top of the leg after the main part has been sawed to shape. These blocks should be left square on all sides in order to clamp them when making the glue joint. By drawing the shape on the inside of the block after it has been glued to the leg, they may be sawed to the shape shown on the pattern.

When two sides of the legs have been sawed to shape, tack the waste to the parts that will be cut off as waste on the remaining two sides. Trace the pattern on the tacked-on waste pieces and saw the last two sides to shape. Once this has been done, the leg may be rounded and shaped as indicated by the cross-sections on the leg shown at the left on Fig. 2.

Now get out stock for rails (C), (D), and (E).

Fig. 1. Queen Anne Pembroke Table. A ROBERT TREATE HOGG REPRODUCTION.

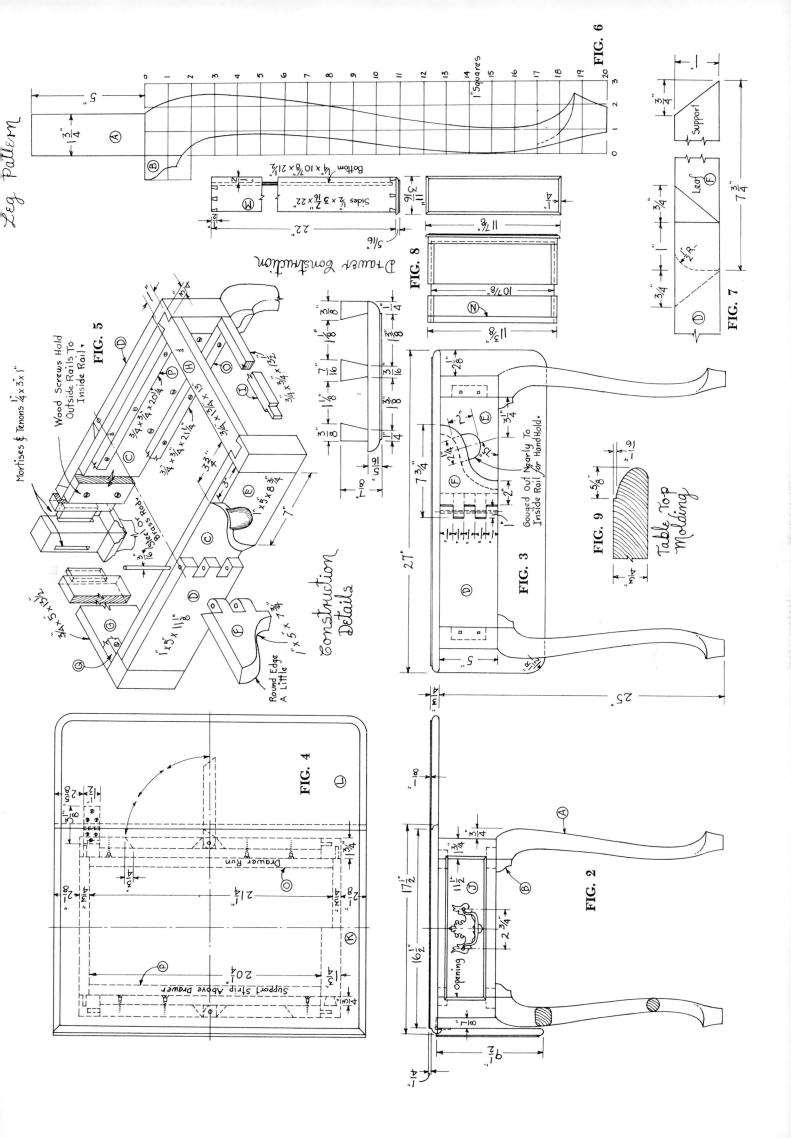

Leg Pattern

1" Squares

FIG. 6

Support

FIG. 7

Drawer Construction

FIG. 8

Bottom ¼ x 10⅞ x 21½.
Sides ½ x 3⅞₆ x 22.

Construction Details

Mortises & Tenons ¼ x 3 x 1"

Wood Screws Hold Outside Rails To Inside Rail.

FIG. 5

Gouged out Nearly To Inside Rail for Handhold.

FIG. 3

Table Top Molding

FIG. 9

FIG. 4

Drawer Run

Support Strip Above Drawer

Opening

FIG. 2

Square, sand, and cut these to shape and to their proper size. Note that the tenons joining the side stretchers to the legs are made on short stretchers (D) and (E). Stretchers (C) are merely butted against the tops of the legs and are not glued or fastened to them. Rails (D) and (E) are screwed to the outside of rails (C). Some glue may be used to help fasten these three pieces together, but it will not be necessary to coat these surfaces entirely with glue if enough wood screws are used to hold them together.

Before gluing rails (D) and (E) to rails (C), the finger-jointed hinges will have to be made and fitted, by which the two tabletop support wings are fastened to rails (D). By careful examination of Figs. 4, 5, and 7, you will note that angles are cut at the backs of these fingers on rails (D), just as they are on the inside of the fingers on wing supports (F), to make room for the corners to make the arc when (F) is swung to a position at right angles to the rails.

The S-curved edge of (F) and its matching curve on rail (E) are cut at an angle, in order to make the handhold gouged into rail (E). This gouged-out portion on rail (E) is shown to go almost as deep as the thickness of the rail, thus making it possible to take a good hold on the back of (F) in order to pull it away from the rails.

Once the finger joints have been made and properly joined and fitted, get out stock for rails (G), (H), and (I). Cut tenons and dovetails on the ends of these, as indicated on the drawings. Make a trial assembly of the table frame, and make the layouts for the dovetail mortises on top of the front legs. Cut these dovetail mortises. You may then glue the table frame together. First glue the side rails to the legs, and then glue rails (G) and (I) to the legs. Rail (H) is glued to the legs after the rest of the frame has been glued together, since it may be slipped into place from the top.

Make strips (O) and (P) for drawer runs and supports. Screw these to the inside of rails (C), as shown in Fig. 5.

Now make the drawer, which goes to the back of the table frame. Details and dimensions to make this drawer are shown in Fig. 8. Fit the drawer to the table frame.

Get out stock to make the tabletop. Leaves are joined to the center section with rule joints, as they should always be on fine drop-leaf tabletops. Two hinges are used to fasten each leaf, and one of these is shown in Fig. 4. As shown in Figs. 2 and 4, the barrel of this hinge must be centered below the line separating the leaf from the tabletop, which you see on the upper side of the tabletop. The special table hinge, having one leaf longer than the other, makes this possible. Such hinges must be mortised into the underside of the tabletop to bring their surface level with this underside. The radius of the molding on the rule joint is $\frac{1}{2}$ inch.

When the rule joints have been made and the hinges have been put on, the hinges may be removed to cut, on the shaper, the molding going around the outside of the tabletop. After this has been done, put the hinges back on and fasten the tabletop to the table frame.

Put the drawer pull on the drawer, and you will be ready to put on the finishing coats. For directions to do this consult the chapter on wood finishing.

BILL OF MATERIAL

Black Walnut or Mahogany

4 Legs (A) $2\frac{1}{2}$" x $2\frac{1}{2}$" x 25"
8 Blocks for legs (B) 1" x $2\frac{1}{2}$" x $1\frac{1}{2}$"
2 Side rails (C) $\frac{3}{4}$" x 5" x $19\frac{1}{4}$"
2 Short side rails (D) 1" x 5" x $11\frac{1}{8}$"
2 Short side rails (E) 1" x 5" x $8\frac{3}{4}$"
2 Tabletop support wings (F) 1" x 5" x $7\frac{3}{4}$"
1 Table rail (G) $\frac{3}{4}$" x 5" x $13\frac{1}{2}$"
1 Table rail (H) $\frac{3}{4}$" x $1\frac{3}{4}$" x 13"
1 Table rail (I) $\frac{3}{4}$" x $\frac{3}{4}$" x $13\frac{1}{2}$"
1 Drawer front (J) $\frac{7}{8}$" x $3\frac{11}{16}$" x $11\frac{7}{8}$"

1 Top (K) $\frac{3}{4}$" x $17\frac{1}{2}$" x 27"
2 Drop leaves (L) $\frac{3}{4}$" x $9\frac{1}{2}$" x 27"

Poplar

2 Drawer sides (M) $\frac{1}{2}$" x $3\frac{7}{16}$" x 22"
1 Drawer back (N) $\frac{1}{2}$" x $2\frac{11}{16}$" x $11\frac{3}{8}$"
2 Drawer runs (O) $\frac{3}{4}$" x $\frac{3}{4}$" x $21\frac{1}{4}$"
2 Drawer supports (P) $\frac{3}{4}$" x $\frac{3}{4}$" x $20\frac{1}{4}$"
1 Strip at back (Q) $\frac{3}{4}$" x $\frac{3}{4}$" x $11\frac{1}{2}$"

Plywood

1 Drawer bottom $\frac{1}{4}$" x $10\frac{7}{8}$" x $21\frac{1}{2}$"

EIGHT

Queen Anne Handkerchief Table

THE walnut table shown in Fig. 1, which fits so nicely into the corner of a room, has legs and feet which are quite unusual even for the Queen Anne style, noteworthy for its beautifully curved cabriole legs. Delicately and gracefully shaped and proportioned, the legs of this table fully live up to William Hogarth's designation of the **S** curve as "the Line of Beauty." The pad foot of the Queen Anne leg is beautiful, but seldom does one find it shaped in so distinctive a pattern as it is in this table and on the legs of the lowboy shown in Chapter 9. The table gets its name from the similarity of the top, when the leaf is down, to a handkerchief folded on the bias.

To build the table, select the very best grade of black walnut wood 2¼ inches square by 27 inches long to make the legs. First draw a full-sized pattern made from the one shown in Fig. 5. Using this pattern, trace the outline of the leg on two opposite sides of the leg stock, after the stock has been cut and squared to the size given in the Bill of Material. Pay no attention to the blocks (G), which are not yet a part of the leg at this time, but which will be added and glued on later. Saw the leg to this shape on the band saw, cutting close to the lines that have been drawn on the two sides.

If the pattern, shown in Fig. 5, is to be used to draw lines on the last two sides, it will be necessary to save the waste pieces which have been cut from the first two sides of the leg and nail them back on the leg. Small brads, driven through waste parts of the stock rather than the leg itself, will fasten the waste to the leg well enough to permit marking and cutting the remaining two sides of the leg to shape. A more detailed description of this process is given in Chapter 6.

When the waste from all four sides of the leg has been cut off on the band saw, the leg will be curved properly lengthwise, but will have to be rounded and shaped as shown in Fig. 1 and as indicated by the cross-section views shown in Fig. 5. This shaping is done with a spokeshave, well-

Fig. 1. Queen Anne Handkerchief Table. A ROBERT TREATE HOGG REPRODUCTION.

sharpened scraper blades, wood files, and sandpaper.

Once the legs and feet have been properly formed, be sure the upper end of the leg, where the rails are to be joined to it, is perfectly squared and smoothed. On the two adjacent inside surfaces of this upper part of the back leg, and on the correct one upper side of each of the front legs, make layouts for the mortises, as shown in Figs. 2, 3, and 4. Cut these mortises on the mortising machine, if such equipment is available, or if not, then with hand tools.

When the mortises have been cut on all legs, make blocks (G) and glue these to the legs. Cut the curves on these after gluing them to the legs. Otherwise it will be too difficult to fasten clamps securely to them for the glue to dry. Even so, the waste pieces cut from the leg tops will be needed under the clamps to do this properly. Cut tenons on both ends of rails (B) and, when these fit the mortises properly, glue the three legs and rails (B) together.

Because of the triangular shape of the table frame, it is not practical to use mortise-and-tenon joints to fasten the front rail (C) to the legs. An angled butt joint is made instead, fitting the ends of (C) into the corners formed by rails (B) and the two legs having only one mortise, as shown in Fig. 6. Fig. 6 also shows how the ends of rail (C) are fastened with glue and wood screws to rails (B). No glue is put on the end face of rail (C) where it butts against the front legs, because shrinkage or swelling would not be alike on rail and legs, since the grain goes in different directions and a glue joint of these two members would not hold. Glue will hold where the end face butts against rail (B), especially when screwed fast as shown in Fig. 6. However, when filler blocks (D) and (E) are glued to rail (C), the joint as we show it in Fig. 6 will be secure. Before fastening rail (C) to the table, cut the groove across it where the gateleg will go when the table leaf is lowered.

The leg on the gate should be joined and glued fast to rail (F). Rail (F) should then be joined with hinges to filler block (E) before the block is glued to rail (C).

Saw ¾-inch-square strips and, after holes are drilled and countersunk for wood screws, fasten them to the tops of the rails to fasten the tabletop after it has been made.

Make the top and table leaf next. Notice the direction of the grain on Fig. 4, when these two pieces are to be glued up. Fig. 8 shows how these pieces may be glued up to save lumber. It is a good idea to cut the rule joint on the table leaf and top, and to join the two together with hinges, before marking the pieces to be sawed to their finished triangular shape. If this is done, the curves at the corners of the triangles may be accurately laid out. Hinges may be removed to do the sawing, of course. The rule joint for table leaves is cut with matching cutters on a shaper or with a portable electric hand router and shaper. For more comprehensive directions showing how the rule joint is made, see Chapter 17.

When the top and leaf have been glued up, planed, sanded, shaped, and joined with hinges, lay these two pieces upon the workbench or on a clean floor, bottom side up. Then place the table frame in its proper position on the tabletop and fasten them together with wood screws, as shown in Fig. 6. This completes the table, except for the finish. For doing the finishing, see Chapter 2 for directions.

BILL OF MATERIAL

Black Walnut

4 Legs (A) 2¼" x 2¼" x 27"
2 Rails (B) ⅞" x 5½" x 21¼"
1 Rail (C) 1⅜" x 5½" x 28¾"
1 Rail (D) 1⅛" x 5½" x 6¾"
1 Top (H) ¾" x 19¾" x 38½"   ⎫ Make from:
1 Leaf (I) ¾" x 19¼" x 38½"   ⎬ (See Fig. 8)

1 Rail (E) 1⅛" x 5½" x 3¼"
1 Rail (F) ⅞" x 5½" x 19¼"
8 Leg knee blocks (G) ¾" x 2¼" x 1¾"
3 Strips to fasten to frame (J) ¾" x ¾" x length as needed.
2 pcs. ¾" x 7" x 40"
2 pcs. ¾" x 7" x 27"
2 pcs. ¾" x 7" x 14"

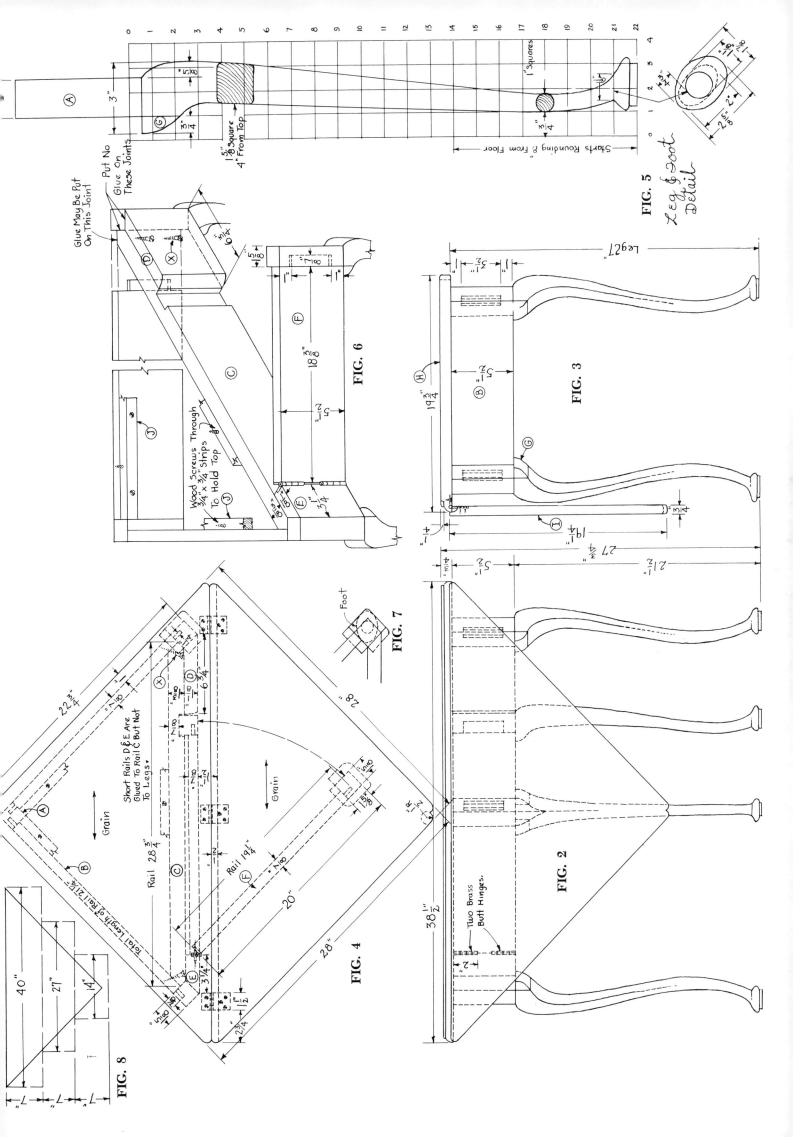

FIG. 5 *Leg & Foot Detail*

FIG. 6

FIG. 3

FIG. 7

FIG. 2

FIG. 4

FIG. 8

NINE

Queen Anne Lowboy

MOST students of antique furniture seem to agree that lowboys of the William and Mary, Queen Anne, and Chippendale styles were intended to be used as dressing tables in the bedroom or boudoir. They are usually shown with a mirror hung on the wall above them, as we do here.

The design of most of the lowboys of these periods was exquisite. They were low in height and almost invariably well proportioned. The Queen Anne Lowboy under consideration here has unusually graceful lines and proportions. In addition to its beautifully shaped legs, the shape of the feet on this example is unique. No finer, more gracefully shaped foot has ever been seen by the author on a piece of Queen Anne furniture.

Genuine lowboys were always low in height, almost never exceeding 30 inches, and not very wide nor deep. Bases of highboys, designed in patterns to match, were nearly always higher and wider, and any piece of furniture, passed off to be an antique lowboy exceeding 30 inches in height, should be suspected of having been converted from an old highboy base from which the upper part has been lost or removed. Such converted pieces are seldom worth the price asked for them. A genuine antique lowboy of good design brings a very high price in today's antique market, for they are exceedingly desirable and rare and scarce as "hen's teeth."

Students of antique furniture have been somewhat puzzled by their purported function as a dressing table, in spite of their handsome appearance. Because of the low aprons on nearly all of them, it is next to impossible to sit close to one and be comfortable when dressing and primping in the mirror hung above a lowboy. Chances are that, if they were used as dressing tables, milady had to turn her chair sideways to the front of the table and use the mirror on the wall to reflect side and rear views mostly, while using a hand mirror to "fix her face." Be this as it may, the lowboys of these three periods were more than ordinarily handsome pieces of furniture, as this very fine example proves.

To build the lowboy, first make a full-sized pattern of the leg from the drawing in Fig. 5. Stock for these legs measures 2⅝" x 2⅝" x 29½". Blocks (B) need not be made a part of the pattern at this time, since these are not glued to the legs until every other operation needed to make the leg ready for use has been completed. When making the full-size pattern it is best to include the squared upper part of the leg as well as the part we show in Fig. 5. Using this pattern, mark the outline of the leg on two opposite sides of all four legs, and then saw off waste stock very close to these pattern lines on the band saw. Save the waste and, with small brads, nail it back into the place whence it came. Drive brads only into parts of the leg that will become waste when the other two sides are sawed off. The waste of the first two sides needs to be returned to the leg so the pattern may be drawn on the remaining two sides, and also to hold the leg level on the saw table to saw the last two sides.

When the four sides of each leg have been sawed to shape, the legs will be almost fully formed vertically. Rounding and shaping the legs, as indicated by the cross-sections shown on the pattern in Fig. 5, remain to be done to make the leg and foot look as it does in Fig. 1. This shaping should now be done, using a spokeshave, properly sharpened hand-scraper blades, wood files, and sandpaper.

When the shaping of the lower parts of the legs and feet has been completed, make layouts on the squared upper sections of the legs for the mortises to be cut on all four legs. Notice that while mortises are alike on the two adjacent sides of the back legs on the inside, the layouts will differ on the two adjacent sides of the front legs. This is clearly shown on our drawings in Figs. 3 and 8. Do not lay out or cut the mortise members of the dovetail joints on top of the front legs at this time; leave these to be traced from the tenon members of the dovetail joints themselves after these have been made on both ends of rail (C). All other mortise-and-tenon joints should be made and fitted before

Fig. 1. Queen Anne Lowboy. A ROBERT TREATE HOGG REPRODUCTION.

you lay out and cut the dovetails on top of the front legs, but these should be cut before any of the other joints are glued together.

If leg mortises are to be cut on a mortising machine, strips of wood 1⅛ inch thick should be placed under the part of the leg being mortised to hold it in a level position while the mortising is being done. If boring and chiseling must be done with hand tools, the leg may be held in a vise to do the job. Cut blocks (B) to the size given in the Bill of Material and glue these to the legs just prior to gluing front, back, and ends together. Shape these after gluing them to the legs.

When the legs have been made, glue up stock for the back and ends of the lowboy. Plane and sand these to the sizes given in the Bill of Material. Then cut, plane, and sand rails (C), (D), stile (F), rails (T-1), (U), and (V). Lay out and cut tenon members of the dovetails on rail (C). Lay out and cut the mortises to which stile (F), and rails (T-1), (U), and (V) are to be joined on rails C and D. Then lay out and cut the tenons on rails (D), (T-1), (U), and (V), and on stile (F). Be sure all rails, ends, back and stile are exactly right in size and perfectly squared on all sides and edges before laying out and cutting tenons, for upon this as much as anything will depend proper squaring and fitting of the lowboy frame when it is glued up.

Front apron (E) should now be made. A pattern for half of this apron is shown in Fig. 6. Cock beading is glued to the apron around the entire lower edge as shown in Fig. 2. Cock beading * also is glued to the bottom edge of both ends, as shown in Fig. 3. To make cock beading for this purpose, cut strips of walnut from stock that has first been planed and sanded to a thickness of ³⁄₃₂ inch and a width of ¹³⁄₁₆ inch, and round one edge. It protrudes from the face of the board only ¹⁄₁₆ inch when glued to it. Cauls to clamp the pieces fast to these curved edges can be made by cutting the edges of other boards to the shape of the waste which has been removed from the ogee-curved arches. The edges of these cauls must however be

---

* To steam and bend cock beading for the Lowboy, run two or three heavy wires through stovepipe as shown in Fig. 13 in the chapter on the Windsor Side Chair. Upon these place wire mesh to hold the cock-bead strips so they can be steamed.

sawed so they clear the curved arches by exactly as much as the thickness of the cock beading, so that clamps and cauls will pull glue joints tight when pressure is applied. It is also a good idea to place pieces of felt between the caul and the cock beading when clamps are applied to help exert pressure equally over the entire surface. It is also easier to clamp the cock beading to the apron before drawer openings are cut out of the apron. Ends of the cock beading are mitered where they join. Steam the strips long enough to make them flexible before gluing them fast, one or two at a time.

Cut out openings for the drawers on apron (E). Then lay out the mortises on the back (H), which are to be cut through the back to support the drawer runs and drawer guides, excepting those fastened to the ends of the lowboy. Sometimes drawer runs fastened to the middle of a back like this are supported on strips or blocks of wood screwed to the inside of the back, instead of doing it the way we show here. The drawers can be made longer doing it the way we show it in our drawings.

Now with glue and wood screws fasten rail (D) to apron (E), as shown in Fig. 8. Make a trial assembly of (D), (E), and the two front legs, and with these pieces clamped together, and placing rail (C) on top of the front legs, it will be possible to get an accurate layout to cut the mortise members of the dovetail joints on top of the front legs. Remove the clamps and separate the legs from (D) and (E), and cut the dovetail mortises on top of the front legs. Now make another trial assembly of these members, but this time also add stile (F) to the other members when you do it. When all these members fit together, the front members consisting of legs (A), rails (C) and (D), stile (F), and apron (E) may be glued together. Back (H) and the back legs may be glued together next, after first cutting out the arch at the bottom of (H).

Make drawer guides (R) and screw them fast to the ends (G). Now glue the ends (G) to the assembled front and back of the lowboy. Be very sure to check this assembly to make sure the frame is square when gluing it together, since the frame will have to be square so the drawers will slide in and out easily. Make and screw rails (Q) and drawer runs (S) and (T) to the ends next. All holes for screws in these should be drilled and countersunk so the screws may be pushed through them without binding in the holes.

Now assemble runs, rails, and guides in the following order: make drawer runs (X) and (Z), drawer guides (Y) and (Z-1), supporting stiles (Z-2) and rails (Z-3). See that drawer runs (U), (V), and (Z) slide through the mortises you have cut in back (H) without binding. Then screw stiles (Z-2) to the inside of apron (E). Fasten drawer run (Z) to stile (Z-2) with glue, then screw drawer guides (Z-1) to drawer runs (Z). Next, screw rail (Z-3) to the inside of the apron, and screw rails (X) to it. Slip drawer guides (Y) through their mortises in the back and screw them fast to drawer runs (X). Glue may be brushed on the last ¾ inch of (Y) to join them securely to these mortises. Now slide rails (T-1) and drawer rail (V) through their respective mortises from the back of the lowboy, and glue both ends of these to the mortises which hold them. Then screw drawer guide (W) to the top of drawer run (V). Finally, glue and screw rail (U) into place on top of the frame. The frame has now been completely assembled, and you are ready to make the drawers. Details for making these will be found in Fig. 10.

Drawers on good antique furniture of this period are always dovetailed together. In place of plywood drawer bottoms which we tell you to use here, bottoms on lowboys of this period would have been made of ⅜-inch or ½-inch walnut—or possibly oak or some other wood—and would have been beveled underneath at the edges to fit into grooves in the drawer sides. The grain of these bottoms ran crosswise on drawers, so that any swelling would not make the drawer bind in the opening.

Plywood is much better to use for drawer bottoms and is substituted here, since frankly this is a reproduction rather than a genuine antique, and there is justification for substituting when it improves the product. However, for those wishing to stick faithfully to old methods of construction, the substitution should not be made. Furthermore, if one is not strictly bound by precedent, yellow poplar used for drawer sides and backs, or even white oak, contrast beautifully with black walnut fronts when drawers are pulled out. The author prefers this contrast of two kinds of wood.

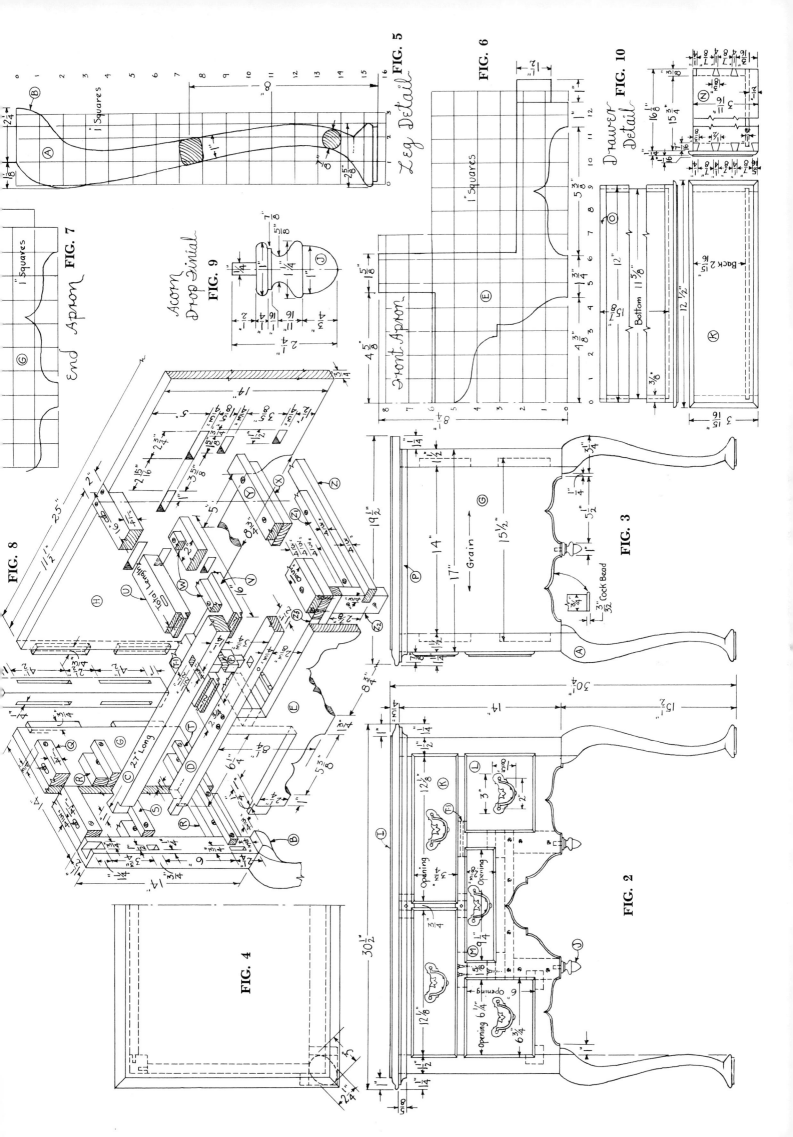

FIG. 5 Leg Detail

FIG. 7 End Apron

FIG. 9 Acorn Drop Finial

FIG. 6 Front Apron

FIG. 10 Drawer Detail

FIG. 8

FIG. 4

FIG. 3

FIG. 2

To build the drawers, cut all drawer fronts, and plane and sand them to size. On the shaper, or using a portable electric hand router and shaper, cut the molding on all four edges of the drawer fronts. Rabbet the ends and upper edges to form the lips on three sides of each drawer front, as shown in Fig. 10. No lip is cut on the bottom edges of the drawer fronts.

Make drawer sides and backs next, sanding these smooth as you did the fronts. Make dovetail layouts for all drawer sides. The layouts for dovetails shown in Fig. 10 are for the upper two drawers. If walnut is used for the sides the $\frac{1}{16}$-inch drawer clearance in the opening will suffice. If softer wood is used for sides, $\frac{1}{8}$-inch clearance is better. Dovetails on drawer sides may be cut with a sharp band saw, if the teeth on the blade do not have too much set. A properly sharpened hand dovetail saw and sharp chisel may be used instead.

Place the cut dovetails of the drawer sides upon the drawer front ends and upon the ends of the drawer backs, and with sharp pencil, awl, or knife point, mark the layouts for cutting the dovetails on the drawer fronts and backs. Follow more detailed directions given in Chapter 1 to make dovetail joints. Then cut grooves in drawer sides and drawer fronts to hold the bottoms. Such grooves may be cut on the table saw with a dado head, or by using an electric hand router with a $\frac{1}{4}$-inch router bit. Drawer bottoms need to be glued into the grooves of the drawer fronts only, and not into the grooves cut in the sides. Gluing the dovetails will hold it at the sides. Assemble all drawers and try them in their respective openings before gluing them together.

When all drawers have been made and fitted, glue up the top. Plane and sand it to size, and then cut the molded edge on a shaper. With drawers removed, place the frame upside down on the top's lower side and fasten the top to the frame with wood screws. Then fasten the molding under the edges of the top on three sides.

Turn the acorn-shaped drop finials, shown in Fig. 9, on the lathe, and glue them to the ends and bottom of the front apron. Complete the lowboy by putting suitable pulls on the drawers.

BILL OF MATERIAL

Black Walnut

4 Legs (A) $2\frac{5}{8}$" x $2\frac{5}{8}$" x $29\frac{1}{2}$"
8 Blocks (B) to glue to curved part of leg at top $\frac{3}{4}$" x $2\frac{5}{8}$" x $1\frac{5}{8}$"
1 Rail (C) $1\frac{1}{4}$" x $1\frac{1}{2}$" x 27"
1 Rail (D) $\frac{3}{4}$" x $1\frac{1}{2}$" x 27"
1 Apron (E) $\frac{3}{4}$" x $8\frac{1}{4}$" x 27"
1 Short stile (F) $\frac{3}{4}$" x $1\frac{1}{2}$" x $5\frac{3}{4}$"
2 Ends (G) $\frac{3}{4}$" x 14" x $15\frac{1}{2}$"
1 Back (H) $\frac{3}{4}$" x 14" x $26\frac{1}{2}$"
1 Top (I) $\frac{3}{4}$" x $19\frac{1}{2}$" x $30\frac{1}{2}$"
4 Drop finials (J) $1\frac{1}{4}$" diam. x $2\frac{1}{4}$"
2 Drawer fronts (K) $\frac{3}{4}$" x $3\frac{15}{16}$" x $12\frac{1}{2}$"
2 Drawer fronts (L) $\frac{3}{4}$" x $6\frac{3}{16}$" x $6\frac{5}{8}$"
1 Drawer front (M) $\frac{3}{4}$" x $2\frac{9}{16}$" x $9\frac{5}{8}$"
4 Drawer sides (N) $\frac{3}{8}$" x $3\frac{11}{16}$" x $16\frac{1}{8}$"
4 Drawer sides $\frac{3}{8}$" x $5\frac{15}{16}$" x $16\frac{1}{8}$"
2 Drawer sides $\frac{3}{8}$" x $2\frac{5}{16}$" x $16\frac{1}{8}$"
2 Drawer backs (O) $\frac{3}{8}$" x $2\frac{15}{16}$" x 12"
2 Drawer backs $\frac{3}{8}$" x $5\frac{3}{16}$" x $6\frac{1}{8}$"
1 Drawer back $\frac{3}{8}$" x $1\frac{9}{16}$" x $9\frac{1}{8}$"
Molding (P) $\frac{5}{8}$" x $\frac{7}{8}$" x about 70"

Cock beading for Ends & Apron $\frac{3}{32}$" x $1\frac{3}{16}$" x lengths as needed.

Poplar or Some Harder Wood Like Oak

2 Inside rails (Q) $1\frac{1}{4}$" x $1\frac{1}{4}$" x $14\frac{3}{4}$"
4 Drawer guides (R) $\frac{3}{4}$" x $1\frac{1}{2}$" x 14"
2 Drawer runs (S) $\frac{3}{4}$" x $\frac{3}{4}$" x $14\frac{3}{4}$"
2 Drawer runs (T) $\frac{3}{4}$" x $\frac{3}{4}$" x $15\frac{1}{2}$"
2 Rails (T-1) $\frac{3}{4}$" x $2\frac{3}{4}$" x 16"
1 Rail (U) $1\frac{1}{4}$" x 2" x 16"
1 Rail (V) $\frac{3}{4}$" x 2" x 16"
1 Drawer guide (W) $\frac{3}{4}$" x $\frac{3}{4}$" x $14\frac{3}{4}$"
2 Drawer runs (X) $\frac{3}{4}$" x $2\frac{1}{4}$" x $15\frac{1}{2}$"
2 Drawer guides (Y) $\frac{3}{4}$" x $1\frac{5}{8}$" x $16\frac{1}{4}$"
2 Drawer runs (Z) $\frac{3}{4}$" x $1\frac{1}{2}$" x $16\frac{1}{4}$"
2 Drawer guides (Z-1) $\frac{3}{4}$" x $\frac{3}{4}$" x $15\frac{1}{2}$"
2 Supporting stiles (Z-2) $\frac{3}{4}$" x $1\frac{3}{4}$" x $4\frac{1}{4}$"
1 Supporting strip (Z-3) $\frac{3}{4}$" x $\frac{3}{4}$" x $12\frac{1}{2}$"

Plywood

2 Drawer bottoms $\frac{1}{4}$" x $11\frac{5}{8}$" x $15\frac{7}{8}$"
2 Drawer bottoms $\frac{1}{4}$" x $5\frac{3}{4}$" x $15\frac{7}{8}$"
1 Drawer bottom $\frac{1}{4}$" x $8\frac{3}{4}$" x $15\frac{7}{8}$"

TEN

Small Sheraton Table

THE delightful little table shown in Fig. 1 may be used as a bedside table, an end table by a sofa or easy chair, or as an occasional table for a variety of purposes. Small tables like this, having a drawer or two, are household items that have utilitarian value almost beyond measure, and such a table will be cherished for as long as it remains in one's possession.

To build the table, saw four legs and plane and sand them to the size given in the Bill of Material. The upper end of the leg, where it is not turned, must be squared perfectly to keep the table square and to make good mortise-and-tenon joints.

Turn the legs and then cut the reeds on a shaper. To do the shaping, the legs should be mounted on a jig having an index head, as shown in Fig. 10, page 179. Reeding, on a shaper, is easily done with such a jig. Some woodturning lathes come equipped with an index head built into the headstock, and the author has used the index head on his lathe to make layouts for reeding and fluting on turned legs and columns. It is possible to rig up a jig with a table which may be fastened to the lathe in such a manner that a portable electric hand router and shaper may be used to do the shaping or reeding on the legs while they are being held between the lathe centers. (See Fig. 8, page 98.)

If the right machinery is not available to cut the reeds on these legs, they are not difficult to carve by hand on the lathe. Lay out lines on the leg by

Fig. 1. Small Sheraton Table. A ROBERT TREATE HOGG REPRODUCTION.

first wrapping narrow strips of paper around the leg at the upper and lower ends of the leg where the reeding is to be carved. Cut the strips of paper at the exact point where the two ends meet, and then remove them from the leg and, by the method shown in Fig. 10, divide the length into sixteen equal parts. Rewrap the marked strips back around the leg, and transfer these marks to the leg. Be sure the first mark at the top and bottom, where the reeding is to go, lines up with a center line drawn on one side of the leg where it remains square. This is a precaution needed to keep the reeds from leaning at an angle after they have been carved. When the lines are drawn, make V-cuts with a wood-carver's parting tool, from the top to the bottom of every line, shallow at first, and deeper as the area between the lines is rounded over with the heel of a wood-carver's skew chisel to form the reeds. Finish the rounding and shaping with a piece of 6/0 garnet paper folded over a thin strip of wood about four inches long, one edge of which has been trimmed to a knifelike thin edge. The sanding with this homemade tool will straighten the reeds as well as smooth them.

When the reeding has been shaped or carved, make layouts on all four legs for the mortises. These will all be alike on one side of both front legs and on two adjacent sides of both back legs, where ends and back are to be joined to the legs. Three small mortises will go into one side of both front legs, as shown in Fig. 6. Cut these mortises on the mortising machine, or by hand, as shown in Figs. 25 and 28, Chapter 1.

Make the ends, the back, and the three rails that go across the front of the table. Plane and sand these to size; then lay out and cut the tenons. When tenons have been cut on rail (E), make a full-sized pattern to cut the apron to shape, as shown in Fig. 7. Cut it to shape on the band saw, and file and sandpaper the band-sawed edge smooth.

Make a trial assembly of legs, ends, back, and three front rails. Glue the ends to the legs. Then saw out, plane, square, and sand drawer runs and guides (B), (C), and (D). Screw these to the assembled ends, and make sure they line up and are level, with the tops of the rails on the table

front. This is essential if drawers are to slide easily.

Glue front rails and back to the legs. Clean up the glue joints, and then cut a ⅛-inch groove all the way across the front of the table. In this groove glue the cock beading shown below the bottom drawer. The groove may be cut by setting the circular saw ⅛ inch above the surface of the saw table, and by placing the top of the table frame against the rip fence of the table saw. Then run the table frame across the saw.

Make the drawers. A dovetail layout for the upper drawer is shown in Fig. 8. To make the dovetail layout for the lower drawer, keep all pin sizes like those on the upper drawer, but lay out each dovetail ¼ inch wider. Dovetail layouts should first be made on drawer sides, using the dimensions given in Fig. 8. These may then be cut to shape on the band saw, or by tilting the table saw to cut them as we have described it in Chapter 1.

Saw, plane, and sand drawer fronts to the sizes given in the Bill of Material. Cut molding on all four edges on the shaper or with a portable electric hand shaper. Then rabbet top and ends of the drawer fronts. Laying the cut-out dovetails of the drawer sides upon the rabbeted ends of the drawer fronts, transfer their shapes to the ends of the drawer fronts. Make layouts for depth of cuts on the backs of the drawer fronts; saw and chisel out the waste so sides and fronts will go together.

Cut grooves into the drawer fronts and sides to hold the bottoms and backs. Make trial assemblies of both drawers and make sure the drawers will slide in and out freely before you glue the parts together. Glue up the drawers. The drawer bottom is glued to the groove in the drawer front, but not to the grooves in the drawer sides. Glue the drawer backs into grooves that have been cut into the drawer sides for them, and also glue the drawer bottom to the lower edge of the drawer back. Reinforce joints with triglyph-shaped glue blocks rubbed fast under the drawer to hold front, sides, and bottom from coming apart, and behind the drawer backs to hold bottoms and sides from coming apart.

Now glue up, plane and sand the tabletop. Even if you find a board this wide in one piece, it should be ripped into several pieces and reglued. This re-

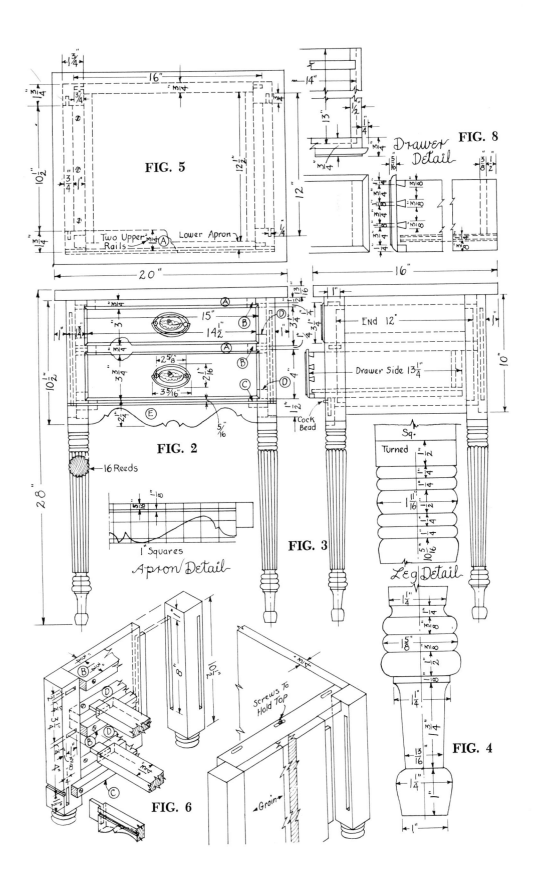

FIG. 5

FIG. 8

Drawer Detail

FIG. 2

16 Reeds

1" Squares

Apron Detail

FIG. 3

Sq.
Turned

Leg Detail

FIG. 4

FIG. 6

Screws To Hold Top

Grain

Two Upper Rails

Lower Apron

Cock Bead

End 12"

Drawer Side 13¼"

lieves stresses and strains in the wood structure, which can cause tops to warp or split apart later. Regluing is the proverbial "stitch in time."

Wood screws through strips (B), as shown in Fig. 6, will hold the top to the frame. A wood screw through the upper front rail, and one more through a strip screwed to the upper edge of the back on the inside, will help to hold the top that much better.

Put drawer pulls on both drawers. These should be removed before applying any part of the finish for which the table should now be ready.

BILL OF MATERIAL

Mahogany

4 Legs 1¾" x 1¾" x 27³⁄₁₆"
2 Ends ¾" x 10" x 12"
1 Back ¾" x 10" x 16"
1 Shaped apron (E) ¾" x 2¼" x 16½"
2 Rails (A) ¾" x 1¾" x 16½"
1 Upper drawer front ¾" x 3¼" x 15"
1 Lower drawer front ¾" x 4" x 15"
1 Tabletop 1³⁄₁₆" x 16" x 20"
Cock bead ⅛" x ⅛" x 18"

Poplar

4 Drawer runs (B) ¾" x 1¾" x 11½"
2 Drawer runs (C) ¾" x 1¾" x 12½"
4 Drawer guides (D) ¾" x 1" x 10½"
2 Drawer sides ½" x 3¾" x 13¼"
2 Drawer sides ½" x 3" x 13¼"
1 Drawer back ⅜" x 2⅜" x 14"
1 Drawer back ⅜" x 3⅛" x 14"

Plywood

2 Drawer bottoms ¼" x 13" x 14"

ELEVEN

Sheraton Bench

THE small Sheraton Bench shown in Fig. 1, with its saddle seat, is a bit different from the usual bench one finds. Small and gracefully formed, it is comfortable, too, and might be used as a piano bench. The flared legs give it adequate stability despite its small size.

To build the Sheraton Bench, first cut stock for legs (A) and for stretchers (B) and (C). Turn these on the lathe. After legs and stretchers have been turned, reeds should be cut on them. Most of this may be done on a shaper by using a special jig fitted with an index head, much like the jig shown with the drawings for the Salem Chest of Drawers in Fig. 10, Chapter 32. In this case, however, cutter knives to do reeding instead of fluting must be used. On legs (A), all of the reeding could be done on the shaper with such a jig, except the ends of the area to the left of the thickest part of the turning in Fig. 6. This part would have to be finished by hand with wood-carving chisels.

In the event machinery and equipment for doing the reeding are not available, the job of carving the reeding entirely by hand is not too difficult a task, once the layout for the reeds has been properly done. As stated in other chapters of the book, wood-turning lathes sometimes come equipped with an index head that makes laying out reeding or fluting fairly easy. If your lathe does not have an index head, cut narrow strips of paper and wrap them around the column so the ends meet exactly. Unwrap the strips and with a pencil divide them into the number of segments to correspond with the number of reeds needed on the column. Where these segments must be marked off two or more

times on the same column, as they must be on (A), (B), and (C) because of the differences in diameter from one end to the other, be careful the first line you draw lines up with the center line of the column, as shown in Figs. 6, 7, and 8. This is to prevent lines from spiraling partway around the column after all of them have been drawn.

Once the lines dividing the reeds have all been drawn on a column, shape or carve them. If you use wood-carving chisels to do them by hand, cut out the lines with a V tool, being careful not to cut very deep the first time. Follow with deeper cutting on the second time over the line, and then begin rounding the reeds with the heel of a skew chisel. Keep alternating these two operations until the reeds are shaped as we show them in the cross-section view in Fig. 6. To those who feel this to be a tedious and long-drawn-out process, we can only emphasize that this is the way such work was done before machinery now used to do this work was available.

When the reeds have been carved or shaped, they may be sanded smooth by wrapping pieces of 6/0 or 8/0 garnet paper around a short stick which is about ⅛ inch thick by ¾ inch or more wide and one edge of which has been thinned down to almost knife-blade thickness. With this, smooth the rounded parts of the reeds and straighten the lines between.

When legs and stretchers have been turned and

Fig. 1. Sheraton Bench. A ROBERT TREATE HOGG RE-PRODUCTION.

carved, drill holes into the legs and into stretchers (C) to join them together. The best way to do this is on a drill press, with the special bits made to be used on one.

Seat rails (D) and (E) should now be made. Rail (D) is fairly simple to make. A full-sized pattern for it may be made from Fig. 9, and it may be cut to shape on the band saw. End rails (E) may be turned on the lathe, and one side flattened on the jointer to the shape shown in Fig. 5. Here you also have the option of turning a 1-inch dowel on each end, and drilling holes into rails (D) to join the rails together instead of using the mortise-and-tenon joint we show in Figs. 2, 3, 4, and 5. With the mortise-and-tenon joint there is no danger of (E) turning on its axis should the glue come loose in the joints.

Mortises should be cut into rails (D) to hold the middle rail (F), which holds down and supports the seat. Mortises, or round holes, as the case may be, should also be cut at this time for end rails (E) to be joined to side rails (D). The shape of rail (E) is shown in Figs. 2 and 5. After the inside of rail (E) has been flattened on the jointer, the rabbeting on top to hold the seat board (G) is done with a dado head tilted at an angle of 10 degrees on the table saw.

Make rail (F), cutting the tenons on both ends to join it to rails (D). Drill three holes for the stove bolts, or carriage bolts, you will use to pull the seat to the curvature shown in Fig. 2. Other strips, or small blocks of wood, not shown in our drawings, may be glued to the insides of rails (D) to help support the seat should this prove desirable.

When all legs and stretchers have been made, fitted to each other, and a trial assembly made to check them out, the bench may be glued together. Glue stretcher (B) to stretchers (C) first. Then glue the legs to rails (D). After this glue rails (E) and rails (C) to the parts that have already been glued up. The above sequence in gluing up the pieces will give the least trouble in seeing that the angle at which the legs should be tilted is right.

After gluing the joints on the bench, angle the bottoms of the legs so they will rest flat upon the floor. If the 15-degree angle shown in Fig. 6 has been cut before the legs are glued to the other parts of the bench, very little or no trimming should be necessary. Should some trimming have to be done, it may be done with a fine-toothed panel handsaw if a piece of plywood is placed under the bench and each leg in turn is held with one hand while you saw between the bottom of the leg and the plywood with the other.

The seat board should be made next, and once it has been checked out to see it fits properly, a finish may be put on the bench. To do this consult the chapter on Wood Finishing.

To upholster the seat, first be sure the board ance at all four edges of the board to pull the up-bolts are in place and that you have $\frac{1}{8}$-inch clearance at all four edges of the board to pull the upholstery material down under to tack it. Glue a piece of 2-inch-thick foam rubber to the top of the seat board and trim it exactly even with the edges of the seat board. Then with upholsterer's shears trim the edges to round them, and over the foam rubber pull a piece of unbleached muslin and tack it to the bottom of the seat. Tack from the middle of each side to the corners of the seat with 3-ounce tacks. Over this fasten the upholstering material, which should have either no figure at all or small-scale figures to conform to the delicacy of scale found in the turnings on the bench. Sheraton furniture was often upholstered with striped materials, and if stripes run lengthwise on the seat, such material would be suitable, provided the scale is in keeping with the scale of the piece itself. The choosing of a suitable material requires good judgment.

When upholstering is all in place, the seat may be bolted fast to the bench to complete the job.

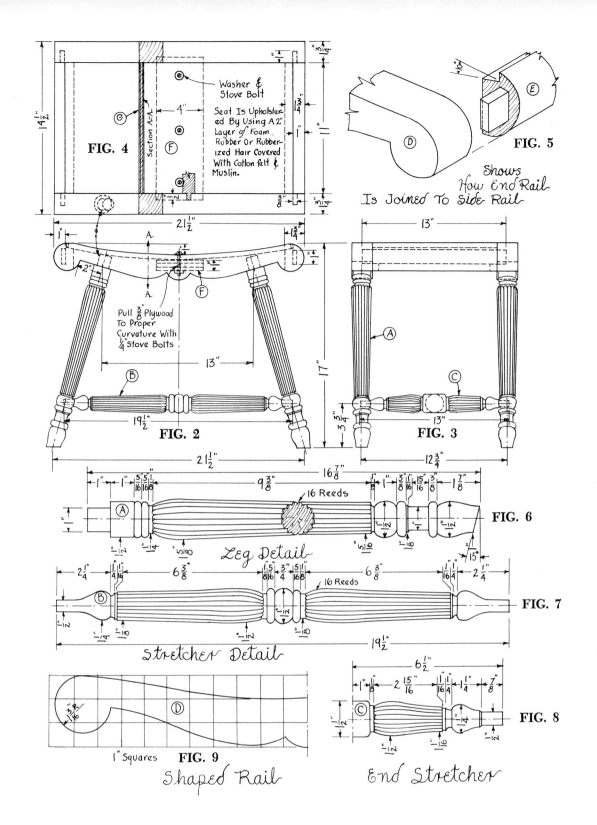

FIG. 4

Washer & Stove Bolt

Seat Is Upholstered By Using A 2" Layer of Foam Rubber Or Rubberized Hair Covered With Cotton felt & Muslin.

Section A-A

FIG. 5

Shows How End Rail Is Joined To Side Rail

Pull ⅜" Plywood To Proper Curvature With ¼" Stove Bolts.

FIG. 2

FIG. 3

16 Reeds

Leg Detail

FIG. 6

16 Reeds

Stretcher Detail

FIG. 7

1" Squares   FIG. 9

Shaped Rail

End Stretcher

FIG. 8

BILL OF MATERIAL

Mahogany

4 Legs (A) 1⅝" diam. x 16⅞"
1 Long stretcher (B) 1½" diam. x 19½"
2 Short stretchers (C) 1½" diam. x 13"
2 Shape side rails (D) 1¾" x 3" x 21½"
2 End rails in seat (E) 1¾" x 2⅜" x 13"

Oak, Maple, or Some Other Hardwood

1 Middle rail to hold seat (F) 1" x 4" x 12"

1 Seat board (plywood) (G) ⅜" x 10¾" x 19¼" *

NOTE: Turnings are dimensioned actual size, and stock from which they are to be made should be great enough in size to turn them down to the diameters given.

* ⅛-inch clearance on all four sides of the seat board is allowed to pull upholstering materials around each edge and tack them to the bottom of the board.

TWELVE

Kneading Trough

THIS kneading trough, or dough table as these pieces of furniture are sometimes called, is as good a one as the author has ever seen. It belongs to his sister, Mrs. I. Y. Stauffer, and is a treasured family heirloom handed down from the late Mr. Stauffer's side of the family. It was rescued from the damp basement of the nearly two-hundred-year-old house in which it is now a restored and treasured item in the living room, as you can see in Fig. 1.

The canted, hand-turned legs of the supporting frame, the hand-dovetailed joints at each corner of the hopper-shaped trough, and the long running dovetail joints holding the cleats to the top are clear evidence of the superb craftsmanship embodied in this fine antique example of the cabinet-maker's art.

Yellow poplar, sometimes called tulipwood, was used to build this piece. It is a native wood in the part of Pennsylvania where the table was built. Trees can still be found with heavy trunks from which boards can be cut in one piece wide enough to make sides and ends like those of this trough. Other reasons why poplar was used to make kneading troughs were that it is an excellent wood for turning and dovetailing, being neither very hard nor very soft, and it does not give off an objectionable odor or flavor, which could be transmitted to the dough placed in the trough for kneading. This is a very important consideration, since the table's

chief function was originally to hold dough. Many such tables are smaller than this one and not nearly as handsomely designed. If a reproduction is to be made, and kneading of bread dough never intended as a function, black walnut or even mahogany could be used to build it instead of poplar. Both these fine cabinet woods would serve the purpose very well if the trough is to be used as a table in the library or living room. The box under the lid would provide additional storage, an idea not to be overlooked.

To build the kneading trough, cut stock to size for the legs. Square and sandpaper these, since the upper ends must be square to make good joints with the rails. Then turn them on the lathe to the shape shown in detail in Fig. 5. The top of each leg should be slanted 12 degrees from the high point on the inside corner of the upper end to the nearest two corners, and then 12 degrees again from these two corners to the low outside corner. Then lay out and cut mortises on the two sides of each leg where they are needed.

Make the four rails for the supporting frame next. Plane and sand these to the size given in the Bill of Material. Then lay out tenons on both ends, cutting shoulders and tenon ends to an angle of 78 degrees with the lower edges of the rails. The bead molding around the lower edges may be cut with an electric hand shaper, or if one of these is not available it may be done by hand with a woodcarver's V tool and skew chisel. Make a trial fitting and assembly of the supporting frame and, when all is ready, glue legs and rails together, and, with bar clamps still in place, drill ¼-inch holes through each joint for the square pegs with which you reinforce the glued-up mortise-and-tenon joints. Three-quarter by seven-eighth-inch fastening strips are screwed to the top of the rails on the inside to fasten the supporting frame to the box.

The hopper-shaped trough, or box, is the most difficult part to make. Cutting dovetail joints like these is more difficult than the ordinary kind, but if layouts for them are carefully and accurately made, anyone who has made through dovetail joints for a drawer can also do a good job on these.

Once boards for the sides and ends have been cut to the sizes given in the Bill of Material, planed, and sanded, they all should be cut to shape at both ends. The angle is 102 degrees for both ends on every one, as shown in Figs. 2 and 3. For bottom edges, the angle made with the inside of the trough is 78 degrees on ends and sides, and for top edges the angle is 78 degrees with the outside of the trough ends and sides. These edges should be planed to this angle before laying out tails and pins on the trough sides or ends. Or, if you prefer laying out this angle from opposite sides of these four pieces, the angle will be 102 degrees.

Fig. 6 gives clear directions for laying out tails on the trough ends. Not being able to take the trough apart to show the dovetailing and joint lay-out more clearly, we have made a three-tail model of the joint to get pictures and help you understand it better. Notice that the 78-degree and 102-degree angles prevail to lay out the ends of the tails as well as the sides, as shown in Figs. 7A and B. Once the tail layouts have been made on the ends of the trough, they should be cut.

A simple way of removing the pin areas from the ends is to tilt the band saw table 12 degrees, then saw the tail members to shape on the band saw, as we show it being done in Fig. 8. If this part of the work must be done entirely with hand tools, use a dovetail saw or a fine-toothed backsaw to make the long cuts going with the grain, and then chisel out the waste. Removing the waste for the pins by this method will be made easier if a ⅜-inch hole is first drilled halfway through the waste area from each side before saw cuts are started. But remember, these holes must be drilled or bored at the 72-102-degree angle.

Pins, on the sides of the kneading trough, may be sawed to shape on the band saw in the same way by tilting the band saw table. It will be found best to saw to the lines of the pins, going in the same direction as the grain, with a dovetail saw before band sawing. The remaining waste material may then easily be removed on the band saw.

If dovetail layouts have been carefully made, and if the waste has been sawed and removed exactly to these lines, the joints should now go together perfectly. When assured they will do this by trial assemblies of each corner of the trough, the joints may be put together with glue. No

clamping should be necessary, for if the joints fit as they should, being neither loose nor tight, it will be possible to lay strips of wood over the tails on the ends of the trough and tap the joints into place with light hammer strokes on these strips of wood.

Fig. 1. Kneading Trough. PROPERTY OF MRS. I. Y. STAUFFER, BOYERTOWN, PENNSYLVANIA.

A floor for the trough should now be made, the edges rounded on the shaper or with a hand plane and sandpaper. This floor should then be screwed fast to the bottom of the trough. Then place the trough upside down on the floor and screw the supporting frame to the floor of the trough, as shown in Figs. 2 and 3.

Saw out stock for the top. To help prevent warping, it is best to rip well-seasoned stock into narrow boards and glue these together to make a top as wide as this one. One of the best ways to make the running dovetail joint groove is with a radial-arm saw. The radial-arm saw is an ideal machine to make precision miter cuts on wide boards. There are several ways of doing it, one of which is shown in Fig. 9. Set the radial arm at right angles to the table fence and, after placing the tabletop upside down on the saw table, tilt the motor to the angle you have laid out on the edges of the tabletop for one side of the cut. Then adjust the saw to get the proper depth of cut, testing for both the angle and depth of cut on a narrow strip of wood first, to make sure all settings have been correctly made before actually making the saw cut across the top itself.

Since the radial-arm saws usually found in small shops have a track too short to cut all the way across a top as wide as this one, the cut should be made as far across as the length of the arm will allow the saw to go; then the top must be swung around with its other edge against the table fence, or backstop, to complete the cut. This cut must be completed with the motor tilted in the opposite direction. Do as much of the first saw cut as you can on both ends of the tabletop before resetting.

Another method which could be used is to glue up the top in two parts, each being approximately half the width, say 14 inches or a little more. Cuts can be made all the way across boards this wide, and after the grooves have been completely cut out, the two pieces can be glued together. To line up the grooves accurately when the edges of the two boards are glued together, a short strip of wood no more than 1 inch long and shaped like the dovetail is placed into the grooves where the two come together to make the glue joint. These may be removed quite easily once the glue has set sufficiently so the grooves will no longer get out of line.

Still another way of doing it is to revolve the motor 90 degrees on the index at the top of the motor, so the saw blade is parallel to the fence instead of perpendicular to it as shown in Fig. 9. Lock it in this position and adjust it to the proper angle and depth to cut one side of the dovetail. With a top as wide as this one, it will then be safe to run the board through under the saw with the end of the tabletop against the fence or backstop. A pusher stick should be used to finish the cut, and care should be taken to keep the table end snugly against the fence at all times when making the cut.

Fig. 7A.

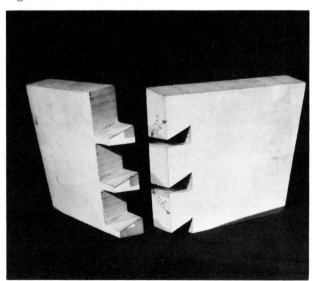

Fig. 7B.

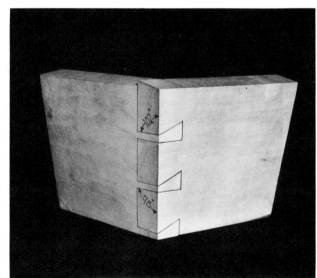

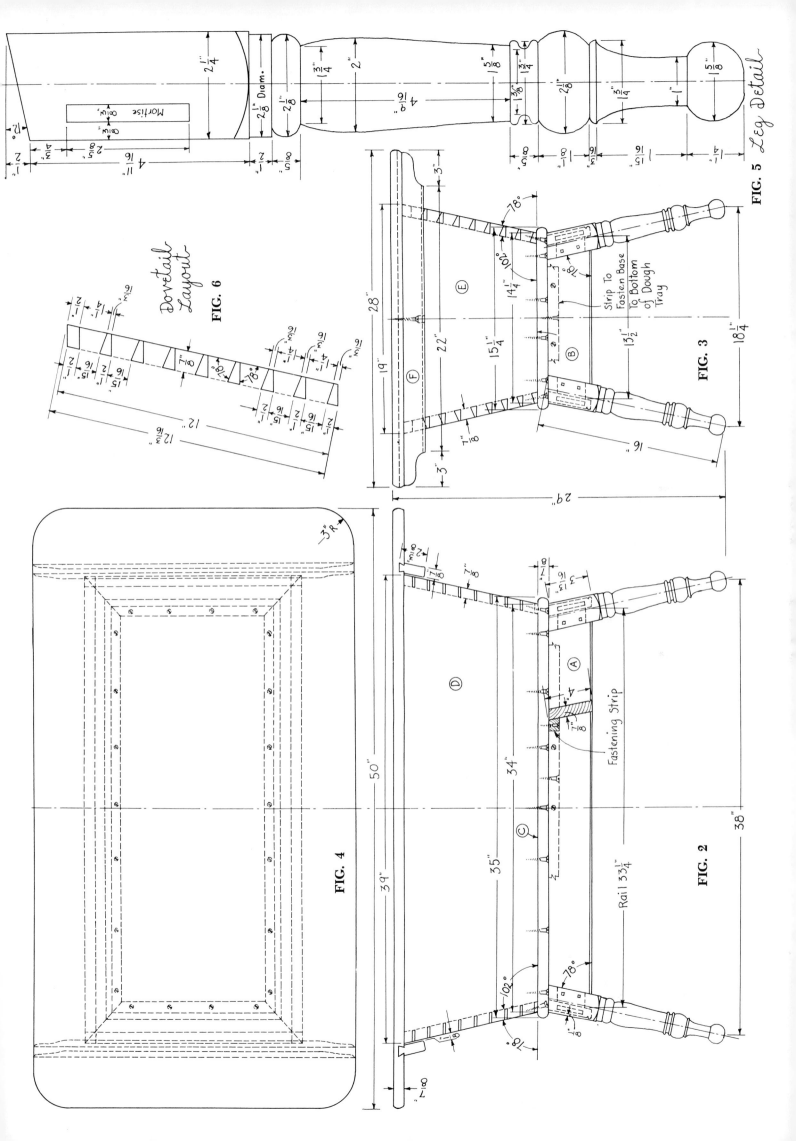

FIG. 5 *Leg Detail*

FIG. 6 *Dovetail Layout*

FIG. 4

FIG. 3

FIG. 2

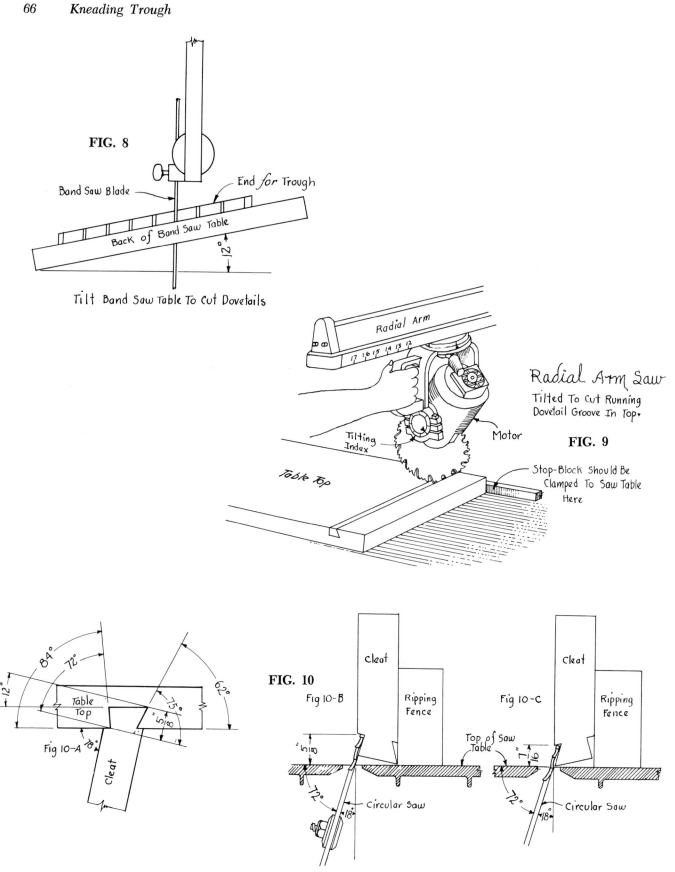

FIG. 8

Band Saw Blade

End *for* Trough

Back of Band Saw Table

12°

Tilt Band Saw Table To Cut Dovetails

Radial Arm

17 16 15 14 13 12

Radial Arm Saw

Tilted To Cut Running Dovetail Groove In Top.

Tilting Index

Motor

FIG. 9

Table Top

Stop-Block Should Be Clamped To Saw Table Here

84°

72°

12°

62°

Table Top

75°

5/100"

Fig 10-A

18°

Cleat

FIG. 10

Fig 10-B

Cleat

Ripping Fence

5/100"

72°

18°

Circular Saw

Fig 10-C

Cleat

Ripping Fence

Top of Saw Table

7/16"

72°

18°

Circular Saw

This grooved part of the running dovetail can also be made with a portable circular saw by tilting the saw as shown in Fig. 11. A guide strip may be clamped to the tabletop to make sure the saw cuts in a straight line across the top.

When both side cuts with the motor tilted at an angle have been made, reset the motor to a 90-degree angle to remove the waste between the two angle cuts, thus completing the dovetail groove part of the joint.

Saw out, plane, and sand stock to make the cleats, on one edge of which the male member of the running dovetail joint must be made. This part of the dovetail joint may be made most easily on a table saw having a tilting saw arbor. Setups for doing it are shown in Figs. 10-B and 10-C. These cleats are not glued to the tabletop, but are held from sliding back and forth by a single screw through the cleat in the middle, holding it in its correct position. On a joint as long as this there is little likelihood the joint would slide anyhow, even if no screw was used to hold it.

Except for these cleats, the top is not fastened to the top of the trough, since it was necessary to remove and replace it frequently when such troughs were used for kneading dough.

Before fastening the cleats to the top, round the edges and ends of the top, using the same method for doing it as you did when rounding the edges

of the floor of the trough. When the cleats are in place, all that remains to be done is to put on the finish. For doing this see Chapter 2.

Fig. 11.

BILL OF MATERIAL

Poplar
(make of white pine if dough is to be used)

4 Legs 2¼" x 2¼" x 16"
2 Rails (A) ⅞" x 4" x 33¼"
2 Rails (B) ⅞" x 4" x 13½"
1 Trough bottom (C) ⅞" x 15¼" x 35"

2 Trough sides (D) ⅞" x 12¾₆" x 39"
2 Trough ends (E) ⅞" x 12¾₆" x 19"
2 Cleats with running dovetails (F) ⅞" x 2⅜" x 28" *
1 Top ⅞" x 28" x 50"

* These cleats are not glued fast to the top. Careful joining and one wood screw in the center hold them in position.

THIRTEEN

Snake Foot Tilt-Top Table

The chisels used to turn so large a top should be fairly heavy and rugged, because turning it will put considerable strain upon turning tools, even when the tool rest is placed as close to the work as possible. A long, heavy, flat chisel, sharpened at the end to a roundnose shape, will be the tool most needed. Such tools are sometimes fashioned from long, heavy mill files if regular turning tools are not at hand, and such tools hold their cutting edge very well. Do not use a gouge to turn a top this size. Even on tops of smaller sizes, the use of a

Fig. 1. Snake-Foot Tilt-Top Table. A ROBERT TREATE HOGG REPRODUCTION.

TILT-TOP tables with tops as big in diameter as this one are not plentiful. One reason why this is true is the difficulty of turning so large a top on the lathe. If a sturdy lathe is available with a strong enough motor to rotate so large a top, the project will be very much worthwhile attempting, for these tables are strikingly handsome in appearance as Figs. 1 and 2 show.

If the top is to be turned on the lathe, the glued-up stock should be cut as near perfectly round as possible on the band saw. It should then be mounted on a large faceplate, and this faceplate must then be screwed to the shaft of the headstock at the end of the lathe. The tool rest used to support the lathe tools while turning the top must be mounted on a sturdy floor stand, and the lathe spindle must be rotated at the slowest possible speed.

At two of the schools where the author has taught cabinetmaking, heavy-duty lathes such as would be required to turn such a top were available, and they were equipped with faceplates more than a foot in diameter. Floor stands to use in turning such a top were also part of the equipment. If a 6-inch faceplate is the largest size you have, a piece of ⅝-inch or ¾-inch birch plywood may be bolted to it, and then a top of this size may be screwed to the enlarged faceplate. The heavy floor stand to hold the tool rest is essential, however.

gouge would be very dangerous because of its tendency to hook into the wood. A flat chisel, which scrapes the wood away in the form of sawdust rather than in the form of a ribbon, as a gouge would tend to do, is suitable.

To build the table, first get out stock for the column. This requires a 4-inch-square piece of solid stock. Turn it on the lathe. Make the layout for the mortise into which the key is fitted to hold the crow's nest in place on top of the column. Cut this mortise all the way through near the top of the column, as shown in Figs. 4 and 6.

Get out stock for the three legs, cutting them from a 2-inch plank. Be sure the grain goes in the right direction to make the leg as sturdy as possible, as shown in Fig. 7. A word or two explaining the manner of joining these legs to the base of the column is in order here. In Figs. 5 and 7 we show two different ways in which this may be done. The usual method of joining such legs to columns on tables of this sort is with running dovetail joints, as is shown for two of the legs in Fig. 5. Mortise-and-tenon joints would be better here, but the reason they are not used is the difficulty of clamping legs like this tightly to the column when gluing up the joints. With dovetail joints, clamps are not needed, since the dovetail slides into the column from the bottom and is then held there by the glue.

Our objection to the dovetail joint is that the column has a greater tendency to split when too heavy a weight is placed upon it, or as a result of carelessly moving it about. A properly fitted mortise-and-tenon joint would be less likely to do this. The difficulty encountered in applying clamps to a mortise-and-tenon joint on a leg of this kind may be overcome by keeping the leg square at the knee on the outside, as we show it on the left leg in Fig. 3, until the joint has been glued up. A hollowed-out block of wood placed over the opposite side of the column makes it possible to clamp the leg tightly to the column until the glue hardens. After each leg has been glued to the column, the unwanted square part may be cut off the knees by hand with a coping saw, and the knee may then be trimmed to its proper shape with chisels, a file, and sandpaper.

The crow's nest should be made next. The colon-

nettes should be turned on the lathe. Pieces of wood several inches longer than the actual height of the colonnette should be used to turn each one. Once turned, the waste at both ends may be cut off. The upper board of the crow's nest has dowels ¾ inch in diameter by ⅞ inch long. These act as a fulcrum for the top to be swung to the vertical position shown in Fig. 4. These dowels are made on both ends of the board and must be rounded by hand. Holes in cleats (F) should be large enough for the top to be raised or lowered without any trouble, but not too loose fitting. The same is true of the holes bored through boards (D) and (E) so they may be rotated around the column and be neither too loose nor too tight.

In making the table, the part you will probably have the greatest difficulty with is the top, because of its raised rim. Since we have already discussed

Fig. 2.   Front View Tilted.

the manner in which this is usually done, we will not repeat the instructions already given here. However, the proverbial reminder that "there is more than one way to skin a cat" applies here. This being the case, one or two alternate methods of accomplishing the job may be offered here as suggestions.

Once the top is made round, a jig for routing out the section within the rim may be rigged, so that a high-speed electric hand router may be used to do the job. Such a jig might consist of two parallel bars of wood with an opening cut lengthwise down the middle for the routing bit to go through and do the cutting. A way might even be found to rotate the parallel bars around the center of the tabletop, such as gluing a small disk of wood to the center of the tabletop and screwing one end of the bar to it, so the other end carrying the router would rotate around the top. If this were done, it would also be possible to cut the molding to shape on the inside of the rim with a shaper bit by fastening the router to one end of the arm at the proper distance from the center. The outside of the tabletop could very easily be formed on a spindle shaper afterward.

Another method that suggests itself would be to screw the tabletop to a 6-inch faceplate, fasten this to the outside of the lathe, and then rig up a substantial mount for the portable electric hand router and shaper to hold it the proper distance above the floor of the workshop to shape the rim as it is slowly rotated on the lathe by hand. The "dishing out" in the center may be accomplished without the use of a jig, with the hand router, if large portions of

the surface are routed out between tracks of raised portions which are left level with the upper level of the tabletop. These remaining raised portions can then easily be chiseled down level with the surface at the bottom of the dished-out surface.

The inside of such a rim may be hand carved to shape, if one is very careful and if no better method is available to the person wishing to build the table.

Once the top has been made, the two cleats (F) should be made and fastened to it across the grain. They must be joined to the dowels on top of the crow's nest before the second cleat is screwed to the underside of the table top. The wooden washer shown in Fig. 9 and the wooden key shown in Fig. 10, used in holding the tabletop to the column, should also be made and fastened in place at this time. The brass spring catch, shown in Figs. 5 and 8, to hold the top in place when it is level with the floor, may then be fitted in place. This catch is also shown as #7 on the plate showing examples of hardware used on the furniture in this book.

FIG. 8

BILL OF MATERIAL

Black Walnut

1 Column (A) 4″ diam. x 22⅜″
4 Colonnettes (B) 1¼″ diam. x 5⅝″
3 Legs (C) 2″ x 4½″ x 18″ *

* 2″ x 6½″ x 18″ if tenons instead of dovetails are used to fasten legs to column.

1 Bottom of crow's nest (D) 1″ x 7″ x 7″
1 Top of crow's nest (E) 1″ x 7″ x 8¾″
2 Cleats (F) 1¼″ x 1¾″ x 29″
1 Top (G) 1¼″ x 34″ diam.
1 Wooden key (H) ⅜″ x 1¹⁵⁄₁₆″ x 4½″
1 Wooden washer (I) ½″ x 4″ diam.
3 Pieces to glue to bottom of feet (J) ¼″ x 2¼″ x 4″

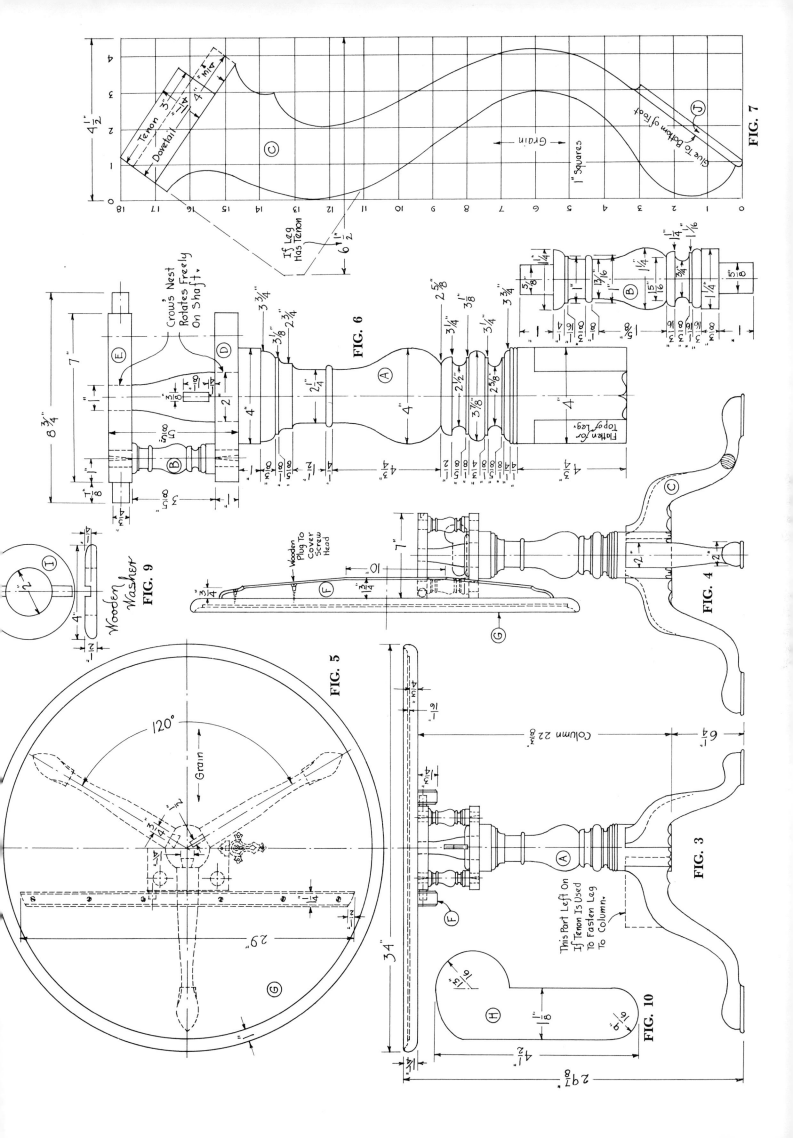

FOURTEEN

Duncan Phyfe Library Table

WHILE this walnut library table is patterned after the designs of Duncan Phyfe, the author's adaptation takes liberties which adherents to the cult of strict copy, as it applies to reproducing the work of old masters, might not approve.

One such innovation in this design is a ball-and-claw foot of wood, a modified, characteristically Chippendale motif, which to the best of the author's knowledge Duncan Phyfe never put on his furniture. Duncan Phyfe's choice of animal feet usually ran to dogs' or lions' feet, and these were for the most part cast-brass sheaths fastened with screws to the wooden legs. One must judge for himself whether the substitution is or is not as happy or tasteful a choice as what Phyfe had to offer in its place. We think it is. Other innovations are the use of walnut instead of mahogany and wooden drawer pulls in place of the brass pulls which Phyfe used almost invariably.

Scale and proportions on this table are in the best Phyfe tradition, and we think cannot be greatly improved upon. Reeding and turning are characteristic of Phyfe's work, but our holly leaf is modeled somewhat differently from similar leaf motifs which Phyfe rather consistently used.

To build the table, first get out stock for the feet (A). A full-sized pattern for these may be made from the foot drawn to scale on the graph squares in Fig. 6. Each foot should be cut from blocks of wood so the grain runs as nearly parallel to the long curve of the foot as possible, as shown in Fig. 7, to give it maximum strength. When band sawing feet like these to shape, it will be found a good idea to keep on the foot the part we have indicated with dotted lines in Fig. 7. This part can then be used to hold the bar clamps, and to pull feet (A) and block (B) tightly together when gluing up the base to which the columns are fastened. In Fig. 13 we show this being done on a base similar to this one. Once these pieces have been glued together, the waste indicated by the dotted lines in Fig. 7 may be sawed off.

The ball-and-claw feet may be carved before the feet and block (B) are glued together, though it is easier to fasten the feet in a vise to carve after the three pieces have been glued together. After sawing the foot to shape on the band saw, as shown in Fig. 7, it should be trimmed to a thickness of 1¼ inches at the ankle, as we show it in the top view of Fig. 6.

The rough outline of the ball-and-claw carving may then be drawn on top and underneath where the foot rests upon the floor. Still referring to the top and bottom views of Fig. 6, roughly outline the three toes, drawing lines for these as far apart as their greatest width. Correct these toe outlines until you feel them to be spaced and arranged about as we show them.

This outline should be a nearly straight line for the toe in the center of the foot, when viewed from above; and for the two toes on the outside they should be gently curved outlines, free of the indentations which must later be made when individual knuckles are formed.

Now, starting at one side of the ball-and-claw, draw three horizontal lines which are parallel, or nearly so, to indicate where the high point of each knuckle is to go. Then with a wood-carver's V tool outline each toe from top to bottom. Pare away the waste between the toes and in back of the outside toes, forming the ball under the toes as you do this. When in your judgment you have pared away this waste to the depth you think you will need to begin forming the toes, start shaping them. Once shaping the toes has begun you will soon know how much deeper you will have to cut around them to get good modeling.

Draw a full-sized pattern of the holly leaf, which must now be carved on the upper part of the foot. Once the leaf has been drawn, outline it and the leaf veins with a V tool. Then pare away the wood to shape the leaves. The rippled surface, which forms a rectangular panel on the outside of the block between the feet, is carved with a shallow wood-carver's gouge about ½ inch wide.

Get out stock to turn the columns and stretchers. When these have been turned on the lathe, keep each one there to carve it. While the reeding could be partly done on a shaper, we think you will find it easier to carve the reeds as well as the leaves by hand, with wood-carving chisels, as was done on the table shown in Fig. 1.

A layout to make a pattern for the leaves and reeding is shown in Fig. 10. To draw lines for the reeds on the column, wrap a narrow strip of paper around the top of the column, so its ends just meet. Remove the paper strip and draw pencil lines across the strip to divide it into 24 equal parts. Wrap the strip around the column once more to mark the width of each reed on the column. Do

the same to lay out the reeding at the bottom. When doing this be sure the first line you draw is perfectly plumb, so all lines dividing the reeds, and the reeds themselves, will be plumb. Follow the directions we gave for carving the leaves on the feet to carve the leaves on the columns.

Cut out stock for table ends (E). Shape, plane, and sand these. Lay out and cut the mortises for the rails. Then bore holes into the bottoms of ends (E) to join the tops of the columns to them.

Make rails (N), drawer runs (O), drawer guide (Q), and supporting strip (P). Lay out and cut tenons on rails (G) and (N). Fit the tenons to the mortises and make a trial assembly of ends (E), rails (G) and (N), and stile (H), to make sure these fit together perfectly.

To assemble the above pieces, proceed as follows: first screw drawer run rails (O) to ends (E). Then screw supporting strip (P) to back (M). Screw drawer guide (Q) to the bottom drawer run rail (N), as shown in Fig. 5. Then glue stile (H) to rails (G). Glue rails (N) to rails (G). Then glue rails (G) and back (M) to ends (E). Finally screw the rear end of drawer runs (N) to supporting strip (P).

Fig. 1. Duncan Phyfe Library Table. DESIGNED BY THE AUTHOR AND BUILT IN THE BERRY COLLEGE SHOPS.

Bore holes into blocks (B) on the inside for the stretchers, and glue the stretchers to the foot assemblies. Make blocks (C) and glue them to the tops of the foot assemblies. Bore holes through these and into blocks (B) and glue the columns to the feet and to ends (E).

Make facing blocks (F) and glue them to the ends of (E); then carve these facing blocks.

Make the top. After cutting it to size, and rounding the corners as shown in Fig. 4, sand it smooth and then cut molding around all four edges. Use a shaper to do this if you have one; if not, the molding can easily be carved with a wood-carver's V tool and a skew chisel, as was the edge of the tabletop shown in Fig. 1.

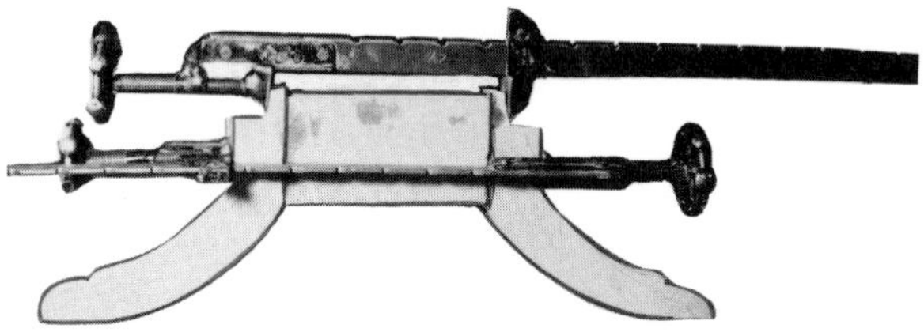

Fig. 13.

Make and fit the drawers before fastening the top to the table frame. Details for making the drawers, and for laying out the dovetail joints, will be found in Fig. 11. Lay out and saw dovetails on drawer sides first. Then using these as templates, transfer the dovetail layouts to the ends of the drawer fronts, and with a dovetail saw and sharp thin-bladed chisel, cut out the waste to join the fronts to the sides.

Dado drawer sides to hold drawer backs, and groove drawer sides and drawer fronts to hold drawer bottoms, as shown in Fig. 11. Make trial assemblies of both drawers and fit them to the openings. Glue up the two drawers. Turn four drawer pulls, as shown in Fig. 12, and fasten them to the drawer fronts.

Lay the top upside down upon the workbench or across two sawhorses. Place the table frame upon it and fasten it to the top with wood screws.

Putting a good finish on the table is the final step in building it.

BILL OF MATERIAL

Walnut or Mahogany

4 Feet (A) cut from stock 1⅞" x 4" x 12"
2 Blocks to which feet are joined (B) 1⅞" x 3½" x 6½"
2 Blocks on which columns rest (C) ½" x 2" x 7"
4 Columns (D) 1⅞" diam. x 18½"
2 Ends of table (E) 1⅞" x 6¼" x 21½"
4 Blocks to veneer ends (F) ¼" x 1⅞" x 4½"
2 Rails (G) ⅞" x 2" x 31¾"
1 Stile (H) ⅞" x ⅞" x 4½"
2 Turned stretchers (I) 1½" diam. x 31¾"
2 Drawer fronts (J) ⅞" x 2$^{11}/_{16}$" x 14⅛"
1 Tabletop (K) ⅞" x 24" x 47"
4 Drawer pulls (L) 1" diam. x 2⅛"
1 Back (M) ⅞" x 4½" x 31¾"

Poplar

2 Drawer run rails (N) ⅞" x 2½" x 19⅝"
4 Drawer run rails (O) ¾" x ⅞" x 18⅝"
1 Supporting strip for rails and drawer runs (P) ¾" x 2¾" x 29¼"
1 Drawer guide (Q) ¾" x ⅞" x 17⅞"
4 Drawer sides (R) ½" x 2$^{11}/_{16}$ x 19⅝"
2 Drawer backs (S) ⅜" x 2$^{1}/_{16}$" x 13⅝"

Plywood

2 Drawer bottoms ¼" x 13⅝" x 19⅜"

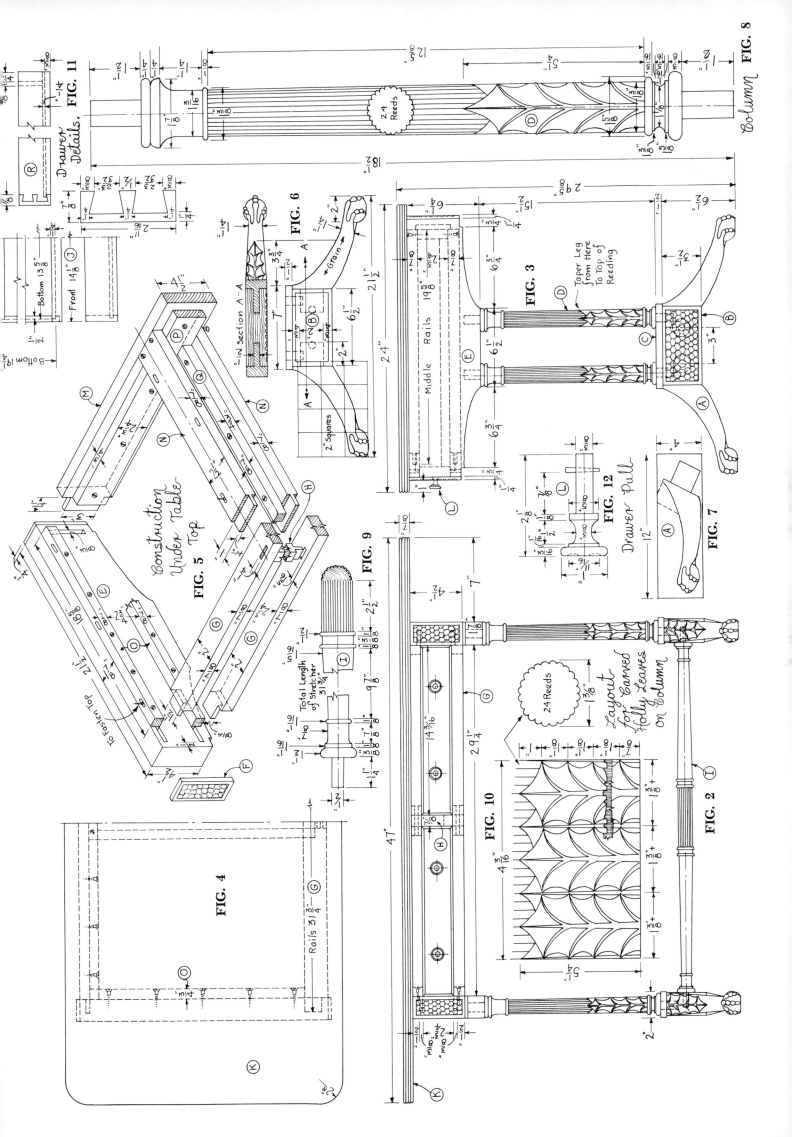

FIG. 11

Drawer Details.

Column FIG. 8

24 Reeds

Taper Leg from Here To Top of Reeding

Middle Rails 19⅝"

FIG. 3

FIG. 6

In Section A-A

2" Squares

Drawer Pull

FIG. 12

FIG. 7

Construction Under Table Top

FIG. 5

Total Length of Stretcher 31¾"

FIG. 9

24 Reeds

Layout for Carved Holly Leaves on Column

FIG. 10

FIG. 2

Rails 3¾"

FIG. 4

FIFTEEN

Duncan Phyfe Dining Table

THE superb mahogany table shown in Fig. 1, when fully extended, makes an impressive banquet table in the dining room of the most elegant home. It fully measures up to three things necessary, in the opinion of the author, to determine quality in a piece of furniture: utility, good construction, and beauty.

Utility in a dining table presupposes a combination of certain definite attributes. So many otherwise fine dining tables lack one or more of these. These are: a table surface that may readily be varied in size to suit the demands of the occasion. Since this table is so constructed that any two sections of the top may be joined together, this demand has been met. In order to bring this about, thin chips of wood, by means of which the sections are aligned when brought together, must be fastened exactly the same distance apart on the edges of the top where the five sections join each other. See drawing. They must be fastened with glue to the proper edge of each section so that any two sections will make a pair. For illustration, if the two end sections are to be brought together it follows that the chips must be fastened to the edge of the top of one of them, and mortises must be cut into the edge of the mating end.

Naturally no one expects to make a setup using a section to which a pedestal is fastened, with a leaf to which no pedestal is attached to support it. Nevertheless, the leaf that mates with the part having the pedestal must have the mortises if the top on the pedestal has the chips glued to its edge. This being the case, it also follows that if one end has the chips glued to its edge, the opposite end of the table must have mortises cut into the edge of the top, so the two can be used together if so desired.

A second important attribute such a dining table should have is a sound and sturdy supporting structure, or underframing, which must have its parts so arranged and placed that it will not interfere with comfort or freedom of movement of anyone seated at the table. It will readily be seen this table is almost ideal in this respect.

A third important qualification: the table must be a comfortable height for the average-sized person to sit at. Thirty inches, which is the height of this table, is just about right. The table has stability, and adequate support is provided for the wide boards which may be added between the three tabletops supported by the pedestals. This is provided by the short brackets which may be swung into place to help support these wide boards. The five parts, or any three of them, can be locked together with brass keepers, a detail of which is shown in Fig. 5.

Such a table should be made of the best grade of mahogany available. Unfortunately, Cuban mahogany, a very superior grade of mahogany used by Duncan Phyfe almost exclusively, is no longer available to cabinetmakers at the present time, but top quality Honduras mahogany is almost equal to it in quality and hardness.

To start construction, make the pedestals first. This requires three heavy pieces of solid stock, 5 inches or more square and 21 inches or more long. When turned, three areas on the pedestals at the end, and four areas on the pedestal in the middle, should be flattened at the bottom where legs are to be joined to the columns. This can be seen if Fig. 6 is examined.

Legs for these pedestals customarily are fastened to the columns with running dovetail joints as we show them here. Unfortunately, the great weight that such pedestals are often called upon to bear sometimes causes the column to split apart at these joints; to prevent this we advise reinforc-

76

ing of this joint with a metal plate like the one we show in Fig. 6. Mortise-and-tenon joints may be substituted for the dovetail joints shown. Indeed, the author considers mortise-and-tenon joints, at this place, superior to the dovetail joints shown here. Such a joint is shown in a situation similar to this one as an alternative to the use of the running dovetail on the pedestal of the Tilt-top Table in Chapter 13.

The principal reason for using the dovetail joint in the first place is the difficulty encountered in clamping the legs to the pedestal until the glue has dried if the mortise-and-tenon joint is used. The author has overcome this difficulty many times on tables like this, which he has built, by the simple expedient of leaving a squared section on the upper part of the knee on such legs to which clamps may be fastened to pull the leg tightly against the column and hold it there until the glue has dried. This squared section may then be removed with hand tools after all legs have been glued to the

column. The running dovetail does not require the use of clamps to fasten it to the column. A large dowel, 2 inches or more in diameter, is turned on top of the column to fasten it to the heavy oak plank that supports the top.

The frames that support the tabletops are made up of several members of oak. Note that the pieces marked (F) and (G) on the drawings are quite wide and thick. To the ends of these pieces are fastened other supporting members (H) and (I). The long supporting rails (H) are joined to the heavy planks (F) and (G) with mortise-and-tenon joints, as shown in the detail drawing, Fig. 8. Fastened to both ends of rails (H) by means of a wooden hinge arrangement are brackets (I), put there for the purpose of giving adequate support to boards (E) when they are being used.

Table boards are fastened to planks (F) and (G) with metal angle brackets screwed fast to both supports and tops with wood screws. The brass keepers, of which a detail is shown in Fig. 5,

Fig. 1. Duncan Phyfe Dining Table.

hold the sections together and lock them in place where the tabletops come together.

The casters are a part of the brass foot guards. These are made like a sheath or sleeve and may be bought from firms specializing in custom-made cabinet hardware. We show these on a photograph with other hardware on page 34.

With the final quality of beauty, this table is richly endowed. It is a superb example of elegance and dignity. The table is not fancy. The lines are simple, the turnings plain, the carving unpretentious. A simple holly leaf is carved in low relief on the knee of each leg, and there is reeding below it to the foot guard, as shown in Fig. 7. The exposed edges of the top are also reeded, and this reeding may be done on a power shaper.

To put a suitable finish on the table consult the chapter on wood finishing.

BILL OF MATERIAL

Mahogany

3 Columns for pedestals (A) 5″ diam. x 21″
10 Legs (B) 2″ x 6½″ x 19″ (See Fig. 3)
Tabletop 2 pcs. (C) ⅞″ x 24″ x 48″
      1 pc. (D) ⅞″ x 30″ x 48″
      2 pcs. (E) ⅞″ x 24″ x 48″

White Oak

1 Supporting plank for tabletop (F) 2″ x 8″ x 29″
2 Supporting planks for tabletop (G) 2″ x 8″ x 19¼″
4 Rails in supporting structure (H) 1¼″ x 2⅝″ x 31⅛″
8 Swinging brackets (I) 1¼″ x 2⅝″ x 7⁹⁄₁₆″
12 Chips to align tops (J) ¼″ x 1″ x 1¾″

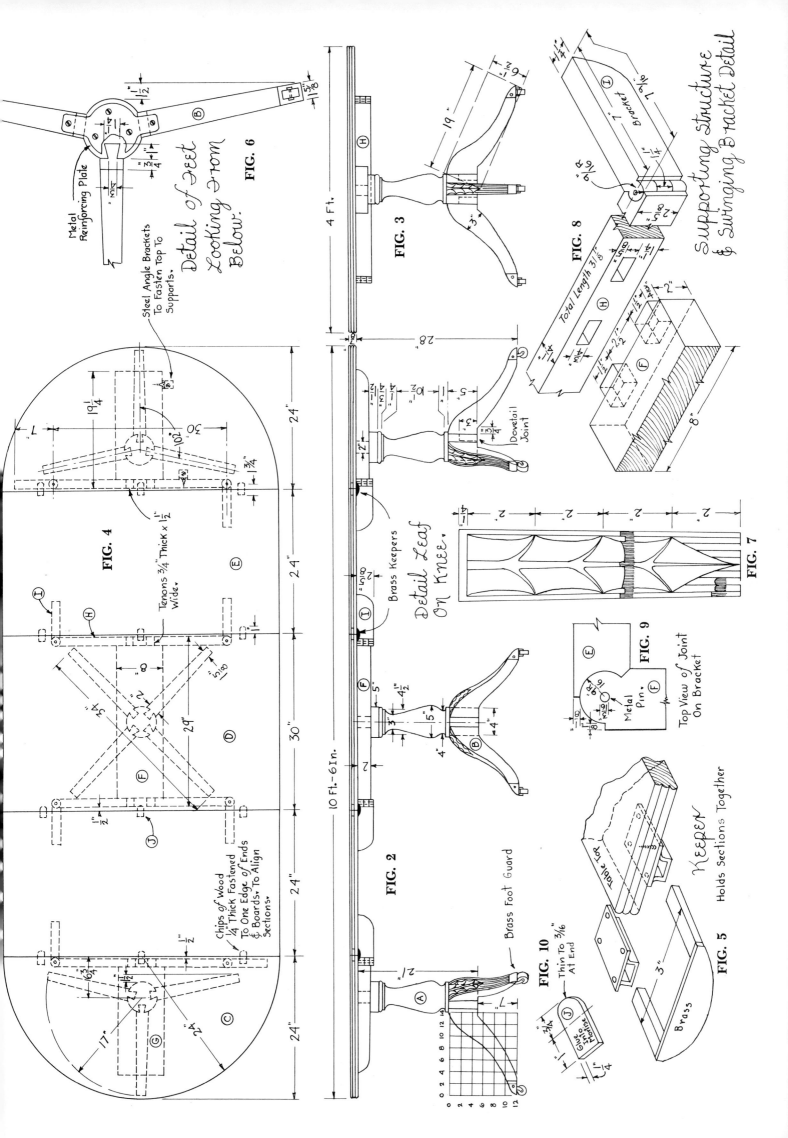

Metal Reinforcing Plate

Steel Angle Brackets To Fasten Top To Supports.

Detail of Feet Looking From Below.

FIG. 6

FIG. 4

Tenons 3/4" Thick x 1 1/2" Wide.

Chips of Wood 1/4" Thick Fastened To One Edge of Ends & Boards. To Align Sections.

19 1/4"

30"

24"   24"   30"   24"   24"

FIG. 3

4 Ft.

28"

Dovetail Joint

FIG. 8

Total Length 31 1/8"

8"

Bracket

Supporting Structure & Swinging Bracket Detail.

FIG. 7

2"   2"   2"   2"

Detail Leaf On Knee.

Brass Keepers

19"

3"

10 Ft.-6 In.

FIG. 2

Brass Foot Guard

21"

5"   4 1/2"

3"   5"   4"   4"

FIG. 9

Top View of Joint On Bracket

Metal Pin.

E

F

FIG. 10

Thin To 3/16 At End

Glue in to Mortise

KEEPER

Table Leaf

Brass

3"

Holds Sections Together

FIG. 5

SIXTEEN

Sheraton Drop-Leaf Dining Table

FIG. 1 shows a sturdy drop-leaf table in the Sheraton style. Legs are gracefully turned and reeded, and although there are eight legs on this table, the table is so designed that they are not in the way when people are seated close together on all four sides. This is the case because the four legs in the middle are set well back from the sides, and also because the legs on the gates, which swing out to support the leaves, can be placed in positions to give ample legroom. They do this and still furnish adequate support for the wide and heavy drop leaves.

Leaves on this table are a full inch thick. This, together with the generous width and length of the table, gives it a solid and substantial aspect without sacrificing good scale and beautiful proportions.

To build the table, start with the frame below the top. Rails for this are all 5½-inch-wide solid mahogany. Cut out, dress to size, and sand the long rails (D) and crossrails (E) and (F). Then lay out grooves and mortises going across rails (D), where rails (F) are joined to them. After cutting tenons on the ends of rails (F) and drilling a hole for the bolt to hold each leg as shown in Fig. 4, these parts may be glued together.

Now get out stock for the legs. After squaring these to the sizes given in the Bill of Material, turn them on the lathe to the shape shown in Fig. 6.

Four of these legs have ¼ inch cut away on two adjacent sides at the top of the leg, to fit into the corners as shown in Fig. 4. Only the lower ½ inch of the square part of the leg at the top remains 2¼ inches thick. The 5½ inches at the top will be only 2 inches square when this has been done. At this time, these four legs may be bolted to the frame as shown. When this has been done make sure all four legs rest solidly upon the floor, so the table will not rock. The remaining four legs are fastened to the gate rails (G), so the gates may be swung back against the frame when the leaves are dropped and away from the frame when the leaves are raised.

One end of the gate rail is fastened to the leg with a mortise-and-tenon joint. The other end of the gate rail is hinged to a short block of the same width and thickness with a finger joint, so called because the parts where the two are fitted together resemble fingers of two hands intertwined to form a swivel joint. The joint may be held together with a steel pin, acting as a fulcrum; for this purpose a forty-penny nail may be used if nothing better is available. Graphite, or one of the newer waxlike preparations used to make drawers slide more easily, which come in pressurized spray cans, may be used to make the joint work more freely and prevent squeaking when the table has been completed.

Construction details for making the finger joints are shown in Fig. 7. These are designed so none of the surfaces will bind if properly made. Arcs at the backs of the fingers on the blocks may be chiseled to shape with very little difficulty. Finger joints should be carefully laid out, cut, and fitted together, and when this is done they work beautifully.

Strips ⅞ inch square may be screwed to the inside of the frame and to the top underneath, to hold them together. This is shown in Fig. 4. Top and leaves are joined with rule joints. The arc on this joint has a ⅝-inch radius, and four hinges are used to hold each leaf to the top, since the 1-inch-thick leaves are quite heavy.

One leaf is longer than the other on drop-leaf table hinges, so the wood screws fastening them to the leaves may be driven into the wood below the groove of the rule joint. The hinge must be positioned so the middle of the barrel falls directly below the joint line on top of the table. See Figs. 2 and 4. The hinges must be mortised into the undersides of the top and leaves, to make leaves, top, and hinges flush with each other.

Boards used to make tops and leaves should be ripped into narrow widths and reglued. This reduces strains and stresses which make wide boards warp, check, or split apart. Putting the same number of coats of finish on both sides of leaves and top is a necessary precaution to help prevent warping in wide boards, especially on tabletops and leaves.

BILL OF MATERIAL

Mahogany

8 Legs (A) 2¼" x 2¼" x 29"
1 Tabletop (B) 1" x 25¾" x 48"
2 Drop leaves (C) 1" x 25½" x 48"
2 Long rails under top (D) 1" x 5½" x 42¼"
2 End rails (E) 2¾" x 5½" x 19¼"

2 Crossrails (F) 1¾" x 5½" x 19¼"
4 Gate rails (G) 1¾" x 5½" x 18⅜"
2 Blocks (H) 1¾" x 5½" x 8¼"
Strips to hold top (See Fig. 4) ⅞" x ⅞"
8 2"-steel drop-leaf table hinges
4⅜" x 5" carriage bolts to fasten legs to frame
4⅜" x 3½" carriage bolts to hold blocks to frame

Fig. 1. Sheraton Drop-Leaf Dining Table. A ROBERT TREATE HOGG REPRODUCTION.

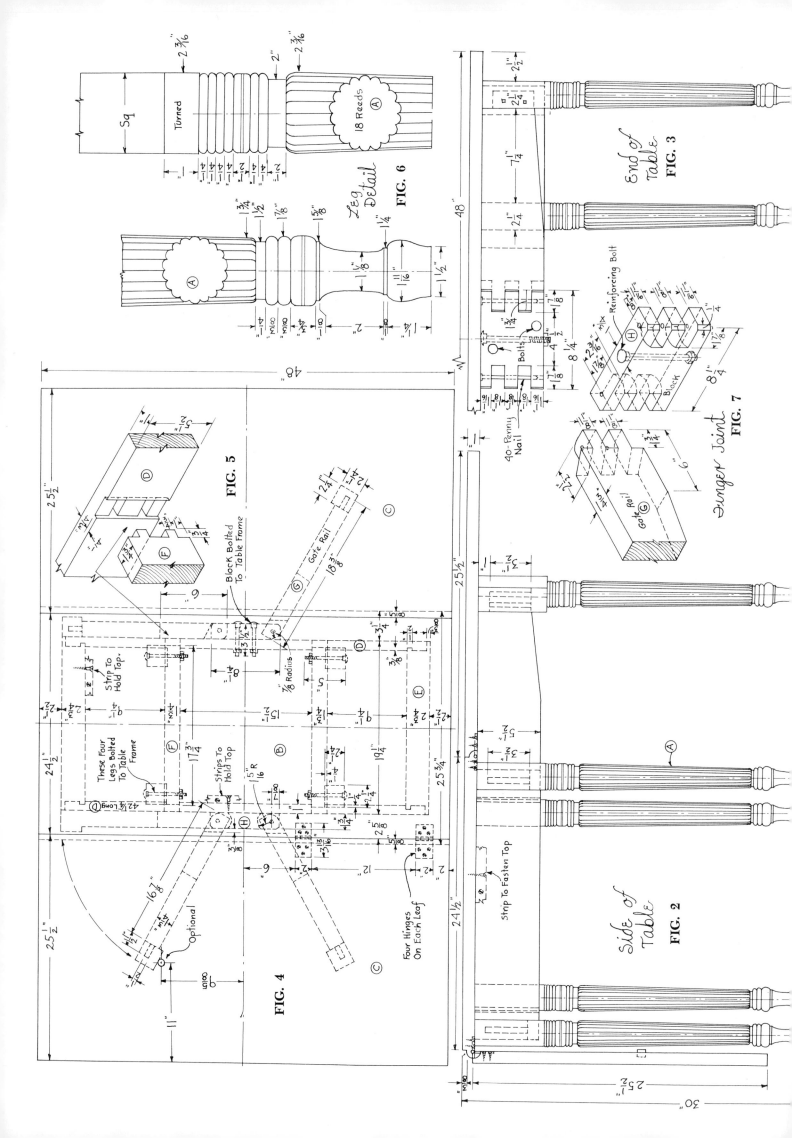

SEVENTEEN

Sheraton Coffee Table

IN addition to its attractive appearance, due to its clean-cut lines, refined ornament, and well-scaled proportions, the Sheraton Coffee Table shown in Fig. 1 provides greatly appreciated storage space in its generously sized drawers. Its table-top area may be reduced or enlarged to suit the occasion by raising or lowering one or both drop leaves. A good c fee table is an almost indispens-

able piece of furniture for anyone who does even a small amount of entertaining; and for a home furnished with any of the traditional eighteenth-century styles, one cannot go very far wrong with this fine little table. Mahogany is the only proper wood to use to build it.

First get out stock to turn the four legs. Delicately proportioned bead turning and reeding are distinguishing features on these legs. They should first be planed, squared, and sanded to the size of the upper end which remains square; then the lower part may be turned as shown in Fig. 6.

The reeds may be formed on a shaper if the leg is held in a jig having some kind of index head to divide the circumference into the required number of parts. See Fig. 8, page 98, for instructions on how to do this work. If a shaper is not available, the reeds may be carved by hand with wood-carving chisels (a V tool and a skew chisel) while the leg is held in the lathe. After hand-carving the reeds, use a piece of fine grit Open Kote garnet paper to finish shaping and smoothing them. Wrap it around a short stick, one edge of which has been beveled until it is sharp enough to run the sand-

Fig. 1. Sheraton Coffee Table.
A ROBERT TREATE HOGG REPRODUCTION.

paper to the bottom of the V cuts. Sanding with this tool will straighten the dividing lines as well as smooth and round over the reeds.

When the legs have been fully shaped and carved, lay out mortises on all four legs. Front and back legs will not be alike when it comes to laying out mortises. With the exception of the mortise-and-tenon joints at the top and bottom of stile (K), all mortises and tenons on the table are ¼ inch thick. The drawings will show how the mortises should be laid out on the legs to cut them. Both table ends are set back to come flush with the insides of the legs. The reason for doing this is to enable one to take hold of the finger grips on the slide supports which hold up the table leaves, and to allow the slide supports to stick out far enough so this may be done without interfering with the leaves when they have been dropped. A study of Figs. 4 and 5 will make this clear.

When all mortises on the legs have been laid out and cut, get out stock for front rails (B), ends (C), back (D), stile (K), and drawer run (L). Plane, square, and sand these to the sizes given in the Bill of Material. Make layouts on the above pieces to cut the mortises in rails (B) and to cut tenons on one end of (L) and on both ends of (B), (C), (D), and (K). When these tenons have all been cut and fitted into their respective mortises, make a trial assembly of rails and legs.

Get out stock to make two slide-support holders (G), drawer guide (N), drawer runs (M), and strips (P) and (Q), and block (V). Plane and square all of these to the sizes given in the Bill of Material.

Now make layouts in the middle of the upper edges of both ends (C) to cut out places to hold two slide supports and the two strips (G) that help to hold them in place. When these have been cut out, screw block (V) to the back. Then you will be ready to begin assembling.

To glue up the frame, first glue stile (K) to rails (B). Then glue rails (B) and back (D) to the legs. Glue the front of drawer run (L) to lower rail (B), and then glue ends (C) to the legs. You can then fasten the back end of drawer run (L) to the bottom of block (V) with wood screws. After drilling and countersinking the holes, screw

drawer guide (N) to drawer run (L) and screw blocks (O) to drawer guide (N).

Make slide-support stopblock (F) and fasten it at an angle of 45 degrees to the top of drawer guide (N) with a wood screw as shown in Figs. 4 and 5. Fasten drawer runs (M) to the table ends with wood screws. Make strips (P) and (Q); drill and countersink them for wood screws and fasten them to ends (C) to hold the drawers level when they are pulled out.

Now make slide supports (E) and groove them, and make strips (G) to hold them in place. Tongue-and-groove joints for these should be made so there will be a sufficient amount of clearance to make it easy to push or pull the slide supports in and out. Special preparations to put on sliding surfaces and reduce friction, which may be sprayed from pressurized spray cans, are now available in hardware stores, and we recommend that such preparations be used if the sliding joints have a tendency to stick. Make sure the slide supports work properly before fastening the tabletop to the table frame.

Drawers should be made and fitted next. Dovetail layouts for these are shown in Fig. 8. Make drawer fronts first, and cut molding on all four edges on a shaper. With a dado head on the table saw, cut lips on upper edge and both ends of the drawer fronts. Plane and sand drawer sides (R) to size, and lay out and cut dovetails on these.

From the drawer sides transfer the shape of the dovetails to the ends of the drawer fronts and drawer backs, and complete the dovetail joints. With a dado head on the table saw, cut grooves into drawer fronts and drawer sides to hold the drawer bottoms. Glue up and assemble the drawers, after first making trial assemblies to be certain the drawers will slide properly in the openings.

Make top (I) and leaves (J). Notice that the grain on the leaves runs in the opposite direction from the grain on the top. Matching shaper-cutters to make the table-leaf joints should be used, and a shaper-cutter should be used to put molding around the edges of the tabletop. Table-leaf hinges having one leaf longer than the other should be used and put on before the top is screwed to the frame. These hinges are shown in Fig. 4. When you make

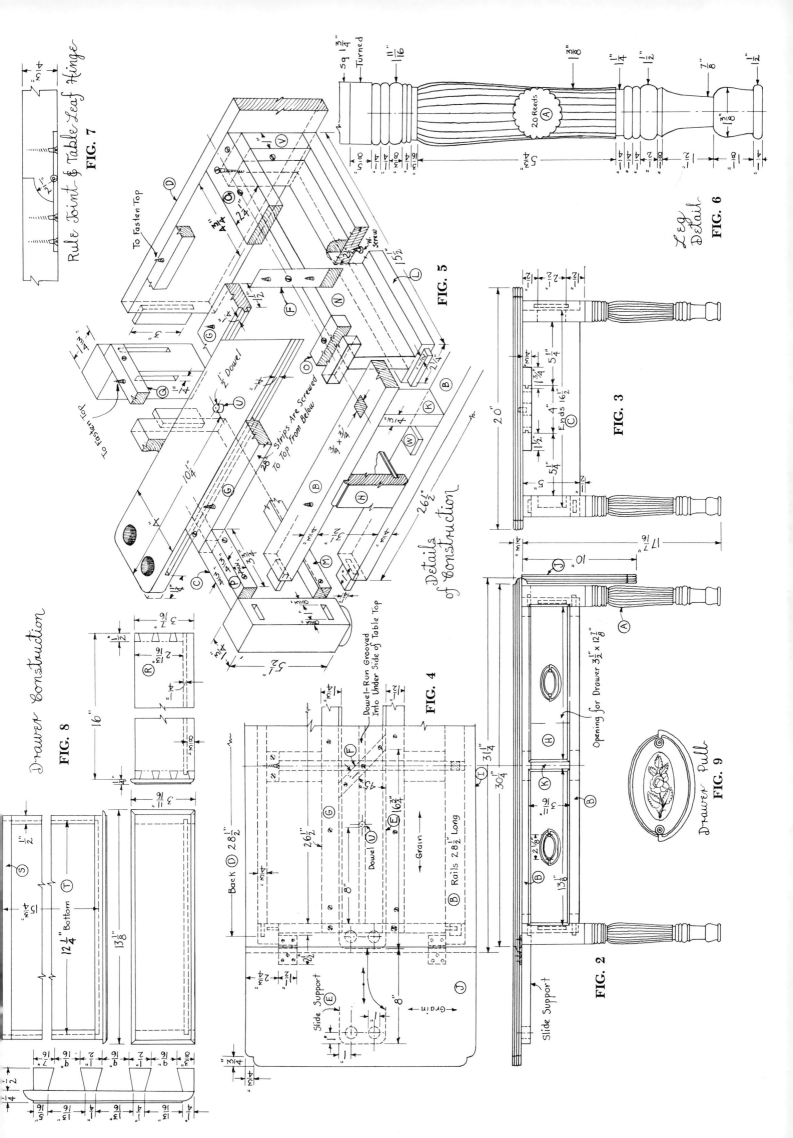

Rule Joint & Table Leaf Hinge
FIG. 7

Leg Detail
FIG. 6

20 Reeds (A)

Details of Construction
FIG. 5

FIG. 3

FIG. 4

FIG. 2

Drawer Construction
FIG. 8

Drawer Pull
FIG. 9

the top, and before you fasten the leaves to it, be sure the leaves can be dropped so as not to come in contact with the ends of the slide supports when the slide supports have been pushed in as far as they will go. Also cut a groove into the top, in which the ½-inch dowels fastened to the tops of the slide supports can move freely back and forth. This groove ends just inside the table ends (C), on the bottom of the tabletop, to keep the slide support from being drawn too far out of the table frame.

When top (I) and leaves (J) have been put together, lay them upside down on top of the workbench and screw the frame to (I). Then fasten drawer pulls to the drawer fronts. This completes the table except putting on the finish.

BILL OF MATERIAL

Mahogany

4 Legs (A) 1¾″ x 1¾″ x 17⁷⁄₁₆″
2 Front rails (B) ¾″ x 1¾″ x 28½″
2 Ends (C) ¾″ x 5″ x 16½″
1 Back (D) ¾″ x 5″ x 28½″
2 Slide supports (E) ¾″ x 4″ x 16¾″
1 Slide support stopblock (F) ¾″ x 1″ x 6¾″
2 Strips to hold slide supports (G) ¾″ x 1¾″ x 28″
2 Drawer fronts (H) ¾″ x 3¹¹⁄₁₆″ x 13⅛″
1 Tabletop (I) ¾″ x 20″ x 31¼″
2 Table leaves (J) ¾″ x 10″ x 20″
1 Stile between drawers (K) ¾″ x 1¾″ x 5″

Poplar

1 Rail to support drawers (L) ¾″ x 2¼″ x 16″
2 Drawer runs (M) ¾″ x ¾″ 15½″

1 Drawer guide (N) ¾″ x 3½″ x 14½″
1 Block (O) ¾″ x 2¼″ x 3¾″
1 Block (O) ¾″ x 2¼″ x 4¾″
2 Strips (P) ¾″ x ¾″ x 3¾″
2 Strips (Q) ¾″ x ¾″ x 4¾″
4 Drawer sides (R) ½″ x 3⁷⁄₁₆″ x 16″ *
2 Drawer backs (S) ½″ x 2¹³⁄₁₆″ x 12¾″ *
1 Block (V) 1″ x 3½″ x 2¼″
4 Drawer stopblocks (W) ¼″ x 1″ x 1″

Birch or Mahogany-veneered Plywood

2 Drawer bottoms (T) ¼″ x 12¼″ x 15¾″
2 Birch dowels (U) ½″ diam. x 1⅛″

* Mahogany may be used for these in place of poplar, if so desired.

EIGHTEEN

Sheraton Dressing Table and Mirror

A DRESSING table, to be functional, should be constructed in such a manner that the son using it may be seated close to it in comfort. This makes it possible to see details of makeup in the mirror with little or no difficulty. The high arch in the middle of the front apron makes it possible to sit as close to this dressing table as one wants to.

The lines are clean and the design, inspired by Sheraton's earlier and better designs, which he adapted from classical and Louis XVI models, is dainty and in good taste. All in all this adaptation, which the author designed and built for his sister, has proven to be a lovely and highly cherished wedding gift.

The wood, of course, is and should be mahogany, with inlay banding of holly to accentuate important areas on both pieces.

To build the table, first turn the four legs. The two front legs are hand-carved as are the brackets under the drawers at both ends. Back legs have been left without carving or fluting, though they as well as the front legs may be carved if the one building the table wishes to go to the extra trouble it takes to carve another pair. Fig. 2 shows carving in progress on one of these legs. The carving is most easily done with the leg mounted between lathe centers, as shown in Fig. 2, which permits rotating it to facilitate the work. Both legs, includ-

ing the fluting, were carved entirely by hand. Flutes on hand-carved legs may be sanded smooth and the flutes made perfectly straight after carving with a short thin stick of wood having one edge over which the sandpaper is stretched, rounded to fit the narrowest parts of the flutes.

When the legs have been turned, carved, and sanded smooth, make layouts to cut the mortises and the dovetails on top of the front legs. Dimensions for these are shown in Fig. 6. Cut these mortises by hand, or on the mortising machine.

Now make rails (A), (B), (C), (E), and (F). Lay out and cut mortises into rails (B) and (C) and into back (F). Then lay out and cut tenons on

Fig. 1. Sheraton Dressing Table and Mirror. DE-SIGNED AND BUILT BY THE AUTHOR.

Fig. 2. Dressing Table Leg Being Carved.

rails (C), (E), and (F), and the tenon members of the dovetail joints on the ends of rail (B). Make stiles (D). When the joints on the above members have been fitted, make a trial assembly of the legs, rails, and stiles.

Saw and smooth the arches on rail (A) and back (F). Drawer runs (R), (U), and (T) and drawer guides (Q), (S), and (V) should be made. Also at this time make rails (P) and (W); strips (X) and strips (T-1). Rails (P) and (W) keep drawers level when pulled out by giving support on top, and they and strip (X) are used to fasten the table-top to the frame. Strips (T-1) support drawer run (T) behind rail (A) and hold rails (A) to stiles (D) with wood screws.

Make and carve the two brackets, a detail of these being shown in Fig. 9. These are fastened to the legs with short mortise-and-tenon joints, as shown in Fig. 3. They are not glued to the frame until after the table frame has been assembled and glued together. Be sure to cut the grooves into the bottoms of rails (C) before assembling the frame, so the short tenons on top of bracket (J) may slide into place in this groove when you glue the tenons to the mortises in the legs. These grooves are shown in Fig. 3.

To glue up the frame and legs, first glue stiles (D) to rails (C). Then glue rails (C) to the front legs. Glue back (F) to the back legs. Then glue ends (E) to the front and back legs. Now glue rail (B) to stiles (D) and to the tops of the front legs. Be very careful to see that the frame is squared when the above pieces are glued together. Screw strips (T-1) to rail (A), and then screw strips (T-1) to stiles (D).

Drill and countersink holes, and screw drawer guides (Q) and rails (P) to ends (E). Then drill and countersink holes, and screw drawer guides (V) to drawer runs (U). Screw drawer runs (R) to drawer guides (Q). Then glue drawer guides (S) and drawer runs (U) to the mortises in the back. Screw drawer runs (T) to drawer guides (S) and glue them to strips (T-1), and screw drawer guides (V) to rail (C). Then screw strip (X) to the back. This completes the table frame assembly.

Make the drawers next. A detail of one of the side drawers is shown in Fig. 8. The middle drawer front and sides may be joined together with two tails, and with three pins the same size as those we show in Fig. 8. Make drawer fronts first and cut grooves for the inlay banding with an electric-powered hand router, or outline the grooves with a thin-bladed sloyd knife, sharpened on the skew, and then chisel out the waste between the knife cuts to make the shallow grooves for the inlay banding.

Lay out the dovetails on the drawer sides first. Then after they have been cut out transfer the shapes from the sides to the ends of the drawer fronts and drawer backs. When dovetail joints have been made and fitted, cut grooves with a dado head into sides and fronts to hold the drawer bottoms. Then glue up the drawers. Glue drawer bottoms to the grooves cut into the drawer fronts only, and not to the grooves cut into the drawer sides. Drawer bottoms may be nailed to the lower edges of the drawer backs. Fit the drawers carefully to the openings, being sure they slide in and out easily.

Glue up and make the tabletop. The molded edge may be formed on a shaper, or with a shaper-cutter on the drill press using a setup like the one shown in Fig. 14. The groove between the beads may be cut out with a dado head on the table saw, and the beads may then be rounded over with a wood-carver's skew chisel and sanded smooth and round. Screw the tabletop to strips (P), (X), and to rail (B) from below. Strips (W) may then be screwed fast to the tabletop from below to keep the drawers level when they are pulled out. Put the drawer pulls on the drawer fronts. This completes the table construction.

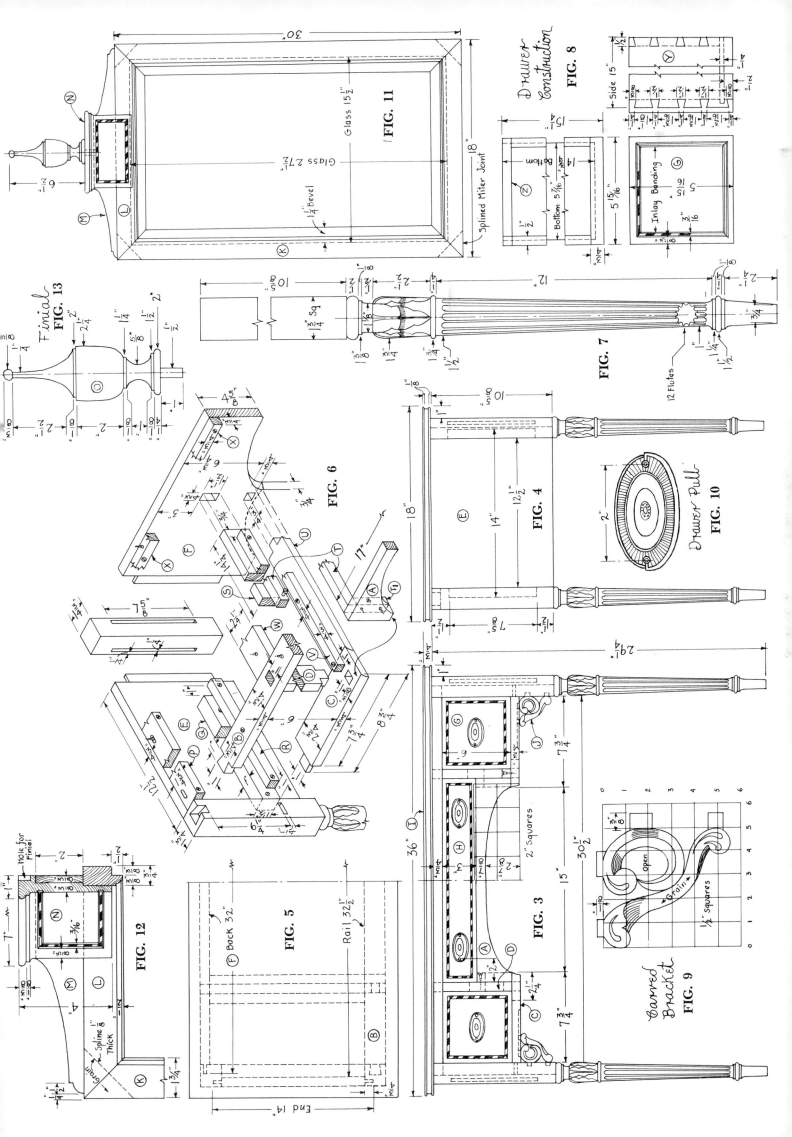

Drawer Construction FIG. 8

FIG. 11

Glass 27½"

Glass 15½"

¼" Bevel

Splined Miter Joint

30"

18"

Inlay Banding G

Side 15

Bottom 5/16

Bottom 14

Z

FIG. 13 Finial

O

FIG. 7

12 Flutes

FIG. 6

X X F S U T A I1 W V D C E G B R P

FIG. 12

Hole for Finial

N L M K

Spline 1/8" Thick

Grain

FIG. 5

Back 32" F

Rail 32½"

End 14

B

Drawer Pull FIG. 10

FIG. 4

14"

12½"

10 5/8"

7 5/8"

29¼"

36"

18"

17"

Carved Bracket FIG. 9

Open

Grain

½ squares

FIG. 3

G A H D C J

2" squares

15"

30½"

7¾"

L M N

Fig. 14.

across the corners of the joints for splines, shown

To build the mirror frame, cut out, plane, and sand stiles (K) and rails (L) to the sizes given in the Bill of Material. With a dado head on the table saw, cut rabbets on one edge of these. Cut the ends at a 45-degree angle in the miter box. Be sure these joints come together perfectly tight, and glue them together. You may do this with four bar clamps— two going across and two lengthwise on the opposite side of the frame, to pull the joints together. When the glue joints have dried, cut grooves

in Figs. 11 and 12. The method used for cutting grooves for splines in corners of a frame is shown in Fig. 6 (Chippendale fretwork mirror frame) in Chapter 33. Splines, or feathers as they are sometimes called, are glued across miter joints in frames having to bear heavy objects, such as a mirror like this, to reinforce them.

The shaped top (M) should now be made and fastened to the top of the frame with glue and several brads. Then make the small fascia board (N) with the molding on top. Fit it to the frame and shaped top (M), as shown in the cross-section in Fig. 12. Cut grooves into the face for the inlay banding, and glue the banding into the grooves. Sand the surface carefully to smooth it, then glue the fascia to the frame.

A beveled plate-glass mirror like the one shown in Fig. 1 should be used; it should not be put into the frame until all the wood finishing on both pieces has been done.

It should be noted here that both of these pieces of furniture were given their beautiful red mahogany color by first whitewashing them with quicklime dissolved in water. The advantage to using this instead of a mahogany oil or water stain to color the wood is that it does not affect the color of the inlay when it is applied. When dry, it may be wiped off clean with burlap or cotton waste, and the surface cleaned off by washing it with boiled linseed oil thinned with turpentine. Wood filler, needed for a good finish on mahogany, should be applied after the whitewash has been cleaned off. If the filler is colored, masking tape will have to be used over the inlay banding to protect it, and this masking tape should be somewhat wider than the banding to prevent any of the color from staining it.

BILL OF MATERIAL

Honduras or Santo Domingo Mahogany

4 Legs 1¾″ x 1¾″ x 29¼″
1 Arched rail (A) ¾″ x 3″ x 17″
1 Rail (B) ¾″ x 1¾″ x 32½″
2 Rails (C) ¾″ x 2¾″ x 8¾″
2 Stiles (D) ¾″ x 1¾″ x 7½″
2 Ends (E) ¾″ x 10⅝″ x 14″
1 Back (F) ¾″ x 10⅝″ x 32″
2 Drawer fronts (G) ¾″ x 5¹⁵⁄₁₆″ x 5¹⁵⁄₁₆″
1 Drawer front (H) ¾″ x 2¹⁵⁄₁₆″ x 16¹⁵⁄₁₆″
1 Top (I) ¾″ x 18″ x 36″
2 Carved brackets (J), carved from stock ¾″ x 2⅛″ x 4″
2 Mirror frame stiles (K) ¾″ x 1¾″ x 30″
2 Mirror frame rails (L) ¾″ x 1¾″ x 18″
1 Piece for top of frame (M) ⅜″ x 2″ x 17½″
1 Inlaid fascia board (N) 1″ x 4″ x 7″
1 Finial (O) 2¼″ diam. x 7½″

Poplar

2 Rails (P) ¾″ x 1¾″ x 12½″

2 Drawer guides (Q) 1″ x 1½″ x 12½″
2 Drawer runs (R) ¾″ x ¾″ x 12½″
2 Drawer guides (S) ¾″ x 1½″ x 14¼″
2 Drawer runs (T) ¾″ x ¾″ x 14½″
2 Strips (T-1) ¾″ x ¾″ x 2¼″
2 Drawer runs (U) ¾″ x 2¼″ x 13¼″
2 Drawer guides (V) ¾″ x ¾″ x 13½″
1 Rail (W). Screwed to underside of top. ¾″ x 2¼″ x 12⅝″. Not joined to front rail or back
1 Strip to which top is screwed fast (X) ¾″ x ¾″ x 30½″
2 Drawer sides ½″ x 2¹⁵⁄₁₆″ x 15″
4 Drawer sides (Y) ½″ x 5¹⁵⁄₁₆″ x 15″
1 Drawer back ½″ x 2³⁄₁₆″ x 16¹⁵⁄₁₆″
2 Drawer backs (Z) ½″ x 5³⁄₁₆″ x 5¹⁵⁄₁₆″

Plywood

1 Drawer bottom ¼″ x 14¾″ x 16⁷⁄₁₆″
2 Drawer bottoms ¼″ x 5⁷⁄₁₆″ x 14¾″

NINETEEN

Hepplewhite Four-Poster Bed

FOUR-poster beds with high posts are always very impressive pieces of furniture, especially when made up with an attractive coverlet. Even without a canopy, a bed of this type, if it has well-designed posts, is a very distinctive object to behold and almost invariably is the main feature in an attractive bedroom. The handsome bed shown in Fig. 1 will fully bear us out in this assertion.

The bed shown in Fig. 1 was made by students at Berry College in Georgia, under the author's direction. The wood is mahogany. The octagon-shaped posts are a distinctive feature and are a very attractive variation of the more commonly found turned posts found on most beds of this kind.

The bed is designed for a standard-sized double-bed box spring and mattress which measures 54 by 75 inches. The design could easily be adapted to a three-quarter-size box spring and mattress, which would measure 48 by 75 inches, or to a "longster" for which the above widths would remain the same, but the length would be 80 inches. The 78-inch rail length on each side of the bed gives about the right amount of extra room to make tucking in of covers easy.

To build the bed, get out stock for the posts first. As shown in the Bill of Material, even though the posts are quite slender, it still takes pieces of mahogany 3 inches square to make one. If a lathe with a long enough lathe bed is available, it is best to make the post in one piece except for the finial,

which is always turned separately. If such an exceptionally long lathe is not available, then the post must be made of two pieces, joined to each other, as shown at C in Fig. 3, with a large dowel turned on the lower end of the upper part. If properly joined, this will never be noticed on the post after the two parts have been glued together, and most bedposts as long as this one are designed so they may be made in two or more parts. Thus the upper part will need to be 47 inches long and the lower part, which has no turning on it, will be 24 inches long.

Step 1 in Fig. 4 gives an indication of how the

Fig. 1. Hepplewhite Four-Poster Bed. BUILT IN THE BERRY COLLEGE SHOPS.

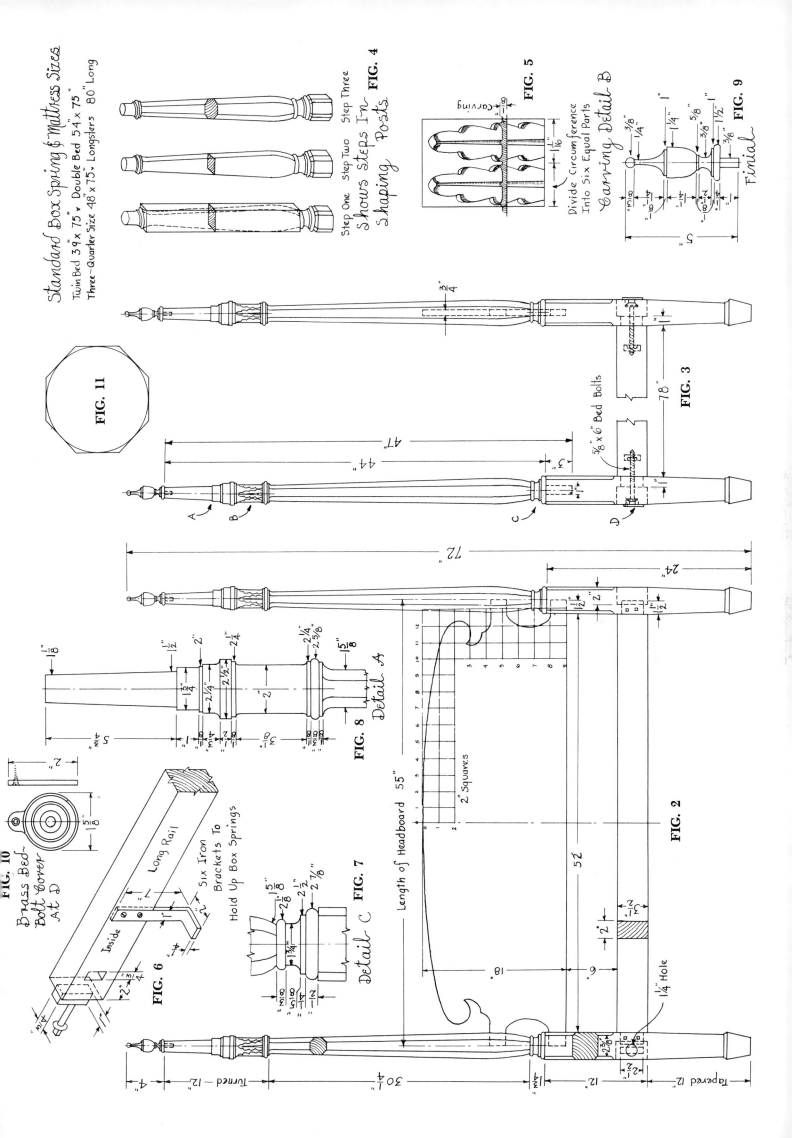

upper part of the post must be turned before giving it the octagon shape shown in Step 3. To shape the post, after it has been turned, cut it roughly to shape as shown in Step 2, Fig. 4, before finishing it as shown in Step 3. A cardboard pattern laid on each side to trace the outline, as shown in Step 2, will be a great help in doing this part of the work correctly. After cutting the post to the shape shown in Step 2, draw two octagons on a piece of paper. One needs to be 3 inches across the flats, which will give you an octagon, the sides of which are as long as the width of one side of the octagon post at its greatest width; and the other will have to be 1⅝ inches across the flats for the upper and lower ends of the octagon-shaped part. This will give the approximate width of each of the sides at these places on the octagon-shaped part, which you will need to know to cut them to the proper shape.

Lay out your octagons by first drawing a circle having the same diameter as the distance across the flats, and then with T square and 45-degree triangle you can draw the octagon about the circle by making all sides tangent to the circle as shown in Fig. 11.

When all posts have been cut to the octagon shape, mount them between the lathe centers to carve the leaves. A full-sized pattern for these leaves may be made from the sketch shown in Fig. 5. To carve the leaves, outline each one and the vein going up its center with a wood-carver's V tool, and then cut backgrounds and do shaping with small shallow gouges. The modeling on these does not exceed ⅛ inch at the deepest part.

Make and shape the lower part of the post, as shown in Figs. 2 and 3. Some of the shaping on these may be done on the band saw, but it must be finished by hand with chisels and a gouge. Sandpaper all parts, and then bore holes to join the two parts of each post together if the posts have been made in two parts. The best way to bore these holes is by using a 1-inch bit in a floor-model drill press. It is essential to hold the part to be drilled in a vertical position when doing this, so the upper part will not lean to one side or the other when it has been glued to it. Even the slightest degree off from being straight will show on a post as tall as these, so absolute accuracy is essential here.

To hold the lower part of the post in a vertical position, draw center lines on two adjacent sides and then fasten several large hand-screw clamps to the bottom of the post, turning each alternate clamp with its tightening screws going in the opposite direction from the one put on just under it. Then use a plumb line to be sure the center lines are lined up with the plumb line to bore the hole.

Glue the two parts of the post together. When doing this it is essential to make sure a flat side of the octagon-shaped part is lined up to be level with, or at least parallel to, a flat side of the squared upper section of the lower part of the post so that the two mortises which hold the headboard may be cut into sides properly lined up with each other. Then turn the finials to go into the tops of the posts, as in Fig. 9.

Mortises for the headboard should now be laid out on two of the posts, and mortises for the side and end rails should be laid out on all posts. These may be cut on the mortising machine, or if none is available, with hand tools. Mortises for side rails are short, so bed bolts which hold them in place will have enough solid wood left to make the joint strong. These bed bolts are specially made with big heads, so the bearing surface against the wood is quite large in diameter. Holes for these bed bolts are covered—especially at the foot end of the bed, where they would detract from the appearance if left exposed—by brass bed-bolt covers like the one shown in Fig. 10. It is not absolutely essential that covers be used at the headboard end of the bed, since this is usually hidden from view.

Make the headboard. Lay out the graph squares shown in Fig. 2 full size on a large piece of paper or plywood, and on these graph squares draw the full-sized pattern. When boards for the headboard have been glued together, plane and sand the headboard, and then saw it to shape on the band saw. File and sand all edges smooth, and fit the tenons to the post mortises.

Make the four rails and cut tenons on both ends of each. Tenons on the short rails should fit tight, and it is a good idea to reinforce these joints with wooden pegs, as shown in Fig. 2. Tenons on the long rails should not fit mortises as tight as those on the end rails do theirs, because it is necessary to remove these rails to take the bed apart whenever it is to be moved from one room to another. Holes for the bed bolts must be bored into the ends of the long rails. Since the rails are too long to do this on a drill press, an electrically operated hand drill may be used to do this, and lacking this, it must be done by hand with a brace and bit. Mortises must also be cut on the inside of the long rails at both ends for the nut that tightens the bolt and pulls the joint together.

Six or more heavy iron brackets are fastened to the long rails on the inside to support the box spring. If a box spring had to be supported on top of these rails, it would make the bed much higher, since the total thickness of box spring and mattress when put on a bed is about 14 inches.

Fastening the bolt-hole covers completes the bed. They should be removed when the finish coats are applied.

BILL OF MATERIAL

Mahogany

4 Posts 3″ x 3″ x 68″, or 4 pcs. 3″ x 3″ x 24″ and 4 pcs. 3″ x 3″ x 47″

4 Long rails 2″ x 3½″ x 80″
4 Short rails 2″ x 3½″ x 55″
1 Headboard ¾″ x 18″ x 55″
4 Finials 1½″ diam. x 5″

TWENTY

Sheraton Four-Poster Bed

THE Sheraton Four-Poster Bed, shown in Fig. 1, is constructed much like the Hepplewhite Bed in Chapter 19. It was designed by Mr. Monroe Guyton, a colleague of the author's at Berry College, and was built by students under his direction.

If a craftsman wishing to build this handsome bed has a lathe with a lathe bed long enough, the posts may be turned in one piece. At Berry College there is such a lathe, and the posts of this bed were turned in one piece. It is better to turn bedposts in one piece, but since lathes with so long a bed are rarely found in small shops, the author has shown on these drawings how posts for the bed may be turned in two sections on a shorter lathe bed.

Since the construction of this bed is the same in many respects as the construction of the Hepplewhite Bed shown in the previous chapter, we will not repeat those directions for making it that were given for the other bed.

We do want to call attention, however, to several important matters with which the builder of the other bed need not concern himself, but which need to be brought to his attention if he builds this one. One of these is the manner in which the reeding is done on the bedposts. In Fig. 8 we show about as good a method of doing reeding, or fluting, on turnings as has yet been brought to our attention, especially when we bear in mind the

facilities available to small shops lacking the more sophisticated equipment of furniture factories. This is the method used in Mr. Hogg's cabinet shop to do reeding and fluting on all furniture turnings made there.

As can readily be seen when Fig. 8 is examined, a small electric hand router and shaper is fastened securely into a jig in such a manner that the cutter is exactly in line with the lathe centers. Two collars, one above the cutter and the other collar below the cutter, regulate the depth of cut. A homemade index head is fastened to the faceplate of the lathe, and the small stand with the band-iron upright holds the index head and the turning in the proper position to make each cut.

This lathe setup will work on straight or shaped turnings, and the shaping is more easily accomplished than could be done on a spindle shaper.

Fig. 1. Sheraton Four-Poster Bed. BUILT IN THE BERRY COLLEGE SHOPS.

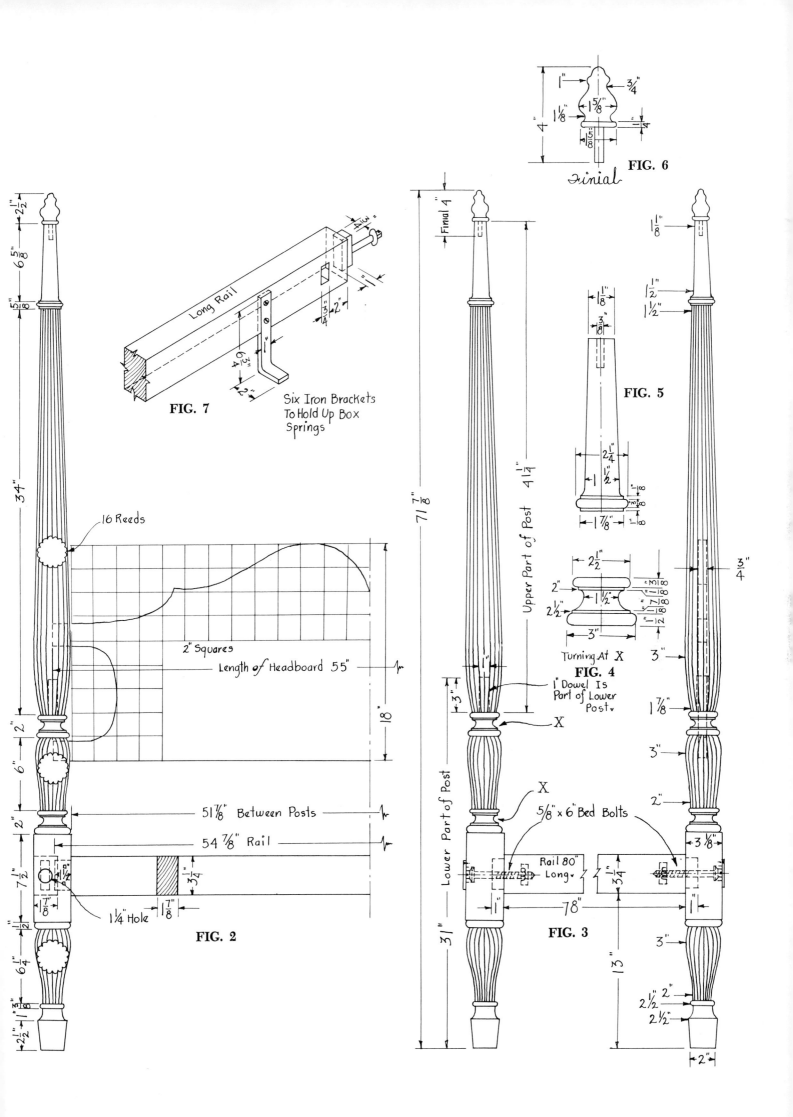

FIG. 6

Finial

FIG. 7

Long Rail

Six Iron Brackets
To Hold Up Box
Springs

16 Reeds

2" Squares

Length of Headboard 55"

51 7/8" Between Posts

54 7/8" Rail

1 1/4" Hole

FIG. 2

Finial 4"

Upper Part of Post 41 1/4"

71 7/8"

Lower Part of Post

31"

X

5/8" x 6" Bed Bolts

Rail 80" Long.

78"

FIG. 3

FIG. 5

Turning At X

FIG. 4

1" Dowel Is
Part of Lower
Post

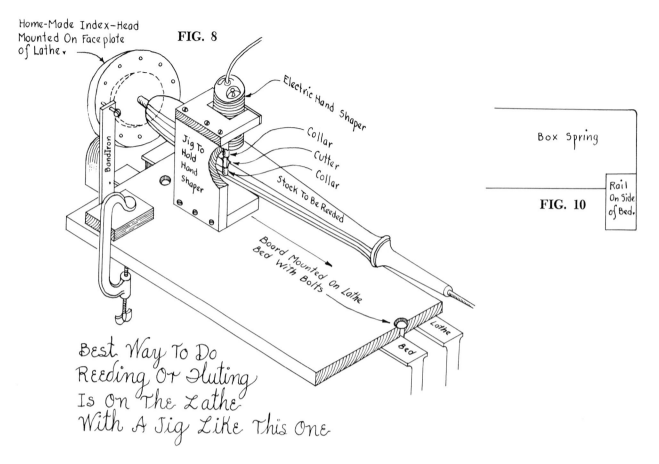

FIG. 8

FIG. 10

Best Way To Do Reeding Or Fluting Is On The Lathe With A Jig Like This One

Fig. 9 shows the type of bed-bolt cover used on beds like this one.

Standard sizes for mattresses and box springs for beds of various widths and lengths are given on the drawing of the Hepplewhite Bed. Should the maker of this bed want a narrower bed than this double bed, all he would have to do is shorten the rails and the headboard at both ends of the bed to make it conform to the smaller-sized standard mattress size. Should he wish to build a longer bed, all he would have to do is lengthen the side rails by as much as the box spring is longer than a standard-length bed.

Attention should be called to the fact that custom-made box springs can be made with a rabbet on both edges on the underside as shown in Fig. 10. This makes it possible to fit such springs to a bed so the sides of the box springs are flush with the outside of the bed rail. With such springs and a mattress to match, the bed covers may be put on the bed so the sides hang vertically. This gives the bed a much neater appearance when it is made up, something the housewife will greatly appreciate.

At Nutting's studio, custom-made box springs for beds were bought having corners built into them to make the box springs fit around the posts at the lower end of the bed. Corners of the mattress were cut to the same pattern to conform to the shape of the box spring, so the coverlet would hang straight on three sides of the bed. Such custom work is expensive, of course, but worth considering if one can afford to have it done.

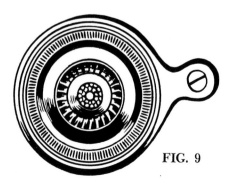

FIG. 9

BILL OF MATERIAL

Mahogany

4 Posts lower part 3⅛″ x 3⅛″ x 31″ *

4 Posts upper part 3″ diam. x 41¼″

* If a lathe with a long enough bed is available, four posts may be turned 69⅝″ long.

4 Finials 1⅝″ diam. x 4″

1 Headboard ¾″ x 18″ x 55″

2 Short rails 1⅞″ x 3¼″ x 54⅞″

Mahogany or Maple

2 Long rails 1⅞″ x 3¼″ x 80″

TWENTY-ONE

Grandfather Clock

Fig. 1. *Grandfather Clock.* COURTESY MALMBERG AN-
TIQUES, BOYERTOWN, PENNSYLVANIA.

GRANDFATHER Clock is the generally accepted nickname for a tall clock, and the
term has come to be almost universally associated
with these regal timepieces. These tall and handsome examples of a noble art flourished in fine
homes of the eighteenth century in Colonial America and were highly esteemed because of the time,
special skills, and expense required to build one.
Such clocks came to be greatly cherished as heirlooms, and, indeed, they continue to stand well at
the top of the list of our most cherished antique
furniture to this very day, with prices of good ones
running into four figures, so that reproducing one
like the fine example we show here is a very worthwhile undertaking.

Tall clocks like these originally were probably
designed to be placed in a hallway, or at the head
of a fine staircase where the ceiling was high
enough to accommodate them. The fact that they
were weight clocks, and the motive power for running the clock depended on the weights descend-
ing from high to lower levels inside the case,
influenced the design of course. For an eight-day
clock the weights naturally had to travel a considerable distance. Sad to relate, it sometimes hap-
pened that such tall clocks, either by inheritance
or otherwise, fell into the hands of a family who
did not have a house with a great hallway or rooms
with ceilings high enough to accommodate them.
Being heirlooms which the owners may have been

loath to part with, or just a useful piece of furniture not readily replaceable except at considerable expense, such clocks at times were mutilated by having the tops of pediments sawed off, having feet and finials removed so a room in the house could accommodate it.

The hall clock in "Oak Hill," home of Martha Berry, founder of the Berry Schools in Georgia, is an example of such a clock, the case of which the author restored. A picture of this fine tall clock appears in *Design for the Craftsman*, an earlier book.

Pennsylvania, especially in the city of Philadelphia or within a fifty mile radius of it, heads the list of states where clockmakers specializing in this type of clock flourished. One of the most famous makers of tall clocks in America was David Rittenhouse of Norristown; scientist, mathematician, astronomer, and member of the Constitutional Convention, who built some very fine tall clocks.

A remarkable fact we should not overlook about these builders of early clocks is that they not only built the fine clock cases, but the works as well. Before the eighteenth century, when metal was harder to come by in the colonies than wood, which was in plentiful supply, works for many of these clocks were made of wood, including the gears, which were whittled and fashioned by hand, as indeed were all other parts. The clocks may not always have kept perfect time, but the craftsmanship was marvelous. Lucky indeed is anyone who possesses a fine antique original grandfather clock in good condition. Reproducing one is an accomplishment of which anyone can be proud. We think the one we show here is a worthy example to start with.*

To build the clock, get out stock for the two ends (A), front (B), reinforcing and backing strips (H), and floor (J), for the lower section. Glue up, plane, and sand these to the sizes given in the Bill of Material. Front (B) is inlaid with strips of holly only ⅟₁₆ inch wide to give a panel effect, as is the door of the middle section. Another strip of inlay is put over the arching of the hood on the pediment facing. The routing out to do this inlaying should be done with a portable electric hand

* See footnote at end of chapter.

router. At the time this clock was built, this routing was most likely done with a scratch stock, which was a tool, often homemade, somewhat resembling a marking gauge. Instead of a steel pin with the pencil-point end, however, the steel was filed to a chisel point, straight across, and with it the groove in the wood could be scraped out. For hollowed corners, such as the ones found on the front of the lower section here, a template was clamped to the board, and the corner could then be scratched to the curve of the template with an awl, the end of which was also filed straight across like a chisel. Small edge moldings like the one shown at the bottom of molding #3 were often cut with tools similar to this, the cutters of which were ground to the shape of the molding to be cut.

Inlay the front, then cut the rabbet along one edge of strips (H). Glue these strips to the back

Fig. 2.

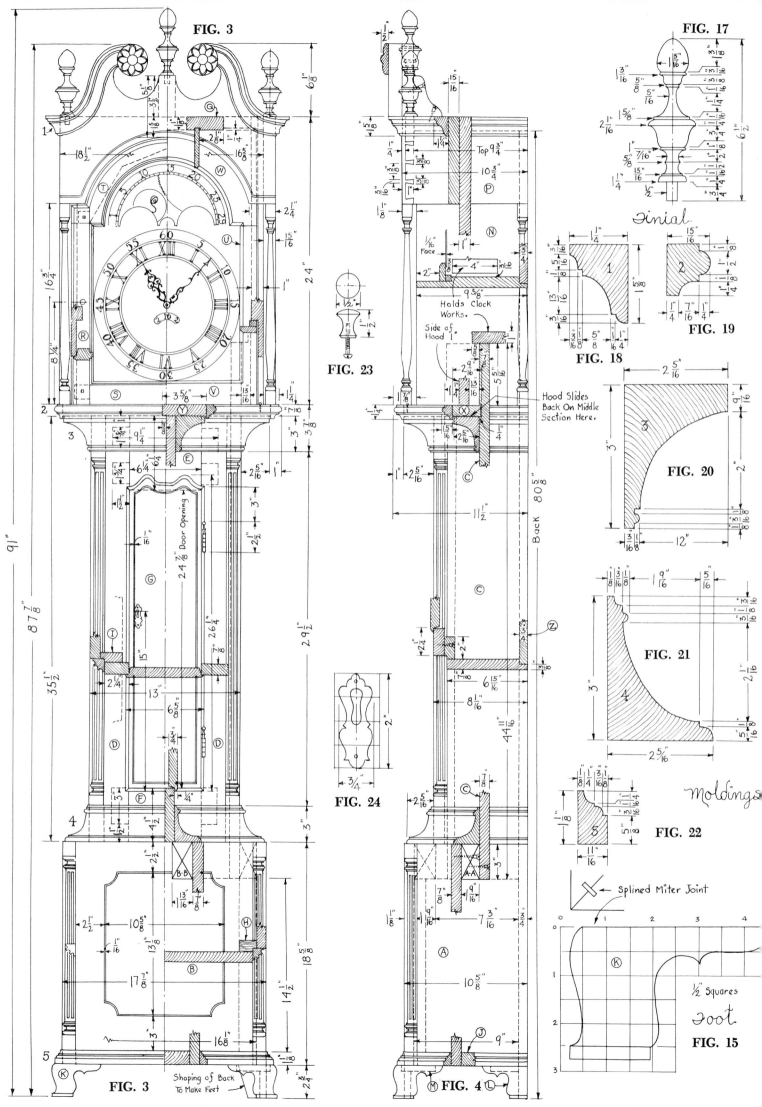

FIG. 3

FIG. 17

Finial

FIG. 18

FIG. 19

FIG. 20

FIG. 21

Moldings

FIG. 22

FIG. 23

Holds Clock Works.

Side of Hood 1"

Hood Slides Back On Middle Section Here.

FIG. 24

Splined Miter Joint

½ Squares

Foot

FIG. 15

FIG. 4

Shaping of Back To Make Feet

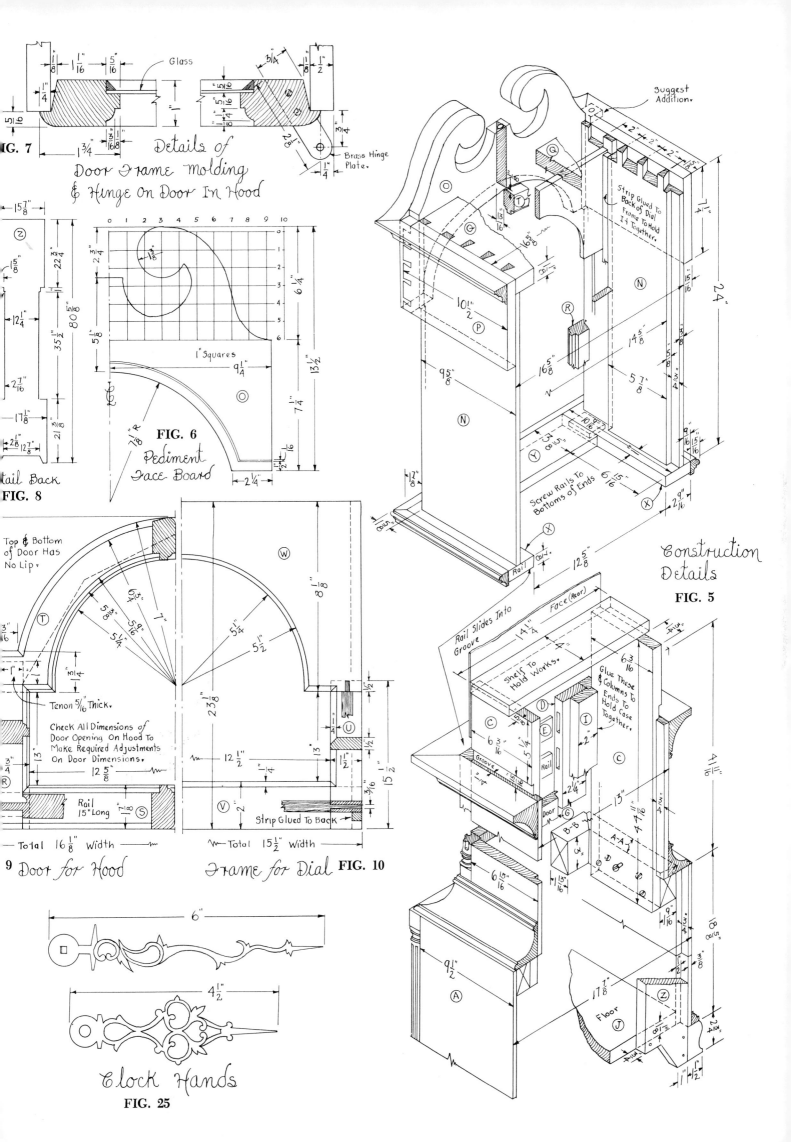

FIG. 7

Details of
Door Frame Molding
& Hinge On Door In Hood

Glass

Brass Hinge Plate.

FIG. 6

Pediment
Face Board

1" Squares

Tail Back
FIG. 8

Top & Bottom
of Door Has
No Lip.

Tenon 5/16" Thick.

Check All Dimensions of
Door Opening On Hood To
Make Required Adjustments
On Door Dimensions.

Rail
15" Long

Strip Glued To Back

Total 16 1/8" Width

9 Door for Hood

Frame for Dial **FIG. 10**

Total 15 1/2" Width

Suggest
Addition.

Strip Glued To
Back of Dial
Frame To Hold
It Together.

Screw Rails To
Bottoms of Ends

Construction
Details

FIG. 5

Rail Slides Into
Groove

Face (Rear)

Shelf To
Hold Works.

Glue These
& Columns to
Ends To
Hold Case
Together.

Groove

Rail

Door

Floor

Clock Hands

FIG. 25

of panel (B), as shown in the cross-section view in Fig. 3. Then nail or screw the front to the floor (J). Now rabbet the back edges of ends (A), then glue them to front (B) and nail them to the floor.

Next get out the spacers A-A and B-B and screw these to the upper ends of (A) and (B) on the inside. These pieces are mitered at the front, and then the corners are notched, as shown in Fig. 5, to fit around the quarter columns.

Now get out stock for ends (C), stiles (D), rails (E) and (F), and reinforcing and backing strips (I) of the middle section. Plane, square up, and sand these to size. Lay out and cut mortises and tenons on rails and stiles to make the doorframe. Glue up this frame and clean glue off the joints.

When the doorframe has been made, it will be a good idea to make the door for it and fit the hinges and lock. If this is done before gluing together the middle section, fitting the hinges and lock will be easier, since the frame may be held in a vise, and fitting the door to the frame will take less time. Once the door has been fitted to the doorframe, it may be removed until the middle section has been fastened to the lower section.

To make door (G), plane and sand it to size and rabbet all four edges; the rabbet on top should be made wide enough to fall below the shaping on top of the door, as shown in Fig. 3. Then cut grooves around the edges of the door face for the inlay strips and glue these in place. After sanding the surface smooth, put hinges and lock on the door and fit it to the doorframe. Then glue the reinforcing and backing strips to the back of the frame. Rabbet back edges on ends (C). Cut grooves across the outside of ends (C) near the top, as shown in Figs. 4 and 5. Cut off the edges of rabbets which have been cut on ends (C) from the bottom of the groove to the top of (C), and for a distance of 3 inches from the bottom. Then glue ends (C) to the outside edges of strips (I); be sure before you do this, however, that the middle section, once it has been glued together, will fit inside the spacer rails A-A and B-B. When all parts of the middle section have been glued together, screw the bottom of ends (C) to the 1 9/16-inch spacer rails at the end, as shown in Figs. 4 and 5.

Glue up and turn the columns for the lower and the middle sections. The way to glue up the columns is shown in Fig. 12, with heavy wrapping paper between four strips of wood, so that when split apart with a chisel and mallet after turning, each strip will be a perfectly formed quarter column. Note, however, that in order to make it as easy as possible to cut flutes in the columns, both the long and the short columns are cut into three segments, either before turning them, or afterward, as shown in Fig. 11. If this is done after turning the column, the diameter will be exactly the same where they are rejoined, so that this is actually the better way to do it. Some may find it easier to turn the top and bottom, using shorter lengths of stock, in which case all three segments should be made longer than we show them, to be turned.

Once the columns have been turned and cut into segments, the shaft of the column may be fluted on a shaper by rotating it in a jig, as shown in Fig. 10 in the chapter describing the construction of the Salem Chest of Drawers. After fluting, the column should be split into quarters with a chisel and mallet, and the quarter columns should be glued into their respective corners.

Feet for the clock case may now be made. A single strip of material, long enough to cut all six sides of the feet from it, may be formed as we show it being done for similarly shaped feet in Fig. 11 in the chapter describing the construction of the Salem Chest of Drawers. Fig. 14 shows how these pieces are put together with a glued miter joint, and a full-sized pattern of the foot may be made from Fig. 15. Fasten the feet to the bottom of the clock with screws and glue.

Before doing any work on the hood, the clockworks should be at hand and may now be fastened to the shelf at the top of the middle section. Shelves like this sometimes have a section cut out of the middle for the pendulum shaft, but on this clock the shelf is only four inches wide and the pendulum drops down behind it. Proper adjustments in the design may be made to fit the works which have been purchased to the hood of this clock case, but it is essential that this be done before the hood is made.

Work on the hood should be started by getting

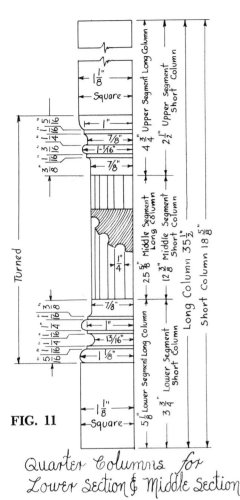

FIG. 11

Quarter Columns for Lower Section & Middle Section

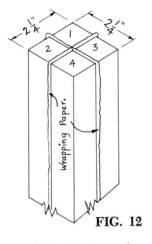

FIG. 12

To Make Quarter-Columns
Glue Four Strips of Wood
Together With Heavy Brown
Wrapping Paper Between.
Turn Columns In Three
Sections As Shown In Fig 11
Then Split Them Apart At The
Wrapping Paper Joints To Make
Quarter Columns. Cut Flutes Into
Middle Sections Before Splitting Them
Apart.

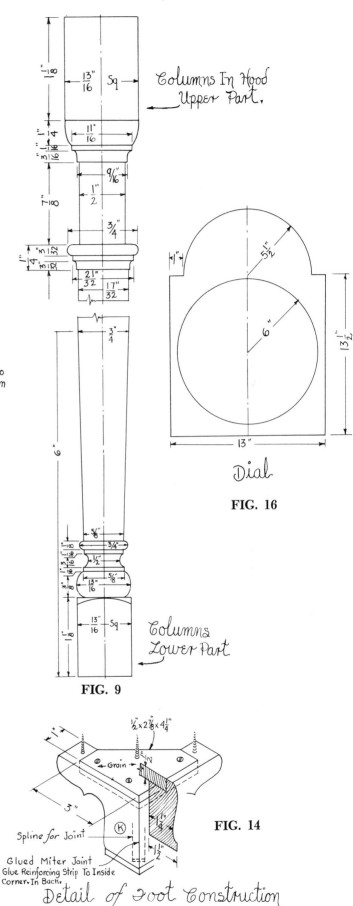

Columns In Hood
Upper Part.

FIG. 9

Columns Lower Part

Dial

FIG. 16

Spline for Joint

Glued Miter Joint
Glue Reinforcing Strip To Inside
Corner. In Back.

FIG. 14

Detail of Foot Construction

out stock for ends (N), pediment face board (O), side pieces (P), and strips (X) and (Y). A top (Q) will also be needed at this time. Once the ends (N) have been cut to size, planed, and sanded, rabbets 3 inches wide and ½ inch deep should be cut on the inside at the front edges, as shown in Fig. 5, and in the cross-sections on both sides of the dial in Fig. 3. The door will close against these front edges and the frame bordering the dial face will fit between the two ends near the back of these rabbets, as shown in Figs. 3 and 5.

Lay out dovetails on the upper ends of (N) and on the top (Q). Cut these to shape as shown in Fig. 5. Cut a groove on the bottom side of (Q) to hold the frame going around the dial. On this clock nothing else except this groove serves to hold this frame in place, and probably nothing more is needed. The frame need not be tightly held when in place, to remain there, though less clearance than we have provided may be allowed. Glue the top to the ends of the hood.

Now cut strips (X) and (Y) and make mortise-and-tenon joints to hold them together, as shown in Fig. 5. Glue them together and after being sure the frame will slide easily into the grooves at the top of ends (C) of the middle section, screw the assembled frame to the bottoms of ends (N).

Make a full-sized pattern of pediment face board (O), from the diagram in Fig. 6. Plane, square, and sand stock to size for this and for the two end pieces (P), which are joined to it with dovetail joints. Lay out, cut, and fit the dovetail joints. Use a template and cut the groove for the inlay which goes around the arch. Then using the pattern, lay out and cut the pediment board to shape on the band saw. Smooth up the sawed edges, and then glue up the dovetail joints, first making sure these three pieces will fit around the ends and front of the previously assembled top and ends. When the dovetail joints have been cleaned up, fasten the pediment with wood screws from the inside of ends (N). The pediment board is reinforced in the middle at the back with a brace, shown at the top in Fig. 4.

Make the dial face frame, as shown in Fig. 10. Through mortise-and-tenon joints hold rail (V) at the bottom to stiles (U). Stub tenons at the top of (U), glued to grooves on the lower edge of (W), hold these pieces together when glued. Two strips of wood glued to both edges at the back of the frame reinforce it and help keep it straight.

Make the door for the hood. Cut stock for stiles (R), arch (T), and rail (S). Mortise-and-tenon joints may be cut on these pieces and the door glued up before cutting the molding on the inside edges, if so desired; the molding may then be cut on a shaper and finished off at each corner with wood-carving chisels. This is easier than making and fitting the coped joints we show in our drawings, though coped joints are better if cutters and facilities for making them are available. Possibly the person making the clock might prefer to have such a door made in a planing mill or a furniture factory, rather than attempting to build it himself, since doing it as we show it in our drawing requires special equipment not usually found in home workshops. However, our first method of putting the doorframe together is possible and quite practical

without such equipment, if care is taken to finish carving the molding at the corners properly.

Rabbeting for the glass on back of the door may be done on the shaper after the frame has been assembled, as may the rounding over on the outside edges. The two inside corners, where the arch begins, must then be finished by hand with carving tools. If the top of the glass is to be cut with straight sides, as shown, the rabbet holding it must be chiseled out to fit.

The door has lips only on the sides. No lips are cut on top of the door, which clears the arch above it by a full eighth of an inch. Hinging at the bottom and top of this door is shown in Fig. 7. The fulcrum of the hinge plate must be placed so when the door is opened it will pull the lip of the door away from the front of the doorstop, so the lip will not be broken off.

Now make the back for the clock and nail it to the two lower sections. (See Fig. 8.)

You are now about ready to make and put moldings on the clock. If any parts of the molding shapes can be cut on a shaper with available cutters, it should be done. However, the lack of proper equipment for accomplishing it by this means need not discourage the craftsman. Molding cutters may be found to fit on circular saws, and if the right ones are available, so much the better. With the exception of the ogee molding at the top of the clock, these shapes may first be roughed out on the table saw, and then finished up by hand with wood-carving chisels. Part of the S-shaped curved molding at the top may be cut on a shaper, but around the rosettes it must be finished off with wood-carving chisels. The rosettes are carved by hand. The top of the ogee under the rosettes may be left flat and kept even with the flat area bordering the upper edge of the molding. The rosettes are carved on pieces of wood ½ inch thick and then glued to these flat areas on the moldings.

Once a molding has been made and carefully sanded, it should be fastened to the clock. Moldings 3 and 4 should not be glued fast, but may be secured by wood screws from the inside of the clock case. Usually they were nailed to the clock case and the holes puttied up with a crack filler of some kind. We prefer to hold nailing to a minimum and keep it from showing as much as possible. The ogee molding at the top may be screwed to the pediment face with wood screws from the back, and with a little glue along the lower edges. All mitered joints should be glued, with a brad or two to hold the joints together until the glue has dried.

Molding #1 at the side may be glued fast, since the grain on the molding parallels the grain on side pieces (P) and will therefore not turn loose as the result of unequal shrinkage. The same cannot be said for moldings #3, #4, and #5, at the sides of the clock, so glue should be used sparingly on these. Brads and small finishing nails should be used instead of glue, and the holes left by heads going into the wood should be carefully filled with colored plastic wood, or crack filler. Molding #3 and molding #4 can be fastened with wood screws from the inside, but molding #5 should be fastened with small brads and glued together at the corners on the front. The finishing coats put on the clock when it has been completed will help hold the molding in place.

Turn and fasten the small colonnettes to the hood. Short pins, made by cutting finish nails to short lengths, will serve to hold the tops of these in place. At the bottom, glue, and a finishing nail driven up from the bottom of the molding, will serve.

Turn the finials and bore holes to hold them. A small platform under the finials on the outside is an improvement from the way they are shown in Fig. 1. We show this at the top of Fig. 5.

NOTE ON GRANDFATHER CLOCK: Before building any tall clock, be sure you can get works for it that will fit the case. As we have pointed out at the beginning of the chapter, most of the antique clock cases were made for works which were often custom made for the clock case into which they were put. Since this is no longer true today, the works should be bought first, and then the case should be made to accommodate it.

Good works for tall clocks are being made in Germany and are being imported by American firms. From these, builders of individual clocks may get works and supplies. Two such firms are: The Modern Technical Tools and Supply Co. whose address is 211 Nevada St., Hicksville, N.Y. 11801; and Mason and

Sullivan Co., 39 Blossom Ave., Osterville, Mass. 02655. Unfortunately not many individuals are left who make clockworks, or if there are, the author his been unable to locate them. Mr. Robert T. Hogg, whose furniture is featured in this book and who builds some clocks, has furnished one name. He is Mr. Jake Reihl, Clocks and Works, Manheim, Pa., R.D. 3. Manheim is near the town of Lititz, in the heart of the Pennsylvania Dutch country. We have not contacted Mr. Reihl at the date of writing this, but we are told that Mr. Reihl prefers selling two or more works at a time to a customer.

In purchasing clockworks, the critical measurements are: 1. Length of pendulum rod. 2. Inside case width for swing of pendulum. 3. Distance weights will drop. 4. Distance from middle of dial to middle of pendulum disk. 5. Measurement of movement. 6. Size of dial (clock face).

Our clock, whose exact measurements we reproduced in the drawings, has a dial which is about 1 inch wider and higher (square section) than dial faces generally available today. Why the larger dials found on most old clocks are no longer available from firms who deal in these works the author has been unable to ascertain, though he has asked the question of a number of firms. However, should it not be possible to obtain a dial the size needed for this clock, it will be a fairly simple matter to make minor changes in the wooden dial frame, shown in Fig. 10 on the right, to make it fit the smaller-size dials which are available. This frame may also be moved forward in the hood to provide greater depth inside the hood for the works, should this be necessary.

On this clock, the waist of the middle section on the inside is too narrow to accommodate the pendulum swing of any of the available grandfather movements shown in the catalogues of the two commercial firms we have listed. However, several of the works for grandmother clocks in the catalogues will fit and are quite suitable to use. It would not be too much trouble to make the middle section of the clock an inch or so wider, and it would then accommodate the greater swing of the pendulum of the grandfather works.

Two of the grandmother works listed in the catalogue issued by The Modern Technical Tools and Supply Co. which will fit this clock are the M 38/1 works and the M 38/3 works. On these the pendulum swing is 9⅛ inches. The distance from the middle of the dial to the middle of the pendulum disk is 26 inches. The largest moon-phase dial available in this catalogue is

11¾ inches wide by 16½ inches high, and this is listed by number as MD 25/A.

The size of the works is 7⅛ inches high, 6¾ inches wide, 5⅞ inches deep. The M 38/1 has Westminster chimes and the M 38/3 has a 12-rod Westminster-Wellington-Winchester chime, and both are made to be used with a moon-phase dial. Both are 8-day movements.

In the Mason and Sullivan catalogue, the H-50 Nathan Hale grandmother movement made for moon-phase dials fits a space 6¾ inches wide, 10½ inches high, and 5¾ inches deep. The pendulum measures 30 inches from hand shaft to center of the 4½-inch polished brass pendulum disk. The pendulum swing is 9 inches and the distance required for the weight run is 51 inches from bottom of movement to floor. The movement has Westminster chimes powered by three weights. The largest moon-phase dial listed in this catalogue is 11 by 15½ inches.

The most suitable dial for a clock like this one is, of course, a hand-painted one like the one shown in Fig. 2. Such dials are not usually available in catalogues of firms that import clockworks, but must be custom made. Sometimes it is possible to find old clock dials in antique shops. One shop near the author's home which has a large number of old works for sale is Merritts Antiques, R.D. 2, Douglassville, Pennsylvania. Or, such dials may be purchased from individuals like Mr. Reihl who makes clockworks. If such sources of supply cannot be found, the only recourses left are either to adapt the size of the dial frame and the door to the size of the dial you are able to purchase, or to try making one yourself, as did the craftsmen who built the old clocks.

BILL OF MATERIAL

Black Walnut, Cherry, or Mahogany

2 Ends of lower section (A) ⅞″ x 9½″ x 18⅝″

1 Front of lower section (B) ⅞″ x 15⅝″ x 18⅝″

2 Ends of middle section (C) ⅞″ x 6¹⁵⁄₁₆″ x 44¹¹⁄₁₆″

2 Stiles in doorframe, middle section (D) ⅞″ x 2¼″ x 35½″

1 Upper rail in doorframe, middle section (E) ⅞″ x 6¼″ x 9¼″

1 Lower rail in doorframe, middle section (F) ⅞″ x 4½″ x 9¼″

1 Door, middle section (G) ¾″ x 6⅝″ x 26¼″

2 Reinforcing and backing strips, lower section (H) ⅞″ x 1½″ x 14½″

2 Reinforcing and backing strips, middle section (I) ⅞″ x 2″ x 35½″

1 Floor, lower section (J) 1⅛″ x 9″ x 16⅛″ (May be made of pine.)

4 Sides for front feet (K) 1½″ x 2¾″ x 4¼″

2 Sides for back feet (L) 1½″ x 2¾″ x 4″

2 Tops for front feet (M) ½″ x 2⅞″ x 4¼″

2 Tops for back feet ½″ x 2¼″ x 3½″

2 Ends for hood (N) 1″ x 9⅝″ x 24″

1 Pediment face board for hood (O) 1″ x 13½″ x 18½″

2 Side pieces at top of hood (P) ¹⁵⁄₁₆″ x 7¼″ x 10½″

1 Top for hood (Q) 1⅛″ x 9¾″ x 16⅝″

2 Door stiles in hood (R) 1″ x 1¾″ x 16¹⁄₁₆″

1 Bottom rail for door in hood (S) 1″ x 1⅞″ x 15″

1 Top for door in hood (T) 1″ x 7⅜″ x 16⅛″

2 Stiles for dial frame (U) ½″ x 1½″ x 15½″

1 Bottom rail for dial frame (V) ½″ x 2″ x 15½″

1 Top for dial frame (W) ½″ x 8⅛″ x 15½″

2 Side rails for bottom of hood (X) ⅞″ x 2⁹⁄₁₆″ x 10⁹⁄₁₆″

1 Front rail for bottom of hood (Y) ⅞″ x 3⅝″ x 15⅝″

Walnut, Cherry, or Mahogany

1 Column to make quarter-columns for middle section 4 pcs. 1⅛″ x 1⅛″ x 35½″ *

1 Column to make quarter columns for lower section 4 pcs. 1⅛″ x 1⅛″ x 18⅝″ *

3 Finials 2¹⁄₁₆″ diam. x 6½″ †

Moldings—sizes not given here, but should be taken directly from drawings. These are numbered 1, 2, 3, 4, 5 on the drawings.

Plywood

1 Back for clock (Z) ¾″ x 17⅛″ x 80⅝″

Pine

2 Spacers for end at top of lower section (inside) A-A 1⁹⁄₁₆″ x 3″ x 9″

1 Spacer for front at top of lower section (inside) B-B 1¹³⁄₁₆″ x 3″ x 16⅛″

* These columns are turned in three sections, as shown in Fig. 11, so that the fluting on the middle sections may more easily be cut on a shaper. The three sections are then carefully fitted and glued together where the fluting ends.

† Cut the stock a little thicker and wider than the diameter given here; also somewhat longer, to provide for waste in turning.

TWENTY-TWO

Queen Anne Chest-on-Frame

THE Queen Anne Chest-on-Frame, shown in Fig. 1, is an extraordinary and unique piece of furniture. Since this piece of furniture is almost sure to create some controversy, we deem it expedient to offer some explanation as to why it has been included in this collection.

In doing so let us begin by saying we believe the piece to be a combination of parts of two old pieces of furniture. The possibility that the carving on the drawer fronts was done when the upper section was originally built is very remote, because the carving is of a much later type found on Victorian furniture. Furthermore, there are indications that some of the drawer pulls have been moved over from where they had been originally. Nevertheless, one cannot help being delighted with the quality of the carving and with the interest it engenders in the overall design. The hardware is correct with the exception of the escutcheons which belong to a different period and should be changed. Obviously escutcheon plates as large as the plates on the drawer pulls, which no doubt were used before the carving was added, could no longer be used afterward, but more appropriate plates like those shown on the right in Fig. 15, Plate 1 in Chapter 3 would be a decided improvement.

Another reason why we believe the two sections did not originally go together is the much too obvious and crude apron ostensibly added to make the lower frame long and wide enough to accommodate the wide molding dividing the two sections in the middle. The piece of furniture would look much better without it. Dispensing with the offset at the middle of the legs, thus slenderizing them by that much, would also improve the appearance of the lower section.

In the light of the obvious shortcomings of this piece of furniture, the author feels obligated to present to the reader some justification for including it in the book, especially so since it will be quite evident to the reader that he went to considerable lengths to show all parts in sufficient detail so it can be reproduced exactly as it appears here. Although he may be criticized for it, he confesses that a number of things about the piece appealed to him greatly when he first saw it. The carving is superbly executed, and no less than six different variations of the design were used by the wood-carver, when he could have done almost as well with only two. Furthermore the author was in-

Fig. 1. Queen Anne Chest-on-Frame. COURTESY MALMBERG ANTIQUES, BOYERTOWN, PENNSYLVANIA.

trigued by the inventiveness and ingenuity of the person who contrived the combination of elements of design so far at variance from accepted practice. Such diversions always impart an element of surprise and enjoyment, and when they give pleasure and excite the interest which they did to the author in this case, he felt it worthwhile presenting it, especially since other lessons of value to the user of this book may be learned from it.

Mr. Richard L. Malmberg, in whose antique shop the author found the piece, agrees that there is little doubt a lot of doctoring was done to achieve these results. Yet when it was sold shortly after the author first discovered it, the new owner, an avid collector of antiques, was quite happy to pay twelve hundred dollars for it.

But aside from the appeal to the aesthetic sense, and respect for the craftsmanship and ingenuity of the entrepreneur who put this piece together, a prime reason for including it in this book dealing with the reproduction of antique furniture is the other lessons one can learn from studying it, which should not be overlooked in a book of this kind.

Fig. 2.

Fig. 2A.

The first of these is that it brings home the importance of knowing what belongs together in order to avoid the pitfalls of chicanery one often meets up with, not only in places where antiques are sold, but in the wider field encompassing decorative art as a whole, which includes building new, as well as reproducing old, furniture.

A second consideration is one the author brings to the reader's attention in several places in this book: it is his belief in the right of a person capable of doing so to make innovations, to improve design, or at least try to do so, and within reason, to combine structural or decorative elements which originators of a style or period may not have thought of. The end results may not always be good, but neither will they always be bad, and in justification of our advocacy of this course, let us remind our readers that almost every great designer we honor today practiced to some extent what we advocate. The only limitations we place upon freedom of choice in such matters is that (1) the person attempting it have the background from having done some study and research along these lines, and (2) that he be truly honest about it and not try to mislead people into believing that what he has done has the approval of those who adhere strictly to traditional forms.

Many crudities of construction, inferior in quality, found on the original piece, have been improved upon in the design we submit here. The

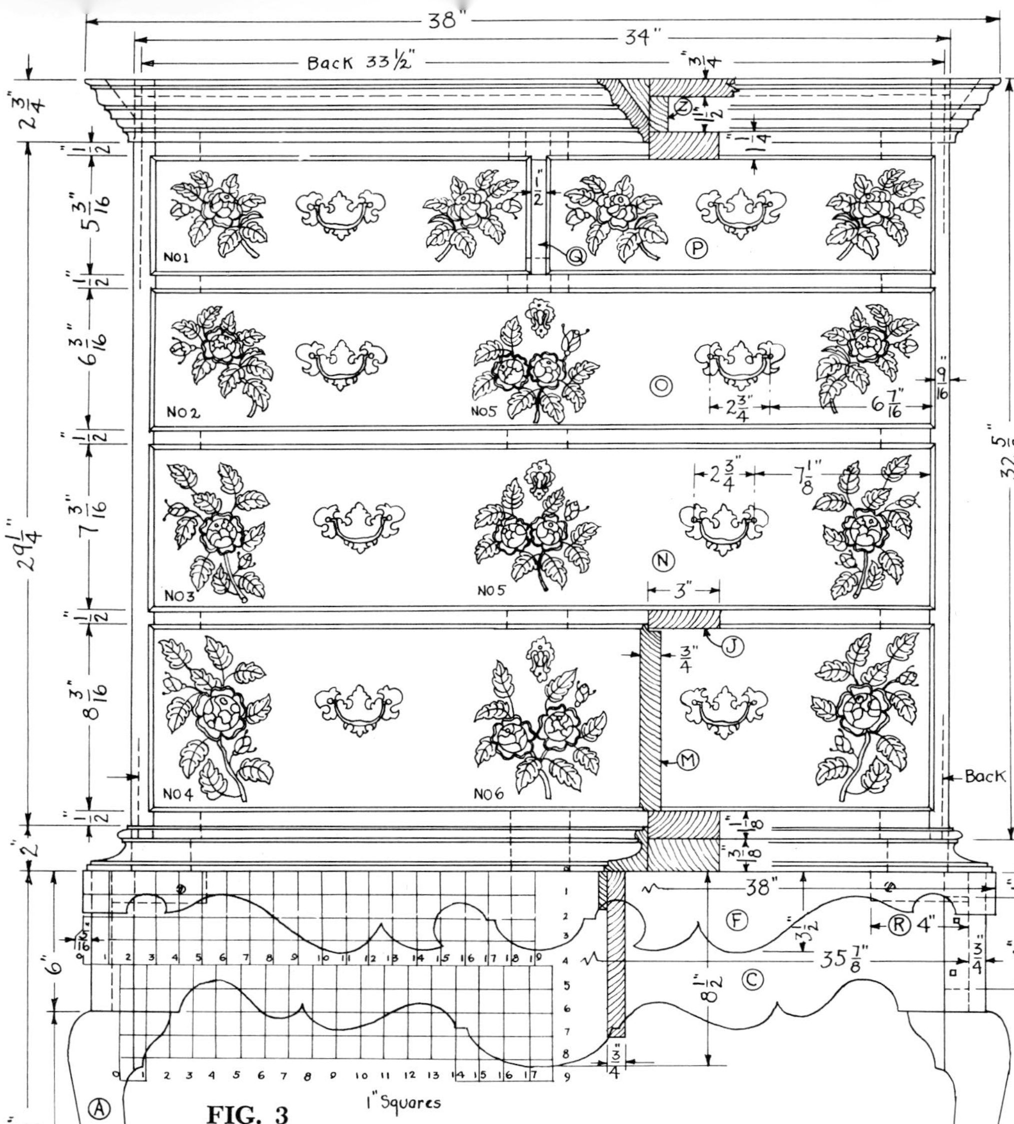
38"
34"
Back 33 1/2"
2 3/4"
29 1/4"
22 1/4"
16 1/4"
32 5/8"
56 1/4"
NO1
NO2
NO3
NO4
NO5
NO6
Back
38"
35 7/8"
1" Squares

FIG. 3

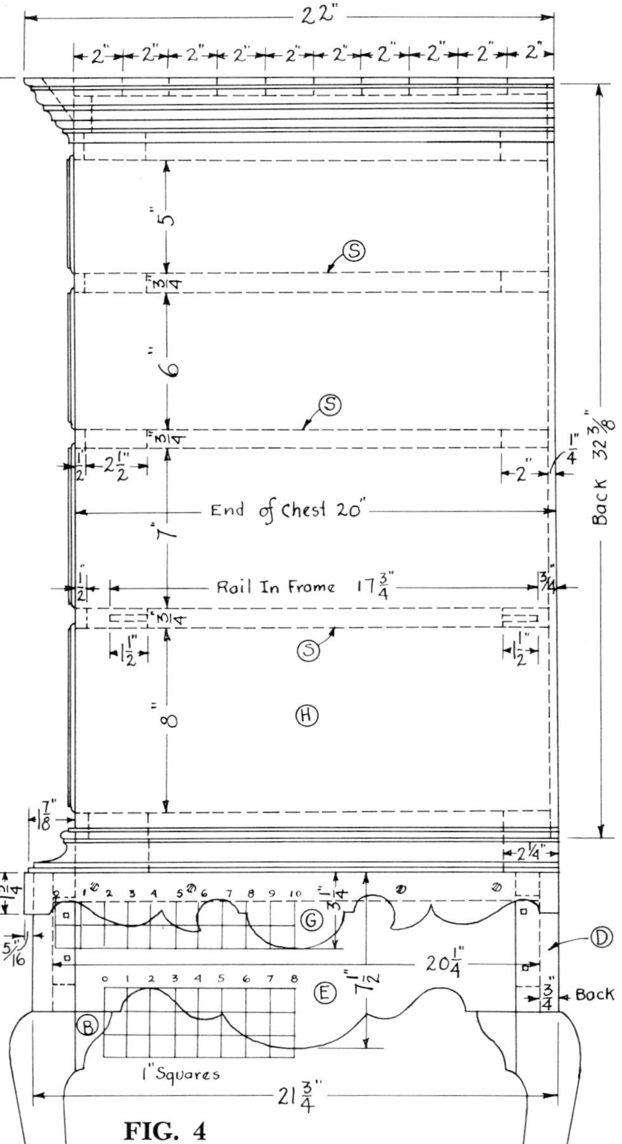
22"
End of Chest 20"
Rail In Frame 17 3/4"
Back 32 3/8"
20 1/4"
21 3/4"
Back
1" Squares

FIG. 4

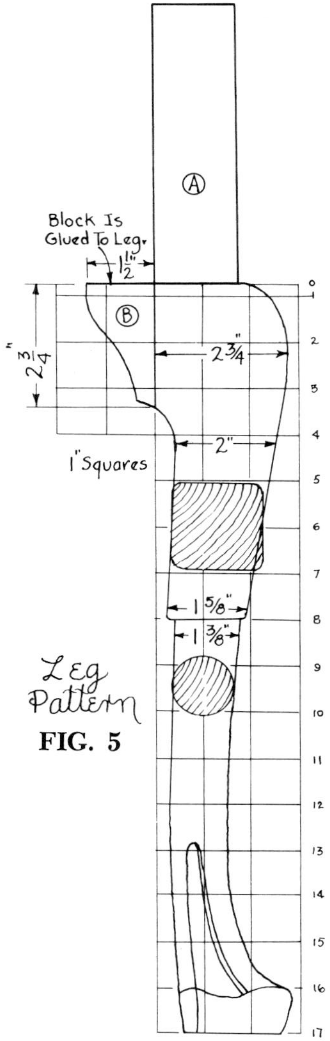
Block Is Glued To Leg.
1" Squares

Leg Pattern
FIG. 5

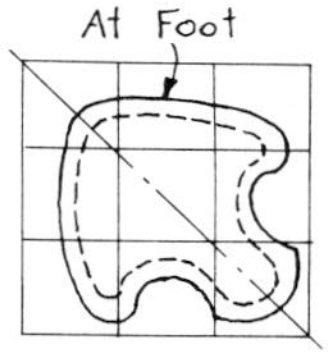
At Foot

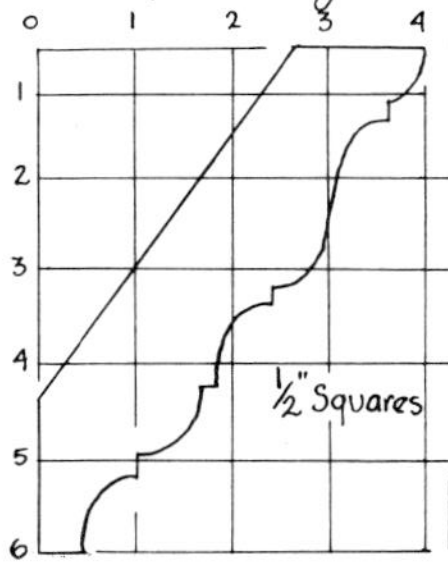
1/2" Squares

FIG. 6
Crown Molding

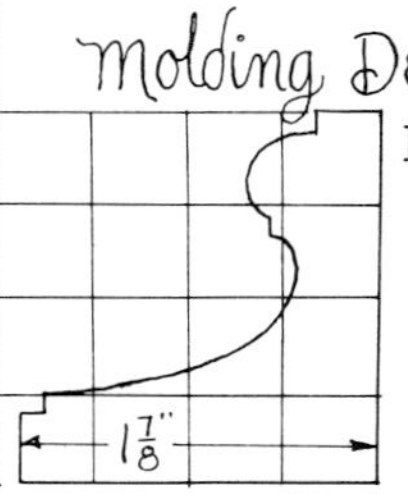

Molding Detail
FIG. 7

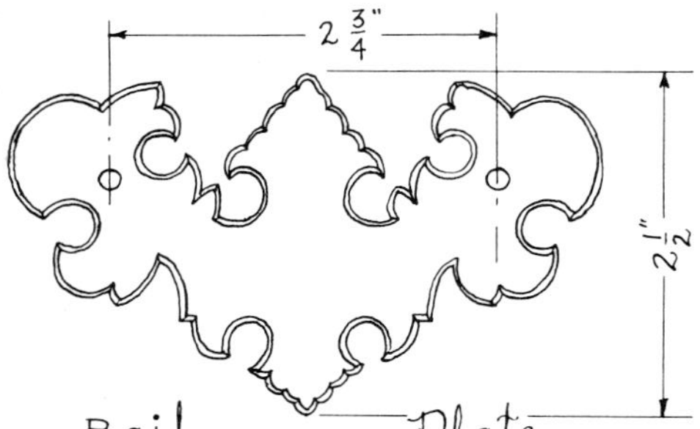

Bail FIG. 8 Plate

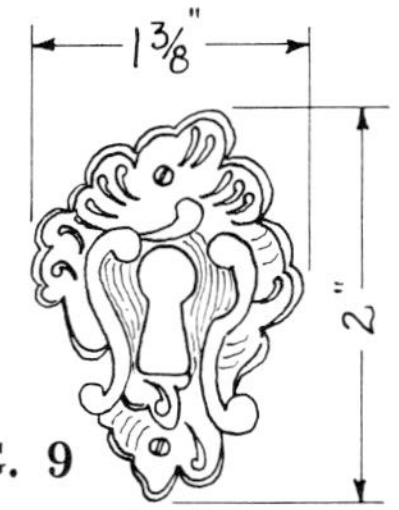

FIG. 9
Escutcheon

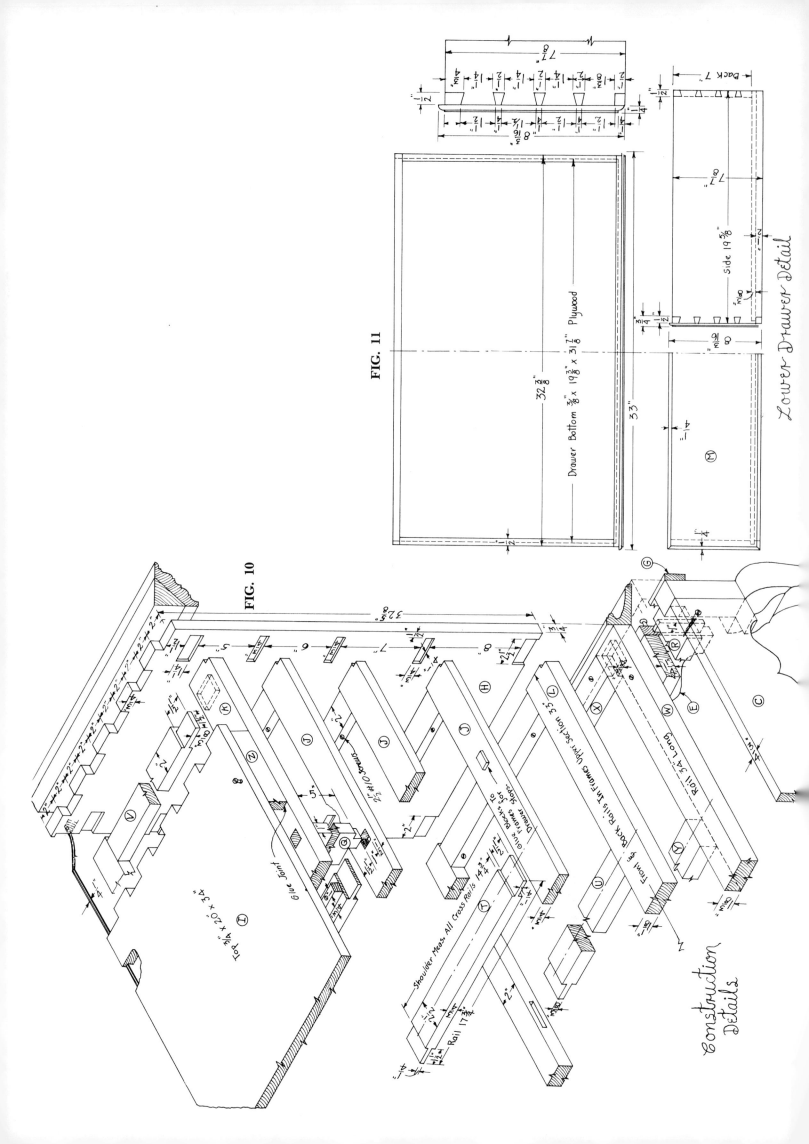

FIG. 11

Lower Drawer Detail

FIG. 10

Construction Details

box joint used for joining the top to the ends is inferior to the dovetail joints one usually expects to find at this place on good highboys of the period, but is good enough so that we left it much as we found it. The spacing of dovetails on drawers has been altered to improve upon those found when we took measurements. In regard to dovetailing, the reader may be interested to know that Mr. Ernst Almendinger, a cabinetmaker of renown in our area, who learned his trade in Germany under the apprenticeship system, lays out all dovetailing almost entirely by eye, and without exact measurements, and scoffs when we do it by the exact measurements we have been taught to make.

We have substituted sturdy frames to support drawers for the rather flimsy and inadequate rails fastened with an insufficient number of screws to the ends of the chest. The back on the original is built up of thin, badly warped boards, fastened to a poorly constructed frame, and for this we have substituted plywood which is far stronger and much better suited to the purpose. But in outward appearance we have changed nothing, preferring to leave the piece as we found it, crude and incongruous though some aspects of it may seem. Any changes made as a result of our suggestions we leave to the person who decides to build the piece.

To build the chest-on-frame, first get out stock for the legs. Make a full-sized pattern on two opposite sides of the 2¾-inch-square stock. Then saw two sides of the legs to rough shape on the band saw. Save the waste pieces to tack back on, so the pattern may be traced on the other two sides, and the legs sawed to shape.

Carve and shape the feet and the rest of the leg with wood-carving chisels, files, and sandpaper. The cross-section views and plan of the foot in Fig. 5 will help you reproduce the leg as shown in Fig. 1.

When the legs, with the exception of blocks (B) which have not yet been glued to them, have been carved and shaped up, make layouts to cut the mortises into the top squared section to which the aprons are to be joined. Cut these mortises on a mortising machine, or with hand tools if power tools are not available. Then fasten glue blocks (B) to the legs and saw and carve them to shape.

Get out stock for aprons (C), (D), and (E), and plane and sand these smooth, squaring them as you do so. Lay out and cut tenons on all of these, using a dado head on the table saw. See to it the joints fit perfectly. Then from where these were laid out on the graph squares in Figs. 3 and 4, make full-sized patterns to cut the bottoms of the aprons to shape on the band saw, and then file and sand the sawed edges smooth. Back apron (D) is only six inches wide and kept straight on its lower edge.

Glue up the bottom or frame of the chest comprised of legs and aprons. Get out stock for two planks (R), which are screwed fast to both ends of the lower section on the inside, to support the upper section. These may be made of almost any kind of wood, since they will not be seen after the upper part has been fastened to them. These planks, and the method of fastening them to the frame with wood screws, is shown in Figs. 3, 4, and 10. A 1⅜-inch-thick frame is made and screwed fast to the tops of these two planks. The molding at the middle of the highboy is glued to the front and both ends of this frame, and it is upon the top of this frame that the upper section rests. Two or more wood screws fastening the 1⅛-inch-thick frame—which holds the lower drawer—to this 1⅜-inch frame fastened to planks (R) will keep the upper section from sliding off the lower section and hold the two together. By removing these screws the two sections may readily be taken apart, if this becomes necessary to move the chest-on-chest to a new location.

Prepare stock to make the three scrolled apron boards which are to be glued to the outside of the front and end aprons. Saw these to shape and make miter joints at the ends where they come together; then glue them to the aprons as shown in Figs. 3 and 4.

If the molding to go around three sides at the middle has not already been made, this should now be done. As we have repeatedly explained in other chapters of the book, these may be shaped with properly ground cutters on the power shaper, but if such equipment is not available, moldings like those found on this piece of furniture may be shaped by hand with wood-carving chisels if preliminary saw cuts on the table saw are made to remove most of the waste. All it takes is painstaking care and patience, and careful sanding after the shaping is done. When this molding has been glued to the 1⅜-inch frame and the frame fastened with wood screws to planks (R), you will be ready to start making the upper section.

Glue up two ends (H) and a top (I), ripping good boards into narrow pieces and regluing them to remove the stresses that make wide boards warp or split. Plane and sand these to the sizes given in the Bill of Material. Then rabbet the back edges to hold the plywood back, as shown in Fig. 10.

Make layouts for the shallow mortises and gains on the inside of both ends, into which the ends of the front and back rails of the frames holding the drawers will be glued. Then make layouts for the box joints used to fasten the top to both ends, and make and fit these joints.

Get out stock for all frames which hold the drawers. Front rails on all of these are black walnut, of course, but for all other rails a different kind of wood, which is cheaper, may be used, provided it is not too soft. Poplar and soft maple are good for this purpose, but oak and other kinds of wood are sometimes used.

Lay out mortise-and-tenon joints on all of these pieces after first planing, squaring, and cutting them to size. The pieces need not be sanded until the frames have been glued up, after which this should be very carefully done so surfaces upon which drawers slide in and out are perfectly flat and smooth.

The drawer guide between the two small drawers at the top must be made and screwed to the middle rail of the second frame from the top; and the short stile (Q), which separates the two upper drawers, must be made and glued to the two upper frames before any of the frames can be glued to the ends.

When all frames have been glued up and sanded smooth, the upper section may be assembled. Glue

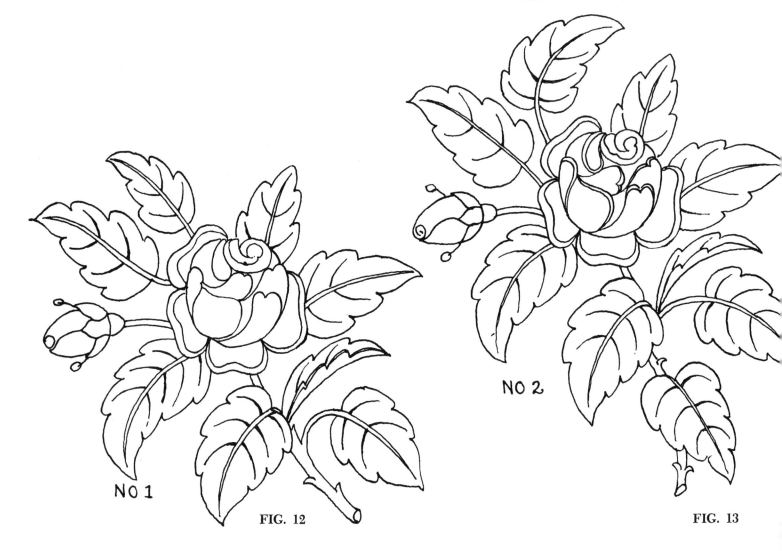

NO 1

NO 2

FIG. 12   FIG. 13

the ends of the front and back rails, which stick out past the end rails, into the mortises and gains that have been made to hold them. Check this upper section carefully when assembling it, to be sure everything is square, so the drawers may be fitted into the openings to slide easily.

After ends and frames have been glued together, glue backing strip (Z) to the top of the upper frame. Then glue the top to the ends of the upper section and fasten it to the upper edge of strip (Z) with a few wood screws. Cut and shape the triangular-shaped backing for the crown molding and glue the crown molding to it. Then fasten the crown molding to the top of the upper section.

On a piece like this highboy, it is always better to make and fit all drawers before putting on the back, and the drawers may be made at this time. Make all drawer fronts first. Because the drawer fronts are to be carved, carefully select good heartwood free of knots. Highly figured wood made from crotch or burl stock should be avoided, since

these would be difficult to carve, and the highly figured grain would compete with the carving for attention. Only kiln-dried or well-seasoned old stock should be used. The carving on the drawer fronts is most easily done before the drawers have been assembled, though it is still possible to do it afterward.

Molding may be cut on all drawer front edges, and dovetail joints may be made and fitted before the carving is started. Details for constructing the largest drawer are shown in Fig. 11. With minor changes in the size of dovetails to accommodate to the various drawer depths, these dovetail layouts may be made very much alike. One should be careful when laying out dovetail joints for drawers to put a tail instead of a pin to cover the groove cut into the drawer front to hold the drawer bottom. Otherwise the groove will run out through the pin and will show.

Patterns for all rose carvings may be traced directly from the pages of this book full size, and

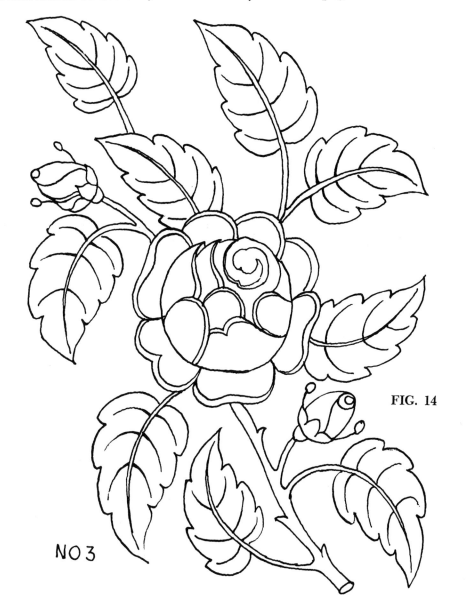

NO 3

FIG. 14

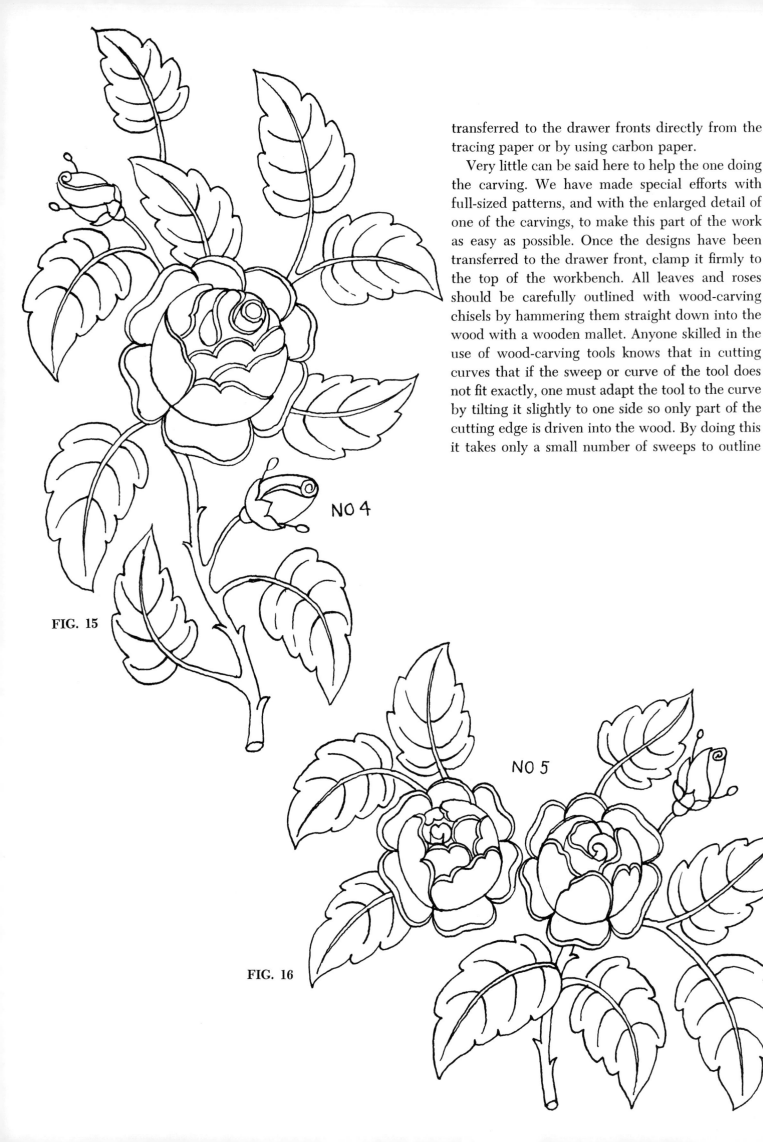

transferred to the drawer fronts directly from the tracing paper or by using carbon paper.

Very little can be said here to help the one doing the carving. We have made special efforts with full-sized patterns, and with the enlarged detail of one of the carvings, to make this part of the work as easy as possible. Once the designs have been transferred to the drawer front, clamp it firmly to the top of the workbench. All leaves and roses should be carefully outlined with wood-carving chisels by hammering them straight down into the wood with a wooden mallet. Anyone skilled in the use of wood-carving tools knows that in cutting curves that if the sweep or curve of the tool does not fit exactly, one must adapt the tool to the curve by tilting it slightly to one side so only part of the cutting edge is driven into the wood. By doing this it takes only a small number of sweeps to outline

NO 4

FIG. 15

NO 5

FIG. 16

almost any carving and to do the actual carving as well.

The author well remembers the exceedingly fine set of several hundred wood-carving chisels owned by the professional wood-carver who first stimulated his interest in this art. This fine friend revealed to the author that while tool collecting was a kind of weakness or hobby, he regularly used only about thirty chisels in this vast collection. The others were kept because of a love for tools and were seldom used except as replacements for worn-out tools.

The most difficult part of these carvings is the fully opened rose. Leaves, buds, and stems will cause little difficulty once one of each has been tried. Walnut carves beautifully if the wood is properly seasoned, for it is firm and crisp under the keen cutting edge of good tools. We advise anyone who does carving like this for the first time to try one of the roses on a piece of scrap wood before attempting it on a drawer front, unless he is sure he has the skill necessary to do the work well.

Once all drawer fronts have been carved, the drawers should be assembled, without gluing the joints at first, in order to make sure they will fit the opening properly without binding. Then glue the joints and clean them up afterward. Locks may be put on the drawer fronts before gluing up the drawers, this being less difficult to do then than after the drawers have been assembled. Drawer pulls may also be fastened to drawer fronts before they are glued to the drawer sides, but these should be taken off to do the finishing. Application of the hardware completes the building process.

To apply a suitable finish, consult the chapter on wood finishing.

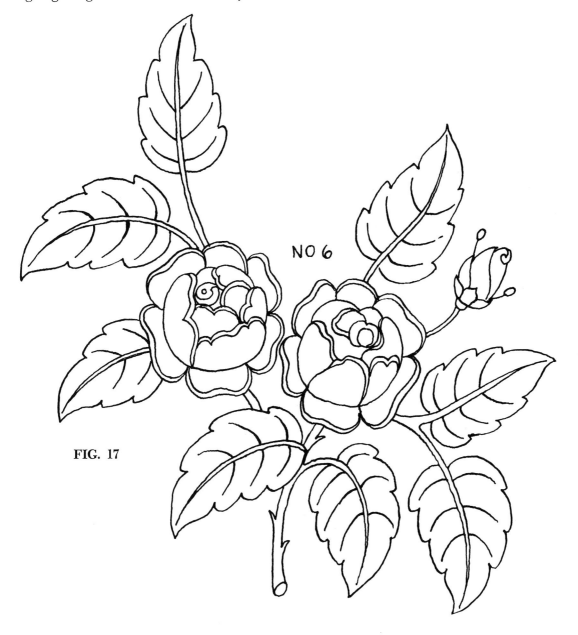

FIG. 17

BILL OF MATERIAL

Black Walnut

4 Legs (A) 2¾″ x 2¾″ x 22¼″

8 Blocks to glue to legs (B) 1½″ x 2¾″ x 2¾″

1 Front apron (C) ¾″ x 8½″ x 35⅞″

1 Rear apron (D) ¾″ x 6″ x 35⅞″

2 End aprons (E) ¾″ x 7½″ x 20¼″

1 Scrolled apron board, applied over front apron (F) 5⁄16″ x 3½″ x 38″

2 Scrolled apron boards, applied over end aprons (G) 5⁄16″ x 3¼″ x 22 5⁄16″

2 Ends (H) ¾″ x 20″ x 32⅝″

1 Top (I) ¾″ x 20″ x 34″

3 Front rails between drawers (J) ¾″ x 3″ x 33″

1 Front rail for top frame over small drawers (K) 1¼″ x 3″ x 33″

1 Front rail for bottom frame of upper section (L) 1⅛″ x 3″ x 33″

1 Drawer front (M) ¾″ x 8 3⁄16″ x 33″

1 Drawer front (N) ¾″ x 7 3⁄16″ x 33″

1 Drawer front (O) ¾″ x 6 3⁄16″ x 33″

2 Drawer fronts (P) ¾″ x 5 3⁄16″ x 16 3⁄16″

1 Stile between upper drawers (Q) 1″ x 3″ x 7″

Crown molding 1 pc. ¾″ x 3 7⁄16″ x 90″ *

Molding around middle 1 pc. 1⅞″ x 2″ x 90″ *

Soft Maple, Poplar or
Some Other Semihard Wood

2 Planks to support upper section (R) 1¼″ x 4″ x 20¼″

6 End rails for three frames between drawers (S) ¾″ x 2″ x 17¾″

3 Middle rails for three frames between drawers (T) ¾″ x 2½″ x 17¾″

2 End rails for frame above small drawers (V) 1¼″ x 2″ x 17¾″

* Includes waste from sawing joints.

1 Middle rail for frame above small drawers 1¼″ x 2½″ x 17¾″

3 Back rails for frames ¾″ x 2″ x 33″

1 Back rail for upper frame 1¼″ x 2″ x 33″

1 Back rail for lower frame in upper section 1⅛″ x 2″ x 33″

1 Front rail for frame upon which upper section rests (W) 1⅜″ x 3″ x 34″

2 End rails for frame upon which upper section rests (X) 1⅜″ x 2″ x 17¾″

1 Middle rail for frame upon which upper section rests (Y) 1⅜″ x 2½″ x 17¾″

1 Back rail for frame upon which upper section rests 1⅜″ x 2″ x 34″

1 Backing strip for crown molding (Z) ¾″ x 1½″ x 32½″

1 Drawer guide between small drawers ¾″ x 1″ x 16¾″

Triangular-shaped backing for crown molding 1¼″ x 1¾″ x 90″ *

Yellow Poplar

2 Drawer sides ½″ x 7⅞″ x 19⅝″

2 Drawer sides ½″ x 6⅞″ x 19⅝″

2 Drawer sides ½″ x 5⅞″ x 19⅝″

4 Drawer sides ½″ x 4⅞″ x 19⅝″

1 Drawer back ½″ x 7″ x 32⅜″

1 Drawer back ½″ x 6″ x 32⅜″

1 Drawer back ½″ x 5″ x 32⅜″

2 Drawer backs ½″ x 4″ x 15 9⁄16″

Plywood

1 Back for upper section ¼″ x 32⅜″ x 33½″

3 Drawer bottoms ⅜″ x 19⅜″ x 31⅞″

2 Drawer bottoms ⅜″ x 15 1⁄16″ x 19⅜″

* Includes waste from sawing joints.

TWENTY-THREE

Chippendale Partner's Desk

THE exceedingly handsome and impressive flat-topped Chippendale desk shown in Fig. 1 is dubbed a "partner's desk," because it is alike on both sides. Presumably such desks were used by partners engaged in business and working together in the same office on more than one occasion, and the desks came to be designated as partner's desks for this reason. The drawers are alike on both sides of this desk, and furthermore the desk has a table surface the size of which is nothing short of fabulous when compared to that found on ordinary desks.

Many things besides its generous proportions make this desk an outstanding piece of furniture. It is made of the best heavy mahogany wood. It has beautifully shaped and handsomely carved cabriole legs. It has distinctive blockfront drawers with decorations carved in bold relief, and fluted quarter columns on all four corners.

The hand-carved gadroon molding around the top and under the drawers and ends; the carved sunbursts and borders giving the highly figured ends of the desk a paneled effect; and the knuckles carved to accent the toes on the claw-and-ball feet, are features intended to improve a design already rich enough without them. The carved gadrooning looks good on the desk, but the claw-and-ball feet would look better if they were carved to look more like the ones found on the Chippendale Wing Chair, and the ends of the desk would be greatly improved if made of solid wood and left perfectly plain.

Quite obviously the desk is modeled after designs created by John Goddard of Newport, Rhode Island, and the Townsends who later carried on in the Goddard tradition. According to the best information available to us today, John Goddard created the first blockfront furniture designs in America, and this unique feature found on early Chippendale furniture made in New England was one of the very few innovations for which American cabinetmakers can claim credit. So far as can be ascertained, blockfronts never appeared on furniture built in England by Chippendale or his contemporaries.

The carving on the drawer front in the middle, while beautifully conceived, as our delineation of it in Fig. 9 clearly shows, is not comparably well executed; the modeling is carved in relief too high above the surface of the drawer front. The carving of the brackets at both ends of the middle drawer

Fig. 1. Chippendale Partner's Desk. PROPERTY OF MERLE M. MILLER, M.D., GERMANTOWN, PENNSYLVANIA.

Fig. 2

and that on the apron below it is better. Carving of this kind in the best tradition should be modeled in relief but should be cut little more than ⅛-inch deep to look its best. Another refinement that should be made to improve the design is to extend the front of the lower rail so the blocking on the lower drawer conforms to the shape of the rail instead of overhanging the rail, which on this desk is straight across the front.

The hand-carved gadrooning on the edges around the top and on the molded edges of the frames under the drawers and ends is not usually found on pieces of this period, though its use here is a feature of some refinement and is not objectionable.

In all other respects, the desk is as fine a piece of furniture as it pretends to be and must be re-garded as a beautiful and impressive example of blockfront construction in the Chippendale style. One expert, whose knowledge of such matters we hold in high regard, hazards the guess the desk may have been built around the year 1800, though the author would not want to put him on the spot by disclosing his name. Whatever the age of the desk, anyone who has seen it will agree, we think, that this is a design well worth reproducing. We would, if we were doing it, however, want to make the few changes we have suggested. A reproduction with these changes would be well worth owning and would be a piece of furniture in whose ownership one could take great pride.

Dr. Merle M. Miller of Germantown, Pennsylvania, owner of this fine desk, informed the author it had been presented to him as a gift from an appreciative patient. Though it may be wrong for the author to assume this, he is of the opinion that it would be hard to find a better way to express appreciation for services rendered to a patient by a doctor.

To build the desk, start with the four legs. These require pieces of mahogany 3½ inches thick and should be made from planks as thick as that. Only the blocks back of the knees are glued on, and even for these stock 2⅜ inches thick is required.

Before cutting the lower part of the legs to shape, it will be best to (1) lay out and cut mortises and (2) remove the corners where the quarter columns are to be glued to the legs. By proceeding in this manner, the mortises may be cut on a mortising machine more easily, and corners may then be cut out nearly to the bottom of the place where they go on the leg with a dado head, or saw, on the table saw. The bottom end of the corner may be cleaned out on the mortising machine. Even if mortises must be cut by hand, this order of procedure will be found most advantageous. The dovetail mortise at the top of the leg should not be cut until the dovetail on rail (D) has been made.

A full-sized pattern of the leg may then be made from the drawing shown in Fig. 8. When the stock has been planed and squared to 3½ inches on all four sides, the pattern is drawn on two opposite sides, and the leg may be sawed to the shape on the band saw. Save the waste and tack it to the part of the leg from which you sawed it, being careful to nail it only to parts of the leg which will be waste when the last two sides of the leg have been sawed to shape.

It should be pointed out at this time that, due to the fact that the ends of the desk are veneered to carry the bold figure of the mahogany veneer to the quarter columns themselves, the tops of the legs have been kept wider at the ends than in front, so the cock-bead molding could be inserted where the legs and ends are joined together. It may also be worth mentioning at this time that anyone reproducing the desk could dispense with the operation of veneering the surface of the desk ends and let this upper part of the leg show with the grain running vertically. The construction would still be the same, but dispensing with the veneering operation on the ends would simplify this part of

the work without detracting too much from the beauty of the desk. However, if the veneer is to be used in order to carry the figure across the whole length of the end, then the veneer covering this part of the leg must be cut from the same sheet of veneer used to cover the end, so the figure of the veneer will be continuous throughout.

When the lower parts of the legs have been sawed to shape, glue blocks (B) to the legs, sawing them to shape on the inside where they and the legs are arched before gluing them to the legs. The blocks may be sawed to shape on the outside after they have been glued to the legs, thus making it easier to apply the clamps needed to fasten them securely when gluing them to the legs.

You should now be ready to shape and carve the legs. Most of the shaping will have to be done to round over and form the cabriole shape, and roughly form the foot, to approximately the shape shown in Fig. 2 on the drawings, before actually carving the shells on the knees, the acanthus leaves on blocks (B), and the toes and ball on the foot. Ball-and-claw feet are not nearly as difficult to carve as they look to be to one who has never tried doing them. Once the leg has been sawed to shape on all four sides to the pattern shown in Fig. 8, it is very easy to transfer the shape of the toes to the wood and to round and shape them with woodcarving chisels.

In addition to gouges and skew chisels ordinarily used for such work, short-bent spoon gouges and V tools will be found most useful and advantageous in carving ball-and-claw feet. With a few such tools at hand, the wood-carver will be surprised at how easy it is to carve such feet, which to an amateur may look to be a most difficult task.

After the legs have been carved, get out stock for ends (C) and rails (D), (E), and (F). Lay out and cut tenons on ends (C), as shown in Fig. 5. Now cut mortises into rails (D), (E), and (F), and then shape them on the band saw. Make and fit tenons and dovetails to the leg mortises, and make a trial assembly of the parts which have been made. Ends (C) of the desk and the upper parts of the legs where ends (C) will be joined to them should now be veneered, if this is to be done. Grooves for the cock beading should then be cut into ends (C) and into the inside edges of the legs,

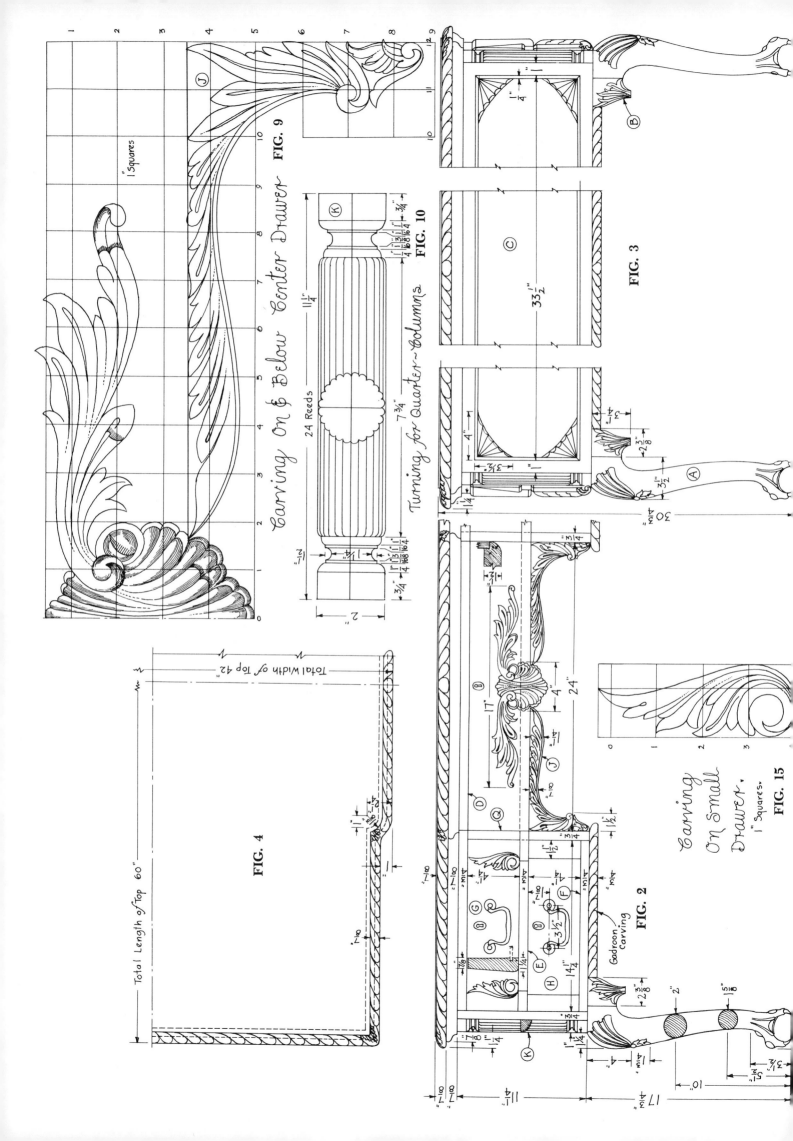

Carving On & Below Center Drawer FIG. 9

FIG. 10

Turning for Quarter-Columns

24 Reeds

FIG. 3

FIG. 4

FIG. 2

Carving On Small Drawer. FIG. 15

Gadroon Carving

as shown at the left end of Fig. 5. This cock beading and the wood for the sunbursts may be glued to the desk after the carcass has been assembled.

To do veneering on ends like these, first cut the veneer to the size needed for the whole end of the desk, including the part to glue to the upper parts of the legs. Then make a caul, which is a heavy plank of pine or mahogany, as large as the end of the desk, and plane and sand one side of this perfectly flat and smooth. If there is the slightest curvature to this caul the hollow side must be on the outside when the caul is clamped to the end of the desk, so that the glue will be driven toward the outside of the panel rather than to the center. Otherwise this would result in blisters under the veneer.

An end as narrow as this may be veneered by clamping the caul with heavy hand-screw clamps and C-clamps, since the distance from edges to center is not great. Wider boards might require a veneer press or special veneer clamps made by passing bolts through both ends of two heavy planks of wood. Adjust the clamps to about the proper distance between jaws, and have sheets of wrapping paper or newspaper ready to place over the veneer under the caul. Glue for veneering should be hot and fairly thin. Caul and end of desk should be heated until they are quite warm. Then spread glue evenly over the surface of the desk end and let it become slightly tacky before placing the veneer on top of it, to prevent the veneer from sliding about. Place paper over the veneer and over the paper a sheet of green felt. Then placing the caul over the felt, clamp caul to desk end, fastening center clamps first and end clamps last, to drive the glue from the center of the panel to the outside edges in order to prevent blisters from forming in the center.

While it would be possible to glue the cock-bead molding to the surface of the ends to form the panel effect, it is better to run $\frac{1}{8}$-inch grooves to glue it fast, in order to hold it better. This may be done after the glue holding the veneer has thoroughly dried, and the scraping and sanding which is necessary has been done.

Rails (R), (S), and (T) should now be made, and tenons cut on the ends to join them to rails (D), (E), and (F).

Cut out stock for partitions (Q). Each partition is composed of three pieces, the main part being $\frac{3}{4}$" x $11\frac{1}{4}$" x $37\frac{1}{2}$" with the grain running horizontally and with ends joined to them with tongue-and-groove joints, so the edges separating the drawer fronts will have the grain running vertically. Glue these up and cut the gains at each end where rails (E) are to be joined to them. Get out strips for drawer runs (U) and (V) and screw these to partitions (Q) on both sides.

To assemble the desk frame, or carcass as such a frame is sometimes called, proceed in the following manner: 1. First glue one rail (E) to one end of both partitions (Q). 2. Then glue rails (T) to rails (F). 3. Now glue rails (T) to the lower edges on the inside of partitions (Q), and drive two wood screws through partition (Q) from the outside to hold rails (F) in place. The heads of these screws will be covered by brackets (J) when they have been fastened to (Q). 4. Now glue the second rail (E) on the other side of the desk to partitions (Q). 5. Glue the ends of rails (S) to rails (E) and rails (F), which you can do since the stub tenons on the ends of (S) may be slipped into the mortises that have been cut on the ends of rails (E) and (F). 6. Now glue ends (C) to the legs. 7. Then glue the assembled ends (C) and the two legs to the ends of rails (E) and (F) and to the edges of rails (S), which should also be screwed fast to the inside of (C).

The upper frame, composed of rails (D) and (R), should now be assembled and glued together. When glue joints have been cleaned up and surfaces leveled with a sander, this frame may be fastened to the top of the legs and partitions with glue and wood screws. Glue and clamps should also be used to fasten edges of rails (R) to ends (C).

Frames for the dust panels, which go under the desk at both ends, should now be made. Details showing how to make these are shown in Fig. 6. Joints holding rails (L), (M), and (N) together are sufficiently strong to hold the frames together, especially when the plywood panel is in place. The frame could be made stronger by adding an inch

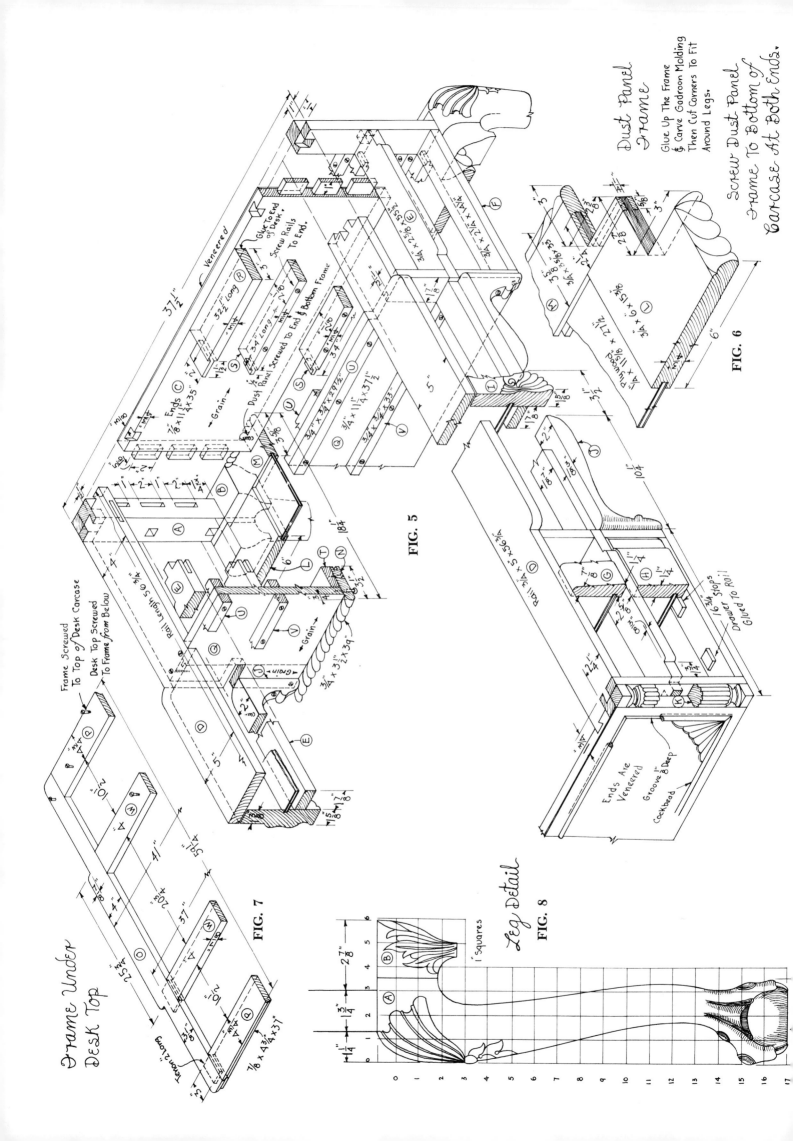

FIG. 5

FIG. 6

Dust Panel Frame

Glue Up The Frame & Carve Gadroon Molding Then Cut Corners To Fit Around Legs.

Screw Dust Panel Frame To Bottom of Carcase At Both Ends.

FIG. 7

Frame Under Desk Top

Frame Screwed To Top of Desk Carcase

Desk Top Screwed To Frame from Below

FIG. 8

Leg Detail

1" Squares

to the width of rails (L) and reducing the length of the plywood panel by 2 inches, but this will hardly be necessary. Once the frame has been assembled and screwed fast to the bottom of the desk, no stress is exerted to separate these joints. The two outside corners of the dust-panel frames are not cut to the shape shown in Fig. 6 until after the molding has been carved and the frames glued up. The plywood panel stays loose and unglued in the frame. Only mortise-and-tenon joints are glued to hold the rails of the frame together.

When dust frames have been fastened to the desk, get out rails (O), (P), and (W) to make the frame that goes under the desk top and serves the purpose of fastening the table board, or desk top, to the carcass of the desk. Dress all lumber for this frame, and after making mortise-and-tenon joints, glue up the frame and flatten all glue joints by sanding them even. Then saw rails (O) to shape if this has not been done before the frame was glued together. Shape the molding around all four edges on a shaper, and then screw the frame to the top of the desk with #12, and possibly even some #14, wood screws. Just possibly the above-mentioned frame should not be fastened to the desk until the drawers have been made and fitted to the desk, so the fitting of the drawers may be that much more easily accomplished.

Brackets (J) may also be made, carved, and glued and screwed fast to the desk before making the drawers, though it might be easier to adjust their length so the ends fit against the shell on the drawer front after the drawer has been fitted to the desk than the other way around. Here you can use your own best judgment.

To make the drawers, first get out stock for the drawer fronts, as indicated in the Bill of Material. All of these are quite thick because of the blocking on the fronts.

While the blocking and carving on the drawer fronts may be done before the dovetailing, we advise doing the dovetailing first, since the fronts may then be held in the vise more easily to do the multiple dovetail joints. Doing it this way also makes damaging the carving far less likely. Lay-outs for the dovetailing on all of the drawers is shown in Figs. 11, 12, and 13.

Drawer backs are also dovetailed to the drawer sides, but since these are through dovetails, all of the work may be done by setups on the circular saw, the band saw, or both. Parts of the waste material of the dovetail mortises on the drawer fronts may be cut out on the mortising machine, and the remainder may easily be chiseled out. Or a dove-tailing saw may be used to start the cuts on the waste side of the line on each dovetail, in the way it was done before machinery came into general use, and the rest chiseled out as we have described the process in other chapters of the book.

When dovetailing has been completed, the ends of the drawer fronts may be reduced in thickness by using a dado head and crosscut fence on the table saw. The rounding of sharp corners at the shoulders, formed by this cutting away, may then be accomplished quite easily using chisels, plane, and sandpaper. The acanthus leaf decorations on the upper drawers should be carved before the drawer is glued together. Locks and drawer pulls should also be fitted to the drawer fronts before gluing up the drawers.

When drawers have been made and fitted, screw the frame shown in Fig. 8 to the top of the desk frame. Then glue up the desk top and cut its edges on the long sides to shape, and carve the gadroon molding. To simplify the process, these edges may be cut to the general shape of a thumbnail molding on a shaper before carving the gadrooning. It should also be pointed out that a top glued up of boards which have first been ripped into narrow widths and then reglued will be less likely to warp or split apart as a result of changes in the atmosphere. Separating the fibers of wood grain, even if they are glued back together exactly as they were before, reduces stresses and pulling which tend to warp such a top. The top, when it is ready, may then be fastened to the two upper frames with wood screws from below.

All that now remains to be done is applying the finish. To do this consult the chapter on wood finishing.

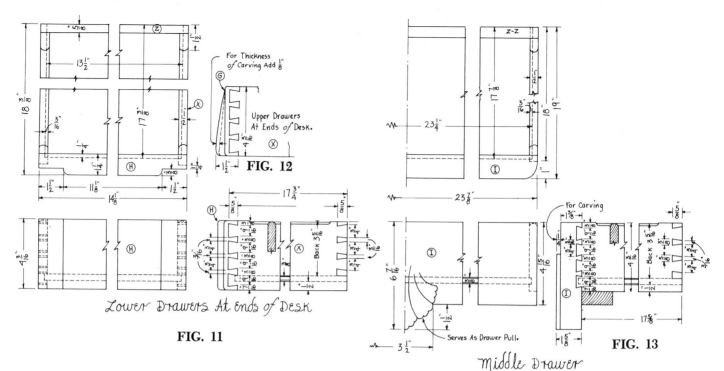

Lower Drawers At Ends of Desk

FIG. 11

FIG. 12

FIG. 13

Middle Drawer

BILL OF MATERIAL

Mahogany

4 Legs (A) 3½" x 3½" x 29"

8 Blocks to glue to legs (B) 2⅜" x 3" x 3¼"

2 Ends of desk (C) ⅞" x 11¼" x 35"

2 Top front rails (D) ¾" x 5" x 56¾"

2 Middle front rails (E) ¾" x 2⅝" x 55½"

4 Bottom front rails (F) ¾" x 2¼" x 14¼"

4 Upper small drawer fronts (G) 1½" * x 4³⁄₁₆" x 14⅛"

4 Lower small drawer fronts (H) 1¼" x 4³⁄₁₆" x 14⅛"

2 Middle drawer fronts (I) 1⅝" x 6⁷⁄₁₆" x 23⅞"

4 Carved brackets under middle drawers (J) 2" x 5" x 10¼"

1 Column for quarter columns (K) 4 pieces 1" x 1" x 11¼"

4 Front rails for dust panel frame (L) ¾" x 6" x 15⅜"

2 Side rails for dust panel frame (M) ⅜" x 3⅝" x 33"

2 Side rails for dust panel frame (N) ¾" x 3½" x 39"

2 Front rails for frame under desk top (O) ⅞" x 4" x 59¼"

2 End rails for frame under desk top (P) ⅞" x 4¾" x 37"

2 Partition boards (Q) ¾" x 11¼" x 34¾" and 4 pcs. ¾" x 1⅞" x 11¼"

* See figure 13.

1 Desk top ⅞" x 42" x 60" (Glue up five or more pieces to make top)

8 Pieces to carve sunbursts on ends ⅛" x 3½" x 4" (Glued to surface, then carved)

Cock-bead molding ¼" x ⅜" x about 15 ft.

Poplar, Soft Maple, or Birch

2 End rails, upper frame (R) ¾" x 3" x 32½"

4 End rails middle frames (S) ¾" x 2⅛" x 34"

2 End rails, lower frames (T) ¾" x 2" x 36" (Tenons on ends are 1½" long)

4 Strips above upper drawers (U) ¾" x ¾" x 29½"

4 Strips to support drawers (V) ¾" x ¾" x 33"

2 Rails for frame under top (W) ⅞" x 4" x 37"

16 Drawer sides for small drawers (X) ½" x 4³⁄₁₆" x 17¾"

4 Drawer sides for large drawers (Y) ½" x 4³⁄₁₆" x 18"

8 Drawer backs for small drawers (Z) ½" x 3⁵⁄₁₆" x 14⅛"

2 Drawer backs for middle drawers (Z-Z) ½" x 3⁵⁄₁₆" x 23⅞"

Plywood

(Use birch or mahogany-veneered plywood)

8 Drawer bottoms ⅜" x 13½" x 17⅜"

2 Drawer bottoms ⅜" x 17⅞" x 23¼"

2 Dust panels ¼" x 11⅝" x 27½"

TWENTY-FOUR

Early American Dresser

AN open-shelf dresser like this can be substituted in the dining room for a sideboard. Such a piece of furniture may be used to display a collection of fine china, either antique or modern, to great advantage, as shown in Fig. 1. Actually, open-shelved cupboards like this one, or others similar to it, were usually found in the generously proportioned kitchens of Colonial homes or taverns, while sideboards and cupboards with glazed doors replaced them in the dining rooms where greater formality usually prevailed.

With a good collection of china or bric-a-brac displayed upon their shelves, the effect can be impressive. Furthermore, these cupboards provide a great amount of storage space. An open-shelved cupboard like this one will make a fine bookcase for the living room or library, and cupboards underneath can provide storage space for records or a host of other items that are in constant use in the home.

The cupboard shown in Fig. 1 was one of two built by senior boys in the Boyertown Area High School, in the author's woodworking classes. This particular one was built of yellow poplar and stained to look like walnut. Maple or walnut are excellent materials for a cupboard like this.

To build the cupboard, first glue up two ends (A), like the one shown in Fig. 4. Rabbet the back edges of each to make a pair of ends: to do this the rabbeting will have to be done on the opposite side on the second end, to make the pair.

Now glue up a partition (B), two floorboards (D), and 2 shelves (E), and plane, square up, and sand them to the sizes given in the Bill of Material. Table board (G) should also be glued up at this time, and the ends cut out as shown at top left in Fig. 6.

Get out stock for partition (C). Before cutting the front edges of ends (A) and partition (C) to the shape shown at the top of Fig. 4, make layouts on these three pieces for the grooves to hold the shelves. These grooves must be lined up with each other on all three pieces, to make the shelves level when glued into the grooves. The best way to cut these grooves is with an electric hand router, using guide strips to work exactly to the lines. See Fig. 33, Chapter 1.

When all the grooves have been cut, make a full-sized pattern from the layouts given at the top of Fig. 4, to shape the front edges of ends (A) and partition (C). These may be cut to shape on the band saw at this time, then filed and sanded smooth.

Fig. 1.   Early American Dresser.

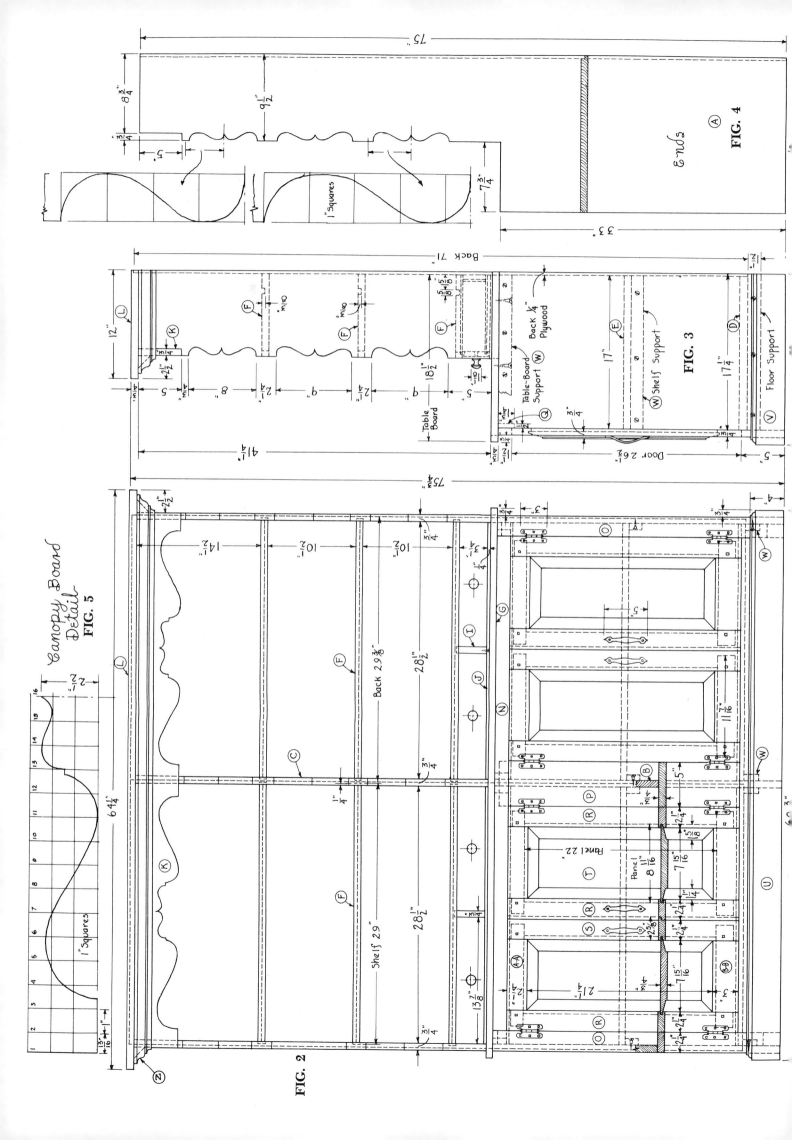

Canopy Board
Detail
FIG. 5

FIG. 4

FIG. 3

FIG. 2

Now cut out twelve strips (W) to support floorboards, table-board, and shelves in the lower part of the dresser. Drill holes in these and countersink them for screwheads. Then screw them fast to the places where they belong on one side of ends (A) and on both sides of partition (B).

Now get out stock for six shelves (F) and for the two partitions (I) that separate the small drawers in the upper section of the dresser. Plane, square, and sand all eight of these pieces to the sizes given in the Bill of Material. Then cut grooves in the underside of two of these shelves to hold partitions (I), as shown in Figs. 2 and 6. Only the upper edge of partition (I) fits into a groove. The bottom edge is fastened with wood screws to ¼-inch boards (J) with short wood screws, and these then rest upon the table-board. These thin boards were added to improve the design after the first dresser shown in Fig. 1 had been built, to keep the drawers from scratching the surface of the table-board when pulled out. Therefore they do not appear in Fig. 1. Cut grooves to hold plates, into all six shelves (F). This is most easily done with a dado head on the table saw. Then glue partition (I) into the grooves which have been cut into the bottoms of the two lower shelves.

Everything should now be in readiness to start assembling the dresser. Lay one of the ends (A) upon the floor of the workshop so the grooves for the shelves are on the side facing you. Then glue one end of the first three shelves into these grooves. Spread glue over the opposite ends of these shelves and into the matching grooves of partition (C); with a rubber mallet tap the partition to pull the shelves into the grooves. Spread glue into the grooves on the opposite side of partition (C) and over the matching shelf ends, and put these together. Now spread glue over the opposite ends of the last three shelves and into the matching grooves in end (A), which is to be joined to these shelves. When all shelves are in the grooves, raise the assembled members to the upright position shown in Fig. 2. Using 2-inch strips of wood 9½ inches long, placed level with each shelf over the outside of ends (A), pull ends (A), partition (C), and shelves (F) tightly together with six long bar clamps.

When bar clamps are being screwed up tight,

check shelves and ends with a try square on the inside to be sure they are exactly at right angles to each other. If not, adjust the bar clamps up or down to make all angles on the inside come to 90 degrees. Care must be exercised not to screw the clamps up too tight, for this may bend the shelves lengthwise and make it impossible to get 90-degree angles either on top or bottom of the shelves, with the two ends and the partition. If the shelves have been fitted properly to the shelf grooves before gluing has been started, it should be unnecessary to put so much pressure on the joints to pull them together.

Now place floors (D), shelves (E), partition (B), and table-board (G) in place; hold these and the dresser ends together with long bar clamps placed level with the shelves and floorboards across the front and back of the dresser. Fasten the shelves, floorboards, and table-board to strips (W) with sixpenny finish nails while the bar clamps hold them together. Use 2-inch strips of wood 17¼ inches long under the clamps to prevent spoiling the outside surfaces of the dresser ends. After nailing, remove the bar clamps and drive several nails through ends (A) into the ends of the table-board. The heads of these will be covered by two cleats (H). These may now be made and nailed fast with fourpenny finish nails. Also put glue on the mitered ends where they join the mitered front corners of the table-board.

Get out stock for the frame to go on the front of the dresser, to which the doors will be fastened. This frame consists of rails (N) and (M) and stiles (O) and (P). Plane and sand these to the sizes given in the Bill of Material and then lay and cut out mortises and tenons to join them together. Glue up this frame with bar clamps and then after cleaning the glue off the joints, nail it to the front of the dresser with sixpenny finish nails.

Make a full-sized pattern from the one shown in Fig. 5 and make the canopy board (K). Drill nail holes and nail to partition (C) and ends (A) with sixpenny finish nails. Then make top (L) and cut a rabbet on the back edge for fastening the plywood back. Nail the top to the partition and ends with sixpenny finish nails.

Make baseboards (U) and (V) next, and cut molding on the upper edge of these, using a spindle shaper or a portable electric hand shaper to do this. Fasten one of the end baseboards first, and then put on (U), and finish by fastening the other base (V). Put glue on the miter joints, and nail them together and to the dresser with fourpenny finish nails.

The crown molding used at the top is a standard molding and may be bought at nominal cost at almost any place where lumber is sold. What is offered for sale is usually made of pine or basswood and is suitable to use on a dresser made of pine or poplar, and could even be used on one made of maple. If you use walnut to make the dresser the molding would have to be made specially, or another kind similar to it and available in walnut would have to be substituted. The author has carved moldings as wide as this by hand with wood-carving chisels on more than one occasion.

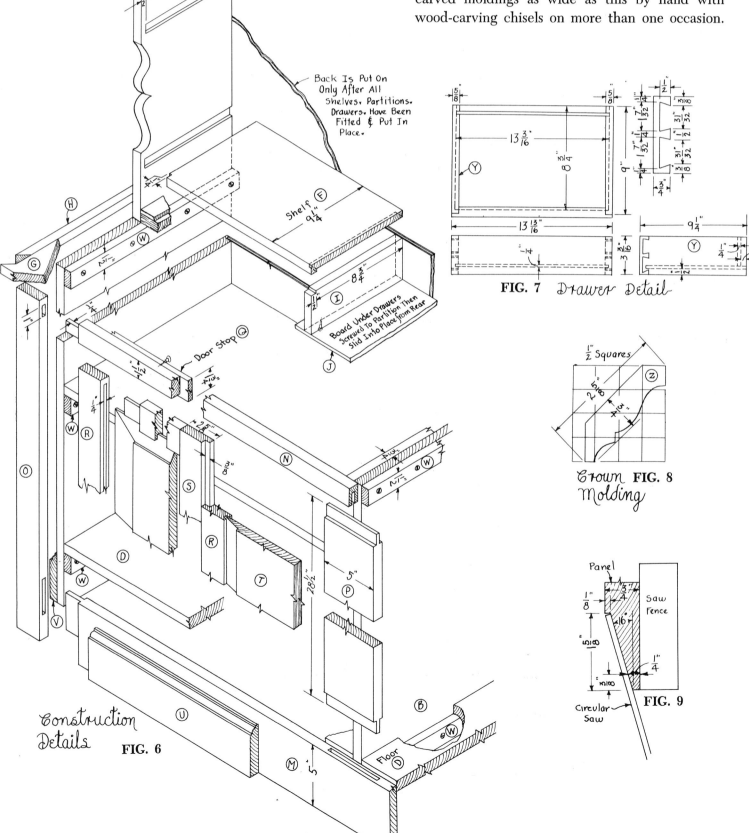

FIG. 7   *Drawer Detail*

Back Is Put On Only After All Shelves, Partitions, Drawers, Have Been Fitted & Put In Place.

Shelf (F) 9¼"

Board Under Drawers Screwed To Partition Then Slid Into Place from Rear

Crown FIG. 8 *Molding*

½" Squares

Panel   Saw Fence

Circular Saw   FIG. 9

Construction Details   FIG. 6

Stock for such a small amount of molding may be partly roughed out on the table saw, and finished off with gouges, chisels, and sandpaper. This method of doing it takes time and patience, but the end justifies the effort if one is unable to purchase it. A molding as wide as this cannot readily be formed on a shaper since the cutters needed to make it would not be safe to use on a shaper.

Crown molding fastened at an angle like this one must be placed into the miter box upside down to saw the mitered ends. To do this, place the lower beveled edge, which you find on back of the molding, flat against the back of the miter box, and the other beveled edge, which you find on top of the molding in back, flat against the bed of the miter box. Then saw the miter at a 45-degree angle. When the miters have been cut, nail the molding to the top of the dresser with brads and small finish nails where the nailheads will show the least. Also spread glue over the miter joints before nailing them together.

Make the drawers next. Fig. 7 gives details for making and assembling the small drawers. When sides and fronts have been cut out, planed, and sanded, cut grooves into them for drawer bottoms and backs. Lay out dovetails on the drawer sides and saw out the tail sections on the band saw. Smooth the saw marks with a sharp chisel; then lay the tails over the drawer front ends on which you trace their shape. Use a dovetail saw to make the first cuts across the end and down the inside of the drawer front, holding the saw at a 45-degree angle and lining it up with the tail layout marks you have made on the inside and end of the drawer front. Use a ½-inch chisel on which both edges are beveled to remove the waste from this part of the dovetail joint. If this is expertly done, the joints will go together perfectly, as can be seen on the drawer which is pulled out in Fig. 1 on our dresser.

Make trial assemblies of all drawers and be sure the drawer slides into place easily before gluing it together. If you have worked to dimensions, very little, if any, trimming should have to be done on these drawers after they have been glued together.

When all drawers have been fitted to the dresser, make the back and nail it to the dresser with three-penny nails with heads, often referred to as lathing nails. Two 6-foot plywood panels, fastened with the facing grain running vertically, will make the back. If the panels are butted together behind the partitions, the joint will not show. The back should be nailed to top, partitions, ends, shelves, and floor.

Now make the doors. First, cut out stock for stiles (R) and (S) and rails (A-A) and (B-B). Grooves to hold the panels should be cut on one edge of all these pieces, but note that the grooves on the stiles go no closer to the ends than the mortises, as is clearly shown on the left door detail in Fig. 6. Cutting the groove clear across on the rails limits the width of the tenon on that side of the rail, so the groove may be cut from one end of the rail to the other. Do not rabbet the doors, where they come together, until the doors have been assembled.

Make the panels by first cutting the stock to the sizes given in the Bill of Material and sanding it. Then raise the panels on the outside by tilting the arbor of the table saw to the 16-degree angle shown in Fig. 9. First make shallow cuts for the fillets on the face of the panel, where the flat face and the slanted edges meet. Do this by running all four edges of each panel, facedown over the saw table, with the saw in its usual position, but raised to a height of only about ⅛ inch. Then make the angle cuts with the saw setup as shown in Fig. 9.

Panels are not glued to door rails and stiles, but are held in place by nothing more than the grooves. The panels should be made about 1/16 to ⅛ inch narrower than the space made to hold them to allow a little for swelling, should it occur.

Clean up the saw marks on the beveled edges with a properly sharpened scraper blade whose cutting edge has been turned with a burnishing tool. Sand the edges smooth, and then assemble and glue up the doors. While bar clamps used for this purpose are still in place, drill 3/16-inch holes for the square pegs with which the joints are reinforced. When all glued joints have been cleaned up, rabbets cut where doors come together, and doors fitted to openings, fasten the doors with H hinges to the frame.

Magnetic door catches, fastened under the shelves on the inside, will hold the doors shut. Fasten door handles and drawer pulls. All hardware should be removed to do the finishing. Consult Chapter 2 to put on a suitable finish.

BILL OF MATERIAL

Poplar, Maple, or Walnut

2 Ends (A) ¾″ x 17¼″ x 75″
1 Partition (B) ¾″ x 17″ x 33″
1 Partition (C) ¾″ x 9¼″ x 41¼″
2 Floors (D) ¾″ x 17″ x 28½″
2 Shelves (E) ¾″ x 17″ x 28½″
6 Shelves (F) ¾″ x 9¼″ x 29″
1 Table-board (G) ¾″ x 18½″ x 60¾″
2 Table-board cleats (H) ¾″ x ¾″ x 18¾″
2 Partitions (I) ¾″ x 9¼″ x 3½″
2 Boards to go under drawers (J) ¼″ x 9¼″ x 28½″
1 Canopy board (K) ¾″ x 5″ x 59¼″
1 Top (L) ¾″ x 12″ x 64¼″
1 Bottom rail (M) ¾″ x 5″ x 57¾″
1 Rail under table-board (N) ¾″ x 1½″ x 57¾″
2 Stiles, front frame (O) ¾″ x 2¼″ x 33″
1 Middle stile, front frame (P) ¾″ x 5″ x 28½″

2 Doorstops (Q) ½″ x 1¾″ x 28½″
6 Door stiles (R) ¾″ x 2¼″ x 26½″
2 Door stiles (S) ¾″ x 2⅝″ x 26½″
4 Door rails (AA) ¾″ x 2¼″ x 11⁷⁄₁₆″
4 Door panels (T) ¾″ x 8¹¹⁄₁₆″ x 22″
4 Door rails (BB) ¾″ x 3″ x 11⁷⁄₁₆″
1 Baseboard (U) ¾″ x 4″ x 60¾″
2 Baseboards (V) ¾″ x 4″ x 18¾″
12 Supports for table-boards, floorboards, and shelves (W) ¾″ x 1½″ x 17″
4 Drawer fronts (X) ¾″ x 3³⁄₁₆″ x 13¹³⁄₁₆″
8 Drawer sides (Y) ⅝″ x 3³⁄₁₆″ x 9″
4 Drawer backs ¼″ x 2⁷⁄₁₆″ x 13³⁄₁₆″
Crown molding for top (Z) 2⅝″ x 8 feet approx.

Birch or Walnut-veneered Plywood

2 Backs for cabinet ¼″ x 29⅜″ x 71″
4 Drawer bottoms ¼″ x 8¾″ x 13³⁄₁₆″

TWENTY-FIVE

Dutch Cupboard

THE Dutch Cupboard shown in Fig. 1 is one the author designed and built to his own specifications for his living room. Since the room is quite large, and the ceiling a little higher than ceilings usually are in newer homes, the cupboard is a little higher than most people might want. And since this cupboard was meant to be a permanent fixture against the particular wall where it was placed, it was assembled right in the living room when the room was added to the house. This being the case, no provision was made to remove the upper section from the lower section should the cupboard have to be moved. Instead, the ends of both sections were made in one piece. If the necessity for removing it from the room should ever arise, the upper section would have to be sawed off the lower section and then rebuilt at the bottom, as shown in our drawings. The height of the cupboard could easily be reduced, either on the upper or the lower section, or even on both, to adapt it to the height of a lower ceiling.

In the working drawings shown here, the author has made provisions for removing the upper section from the lower section and for fastening the two sections together in such a way that they may easily be taken apart if they have to be moved.

To build the Dutch Cupboard, one should start with the lower section. Glue up both ends (A), three partitions (B), and the table-board (G). Also glue up the two floors and the two shelves needed inside the cupboards. Cut rabbets for the plywood back on the rear edges of ends (A) and on the rear edge of table-board (G). Plane and sand all of these, and cut them to size.

Get out stock for the frame which is used on the front of the lower section. This consists of rails (E) and (F), stiles (Q), and rails (R). When these pieces have been cut to size and sanded, cut mortises into rails (E) and (F) to hold the stiles. Lay out and cut all tenons on stiles (Q) and on rails (R). Make a trial assembly of this frame. When gluing it up, first glue rails (R) to the three stiles in the middle, then glue all five stiles to the long rails.

Next, get out stock for all drawer guides, drawer runs, and shelf and floor supporting strips. Dimensions for these may be gotten from the Bill of Material. All of these should be fastened to the ends (A) and to partitions (B) with wood screws before the frame is nailed to the front edges of ends and partitions with sixpenny finish nails. Shelves and floors should also be nailed fast before the frame is nailed to other parts of the lower section. Floors are raised ⅜ inch above rails (F), and they and the shelves serve as doorstops.

Cheaper fir plywood may be substituted for knotty pine plywood to make the back of the lower section, since it will not show enough to justify the greater expense.

Once the back has been nailed fast, get out stock

Fig. 1. Dutch Cupboard. DESIGNED AND BUILT BY THE AUTHOR.

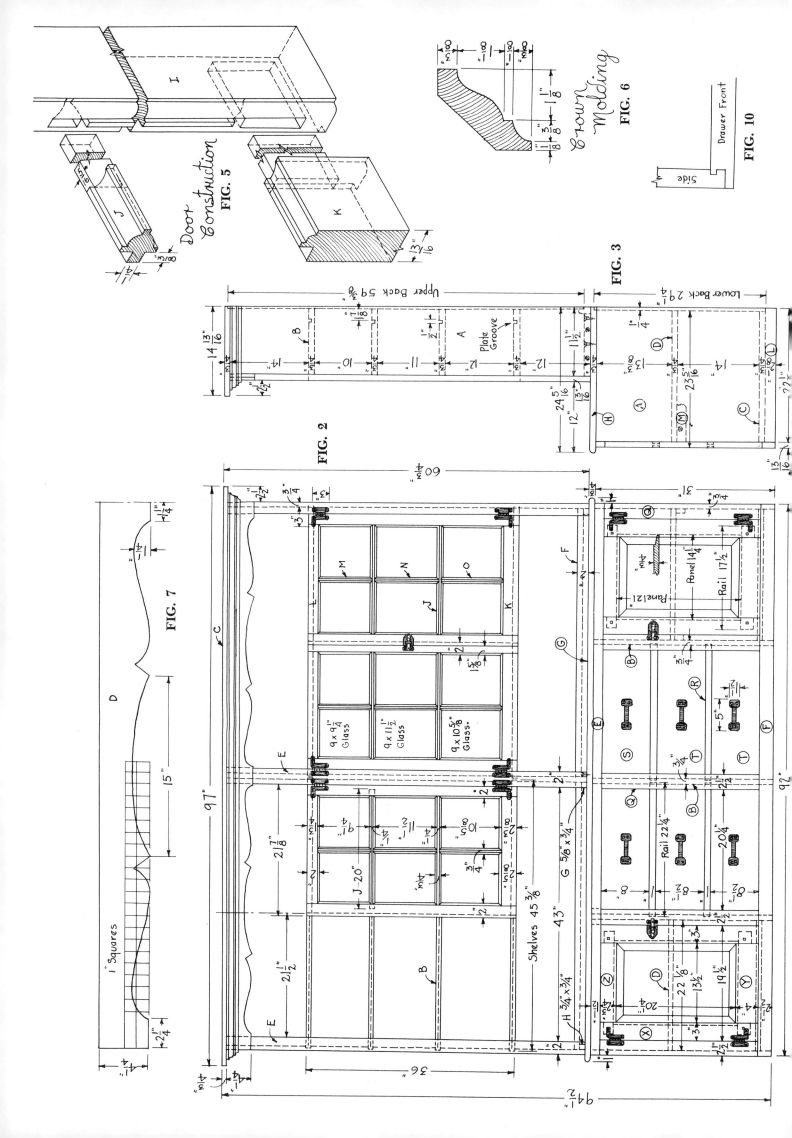

Door Construction FIG. 5

Crown Molding FIG. 6

FIG. 3

FIG. 10

Drawer Front

Side

FIG. 2

Upper Back 59⅜"

Lower Back 29¼"

Plate Groove

FIG. 7

1" Squares

9 x 9¼" Glass

9 x 11½" Glass

9 x 10⅝" Glass.

Shelves 45⅜"

Panel 21

Panel 14¼

Rail 17½

Rail 22¼

Rail 22½

60¾"

97"

94½"

92"

31"

43"

36"

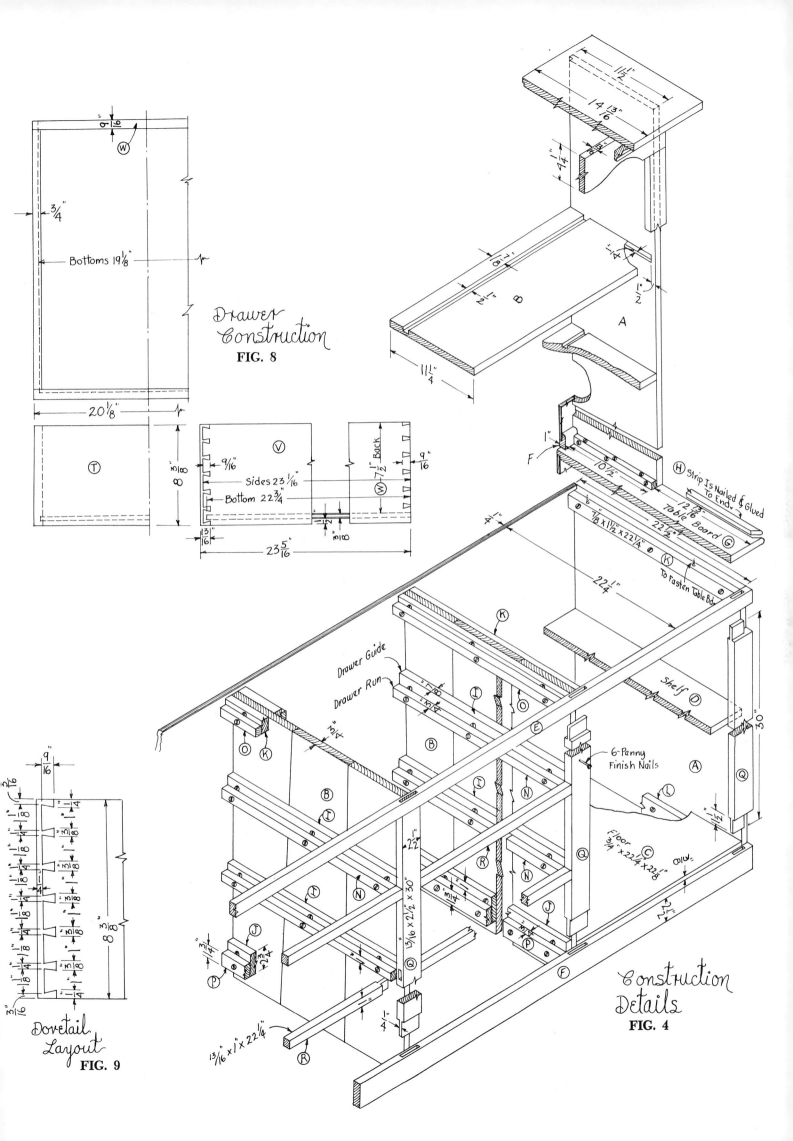

Drawer Construction
FIG. 8

W

3/4"

Bottoms 19⅛"

20⅛"

T

9/16"

V

Sides 23 1/16"

Bottom 22¾"

W 7½" Back

9/16"

8 3/8"

13/16"

3/8"

23 5/16"

Dovetail Layout
FIG. 9

9/16"

3/16"

8 3/8"

1½"

14 13/16"

1¼"

7/8"

2½"

B

A

11¼"

11¼"

½"

¼"

F

1"

H Strip Is Nailed & Glued To End

10½"

12 13/16 Table Board G

7/8 x 1½ x 22¼"

22½"

K

To Fasten Table Bd.

22¼"

4"

Drawer Guide

Drawer Run

K

O

K

B

O

I

E

I

B

I

22"

Shelf D

30

A

6-Penny Finish Nails

N

N

L

R

Floor ¾" x 22¼ x 22⅛"

J

13/16 x 2½ x 30"

Q

Q

P

J

¾"

2¼"

P

13/16" x 1" x 22¼"

R

Construction Details
FIG. 4

for the drawers. To save time, drawers in which sides are fastened to fronts with machine-made tongue-and-groove joints, like the one shown in Fig. 10, may be substituted for drawers made with dovetail joints. We strongly urge, however, making the dovetail joints if skill and time are available, since they add so much to the character and value of such a stately piece of furniture.

When drawers have been made and fitted, make the two doors. Cut out stiles and rails and sand them. Lay out and cut mortises. Then cut tenons and groove the inside edges of rails and stiles for the panels. After a trial assembly, make the panels, raising them as we show it being done in Fig. 17, on page 169, or in Fig. 9 on page 130, for the Early American Dresser. Use wood scraper blades, and sandpaper held on a block of wood, to smooth the borders of the panels. Panels are not glued into door frames, but mortise-and-tenon joints are glued and secured with wooden pegs, as shown in Fig. 2. Fasten the doors to the lower part.

With the exception of the doors, building the upper section poses no great difficulties. Grooves are cut into ends (A) on one side and into the partition in the middle on both sides, to hold the shelves in place. These grooves dispense with the necessity of nailing or screwing strips to these three members to hold the shelves, as was done in the lower section. Rails F, which are not found on the cupboard the author made for himself, are rabbeted on the upper edge, to fasten the lower edge of the plywood panel used for the back to the rails, as shown in Fig. 3.

Doors with panes of glass like these are most easily made in a planing mill, or cabinet shop, where special equipment and skilled workmen who do this kind of work every day are available. Tackle the job yourself if you wish, and if you have the skill and the necessary equipment. For anyone willing and able to try it, the construction details are shown in Fig. 5. Lacking these, we strongly recommend you have the doors made, since the cost should not be prohibitive. Though prices have risen considerably since the author built this cupboard, he had all four doors made in the local planing mill for the very modest price of twenty-eight dollars, not including the glass which he bought and put in himself.

When the doors have been made and fitted to the upper section, you should be ready to apply the finish. No stain was used on the cupboard shown in Fig. 1, since the beauty of knotty white pine is enhanced by letting the warmth of the yellow tones it acquires with aging show through. The author used two coats of the best grade of glossy floor varnish, followed by a coat of satin finish varnish, which was rubbed down and then waxed. This finish has proved to be a highly satisfactory one.

BILL OF MATERIAL

LOWER SECTION

Knotty White Pine

2 Ends (A) ¾" x 22½" x 31"
3 Partitions (B) ¾" x 22¼" x 31"
2 Cupboard floors (C) ¾" x 22¼" x 22⅛"
2 Cupboard shelves (D) ¾" x 22¼" x 22⅛"
1 Upper rail (E) 13⁄16" x 1½" x 92"
1 Lower rail (F) 13⁄16" x 2½" x 92"
1 Table-board (G) ¾" x 24 5⁄16" x 94"
2 Cleats fastened to ends of table-board (H) ¾" x 1" x 24 5⁄16"
8 Drawer guides (I) ⅞" x 2" x 22¼"
4 Drawer guides (J) ⅞" x 2¾" x 22¼"
8 Strips to fasten table-board (K) ⅞" x 1½" x 22¼"
4 Strips to support floor (L) ¾" x 2⅛" x 22¼"
4 Strips to support shelves (M) ¾" x 1½" x 22¼"
8 Drawer runs (N) ¾" x 1" x 22¼"
4 Drawer runs (O) ¾" x ¾" x 22¼"
4 Drawer runs (P) ¾" x 1¾" x 22¼"
5 Stiles (Q) 13⁄16" x 2½" x 30"
4 Rails (R) 13⁄16" x 1" x 22¼"
2 Drawer fronts (S) 13⁄16" x 7⅞" x 20⅛"
4 Drawer fronts (T) 13⁄16" x 8⅜" x 20⅛"
4 Drawer sides (U) ¾" x 7⅞" x 23 1⁄16"

8 Drawer sides (V) ¾″ x 8⅜″ x 23¹⁄₁₆″
2 Drawer backs ⅝″ x 7″ x 20⅛″
4 Drawer backs (W) ⅝″ x 7½″ x 20⅛″
4 Door stiles (X) 1³⁄₁₆″ x 3″ x 27″
2 Door rails (Y) 1³⁄₁₆″ x 4″ x 17½″
2 Door rails (Z) 1³⁄₁₆″ x 2¾″ x 17½″
2 Door panels ¾″ x 14¼″ x 21″

Plywood

6 Drawer bottoms ⅜″ x 22¾″ x 19⅛″

Fir Plywood

1 Back (lower section) ¼″ x 29¼″ x 91½″

UPPER SECTION

Knotty Pine

2 Ends and 1 partition (A) ¾″ x 11½″ x 60″
8 Shelves (B) ¾″ x 11¼″ x 45⅜″
1 Top (C) ¾″ x 14¹³⁄₁₆″ x 97″

1 Canopy board (D) 1³⁄₁₆″ x 4¼″ x 92″
3 Stiles (E) 1³⁄₁₆″ x 2″ x 60″
2 Rails (F) 1″ x 2″ x 45⅜″
2 Strips to fasten upper section to lower section (G)
    ⅝″ x ¾″ x 10½″
2 Strips to fasten upper section to lower section (H)
    ¾″ x ¾″ x 10½″

White Pine Clear of Knots (best grade)

8 Door stiles (I) 1³⁄₁₆″ x 2″ x 36″
8 Door rails (J) ¾″ x 1³⁄₁₆″ x 20″
4 Door rails (K) 1³⁄₁₆″ x 2⅝″ x 20½″
4 Door rails (L) 1³⁄₁₆″ x 2″ x 20½″
4 Muntins (M) ¾″ x 1³⁄₁₆″ x 9¼″
4 Muntins (N) ¾″ x 1³⁄₁₆″ x 11½″
4 Muntins (O) ¾″ x 1³⁄₁₆″ x 10⅝″
Standard crown molding about 130″ (See Fig. 7)

Knotty Pine Plywood

2 Backs ¼″ x 45¾″ x 59⅜″

TWENTY-SIX

Block Front Chest-on-Chest

To build the piece, it will be best to start with the lower section, since the upper section rests upon it and is not fastened to it; it is held in place by the molding around the waist.

First, get out stock for the ends (A). This is glued up of ⅞-inch stock, to a width of 20 inches. When the ends have been made, make layouts for grooves to hold the frames that support the drawers. You may want to make these frames before cutting the grooves, in order to make certain the grooves are as wide as the frames are thick after they have been assembled and sanded. It is always a good idea to make sure of this before cutting grooves into which frames are fitted, if no means

THE very impressive-looking Blockfront Chest-on-Chest shown in Fig. 1 is a remarkably handsome and a very useful piece of furniture. The author made the original drawings for this piece of furniture at the time when he served as an understudy in the studios of Wallace Nutting, where the example shown in Fig. 1 was first built. How many of these chests were built after the author left the studio he has no way of knowing, but only two had been built before he took a position elsewhere.

The piece, impressive though it is, is an adaptation rather than an exact copy of a somewhat taller and larger original. Not now having access to the plans from which the chest shown in Fig. 1 was made, the plans shown on page 140 were drawn from memory and from the photograph in Fig. 1, which also appeared in an earlier book written by the author.* The author makes bold to state, however, that if comparisons should ever happen to be made, deviations in sizes between our drawings and those on the original examples manufactured at the studio in Framingham will be found to be inconsequential and minor ones. Reducing the sizes, and especially the height, from those found on the original chest-on-chest from which measurements were taken makes it a more practical piece of furniture for present-day homes, where low ceilings often will not accommodate very tall pieces.

Fig. 1. Blockfront Chest-on-Chest. A WALLACE NUTTING REPRODUCTION.

* *How to Design Period Furniture.*

138

is at hand to do precision sanding to a predetermined thickness. If a heavy duty drum sander is available to do the job, the thickness of the frame could be made to fit exactly. Once these grooves have been cut, either with an electric-powered hand router or by some other means, the rabbets on the edge at the rear, to hold the plywood back, should be cut.

Get out stock for frames #4 and #5. Mortise-and-tenon joints are used to fasten the parts of all frames together. Stock for a number of these frames are a full inch thick, requiring 5/4 rough stock. Two of the frames on the chest are even thicker, and it may be worth stating here that skimping on lumber is not possible and should not be attempted when building such a fine piece of furniture. Only the front rails need be made of mahogany,* since they will be the only parts of the frames to show. Other parts may be made of poplar, or other less expensive lumber, such as soft maple or even oak. Sizes for all members of these frames will be found in the Bill of Material and on the drawings, in Figs. 10 and 11. Frame #6, shown in Fig. 12, may also be made at this time. The construction of frame #6 is a bit different from the construction used on the other frames, for no end grain should show on the molding that is cut on three of its edges. The front corners are mitered and fastened together with glue and corrugated fasteners. Glues available to the cabinetmaker today are so good that a joint like this should hold if properly put together.

The molding on frame #6 may be cut on a large spindle shaper if proper cutters are available. If not, it may be almost entirely carved by hand, though to start it some of the rough shaping may be done on the table saw. If cut on the spindle shaper, the parts on the front edge where changes in direction occur must still be finished by hand with carving tools.

When all frames for the lower section have been made and fitted to their respective grooves in the ends, these pieces may be assembled. Take great care to square ends to the frames, in order to make sure drawers will slide easily.

Feet should now be made. Make a full-sized pattern from the graph square pattern on the bot-

tom of Fig. 2. Fig. 21 shows how to shape the foot. Be sure the top of the foot at the front conforms to the curve on frame #6. The two pieces of the front feet are joined with a splined miter joint and glued. The feet at the rear are shaped only on the ends of the chest, and a kind of flat wooden bracket is joined to them at the back, as shown in the detail Fig. 4. All the feet may be glued and screwed fast to the bottom of frame #6, after which this frame may be fastened to the bottom of the lower section with wood screws.

Drawers for the lower section may be made at this time, or you may wait to build them when making those for the upper section. Their construction will be discussed later on in the chapter.

To build the upper section, glue up stock for the ends (I). It will not be necessary to groove these ends to hold the frames as you did the ends of the lower section, since gains cut into stiles (J), which are found between the quarter columns and the drawers, will support the frames at the front, and wood screws through end rails and through drawer guides will fasten them securely to the ends of the upper section. Nails through the back will hold them in place there. Rabbets should be cut on the rear edges of both ends for the back, as was done on the lower section.

Cut a dado across the top of end (I) for the top to be joined to it. This dadoed end extends ½ inch above the top (8) so that the edges of the Masonite used to cover the hood will not show after it has been nailed fast.

Make the two stiles (J). These are made of stock 1¼ inches thick and are rabbeted on one side, so the part which shows next to the drawers is only ⅞ inch thick. (See Figs. 6 and 7.) Lay out and cut the gains to hold frames #1, #2, and #3, as shown in Fig. 22. Screw and glue stiles (J) to ends (I). Make frames 1, 2, and 3. Details of construction for these are shown in Figs. 8 and 9. The rail in the middle is added for extra strength and rigidity. Once the frames have been made and sanded, they may be fastened to the ends with wood screws. The front rails of these frames should be glued to the gains in stiles (J).

Make the pediment face board next. Make a full-sized pattern for this from Fig. 5. This face board is fastened to stiles (J) with wood screws, as shown

* With the exception of frame #6.

FIG. 2

FIG. 3

FIG. 4

Grain

Rear of
Back Foot

1" Squares

Frame No 1
Frame No 2
Frame No 2
Frame No 3
Frame No 4
Frame No 5
Frame No 5
Frame No 6

in Fig. 6. When the top (8), and backing strips (6) are added, wood screws will also help to hold the face board more securely in place, though screws will be used only under the ogee molding at the top, where they will not show.

Make stiles (L) to go between the small drawers. These are grooved at the back for the tongue on one end of partition (5), which is to be glued to it, as shown in Fig. 6. When stiles (L) have been glued to partitions (5), these partitions may be fastened with wood screws to frame #1 and to pediment face board (K). Then make and fasten strips (3) and (4) to this partition and to the ends. These keep the small drawers level by supporting them on top when they are drawn out.

Make the end moldings for the top next, and fasten these with wood screws from the inside before putting on top (8). Do not glue this molding to the ends.

Now make top (8) and fasten it to the assembled frame with wood screws, as shown in Fig. 6. Make backboard (7) and backing strips (6) for the return molding, and fasten these where they belong. Make and fasten block (9), which helps support the base of the finial at the middle.

Make the ogee moldings (Z). These are made from stock 2 inches thick, 5½ inches wide, and 20 inches long. Shape them to conform to the shape of the tops of the pediment face board (K), but their upper edges are raised ½ inch above the top of the face board to hide the edges of the Masonite that covers the hood. These ogee moldings may be fastened to the face board with glue and wood screws, after mitering the corners to join them to the end moldings and the return moldings inside the hood.

When the upper section has been made, make and fasten the molding at the waist where the upper and lower sections come together. Fig. 17 shows the shape of these moldings and gives directions for fastening them. Fig. 22 also shows how this is done. Screw strips (10) under frame #3. These act as shoes to slide the upper section into place over the lower section.

Now make the drawers. Details for making a drawer for the upper section are given in Fig. 23, and those for making a blockfront drawer for the lower section in Fig. 24. Drawers for the upper section, with the exception of the carved drawer in the middle of the top, follow the usual pattern used on chests of drawers of the Chippendale style. They have a ¼-inch lip molding on all four edges, but the molding on the bottom does not extend beyond the bottom of the drawer front itself, since it could be too easily broken off.

Blockfronting on drawer fronts is always cut from thick, solid stock. The blocking that extends outward at both ends, and the recessed part in the middle, should never be achieved by gluing pieces on top of each other. For the lower two drawers this will require stock 2⅝ inches thick, and for the upper drawer (B) it will have to be 2¾ inches thick, because of the extra thickness required to carve the beadlike shell ribs. Stock for the small drawer front (X) at the top will have to be 1⅝ inches thick.

While we show patterns to carve these shells in Figs. 18 and 19, they cannot be used to layout the shells to their exact dimensions. The contour shaping of these shells must first be done, and then one rib, or segment, of the shell should be laid out on a piece of Bristol board, and each segment should then be drawn on the wood in turn until the required number have all been drawn. The lines should then be trued up until they look as nearly like our pattern as they can be made. Carve the high ribs first, leaving places between them flat at first. Outlines for the grooves may then be drawn between fillets left flat next to each beaded rib.

An examination of the drawer front in Fig. 24 will show that some of the wood on the inside of drawer fronts (C) and (D) may be gouged out to within about 1 inch of the bottom, to make it lighter at both ends. This trimming out should not be done all the way to where the bottom of the drawer is joined to the groove in the drawer front, for the obvious reason that it will be easier to fit a drawer bottom having a straight edge to the drawer front. No wood is removed from in back of the carved shells on the ends of the upper drawer.

Drawer sides are dovetailed to the drawer fronts. Yellow poplar is as good a wood as can be found for drawer sides, since its color with a natural finish contrasts so beautifully with the mahogany wood

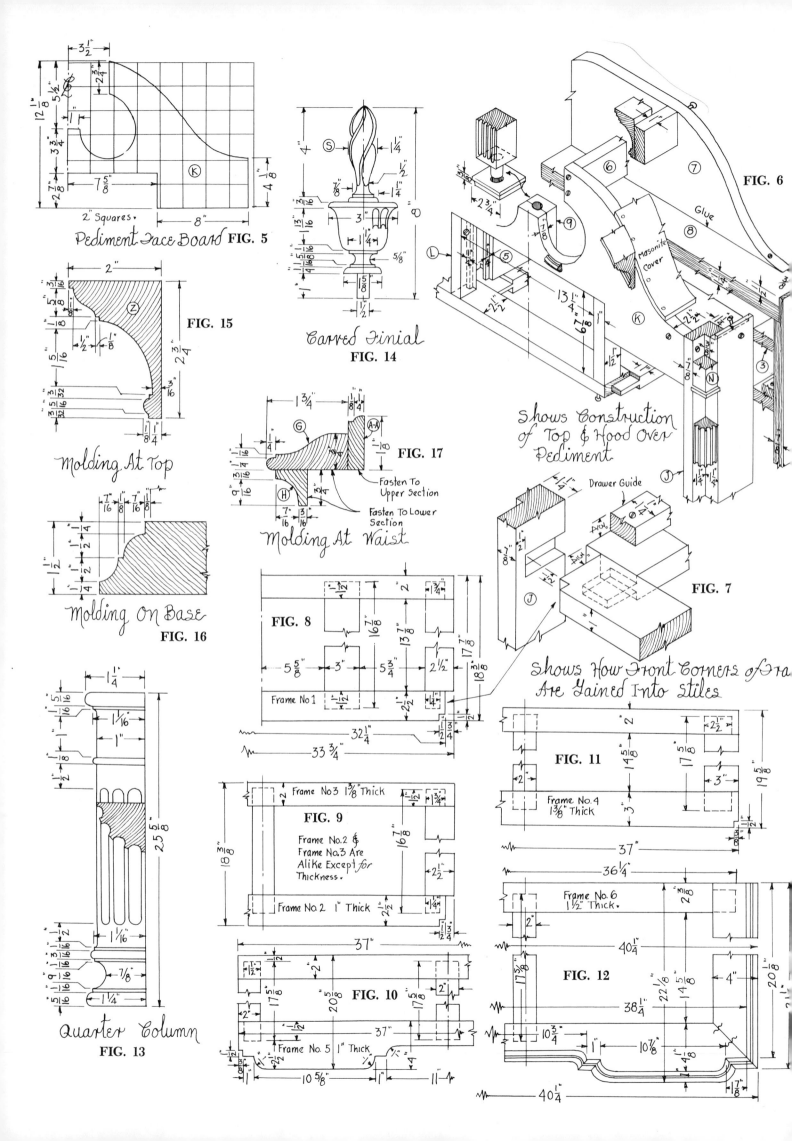

Pediment Face Board **FIG. 5**

2" Squares.

Carved Finial
FIG. 14

FIG. 6

Glue

Masonite Cover

Shows Construction
of Top & Hood Over
Pediment

FIG. 15

Molding At Top

Molding On Base
FIG. 16

Molding At Waist
FIG. 17

Fasten To
Upper Section

Fasten To Lower
Section

Drawer Guide

FIG. 7

Shows How Front Corners of Fra
Are Gained Into Stiles

FIG. 8

Frame No 1

FIG. 9

Frame No 3 1⅛" Thick

Frame No.2 &
Frame No.3 Are
Alike Except for
Thickness.

Frame No 2 1" Thick

FIG. 10

Frame No 5 1" Thick

FIG. 11

Frame No. 4
1⅜" Thick

FIG. 12

Frame No. 6
1½" Thick.

Quarter Column
FIG. 13

Block Front Chest On Chest

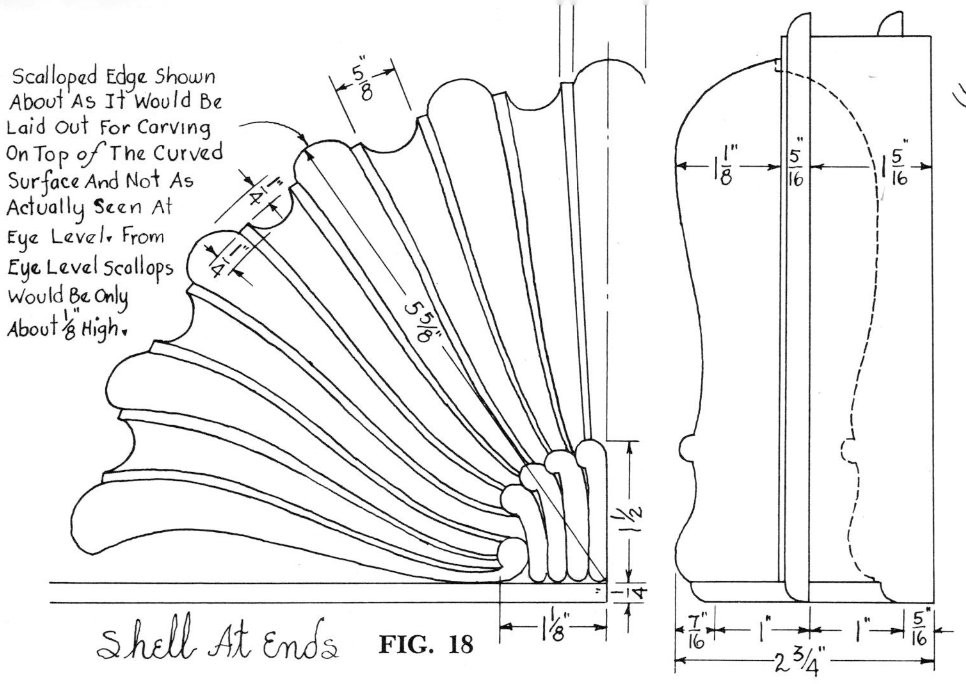
Scalloped Edge Shown About As It Would Be Laid Out For Carving On Top of The Curved Surface And Not As Actually Seen At Eye Level. From Eye Level Scallops Would Be Only About 1/8" High.
5/8"
1/4"
5 5/8"
1 1/2
1/4
1 1/8"
1 1/8"
5/16
1 5/16
7/16
1"
5/16
2 3/4"

Shell At Ends **FIG. 18**

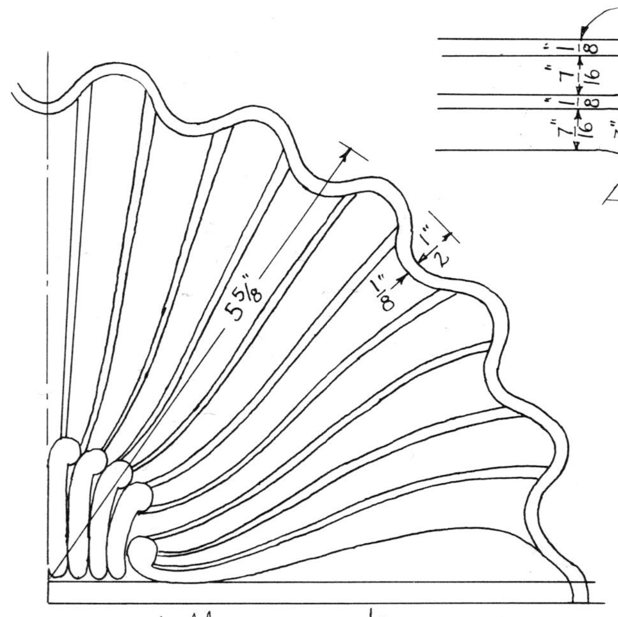
5 5/8
1/8"
1/2"

Shell In Center **FIG. 19**

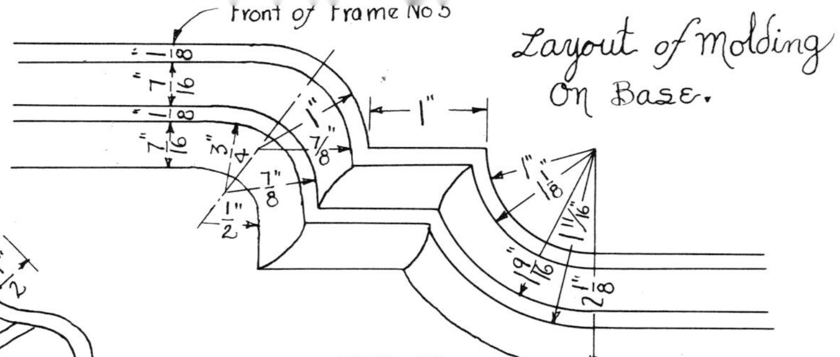
Front of Frame No 5
Layout of Molding On Base.
1"
7/8
1/2"
1 1/8
1 11/16
2 1/8"

FIG. 20

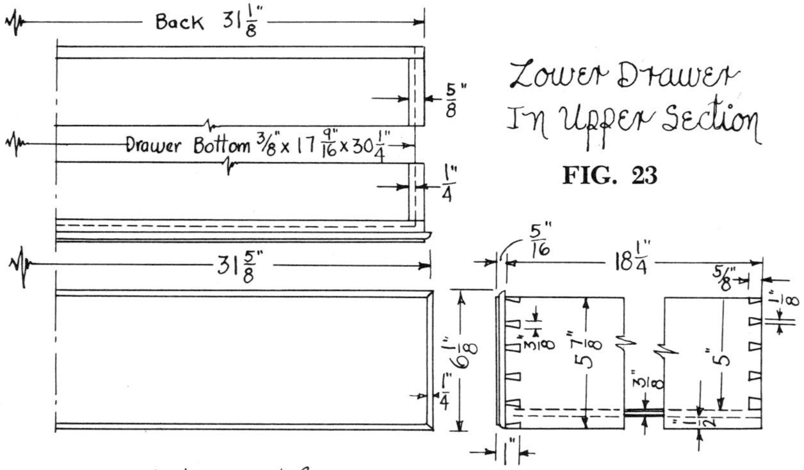
Back 31 1/8"
5/8"
Drawer Bottom 3/8" x 17 9/16" x 30 1/4"
1/4"
31 5/8"
6 1/8"
1/4"
5/16"
18 1/4"
5/8"
1/8"
5 7/8"
5"
3/8"
1/2"
1"

Lower Drawer In Upper Section

FIG. 23

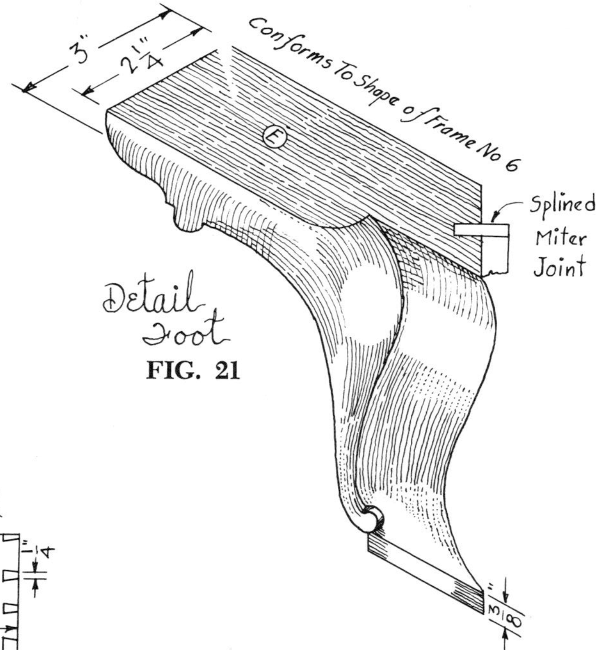
Conforms To Shape of Frame No 6
3"
2 1/4"
Splined Miter Joint
3/8"

Detail Foot

FIG. 21

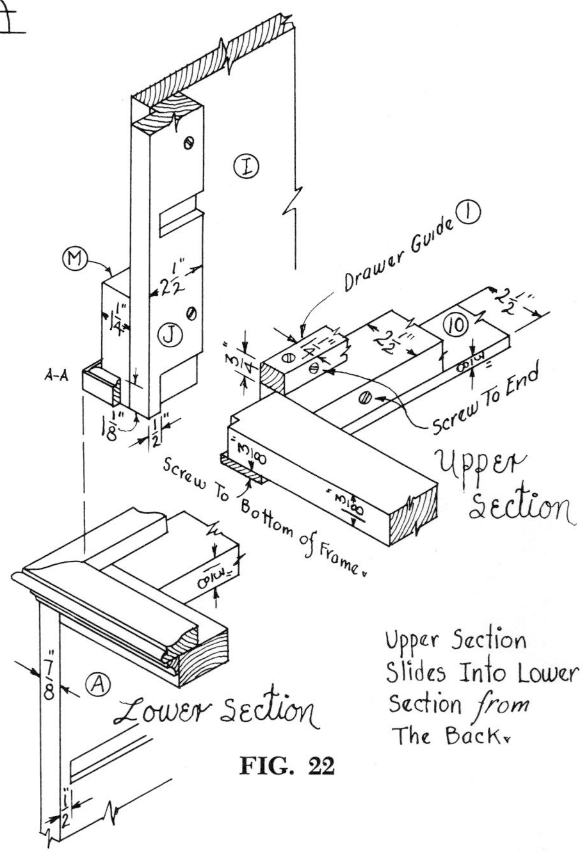
I
M
J
A-A
Drawer Guide 1
1 1/4"
2 1/2"
1 1/8"
1/2"
3/4"
2 1/2"
10
Screw To End
Screw To Bottom of Frame.
Upper Section
A
7/8"
1/2"
Lower Section

Upper Section Slides Into Lower Section from The Back.

FIG. 22

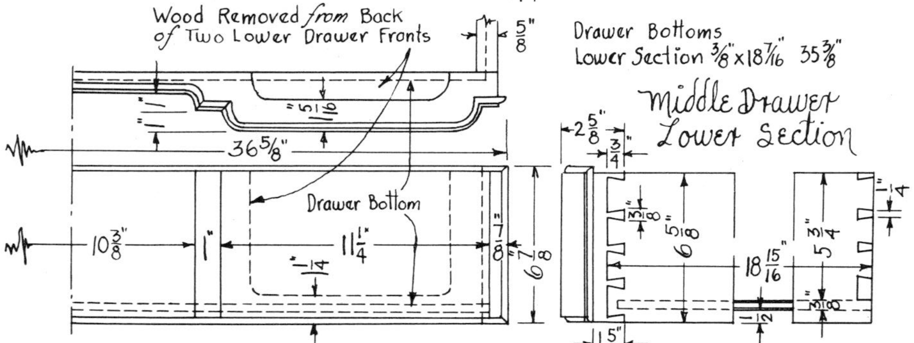
Wood Removed from Back of Two Lower Drawer Fronts
5/8"
5/16
36 5/8"
Drawer Bottom
10 3/8"
1"
11 1/4"
6 7/8
Drawer Bottoms Lower Section 3/8"x18 7/16 35 3/8"
Middle Drawer Lower Section
2 5/8"
3/4
6 5/8
18 15/16
5 3/4"
1 5/16"

FIG. 24

used on the drawer fronts. The best grade of poplar has variegated colors ranging from pale yellow to green, brown, and purple hues, and if left unstained makes a very pretty pattern at the dovetailed joints.

When all drawers have been put together and fitted to the chest, put backs on both sections.

Now glue four sticks together with wrapping paper between them to make the quarter columns. The method for doing this is shown in Fig. 12 in Chapter 21 on building the Grandfather Clock. Turn the column, then split it apart at the paper joints with a chisel. Make base blocks (M) and blocks (N) to go above the columns. Also make caps and bases for the quarter columns; then glue all of these into their respective corners.

Make the base blocks (P) and (Q) for the finials, and their caps (R). The bases (P) and (Q) have a dowel turned or inserted into their bottom ends to fasten them to the top of the chest, as shown in Fig. 6. Turn the finials and carve them and their base blocks, then fasten them in place. Base blocks (P) and (Q) are glued to the top section, but finials are not. In this way they may be removed for cleaning or in order to move the chest without breaking them.

Pieces of tempered Masonite will serve to make a roof for the hood. These are flexible enough to bend to the curve and may be nailed on, then stained the color to match the mahogany wood as closely as possible.

Put on the hardware, which will complete the chest. It should be taken off, however, to put on the finish.

BILL OF MATERIAL

LOWER SECTION

Mahogany

2 Ends (A) $\frac{7}{8}$" x 20" x 25$\frac{1}{8}$"
1 Front rail, frame #4 1$\frac{3}{8}$" x 3" x 37"
3 Front rails, frame #5 1" x 4" x 37"
1 Front rail, frame #6 1$\frac{1}{2}$" x 5$\frac{1}{8}$" x 40$\frac{1}{4}$"
2 End rails, frame #6 1$\frac{1}{2}$" x 4" x 21$\frac{1}{8}$"
1 Carved drawer front (B) 2$\frac{3}{4}$" x 6$\frac{3}{8}$" x 36$\frac{5}{8}$"
1 Blocked drawer front (C) 2$\frac{5}{8}$" x 6$\frac{7}{8}$" x 36$\frac{5}{8}$"
1 Blocked drawer front (D) 2$\frac{5}{8}$" x 7$\frac{7}{8}$" x 36$\frac{5}{8}$"
4 Pieces for front feet (E) 3" x 6$\frac{1}{2}$" x 8"
2 Pieces for back feet (F) 2" x 6$\frac{1}{2}$" x 7$\frac{1}{4}$"
Molding for waist (G) $\frac{3}{4}$" x 1$\frac{3}{4}$" x 82"
Cove molding (H) $\frac{5}{8}$" x $\frac{3}{4}$" x 82"

Yellow Poplar

1 Back rail, frame #4 1$\frac{3}{8}$" x 2" x 37"
3 Back rails, frames #5 1" x 2" x 37"
2 Side rails, frame #4 1$\frac{3}{8}$" x 3" x 17$\frac{5}{8}$"
1 Middle rail, frame #4 1$\frac{3}{8}$" x 2" x 17$\frac{5}{8}$"
6 Side rails, frames # 5 1" x 2" x 17$\frac{5}{8}$"
3 Middle rails, frames #5 1" x 2" x 17$\frac{5}{8}$"
2 Drawer sides, upper drawer $\frac{5}{8}$" x 6$\frac{1}{8}$" x 18$\frac{15}{16}$"
2 Drawer sides, middle drawer $\frac{5}{8}$" x 6$\frac{5}{8}$" x 18$\frac{15}{16}$"
2 Drawer sides, bottom drawer $\frac{5}{8}$" x 7$\frac{5}{8}$" x 18$\frac{15}{16}$"
1 Drawer back, upper drawer $\frac{5}{8}$" x 5$\frac{1}{4}$" x 36$\frac{1}{8}$"
1 Drawer back, middle drawer $\frac{5}{8}$" x 5$\frac{3}{4}$" x 36$\frac{1}{8}$"
1 Drawer back, bottom drawer $\frac{5}{8}$" x 6$\frac{3}{4}$" x 36$\frac{1}{8}$"

Plywood

3 Drawer bottoms $\frac{3}{8}$" x 18$\frac{7}{16}$" x 35$\frac{3}{8}$"
1 Back $\frac{3}{8}$" x 37$\frac{1}{4}$" x 25$\frac{1}{8}$"

UPPER SECTION

Mahogany

2 Ends (I) $\frac{7}{8}$" x 17$\frac{1}{2}$" x 34$\frac{5}{8}$"
2 Stiles (J) 1$\frac{1}{4}$" x 2$\frac{1}{2}$" x 34$\frac{1}{8}$"
1 Pediment face board (K) $\frac{7}{8}$" x 12$\frac{1}{8}$" x 31$\frac{1}{4}$"
2 Stiles between small drawers (L) 1" x 1$\frac{1}{2}$" x 6$\frac{7}{8}$"
2 Quarter columns (make from one column split into 4 pcs.) 2$\frac{1}{2}$" diam. x 25$\frac{5}{8}$"
2 Base blocks under quarter-columns (M) 1$\frac{1}{4}$" x 1$\frac{1}{4}$" x 4$\frac{3}{4}$"
2 Blocks above quarter-columns (N) 1$\frac{1}{4}$" x 1$\frac{1}{4}$" x 3$\frac{1}{2}$"
4 Caps and column bases (O) $\frac{1}{4}$" x 1$\frac{3}{8}$" x 1$\frac{3}{8}$"
2 Bases for finials (P) 2" x 2" x 3$\frac{1}{2}$" } With dowel turned on
1 Base for finial (Q) 2" x 2" x 4" } bottom
4 Caps for finial bases (R) $\frac{3}{8}$" x 2$\frac{3}{4}$" x 2$\frac{3}{4}$"
3 Carved finials (S) 3" diam. x 8"
1 Lower drawer front (T) 1" x 6$\frac{1}{8}$" x 31$\frac{5}{8}$"
1 Drawer front (U) 1" x 5$\frac{1}{2}$" x 31$\frac{5}{8}$"
1 Drawer front (V) 1" x 4$\frac{7}{8}$" x 31$\frac{5}{8}$"
1 Drawer front (W) 1" x 4$\frac{1}{2}$" x 31$\frac{5}{8}$"
1 Drawer front (X) 1$\frac{5}{8}$" x 7" x 13$\frac{5}{8}$"

2 Curved moldings on top of pediment (Z), made from stock 2″ x 5½″ x 20″

2 End moldings on top 2″ x 2¾″ x 20¾″

2 Inside moldings on top 2″ x 2¾″ x 19¾″

Molding at waist (A-A) ⅜″ x 1⅛″ x 80″

1 Front rail, frame #1, 1″ x 2½″ x 32¼″

3 Front rails, frames # 2, 1″ x 2½″ x 32¼″

1 Front rail, frame #3, 1⅜″ x 2½″ x 32¼″

Poplar

2 End rails, frame #1, 1″ x 2½″ x 16⅞″

6 End rails, frames #2 1″ x 2½″ x 16⅞″

2 End rails, frame #3 1⅜″ x 2½″ x 16⅞″

2 Middle rails, frame #1 1″ x 3″ x 16⅞″

3 Middle rails, frame #2 1″ x 2″ x 16⅞″

1 Middle rail, frame #3 1⅜″ x 2″ x 16⅞″

1 Back rail, frame #1 1″ x 2″ x 33¾″

3 Back rails, frames #2 1″ x 2″ x 33¾″

1 Back rail, frame #3 1⅜″ x 2″ x 33¾″

10 Drawer guides for frames 1, 2, and 3 (1) ¾″ x 1¼″ x 15⅞″

2 Guides and supports over small drawers (3) 1″ x 2″ x 17½″

2 Guides and supports over small drawers (4) ¾″ x 1″ x 17½″

2 Partitions joined to stiles between small drawers (5) 1″ x 6⅞″ x 17⅛″

2 Strips to hold return molding, inside on top (6) 1″ x 2¾″ x 16⅞″

1 Back for hood (7) 1″ x 8″ x 31¼″ (approx. length)

1 Top for upper section (8) 1¼″ x 17⅛″ x 34¾″

1 Block to support middle finial back of pediment face board (9) 1⅛″ x 2″ x 2½″

2 Filler strips to act as runners under frame #3 (10) ⅜″ x 2½″ x 18⅜″

1 Filler strip to act as runner under frame #3 (11) ⅜″ x 2″ x 18⅜″

4 Drawer sides for small drawers ⅝″ x 3⅞″ x 18¼″

2 Drawer sides for small drawer with carved shell ⅝″ x 6¾″ x 17¹¹⁄₁₆″

2 Drawer sides for drawer front (T) ⅝″ x 5⅞″ x 18¼″

2 Drawer sides for drawer front (U) ⅝″ x 5¼″ x 18¼″

2 Drawer sides for drawer front (V) ⅝″ x 4⅝″ x 18¼″

2 Drawer sides for drawer front (W) ⅝″ x 4¼″ x 18¼″

Plywood

4 Drawer bottoms, large drawers ⅜″ x 17⁹⁄₁₆ x 30¼″

2 Drawer bottoms, small drawers ⅜″ x 7⅛″ x 17⁹⁄₁₆″

1 Drawer bottom, carved drawer ⅜″ x 12¼″ x 17³⁄₁₆″

1 Back for upper section ⅜″ x 34¾″ x 34⅛″

TWENTY-SEVEN

Carved Shell-Top Corner Cupboard

to size the rear post (A), two end posts (B), and two stiles (C), the overall sizes of which may be gotten from the Bill of Material. End posts (B) have ⅛-inch-deep grooves cut into them to hold and help support shelves (E), as shown in Fig. 5, the detail drawing of the post. One right post and one left post, constituting a pair, will have to be made. Thus the bevels or the rabbet found on an edge on one of the posts will be found on the opposite edge of its counterpart to make the pair. The same will hold true of the two stiles, for one of

Fig. 1. Carved Shell-Top Corner Cupboard. COLLECTION OF THE LATE DANIEL H. UNGER, BOYERTOWN, PENNSYLVANIA.

ONE finds all too few shell-top corner cupboards, and when one does they are often built-in and featured elements in very impressive rooms. One or more such splendid pieces will magically transform even an ordinary room, for a corner cupboard with a carved shell may be compared to a beautiful lady whose crowning glory is a head of lovely well-groomed hair. Wherever such fine pieces are found, they seem to invite the employment of additional out-of-the-ordinary architectural embellishments, like beautifully paneled walls, and classic columns, pilasters, and pediments, on such places as doors, windows, and fireplaces.

In the past, built-in shell-top corner cupboards were usually to be found only in great houses of the wealthy, such as those built by plantation owners, captains of industry or commerce. They were meant to be a symbol of importance and prestige, which indeed they were. Only in rare instances was one ever found in a cottage or modest habitation.

The wood used to build the cupboard is native white pine, and it may have been built by some local cabinetmaker, inspired by designs of the early eighteenth century. It is scaled to fit very nicely into the hall, dining room, or living room of a modest twentieth-century home.

To build the cupboard, first saw, plane, and sand

which a detail is shown in Fig. 4. See models of (B) and (C) in Figs. 13 and 14.

When the left and right posts have been made to the sizes given in the Bill of Material, cut a rabbet from top to bottom of the posts on the edges to which the backs of the cupboard are to be joined. Then make layouts to cut the grooves, which support the shelves, across the inside of these posts. Dimensions for these grooves are given in Fig. 5. These grooves may be cut in a number of ways: on a radial arm saw, or on the table saw with a dado head; with a portable electric hand router; or by sawing both sides of the grooves to a depth of ⅛ inch on a miter box and then removing the waste between the saw cuts with a router plane by hand.

Down 13⅞ inches from the top and up 6 inches from the bottom, make ½-inch-deep saw cuts on the opposite edge from the one on which you have cut the rabbet. See left-hand side of (B) in Fig. 14. Two more such saw cuts are made near the middle of the post, as shown in Fig. 5. Strips of waste ½ inch wide, which you keep, are cut off this edge above and below the 1¼-inch space near the middle. The edges from which the waste has been removed are then beveled on both sides of the post as shown in the third cross-section from the top. The edges of the three protruding parts that have not been cut off are also beveled on both sides, as shown in the cross-section views at the top and bottom of Fig. 5. It is easier to bevel these before sawing off the waste strips between them. The posts are now shaped.

Once the shelves have been glued to posts (B) and nailed or screwed fast to post (A), proceed in a somewhat similar manner to shape the stiles, the two vertical members of the frames which will be glued to the posts, in the manner shown in Figs. 15 and 16.

Most of the groove at the top of (C), where the joint with pediment board (F) is to be made, may be cut with a dado head on the table saw, or on a shaper with the groove-cutting knife of a matching tongue-and-groove set of cutters. At the offset where the groove stops, it may be cut out with a mortising bit on the mortising machine, or the entire groove may be cut out on the mortising machine.

To show the shaping and joining together of a post and a stile more clearly than can be shown on our drawings, we have made and photographed scale models of both. These are shown in Figs. 13, 14, 15, and 16.

When stiles (C) have been completely formed and matched up with posts (B), the top, floorboard, and shelves (E) should be glued up. Plane and sand these, and then cut all six of them to exactly the same shape with the exception of band-sawing the front edges of the two shelves below the shell to shape. A full-size pattern for these may be made from the shelf detail shown in Fig 7. Broken lines in Fig. 7 also show how to glue the boards together to make these, wasting as little wood as possible.

The two shelves below the carved shell may then be sawed to shape on the front, as shown on the plan view drawn on the upper section of Fig. 2. This shaping is also shown in Fig. 7 from which a full-sized pattern may be made. The top, floor, and two other shelves remain straight across the front.

When all six pieces (E) have been cut to the proper size and shapes, you will be ready to assemble posts (A) and (B) and all six pieces (E). Because of the difficulty of fastening clamps to pull the ends of pieces (E) and the posts together when gluing them, some preparations will have to be made before attempting to assemble these pieces. Builders of corner cupboards often used running dovetail joints to fasten ends of shelves to posts, making the use of clamps unnecessary. This is the way it is done on the Queen Anne Corner Cupboard that we show in Chapter 28. The simpler construction shown on this piece is adequate and sound, and nails or screws used to reinforce the glue joints will be hidden under the moldings which are put on later. Begin by first nailing or screwing all pieces (E) to rear post (A). Place pieces (E) with front edges resting on the workshop floor, and hold them upright by screwing a wooden hand-screw clamp, lying on its side, to the bottom of each piece. Be careful to space these exactly the right distance apart when fastening them to the back post. Then screw ¾″ x ¾″ x 73″ strips of wood to each edge at the back of post (A). Put glue into the grooves that you have cut across the inside of posts (B), and on the ends of (E), and

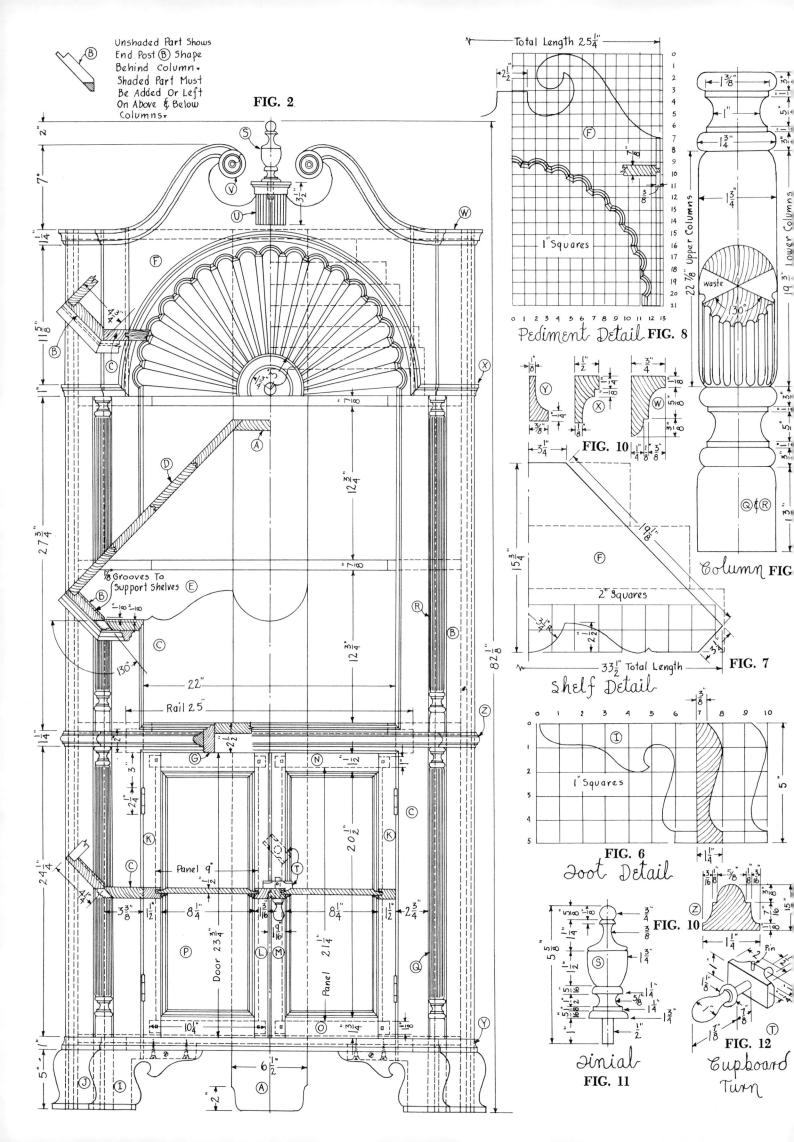

fit the glued ends of (E) into these grooves. Then with nails, screws, or both, fasten floorboard (E) and top (E) to posts (B). Moldings (W) and (Y) will cover these nail- and screwheads after they have been put on.

Use no nails or wood screws to help hold posts (B) to the four shelves between top and bottom pieces (E). Instead, turn what you have assembled to an upright position; then place a board as wide as the post over the face side of the post to keep the clamps from marking its surface, and pull these eight joints together with clamps. The strips you have screwed fast to the back of post (A) will make it possible for you to do so. After the glue in all of these joints has hardened, clamps may be removed and the strips of wood on back of post (A) may be taken off.

The carved shell top should be built up in segments, as shown in Fig. 3, and carved next. California sugar pine is best for this purpose. It is free of grain having layers of annual ring growth that are alternately hard and soft, as is the case with northern and eastern pine-tree boards. Wide and thick planks of California sugar pine are available at most lumberyards where pine is sold. At the end of our Bill of Material we give sizes of segments needed to glue up the shell.

To make correct layouts for the flutes in the shell, it is best first to make pediment board (F) and cut and shape the arc on the lower edge; this then becomes the shell facing after the shell has been carved. A full-sized pattern of the pediment board may be made from the drawing shown in Fig. 8. First cut this board to the size given in the Bill of Material, and after planing and sanding it to this size, cut the tongues on both ends before cutting it to shape on its upper and lower edges. When the arch has been cut to shape and carved, lay it over the front of the glued-up segments of the shell and transfer the shape of the scalloped edge to the shell front. Then describe the 11-inch arc for the fillets, the flat parts dividing the flutes in the carved shell. The 11-inch arc outlines the bottom of the dome on the inside of the carved shell at the front, and this inside of the dome is defined at other points by the three 11-inch radii shown at the top of the cupboard in Fig. 3.

After the arcs with the 11-inch radius have been laid out on the face and on the bottom of the glued-up segments, the inside of the shell may be formed with gouges and scrapers. Use a half-circle template having an 11-inch radius to check the curvature as you trim and smooth the inside of the dome. When shaped, sand it smooth; then lay out radial lines from the center at the back of the dome to carve the flutes. A pattern of heavy drawing paper or Bristol board may be made to use in getting every flute the same size.

On our drawing we show the rosette at the bottom of the shell carved on the glued-up segments from which the shell itself is carved. Sometimes this rosette is turned on the lathe from another piece of wood, and a place is hollowed out for it to be glued to the bottom of the shell. On this shell the outside rim of the rosette is flush with the inside of the dome, where they meet; if a turned rosette is substituted, the rim need not be made flush with the dome, but may be raised slightly higher than the fillets.

When the shell has been carved, it will be an easy matter to fasten it to the upper shelf with glue, since clamping will be easy because of the manner in which the segments have been put together. This should now be done.

The two backs (D) should be made next. On the cupboard shown in Fig. 1, the backs are made of matched boards put together with tongue-and-groove joints, and if authentic construction for old pieces is strictly adhered to, this is the way to do it. A good grade of plywood, veneered with white pine, may be substituted. From the standpoint of good construction, it will be superior to solid stock, since it will neither split, warp, swell, nor shrink. Three-eighth-inch, or even quarter-inch, plywood will be heavy enough. When ready, the backs may be nailed fast to posts (A) and (B) and to all (E)-boards with threepenny lathe nails.

Now make the frame for the front of the cupboard. This is comprised of stiles (C), pediment board (F), and rails (G) and (H). After cutting the top of the pediment board to shape and making tenons on the rail ends, this frame should be glued up. Make a trial assembly before gluing it together, so as to make sure the frame will fit perfectly into

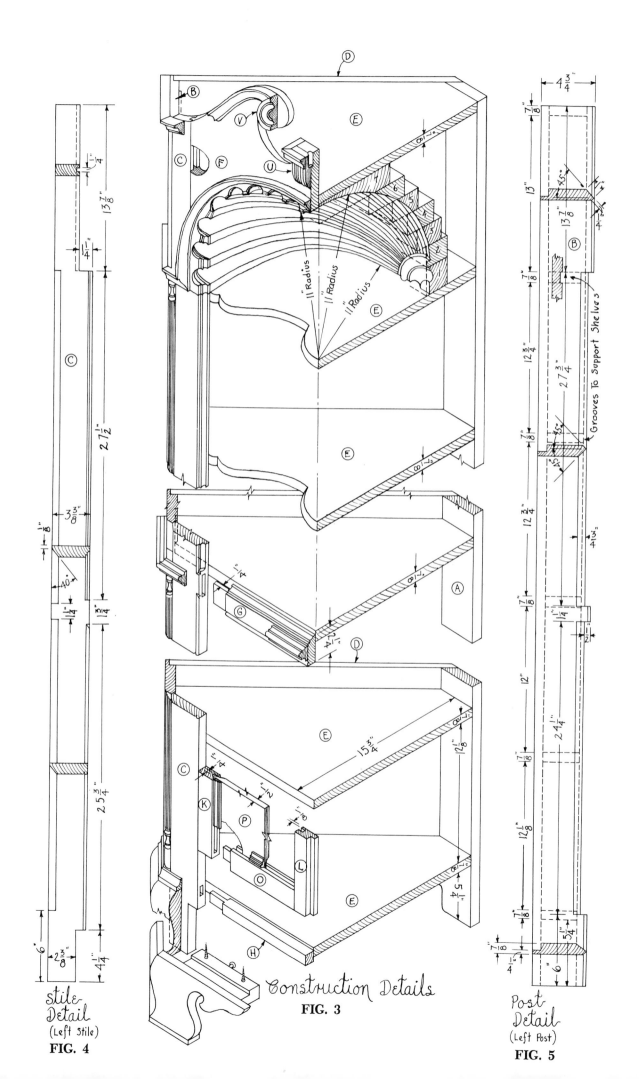

Stile Detail
(Left Stile)
FIG. 4

$13\frac{7}{8}$"

$\frac{1}{4}$"

$\frac{1}{4}$"

$27\frac{1}{2}$"

©

$\frac{1}{8}$"

$3\frac{3}{8}$"

40°

$1\frac{1}{4}$"

$1\frac{3}{4}$"

$25\frac{3}{4}$"

6"

$2\frac{3}{8}$"

$4\frac{1}{4}$"

Construction Details
FIG. 3

Ⓓ

Ⓑ

Ⓒ

Ⓕ

Ⓥ

Ⓤ

Ⓔ

6

5

4

3

2

11" Radius

11" Radius

11" Radius

Ⓔ

$1-8$"

Ⓔ

Ⓖ

$\frac{1}{4}$"

$4\frac{1}{2}$"

Ⓐ

Ⓓ

$1-8$"

Ⓒ

Ⓔ

$15\frac{3}{4}$"

$2\frac{1}{8}$"

Ⓚ

$\frac{1}{4}$"

$\frac{1}{2}$"

Ⓟ

$\frac{1}{8}$"

Ⓛ

Ⓞ

$5\frac{1}{4}$"

Ⓔ

Ⓗ

Post Detail
(Left Post)
FIG. 5

$4\frac{3}{4}$"

$\frac{7}{8}$"

13"

45°

$13\frac{7}{8}$"

Ⓑ

$\frac{7}{8}$"

$12\frac{3}{4}$"

Grooves To Support Shelves

$27\frac{3}{4}$"

$\frac{7}{8}$"

45°

4°

$12\frac{3}{4}$"

$4\frac{3}{4}$"

$\frac{7}{8}$"

$1\frac{1}{4}$"

$2\frac{1}{2}$"

12"

$2\frac{1}{4}$"

$12\frac{1}{8}$"

$\frac{7}{8}$"

$\frac{7}{8}$"

$5\frac{1}{4}$"

$\frac{1}{4}$"

6"

Figs. 13 and 14.   Scale Models of Post and Stile.

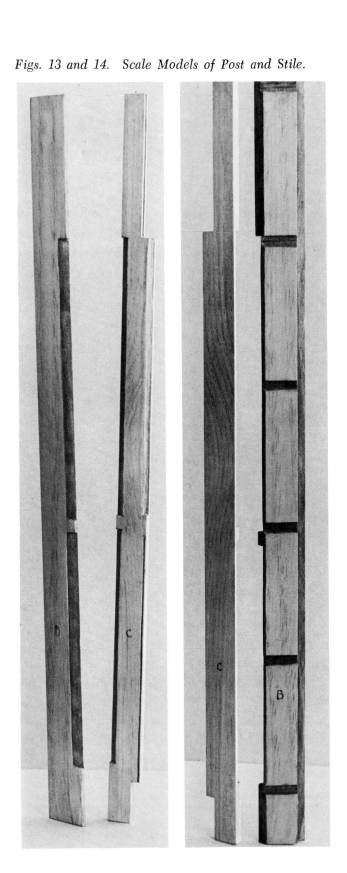

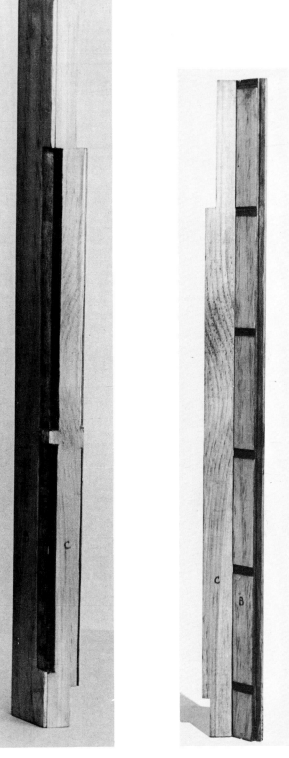

Fig. 15.   Scale Model of Post and Stile Joined To-gether (Outside View).

Fig. 16.   Scale Model of Post and Stile Joined To-gether (Inside View).

the opening between the inside edges of posts (B). The edges of (B) and (C) should be fastened together with glue and fit perfectly at the top. From molding (X) to the floor an imperfect joint would not be so noticeable, since it would be covered by the columns and other moldings.

Once the front is in place, the columns should be turned. Columns on most corner cupboards, for places like these, are usually quartered. When this is so, stock to make them may be glued up with heavy paper in the joints, so they can be split into four quarters after turning. These columns, however, cover a sector of 130 degrees instead of only 90 degrees. By gluing two halves of a column together with heavy brown wrapping paper between and then planing a 50-degree sector off one side of each half after the column has been split in two, you will have the column shaped as you want it for the niche into which it must be fitted. A glance at the cross-section view of Fig. 9 will make this clear.

Make the feet next. From Fig. 6, make a full-sized pattern. Enough foot molding should be shaped as shown in the cross-section in Fig. 6 to make the four pieces needed. This should then be sawed apart in a miter box to make the joints. Screw the feet to posts (B) and stiles (C) from the inside, and fasten the two parts of each foot together with glue. Short, rabbeted blocks of wood, shown at the bottom of Fig. 3, also help fasten the front parts of the feet to the floor of the cupboard.

Moldings (W), (X), (Y), and (Z) and rosettes (V) should now be made and fastened to the cupboard. Block (U), which is shaped and carved to decorate and thicken pediment board (F) at the center so that the finial can be stuck in the top, should also be made at this time and screwed on from the back. Moldings (X) and (W) can be made on a shaper if the right cutters are available; if not, they can be carved by hand with wood-carving chisels. Moldings (Y) and (Z) can be made on a shaper, since they are not curved, but if the right cutters to make them are not at hand, they may be partly shaped on the table saw and then finished by hand with wood-carving chisels

and sandpaper. Shapes for all of the moldings are shown in the cross-section views in Fig. 10.

The doors should now be made. Cut out stock for rails (N) and (O) and for stiles (K), (L), and (M). Also cut out stock for door panels (P). Plane, square up, and sand all of these pieces to the sizes given in the Bill of Material. Then lay out and cut mortises on the stiles. Cut tenons on the rails, and fit the mortise-and-tenon joints. Set up the dado head on the table saw to cut grooves in the rails and stiles to hold the door panels; then cut rabbets on opposite edges of (L) and (M) where the doors come together.

Notice in the detail of (K) in Fig. 3 that the grooves in the stiles are stopped at the mortises and do not go all the way through at the ends. The edges of the panels are feathered or, in other words, planed to a thin edge so they can be inserted into the grooves in the stiles and rails. The panels are not glued into these grooves, but are left free. Only mortise-and-tenon joints are glued, and these joints are reinforced with square wooden pegs. A very thin panel molding is bradded on around the panels on the outside of the doors. Cross-section views showing the shape of this molding are given in Figs. 2 and 3. Stile (M) has a bead cut on the rabbeted edge on the outside of the door.

When the doors have been put together and fitted to the cupboard, fasten them with a pair of sturdy butt hinges. The hinges on this cupboard are of heavy iron with thick leaves. Custom-made hinges of heavy brass or wrought iron are recommended.

Turn the finial and the cupboard turn-handle. Details to make these are shown in Figs. 11 and 12.

The finish on the cupboard consists of little more than a very light colored grayish-brown stain and about two or three coats of thin shellac, finished off with a rubdown of pumice stone, and a beeswax polish. Lacquer may be substituted for shellac, and may be brushed on, but preferably should be sprayed on over a coat of sealer, which should be used over stain if the piece is stained. Lacquer will produce a durable and suitable eggshell gloss, very appropriate for a piece of furniture like this one.

BILL OF MATERIAL

White Pine

1 Rear post (A) 7/8" x 6½" x 73⅛"

2 End posts (B) 7/8" x 4¾" x 73⅛"

2 Stiles (C) 7/8" x 3⅜" x 73⅛"

Backs made of pieces with tongued-and-grooved edges (D) ¾" x approx. 5½" x 67⅞"

Backs could be made of ⅜" or ½" plywood instead 20¾" wide x 67⅞" long

Shelves, floor, and top (E) 6 pieces 7/8" x 15¾" x 33½"

1 Pediment board (F) 7/8" x 21" x 25¼"

1 Rail (G) 7/8" x 2¼" x 25"

1 Rail (H) 7/8" x 1" x 25"

2 Feet (I) 1¼" x 5" x 10"

2 Feet (J) 1¼" x 5" x 5"

2 Door stiles (K) 7/8" x 1½" x 23¾"

1 Door stile (L) 7/8" x 1⁷⁄₁₆" x 23¾"

1 Door stile (M) 7/8" x 1⁹⁄₁₆" x 23¾"

2 Upper door rails (N) 7/8" x 1½" x 10¼"

2 Lower door rails (O) 7/8" x 1¾" x 10¼"

2 Door panels (P) ½" x 9" x 21¼"

1 Turning for lower columns (Q) 1¾" diam. x 24¼" *

1 Turning for upper columns (R) 1¾" diam. x 27¾" *

1 Finial (S) 1¾" x 5⅝"

1 Cupboard turn (T) 1⅛" diam. x 3¼", and 1 pc. ½" x 1" x 2"

1 Carved bracket under finial (U) ½" x 2½" x 3½"

2 Turned rosettes (V) ¾" x 2¼" diam.

Moldings (W), (X), (Y), (Z). Get sizes from drawings.

California Sugar Pine

On the band saw, cut segments to approximately the correct shape on the inside, and then glue the segments together.

Lower segment 2½" x 12¾" x 27"

2nd segment 1¾" x 12¾" x 27"

3rd segment 1¾" x 12¼" x 26"

4th segment 1¾" x 11½" x 24½"

5th segment 1¾" x 10" x 22½"

6th segment 1¾" x 8½" x 20"

7th segment 1¾" x 7" x 15"

* Although the illustration says upper column 22⅞" and lower columns 19⅜", the references are only to the fluted part of the column and not to the column as a whole.

TWENTY-EIGHT

Queen Anne Corner Cupboard

To own such a fine corner cupboard as the cupboard shown in Fig. 1 is a thing greatly to be desired. Corners of rooms frequently are waste areas, where many types of furniture cannot be placed to good advantage. A corner cupboard is a notable exception, and the handsome and imposing Queen Anne cupboard shown and described here is not only an exceedingly useful piece of furniture, but a very impressive one as well. The cupboard is made in two parts, an upper and a lower, and the upper section may be removed from the lower one by sliding it to the rear, off its base. Otherwise it would be difficult to move such a tall piece of furniture from one place to another in a room, and in some circumstances difficult, if not altogether impossible, to raise the cupboard from a horizontal to an upright position, if the ceiling of the room was as low as it is in Fig. 1.

To build the cupboard, start with either section. If you make the lower section first, start by getting out stock for the two end posts (A) and the rear post (O). After squaring, planing, and sanding the posts, make layouts on the inside surfaces and edges for the running dovetail joints that fasten the ends of the shelves to the posts. These may then be cut on the table saw, or on a radial arm saw, by tilting the saw to an angle of about 15 degrees, as shown in Fig. 14. At the same time, cut the rabbet at the top of the post, where the top (J) is joined to it. Then rabbet the rear edges of posts (A) where the plywood back will be nailed to them. When this has been done, cut the front edge

of the post to an angle of 112½ degrees so the quarter columns may be joined to the 90-degree angle this will make when post (A), stile (B), capital and base blocks (Y), and the quarter columns are glued together.

Glue up, plane, and cut to shape the shelf, top,

Fig. 1. *Queen Anne Corner Cupboard.* A ROBERT TREATE HOGG REPRODUCTION.

and bottom of the lower section. If properly planned, not all boards for these need be cut the full length given for the shelves in the Bill of Material; some may be made shorter, like those shown in Fig. 7 on the drawings in Chapter 27 for the Carved-Shell Corner Cupboard. This is done to save material and avoid waste when cutting these members to shape. Still another way in which material may be saved when making these parts is to glue up boards long enough to make two or even three shelves. By drawing patterns on such a long piece so that fronts of alternate shelves—top, bottom, as the case may be—are on opposite edges of the board, even more material will be saved.

Once these three pieces have been cut to shape and the dovetails made on the ends of the shelf and floor, the shelf and floor may be fitted to the posts. No glue need be put on the joints to hold them, and should not be, for fear of not being able to slide the dovetails all the way into the grooves.

Make post (O) and nail or screw it to shelves (I). Make stile (D). Cut out the plywood backs and nail them to posts (A) and (O). Now mortise stiles (B). Make rails (C), and then cut the bead molding around the edges of (B) and (C). Cut tenons on both ends of (C), and a mortise to hold stile (D) into the middle of rail (C) above the doors. Glue together the frame, consisting of stiles (B) and rails (C). Then cut the 112½-degree angle on the outside edges of stiles (B).

Make partition (K) and drawer runs (N). A short ¾-inch square strip of wood is screwed to the front end on the short side of (K) to fasten (K) to the inside of (B). This is shown in Fig. 3. Screw these strips and drawer runs (N) to (K), after which (K) may be fastened to the backs of stiles (B) and to the plywood backs of the lower section with wood screws. Be sure (K) is squared to the front of the frame, so the drawer can be fitted to its opening without any trouble later on.

Now make partition (M), which acts as a drawer guide between the drawers. Make drawer run (L) and screw it fast to the bottom of (M). Then screw (M) and (L) to post (O) and to upper rail (C).

You are now ready to screw and nail the top to the rabbets on the tops of (A) and (B), and to (K), (M), and (O). Glue should also be used to

fasten the top of stile (D) to the mortise in the center of (J) at the front.

Glue up and turn the column from which the quarter columns are made. After splitting it into four parts, glue two of them and blocks (Y) to the corners that have been made for them.

Make and glue the ½″ x 1⅛″ x 34¼″ fill-in strip to the bottom of the floor and to the back of strip (C) under the doors. This strip is shown at the bottom of Fig. 3. Then make rails (E) and (F) in one long piece, cutting the molding on one edge on the shaper before you saw them apart. Fasten these three pieces together with glue and a corrugated fastener or two across each joint, as shown at the bottom of Fig. 3.

Now make the feet. On a two-by-four plank, 30 inches or more long, mold the front of the feet to the shape shown on the outside of (H) at the bottom of Fig. 2. Then cut the miter joint where the feet are glued together at the corners, and make ¼-inch grooves for the splines which help to hold them together. Cut recesses into the tops of the feet for the gusset blocks, which are used to help hold the two parts of the foot together and also to fasten the foot with wood screws to rails (E) and (F). Fasten rails (E) and (F) securely to the bottom of the lower section with wood screws. Some glue may also be used here, especially to fasten rails (F) to the bottoms of posts (A) and stiles (B). Then screw the feet to strips (E) and (F).

Now make the paneled doors. A detail drawing of these will be found in Fig. 11. Stiles for these doors are made first, and a corner of the inside edge on both stiles is rounded to form the quarter round where they and the outside of the panel meet. Grooves and mortises are then cut on the inside edges. The grooves measure ⅜″ x ⅜″. Because the ends of rails, where they fit against the quarter round on the stiles, would make a feather edge so thin it would be impossible to make good coped joints, the quarter-round molding on the stiles is trimmed off at an angle of 45 degrees where the quarter-round molding on the rails meets it. On the paneled doors it is done in the same way we show it in Fig. 9 of Chapter 30 for the doors of the Spice Cabinet. Make the rails, cut

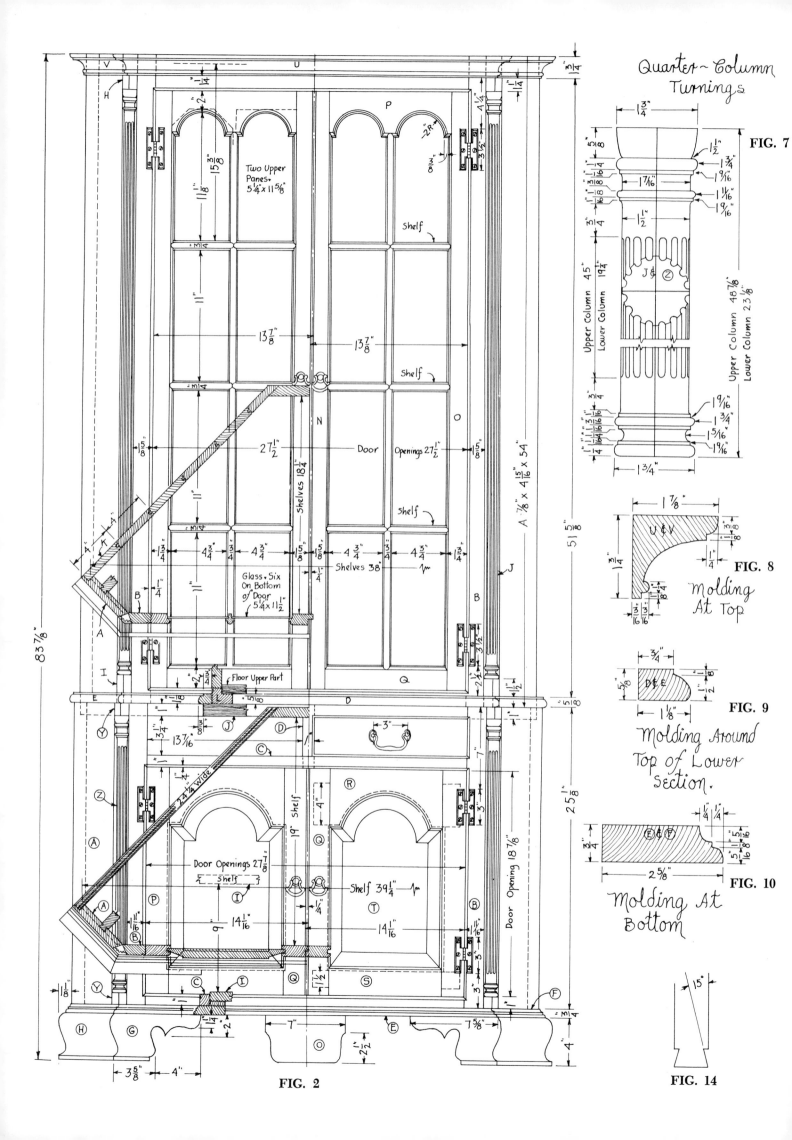

FIG. 2

Quarter~Column
Turnings

FIG. 7

U & V

Molding
At Top

FIG. 8

D & E

FIG. 9

Molding Around
Top of Lower
Section.

E & F

FIG. 10

Molding At
Bottom

15°

FIG. 14

an arch in the top rail (R), and shape the edge to a quarter round on the shaper, as you did the stiles. The groove into which the top of the arched panel fits should also be cut on the shaper.

Panels like these may be raised on the circular saw. Wing cutters for a shaper to make so wide a bevel would be very expensive and would require a very heavy shaper to use them. Straight shaper knives for this kind of cutting would not be at all safe to use, since their length would make them too likely to be thrown from the spindle. Such shaping is fairly easy to do on a circular saw, by tilting the blade as shown in Fig. 17 of Chapter 30 for the Spice Cabinet, though in this case the angle for tilting the saw will not be the same.

To raise these panels, keep the upper edge straight, across the top, and raise the panel on all four edges. Then draw the compass arcs needed, and band-saw the top of the panel to fit the arch on the upper rail. You may then finish the bevel around the curve with wood-carving chisels and wide, very sharp, straight chisels. Smooth up the surface of the bevel all the way around the panel with a sharp scraper blade, and afterward with fine sandpaper on a block of wood. When all members of the doors have been shaped up, and trial assemblies made to be sure they fit together properly, the doors may be glued up. On our dimensions the combined width of the two doors is ⅛ inch less than the opening provided for them. This is about right for the clearance needed to fit them into the opening without binding.

When the doors have been made and fitted to the lower section, get out stock to make the drawers. Drawers for corner cupboards, because of the triangular area into which they must be fitted, are somewhat more difficult to put together than those that are square all around. In many instances, in corner cupboards of this fine quality, such drawers have dovetail joints on all five places where sides and fronts are joined together. When this is the case, the dovetails on two of the joints are a little more difficult to lay out and make than the three joints that are dovetailed in the usual manner. The design of the drawers in this cupboard, taken from the reproduction shown in Fig. 1, has simple, easily made, notched joints, joining the two backs

to the sides. These joints are fastened together with glue and nails, which simplifies the construction considerably. With the details shown in Fig. 6, the construction of the drawers should prove not to be difficult. It should be mentioned in passing that the short side of the right-hand drawer will be on the opposite side from where it appears on our drawing of the left-hand drawer.

The molding shown in Fig. 9, which is fastened to the top of the lower section to hold the upper section in place, should not be made, or at least not be fastened to the lower section, until the upper section has been made. By waiting until then you will be able to make it fit both sections properly.

Start the upper section as you did the lower section, by making the end posts first. Follow the same directions given for doing the lower section so far as making the end posts A, stiles B, back post O, shelves F, and top G is concerned. Notice the bottom rail in the frame that forms the door opening is made with a rabbet at the back to support the floor, as shown at the bottom of the upper section in Fig. 3. The backs K, instead of being made of plywood, are made of matched tongue-and-grooved narrow-width boards. This may be seen quite clearly in the picture of the Sheraton Dining Table, in Chapter 16, which shows this cupboard in the background. This view with the doors open also shows the glass at the top of the doors covered by the wooden arching of rail (P) on the inside, just as it is on the outside of the door.

At the top of Fig. 2 we show two ways of cutting and fitting the upper panes of glass. It should be pointed out here that if a 2-inch-deep saw groove is made, to bring the upper edge of the glass ¼ inch above the arching on these doors, then these two panes of glass must be put into the frame when the frame is glued up. There are two objections to doing this: the first is that the glass must be covered with paper and masking tape while doing the finishing operation to avoid an arduous job of cleaning them up after the finish has been put on; and the second, and still greater, objection is of giving trouble if it should become necessary to replace one of these panes should it be broken.

There are three ways of avoiding these con-

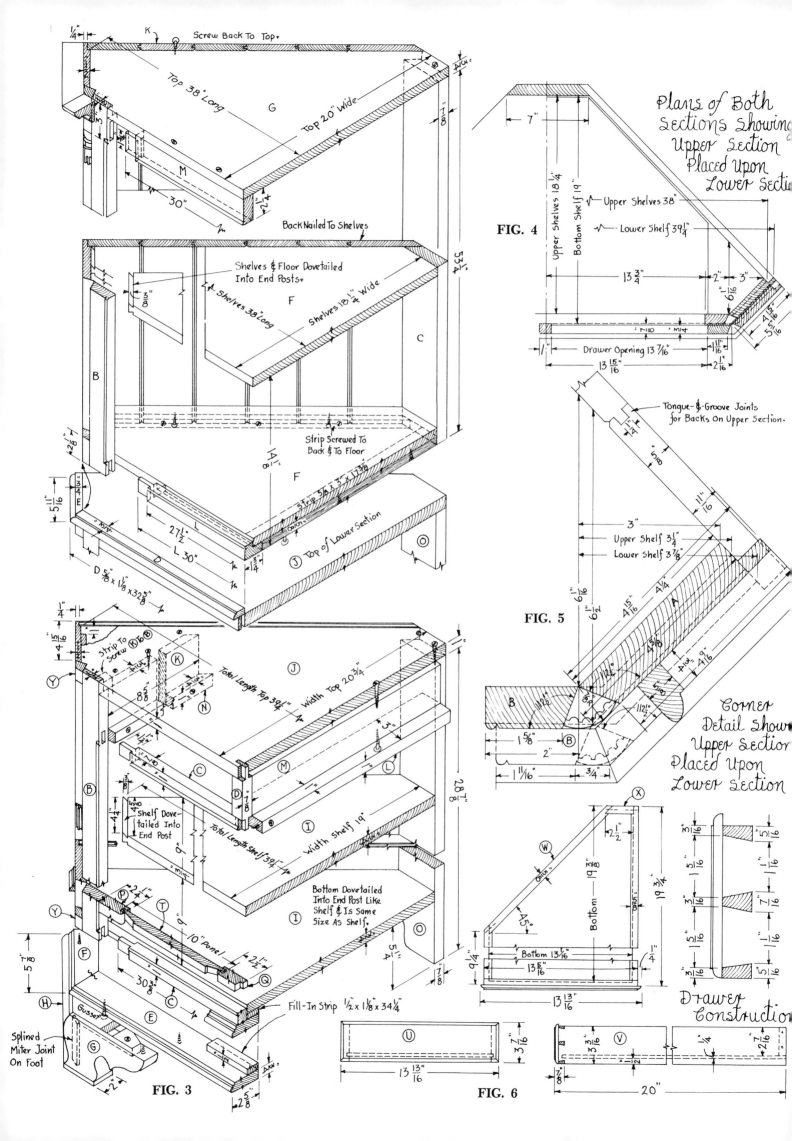

FIG. 4

FIG. 5

FIG. 3

FIG. 6

tingencies. 1. To cut the glass as we show it on the left in Fig. 2 on the left-hand door. 2. By lowering the surface on part of the back of rail (P) behind the arches so it is on a level with the surface on the muntins against which the glass rests, and afterward covering the glass with a thin board having arches cut into its lower edge like those on the outside of the door. These thin boards could be fastened with small brads and just a spot or two of glue, so they can be easily removed should a pane of glass be broken. 3. It is possible to cut the tops of panes of glass to conform to the arching, even including the two inside corners where the arch intersects the two straight lines. We do not advise trying this unless the person attempting it has had professional training as a glass cutter. At shops where custom work in glass cutting is done, such panes of glass may be purchased. Having these, arches on panes may be fastened with segmented quarter-round molding. Quarter-round

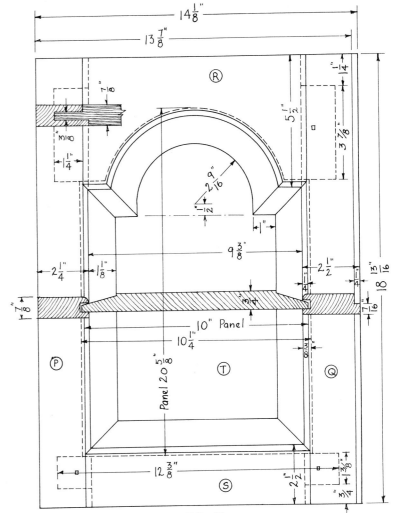

FIG. 11

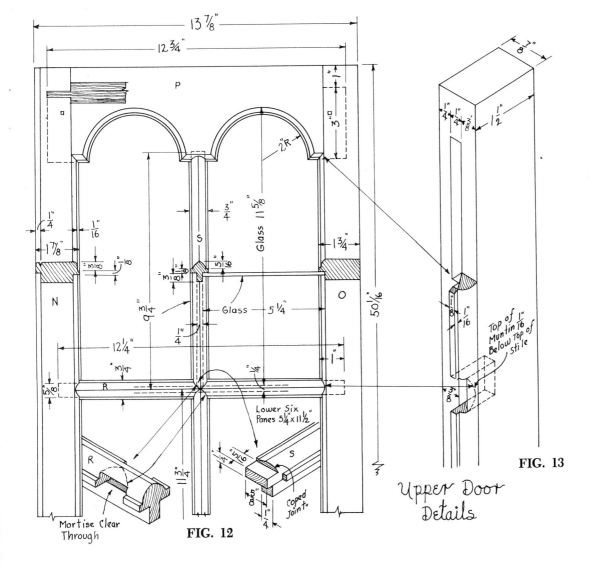

FIG. 12

FIG. 13

Upper Door Details

159

molding is used to fasten glass to the doors on this cupboard. Putty, which could be used, does not look as well.

On glazed doors like these, horizontal muntins should go all the way across the openings and should be tenoned deeply into the door stiles, as we show them in Fig. 12. Vertical muntins, in most doors having small panes of glass, usually are held in place with little more than the coping on the ends, which makes them fit over the molding on the outside of the other molding to which they are joined. The horizontal muntins are usually slightly notched to hold the ends in position, these ends going only far enough to butt against the rib in the middle on the inside of the horizontal molding.

The molding on these doors is a little different from the type used on window sash, which is often used on doors of this kind. Window-sash molding has a slightly raised flat surface on top, which makes it possible to design the coping on the ends of muntins and rails so that they fit over the molding to which they are joined without the ends of the coped member coming to a sharp point. They do so here on the ends of S and R, and they would come to a rough feather-thin edge if we coped the ends of P and Q. To avoid the likelihood of imperfect joints, the ends of rails P and Q have square shoulders back of the tenon, and the molding is trimmed to a miter at the joints, as shown at the top of Fig. 13. Ends of rails R and of muntins S are joined to other members in the manner shown at the bottom of Fig. 13, and in the large details shown in isometric at the bottom of Fig. 12.

When all joints have been made so the parts fit together properly, glue vertical muntins to rails P, Q, and R; then glue all rails to the door stiles.

Quarter columns are made in the same way for the upper section as were those for the lower section. They, and blocks H and I, should be glued to the posts and stiles. Molding like that shown in Fig. 8 should then be made and fastened around the top. Some glue may be used to hold the long piece of molding to the front, and also a few brads, where they will not show too much. Set the brad heads and glue small wooden pegs into the holes instead of using plastic wood or crack fillers, so the holes will show very little. Nail holes that show where the nail was driven, even after the holes are filled, should be avoided as much as possible on fine pieces of furniture like this corner cupboard.

Before permanently fastening the doors, make and fasten moldings D and E, shown in Fig. 9, to the top of the lower section. Then put on all necessary hardware, which should, however, be removed before putting on the finish. Putting glass into the doors is the final step, after all finishing operations have been completed.

BILL OF MATERIAL

LOWER SECTION

Mahogany

2 End posts (A) $\frac{7}{8}$" x $5\frac{5}{16}$" x $25\frac{1}{8}$"

2 Stiles, frame for doors (B) $\frac{7}{8}$" x $2\frac{1}{16}$" x $25\frac{1}{8}$"

2 Rails, frame for doors (C) $\frac{7}{8}$" x 1" x $30\frac{3}{8}$"

1 Short stile between drawers (D) $\frac{7}{8}$" x 1" x $5\frac{1}{4}$"

1 Molding-edged front rail above feet (E) $\frac{3}{4}$" x $2\frac{5}{8}$" x $33\frac{1}{8}$"

2 Molding-edged rails above feet (F) $\frac{3}{4}$" x $2\frac{5}{8}$" x $5\frac{7}{8}$"

2 Blocks for front of feet (G) 2" x 4" x $7\frac{5}{8}$"

2 Blocks for ends of feet (H) 2" x 4" x $6\frac{3}{16}$"

1 Bottom and 1 shelf (I) 2 pieces $\frac{3}{4}$" x 19" x $39\frac{1}{4}$" *

1 Top of lower section (J) $\frac{3}{4}$" x $20\frac{3}{4}$" x $39\frac{1}{4}$" *

2 Partitions in corners to guide drawers (K) $\frac{3}{4}$" x $4\frac{1}{4}$" x $8\frac{5}{8}$"

1 Drawer run (L) 1" x 3" x $19\frac{7}{8}$"

1 Partition between drawers (M) 1" x $3\frac{1}{4}$" x $19\frac{7}{8}$"

2 Drawer runs (N) $\frac{3}{4}$" x 1" x $9\frac{11}{16}$"

1 Back post for lower section (O) $\frac{7}{8}$" x 7" x $28\frac{7}{8}$"

2 Door stiles for paneled doors (P) $\frac{7}{8}$" x $2\frac{1}{4}$" x $18\frac{13}{16}$"

---

* Glued up of several narrower pieces of wood.

2 Door stiles for paneled doors (Q) ⅞" x 2½" x 18¹³⁄₁₆"

2 Door rails for paneled doors (R) ⅞" x 5½" x 12⅜"

2 Door rails for paneled doors (S) ⅞" x 2½" x 12⅜"

2 Door panels (T) ¾" x 10" x 20⅝"

2 Drawer fronts (U) ⅞" x 3⁷⁄₁₆" x 13¹³⁄₁₆"

2 Drawer sides (V) ⅝" x 3³⁄₁₆" x 19¾"

2 Drawer sides (W) ⅝" x 3³⁄₁₆" x 10³⁄₁₆"

2 Drawer backs (X) ⅝" x 2⁷⁄₁₆" x 2½"

4 Capital and base blocks (Y) ¹⁵⁄₁₆" x 1⅜" x 1"

Plywood

2 Drawer bottoms ¼" x 13¹⁄₁₆" x 19⅜"

2 Backs of lower section ⅝" x 24¼" x 24⅝"

UPPER SECTION

Mahogany

2 End posts A ⅞" x 4¹⁵⁄₁₆" x 54"

2 Stiles to which doors are fastened B ⅞" x 2" x 54"

1 Back post C ⅞" x 7" x 53¼"

1 Molding strip fastened to top of lower section to hold upper section D ⅝" x 1⅛" x 32⅝"

2 Molding strips E ⅝" x 1⅛" x 5¹¹⁄₁₆"

4 Shelves and floor F ¾" x 18¼" x 38"

1 Top G ¾" x 20" x 38"

2 Capital blocks H ¹⁵⁄₁₆" x 1⅜" x 3"

2 Base blocks I ¹⁵⁄₁₆" x 1⅜" x 2⅛"

2 Quarter columns J from 4 pcs. ⅞" x ⅞" x 48⅞" ⁕

2 Backs for upper section K ⅝" x 23¼" x 54" †

1 Bottom rail L ⅞" x 1¾" x 30"

1 Top rail M ⅞" x 2¼" x 30"

2 Door stiles N ⅞" x 1⅞" x 50¹⁄₁₆"

2 Door stiles O ⅞" x 1¾" x 50¹⁄₁₆"

2 Door rails P ⅞" x 4" x 12¾"

2 Door rails Q ⅞" x 2" x 12¾"

6 Horizontal muntins R ⅞" x ¾" x 12¼"

2 Vertical muntins S ⅞" x ¾" x 9¾"

6 Vertical muntins T ⅞" x ¾" x 11¾"

Molding at top U 1¾" x 1⅞" x 33¾"

Molding at top V 1¾" x 1⅞" x 6⅛"

⁕ Glue brown wrapping paper between each strip and, after turning, split apart.

† Made of separate tongue-and-grooved boards about 4 inches wide.

TWENTY-NINE

Silver Chest

SILVER chests usually come in small sizes, most of them being mere boxes to be set on top of a sideboard or stored in a drawer. This one is a much larger piece of furniture, and the storage area is much greater. It should hold all of the flat silverware anyone will need and have room for trays and even low pieces of hollow ware.

Should one wish to store taller pieces of hollow ware than these drawers will hold, it would be easy to modify the design and build a high drawer at the bottom to take the place of the two shallow ones. Should this be done, lines to simulate the dividing lines between drawers and rail could be cut into the wide drawer front to keep the design as nearly like the one shown in Fig. 1 as possible. By doing this the more satisfactory spacing of areas shown in Fig. 1 will not be noticeably altered. This change would then provide storage space about 7 inches high in the lower drawer instead of the 3-inch maximum provided by the lower drawer shown in our drawings.

This chest goes best in a room furnished in the Hepplewhite style, though it may be used in a room with any of the traditional eighteenth-century styles, and especially with the plainer American adaptations of these styles.

To build the silver chest, first cut out the four legs (A). Plane, square, and sand them to the size given in the Bill of Material. Then make layouts to cut mortises, and cut these, using a mortising machine, or by the best available means. Legs are tapered on only two sides, as shown in the drawings, and when this has been done and these sides smoothed with sandpaper, cut out, plane, square, and sandpaper rails (B) and (C).

Lay out and cut tenons on these rails, and fit them to the leg mortises. Then glue legs and rails together to make the base.

Now glue up two ends (D) and top (E). Plane, square, and sand these to the sizes given in the Bill of Material. Back edges of ends (D) should be rabbeted to hold the back of the chest, which may be made of ¼-inch plywood.

When rabbets have been cut, make layouts for the gains at the back and for shallow mortises near

Fig. 1. *Silver Chest.* A ROBERT TREATE HOGG REPRODUCTION.

the front on the insides of end boards (D), to which the frames supporting the drawers are joined. These are clearly shown and dimensioned in Fig. 5. Cut these as shown. Some of this work may be done with an electric hand router, but it may be almost as easily done entirely by hand with chisel and mallet, since final trimming around the edges will have to be done this way anyhow.

When the work on the ends has been completed as described above, make the five frames on which the drawers slide in and out. Notice that the upper frame is made of thicker pieces than the four lower frames, since a cove molding put on three sides of the chest under the top covers part of the front rail on this frame. Saw out, plane, and square up front rails (F) and (G), back rails (L) and (N), and end rails (M) and (O). Make layouts for mortises and tenons to put these together. When all are ready, glue up the five frames. Holes for wood screws, to fasten the frames to the ends of the chest on the inside, may be drilled and countersunk before gluing the frames together. Holes for wood screws to fasten the top to the upper frame should also be drilled through rails (O) at this time.

Sandpaper all frames and make sure the top and bottom of every frame is perfectly flat, so drawers will slide easily when this structure, consisting of ends (D) and the five frames, is put together. Then glue and screw the frames to the two ends of the chest. Glue is used only on mortises, gains, and tenons formed at both ends of the frames by extending rails (F) and (G), and by sawing out the two front corners of each front rail, as shown in Fig. 5. Edges of the end rails are not glued to the ends of the chest but are fastened to it with wood screws. If these were glued fast it would cause ends (D) to split apart.

Strips of wood (P) and (Q) are screwed to the inside of the rails at the top of the base. Wood screws through these strips into the bottom frame and ends (D) hold the two parts together.

Molding like that shown in Fig. 8 should now be cut on three edges of top (E), and this top should then be fastened to the upper frame with wood screws, as shown in Fig. 5. An offset screwdriver may be used to do this. If shaper-cutters to make this molding are not available, it can be roughed out on the circular saw and finished with chisels,

spokeshave, and sandpaper, with very little trouble.

Cutters to make the molding shown in Fig. 9, fastened where the base is joined to the part that holds the drawers, and the cove molding under the top are usually to be found in shops having a shaper. Such moldings may be cut on one or both edges of fairly wide strips of wood, or boards, in the home workshop, and then ripped off on the circular saw. If a planing mill is close at hand, perhaps they can be purchased at a reasonable price. If no better way of making or acquiring them can be found, they may be roughed out on the table saw and then finished off by hand with wood-carving chisels. When completed and sanded, they should be nailed to the chest with brads and small finish nails. Nailheads should be set, and the holes filled with pegs of wood or with mahogany-colored plastic wood or crack filler.

Make the drawers. Fronts and backs are dovetailed to the drawer sides, as shown in Fig. 7. These drawers are fairly easy to make because they have no protruding lip on the drawer front. Lay out and cut dovetails on the drawer sides first. Layouts for these will not be alike on all four drawers since drawer fronts and sides are not all alike in width; but by using the methods for laying out dovetail joints described in Chapter 1, the builder of this chest should have little trouble.

Dovetails on the drawer sides may be cut to shape on the band saw. True up saw cuts with a sharp chisel if necessary. Then place each dovetail on the end of the drawer front and drawer back to which it is to be joined and, with a sharp knife blade or scriber, trace its outline on these ends for cutting.

Use a dovetail saw to start these cuts on each drawer front and each drawer back. The cutting on the drawer back joints, to saw out the remaining waste, may be almost entirely completed on the band saw if the band saw table is tilted to remove the waste between the pins. But on the drawer fronts, after outlining the pins with the dovetail saw along the lines made on the drawer front ends and down the inside, the remaining waste must be removed with a sharp chisel. Use a thin-bladed chisel on which the edges are beveled for this part of the work.

When dovetail joints have been made and fitted,

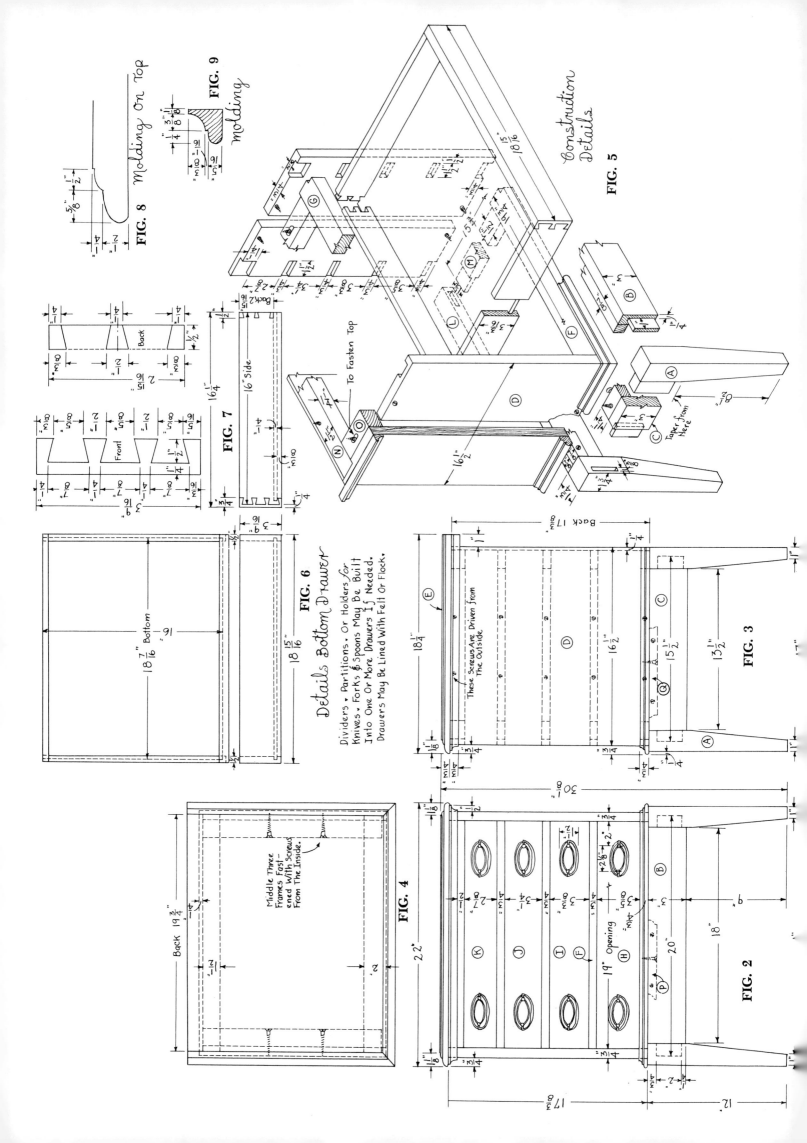

FIG. 8 Molding On Top

FIG. 9 Molding

FIG. 7

FIG. 6

Details Bottom Drawer

Dividers, Partitions, Or Holders for Knives, Forks & Spoons May Be Built Into One Or More Drawers If Needed. Drawers May Be Lined With Felt Or Flock.

FIG. 5 Construction Details

To Fasten Top

FIG. 4

Middle Three Frames Fastened With Screws From The Inside.

Back 19¾"

FIG. 3

These Screws Are Driven From The Outside.

Back 17⅜"

FIG. 2

19" Opening

20"

cut grooves into drawer fronts and sides, to hold the drawer bottoms. Glue drawer bottoms to the grooves in the drawer fronts only, and hold them in place with nails driven through them into the lower edges of the drawer backs. Triangular-shaped glue blocks may be used under each drawer bottom to hold the sides and bottoms together. Wood grain on drawer bottoms should run from one side of the drawer to the other.

Be sure each drawer fits into its respective opening, so it will slide easily even after a coat or two of shellac or other finish has been applied to the drawer sides on the outside. Insides of these drawers may have felt glued to them or may be surfaced with flocking. One can easily blow this on with an inexpensive flocking gun, after first coating the sur-face with a special paint to which the flocking will adhere while the paint is still wet or tacky. Strips of wood, with slots cut partway through across one side, to hold knives, forks, and spoons, may be made and nailed or glued fast to the inside of one or more of the drawers before felt or flocking is put on. If felt or flocking is to be used, no other finish except the glue, or special paint to hold these, should be applied to the inside of the drawer.

When all drawers have been fitted and you are sure they will slide easily, the back may be made and nailed fast to the rabbets that were cut for them in ends (D), and also to the back rail of each frame. Small nails with heads are best here.

Now drill holes and fasten drawer pulls. These must be removed when putting on the finish.

BILL OF MATERIAL

Mahogany

4 Legs (A) 1¾" x 1¾" x 12"
Front and back rails on base (B) ⅞" x 3" x 20"
2 End rails on base (C) ⅞" x 3" x 15½"
2 Ends (D) ¾" x 16½" x 17⅜"
1 Top (E) ¾" x 18¼" x 22"
4 Front rails in bottom four frames (F) ¾" x 2" x 19¾"
1 Front rail in upper frame (G) 1¼" x 2" x 19¾"
1 Lower drawer front (H) ¾" x 3⁹⁄₁₆" x 18¹⁵⁄₁₆"
1 Drawer front (I) ¾" x 3⁵⁄₁₆" x 18¹⁵⁄₁₆"
1 Drawer front (J) ¾" x 3³⁄₁₆" x 18¹⁵⁄₁₆"
1 Upper drawer front (K) ¾" x 2¹³⁄₁₆" x 18¹⁵⁄₁₆"
Molding below lower drawer ¾" x ¾" x 60" approx.
Molding under top ½" x ¾" x 60" approx.

Poplar *

4 Back rails for frames (L) ¾" x 1½" x 19¾"

* Mahogany may be used instead of poplar for drawer sides and backs if so desired.

8 End rails for frames (M) ¾" x 1½" x 15¾"
1 Back rail upper frame (N) 1¼" x 1½" x 19¾"
2 End rails upper frame (O) 1¼" x 1½" x 15¾"
2 Strips to join base to upper part (P) ⅞" x ⅞" x 18"
2 Strips to join base to upper part (Q) ⅞" x 1¼" x 13½"
2 Drawer sides ½" x 3⁹⁄₁₆" x 16"
2 Drawer sides ½" x 3⁵⁄₁₆" x 16"
2 Drawer sides ½" x 3³⁄₁₆" x 16"
2 Drawer sides ½" x 2¹³⁄₁₆" x 16"
1 Drawer back ½" x 2¹⁵⁄₁₆" x 18¹⁵⁄₁₆"
1 Drawer back ½" x 2¹¹⁄₁₆" x 18¹⁵⁄₁₆"
1 Drawer back ½" x 2⁹⁄₁₆" x 18¹⁵⁄₁₆"
1 Drawer back ½" x 2³⁄₁₆" x 18¹⁵⁄₁₆"

Birch or Mahogany-veneered Plywood

1 Back ¼" x 17⅜" x 19¾"
4 Drawer bottoms ¼" x 16" x 18⁷⁄₁₆"

THIRTY

Spice Cabinet

THIS is an unusual design for a spice cabinet in the Queen Anne style. Built of black walnut and exquisitely styled, it is a veritable gem taken from an original design by an unknown artisan of long ago.

As spice cabinets go its size is generous, for pieces of furniture used for this purpose more often than not consisted of a small number of drawers in a frame or cabinet of no great size, hung on the kitchen wall. This one was made something special; if reproduced for present-day use, it is conceivable it might be put to an entirely different use from the one originally planned for it.

To build it, first make legs (A) for the lower part. Cut out, plane, and square up four pieces of the best black walnut you can find, measuring 2" x 2" x 14½". Then from the drawing shown in Fig. 10 make a full-sized pattern and trace this on two opposite sides of each leg. Do not include blocks (B), which will be glued to the legs after all carving, shaping, and mortising has been completed on all four legs. Cut the waste off both sides of the leg, but do it carefully and save the two pieces designated as "waste" in Fig. 10. These two pieces of waste you will want to tack back on each leg with small brads, and on them trace the pattern to saw out the last two sides of each leg.

On the left side of the leg pattern in Fig. 10, we have drawn a broken line to saw to when you do the band sawing, so as to keep enough wood to carve the molding that goes around two sides of the ankle. It is better to carve the molding to shape than it is to attempt to saw it to shape when cutting out the leg.

When all four sides of each leg have been sawed to shape, smooth the surfaces above the molding. This is best done with a sharp chisel. Use a chisel ¾ inch or more in width to do this smoothing up. Then draw lines to carve the foot and ankle, and when these have been completed, sandpaper the curved parts of the leg carefully but thoroughly. Use very fine (6/0) open-coat garnet paper to finish the sanding.

Lay out and cut mortises in all four legs. These mortises will be alike on both sides, where mortises

Fig. 1. Spice Cabinet. A ROBERT TREATE HOGG REPRODUCTION.

go, on the two back legs, and on one side of each front leg. They will be laid out as shown on the square section of the leg at the top of Fig. 7. The front legs have a dovetail mortise cut into their tops for the joint with rail (H). Below this on the same side of the leg are two mortises to which rails (F) and (G) are joined.

When all mortises have been cut, glue blocks (B) to the legs. These should be left square on all six sides until glued fast, after which they may be shaped as shown in the drawings.

Now cut out, plane, and sand ends (C), back (D), and rails (F), (G), and (H). Lay out and cut tenons on both ends of these and make and fit the dovetail to join (H) to the tops of both front legs.

The four drawers in the lower section of the cabinet are supported on drawer runs (J) and (K), screwed fast to ends (C) on the inside; and to drawer runs (L) and (M), screwed to a partition board (E). Above the two upper drawers a ⅝″ x 12¼″ x 15¼″ board (I) is fastened with nails driven through the ends (C), and through back (D) near the top edges. At the ends, these nail-heads should be covered by the ⅜-inch molding that is put on under the larger molding that divides the upper from the lower section. Board (I) should be glued to the back edge of rail (H) before both are fastened to the frame.

Partition board (E) should be made and put in place when the lower frame is put together. The front edge of (E) is notched out to fit over rails (F) and (G).

When all members comprising the lower section have been made and joints fitted, a trial assembly should be made to be sure everything is in readiness for gluing. To do this proceed as follows:

First glue legs and ends (C) together. Then fasten drawer runs and guides (J) and (K) to ends (C) with wood screws, as shown in Fig. 7. The position of these drawer runs should be carefully marked when making the trial assembly so they will line up exactly with rails (F) and (G). Screw rails (L) and (M) to both sides of partition (E). Put partition (E) in place over rail (G), and then glue rails (D), (G), and (F) to the assembled ends; at the same time fasten the back edge of (E)

Fig. 2. *Spice Cabinet with Doors Open.*

to back (D) with wood screws. Partition (E) should not be glued to rails (F) and (G), for it will be held in place at the front by wood screws used to fasten the strip (O-1) to board (I). These wood screws should be #8, at least 1½ inches long. Small glue blocks may be rubbed on at the back of (F) after the frame has been assembled. These glue blocks do not appear in our drawings. Now glue rail (H) and board (I), which has been glued to (H), to the front legs and fasten with nails to ends (C) and back (D). Holes should be drilled for these nails so they do not split board (I). Screw strips (O-1) to the top of (I) and to partition (E), as shown in Fig. 7. Except for the drawers, the lower part has now been completed.

To make the upper section, first glue up ends (P), top (Q), bottom (R), and the four boards

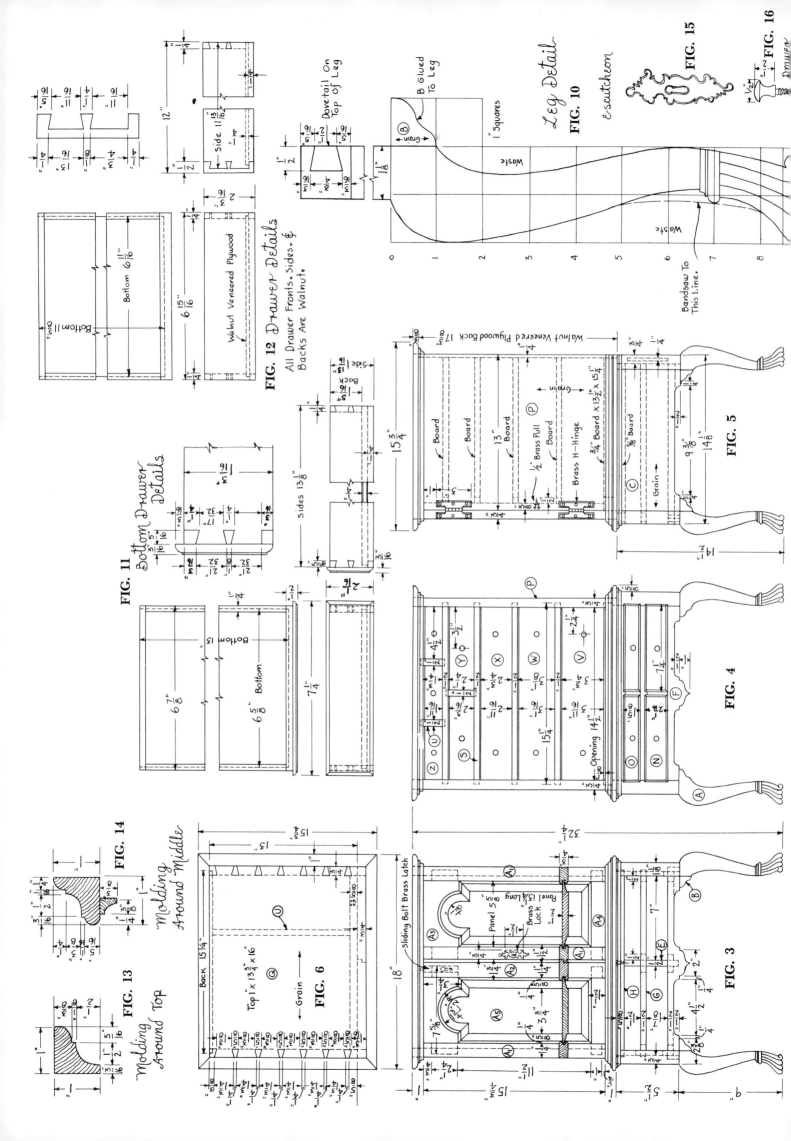

FIG. 12 Drawer Details

All Drawer Fronts, Sides & Backs Are Walnut.

Dovetail On Top of Leg

Leg Detail
FIG. 10

Escutcheon
FIG. 15

FIG. 16

Bottom Drawer Details
FIG. 11

Molding Around Middle
FIG. 14

Molding Around Top
FIG. 13

FIG. 6

FIG. 5

FIG. 4

FIG. 3

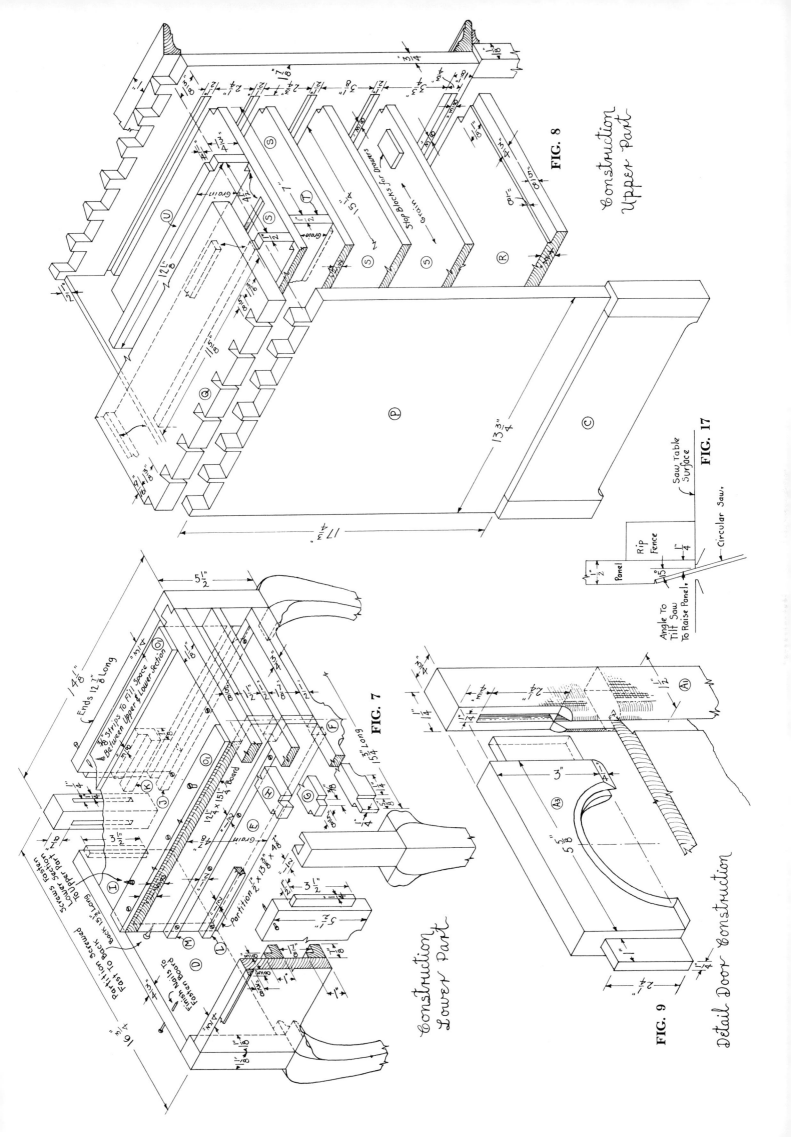

FIG. 8

Construction
Upper Part

FIG. 17

FIG. 7

Construction
Lower Part

FIG. 9

Detail Door Construction

(S). Also cut out partitions (T) and (U). A board 12⅛ inches wide and about 8 inches long may be cut apart to make these three partitions. Plane, square up, and sand all of the above pieces to the sizes given in the Bill of Material.

Lay out grooves on the inside of both ends (P), so the ends of boards (S), which support the drawers, may be glued to the ends of the cabinet. Grooves should also be laid out on the upper two (S)-boards: two grooves on the upper side, and one in the center of the lower side of the top (S)-board; one groove on the upper side of the second (S)-board to hold partitions (T) and (U). Two grooves to hold the top of (U) should be laid out on the lower side of top (Q). All of these grooves may be cut out with a portable electric hand router as shown being done in Fig. 33, Chapter 1. Or it may be done with a dado head mounted on a radial-arm saw or on a table saw. No matter which method is used, the grooves must be finished by hand with a chisel and mallet, where they are stopped in front.

When the grooves have been routed out, cut rabbets on the back edges of the top (Q) and the ends (P), to fasten and hold the back of the cabinet, which should be a ¼-inch piece of walnut-veneered plywood. This rabbet may be cut the full length of top (Q), but those on the back edges of (P) must be stopped ½ inch short of the tops, as shown in Fig. 8.

Now cut front corners out of boards (S) and (R), and cut the shallow rabbet on the front edge of board (R) to make a doorstop. Make a trial assembly of ends (P), boards (S) and (R), and partitions (T) and (U).

Make layouts for the dovetail joints. The layouts for these are dimensioned in Fig. 6, and how they look when cut out may be seen at the top of Fig. 8. To cut the dovetails on top (Q), the circular saw may be tilted to outline the angles of the dovetails, and then the remaining waste may be removed with the saw in its usual vertical position in the table saw. Mr. Hogg, who builds these beautiful spice cabinets in his shop, tells me he cuts this part of the dovetail with dado-head spacer knives, ground to the proper angles and used in the table saw, and they do a beautiful job.

The dovetail pins on ends (P) may be cut by placing this end on the saw table with (P) held vertically against a crosscut fence that has been set at the proper angle. Such setups should first be tried on pieces of scrap wood to make sure they are correct. For setups and ways of doing this, see Chapter 1. With care, all of the sawing on (Q) and most of the sawing on (P), to make these dovetails, may be done on the band saw, an alternate method of doing it.

When all joints go together as they should, glue partition (T) to the upper two (S)-boards. Then glue the ends of the (S)- and (R)-boards to the grooves in ends (P). Also glue the lower ends of partitions (U) into the grooves where they belong. Then fasten ends (P) to top (Q) by gluing the dovetail joints together.

It will be found best to make and fit the drawers before fastening the back to the upper part of the cabinet. At this time, however, the upper part may be fastened to the base, which has already been assembled. Fasten the two together with wood screws from below, through board (I) into board (R).

Make the molding to go around the middle and around the top on three sides. Such molding may be roughed out on the table saw and finished with wood chisels and carving chisels if it cannot be made on a shaper. Details of these moldings will be found in Figs. 13 and 14.

The drawers should now be made. First cut out stock for fronts, sides, and backs. Plane, square, and sand these to the sizes given in the Bill of Material. The four drawers in the lower section have lips on three edges of each drawer front; cutting dovetails on these will be slightly more difficult than it will be to cut them on the drawer fronts in the top section. Layouts for two of the drawers are shown in Figs. 11 and 12, and if the steps for doing dovetailing given in Chapter 1 are followed, the person doing it should have little or no trouble with the remaining drawers.

After all dovetails have been made and the joints fit together properly, cut grooves on one side of the drawer sides and fronts to hold drawer bottoms. This is most easily done on the table saw with a dado head. Make a trial assembly of each drawer, and be sure it will slide in and out easily before gluing the joints. Glue the drawer bottoms into the grooves in the drawer fronts only. When fully assembled, small nails with heads may be used to fasten drawer bottoms to the lower edges of the drawer backs. About four glue blocks shaped like a triglyph may be rubbed fast with glue to the bottoms and sides of each drawer under the drawer bottom, to reinforce it and help to hold it together.

You should now be ready to make the doors. On these the joining of the arched panels to the upper rails, and forming the arch and groove to hold the panel, will be the most difficult part of the work.

First get out all door stock, consisting of four stiles, two upper and two lower rails, and two panels. On the four stiles, cut grooves from the middle of the mortise on one end to the middle of the mortise on the other end, to hold the panels. Then on these same edges lay out and cut the mortises. Details for laying these out will be found on Figs. 3 and 9. Cut grooves to hold panels on the rails, from one end to the other, on the edges to which the panels are to be joined. On the top rails (A-3), this groove should be cut all the way across before the arch is formed. Now cut miters as deep as you have made the grooves on rails and stiles, to make the miter joint on the quarter-round molding which is to be cut on both sides of the groove, clear around the inside of the doorframe. This miter joint, at the top of a door, is clearly shown in Fig. 9 at top right, as is the quarter-round shape of the molding. At the top of the door this miter joint starts 3 inches from the top of stile (A-1). When the miter joints have been made, lay out for tenons on the rails and cut them, then fit them to the mortises in the stiles. Now, using a compass set to a 1¾-inch radius, describe arcs on the lower edges of door rails (A-3) and saw these to shape on the band saw. After smoothing the edges of these arches with sandpaper, cut grooves into the arched edges to hold the tops of the panels. Do this on the shaper with a shaper-cutter, the cutting edge of which is ¼ inch wide, and set the machine to cut a groove ¼ inch deep. When this has been done, put in a shaper-cutter to make the quarter-round molding on both sides of the grooves that hold the panels, and shape this molding.

When the doorframe rails and stiles have been made, make the panels. Boards for these are first cut to the proper length and width, and after sanding them on both sides, a groove about ⅟₁₆ inch deep, and as wide as a circular saw blade will make it, is cut around all four edges of these panels on the face side. Cut these grooves by raising the teeth of the saw only ⅟₁₆ inch above the saw table. The inside edges of the grooves should be ⅞ inch from the four edges of the panel on the face side. Now tilt the table saw to an angle of 15 degrees, and raise it to a height of just under ⅞ inch, to raise the panels on all four edges, including the upper edge which is not yet rounded to fit the arch in the top rail of the door. With a compass set to a radius of 2 inches, draw arcs to round the tops of the panels, and complete the layout for the upper end as we show it in Fig. 3. Saw the tops of the panels to shape on the band saw, and then with wood-carving chisels finish shaping the panel on top so it will fit into the arched groove that was made to hold it. Sandpaper all surfaces smooth. A great deal of smoothing can be done with properly sharpened hand-scraper blades on the beveled edges cut by the saw when it was set at the 15-degree angle. The cutting edge of the hand-scraper blade should be turned with a burnishing tool, and this scraping should be done before these surfaces are sandpapered.

When trial assemblies of the two doors have been made and everything fits properly, the rails and stiles may be glued together, with the panels in place, of course. No glue is put into grooves that hold the panels, but on mortise-and-tenon joints only.

When the doors have been glued up, and joints cleaned and sanded smooth, both doors may be rabbeted to close them together in the center, as shown in Fig. 3.

The way these doors are fastened with H hinges to the cabinet is a bit unusual, but quite easy to do. Put a sliding bolt on the left-hand door at the top to fasten it when closed, and a lock on the right-hand door to keep it closed. Drill pilot holes and screw the small drawer knobs to the drawers. This completes the building of the Spice Cabinet. Remove hardware to put on the finish.

BILL OF MATERIAL

LOWER SECTION

Black Walnut

4 Legs (A) 2″ x 2″ x 14½″
8 Blocks to glue to legs (B) 1″ x 2″ x 1″
2 Ends (C) ¾″ x 5½″ x 12⅞″
1 Back (D) ¾″ x 5½″ x 15½″
1 Partition (E) ½″ x 13⅜″ x 4⅞″
1 Bottom rail (F) ¾″ x 2″ x 15¾″
1 Middle rail (G) ½″ x 1⅛″ x 15¼″
1 Upper rail (H) ⅝″ x 1⅛″ x 15½″
1 Board for top (I) ⅝″ x 12¼″ x 15¼″
2 Drawer runs (J) ⅞″ x 1″ x 12⅝″
2 Drawer runs (K) ⅞″ x 1″ x 12¼″
2 Drawer runs (L) ½″ x ½″ x 12⅝″
2 Drawer runs (M) ½″ x ½″ x 12¼″
2 Drawer fronts (N) ½″ x 2⅙″ x 7¼″
2 Drawer fronts (O) ½″ x 1⅝″ x 7¼″
4 Drawer sides ¼″ x 1¹³⁄₁₆″ x 13⅛″
4 Drawer sides ¼″ x 1⁷⁄₁₆″ x 13⅛″
2 Drawer backs ¼″ x 1⁵⁄₁₆″ x 6⅞″
2 Drawer backs ¼″ x ¹⁵⁄₁₆″ x 6⅞″
4 Drawer bottoms (walnut-veneered plywood) ¼″ x 6⅝″ x 13″
3 Fill-in strips between upper and lower sections (O-1) ⅜″ x 2″ or wider x 12¼″

UPPER SECTION

2 Ends (P) ¾″ x 13¾″ x 17¾″
1 Top (Q) 1″ x 13¾″ x 16″
1 Bottom (R) ¾″ x 13½″ x 15¼″
4 Boards (S) ½″ x 12⅛″ x 15¼″
1 Partition (T) ½″ x 12⅛″ x 2¾″
2 Partitions (U) ½″ x 12⅛″ x 2¼″

1 Drawer front (V) ½″ x 3¹¹⁄₁₆″ x 14⁷⁄₁₆″
1 Drawer front (W) ½″ x 3¹⁄₁₆″ x 14⁷⁄₁₆″
1 Drawer front (X) ½″ x 2¹¹⁄₁₆″ x 14⁷⁄₁₆″
2 Drawer fronts (Y) ½″ x 2³⁄₁₆″ 6¹⁵⁄₁₆″
3 Drawer fronts (Z) ½″ x 1¹¹⁄₁₆″ x 4⁷⁄₁₆″
2 Drawer sides ¼″ x 3¹¹⁄₁₆″ x 11¹³⁄₁₆″
2 Drawer sides ¼″ x 3¹⁄₁₆″ x 11¹³⁄₁₆″
2 Drawer sides ¼″ x 2¹¹⁄₁₆″ x 11¹³⁄₁₆″
4 Drawer sides ¼″ x 2³⁄₁₆″ x 11¹³⁄₁₆″
6 Drawer sides ¼″ x 1¹¹⁄₁₆″ x 11¹³⁄₁₆″
1 Drawer back ¼″ x 3³⁄₁₆″ x 14⁷⁄₁₆″
1 Drawer back ¼″ x 2⁹⁄₁₆″ x 14⁷⁄₁₆″
1 Drawer back ¼″ x 2³⁄₁₆″ x 14⁷⁄₁₆″
2 Drawer backs ¼″ x 1¹¹⁄₁₆″ x 6¹⁵⁄₁₆″
3 Drawer backs ¼″ x 1³⁄₁₆″ x 4⁷⁄₁₆″
3 Drawer bottoms (walnut-veneered plywood ¼″ x 11⅝″ x 14³⁄₁₆″
2 Drawer bottoms (walnut-veneered plywood) ¼″ x 6¹¹⁄₁₆″ x 11⅝″
3 Drawer bottoms (walnut-veneered plywood) ¼″ x 4³⁄₁₆″ x 11⅝″
3 Stiles (A-1) ¾″ x 1½″ x 15¾″
1 Stile (A-2) ¾″ x 1¾″ x 15¾″
2 Rails (A-3) ¾″ x 3¼″ x 7⅝″
2 Rails (A-4) ¾″ x 1½″ x 7⅝″
2 Panels (A-5) ½″ x 5⅝″ x 13¼″

Back and Molding

1 Back (walnut-veneered plywood) ¼″ x 15¼″ x 17⅜″
Molding around top 1″ x 1″ x 70″ approx.
Molding around middle 1″ x 1″ x 50″ approx.
Cove molding under molding around middle ⅜″ x ⅜″ x 50″ approx.

THIRTY-ONE

Bachelor's Chest

THE Bachelor's Chest, an intriguing small piece of furniture of a design adapted from a diminutive chest of drawers, is made to hold and hide from view a telephone in its upper drawer. The area back of the upper drawer is left without a back to permit telephone wires to be hidden behind the chest. A writing board above the upper drawer is very conveniently located for taking notes. At the bottom are two drawers of the conventional type which provide considerable storage space.

The chest is Chippendale, or what is generally accepted as an American interpretation of this style and period, as evidenced by the fluted quarter columns, ogee bracket feet, the richly figured mahogany wood, and the type of drawer pulls used. Not a very large piece of furniture, the Bachelor's Chest is ideally suited to the requirements imposed by space limitations and restrictions frequently encountered by dwellers in apartments and small houses.

To build it, first glue up two ends and plane, square, and sand them to the sizes given in the Bill of Material. At the lower ends cut these to the shape shown at bottom left in Fig. 6. Then rabbet the edges at the back to the height needed for the plywood back that goes behind the two bottom drawers of the chest. Rout out short gains to support the back rails of the frames that support the drawers and hold the writing board.

Get out stock for two stiles (B). Two sides of these are cut away at the bottom to keep from showing behind the front feet. Stopped grooves and gains are routed out on these on the inside to support front rails of the frames that hold drawers

and writing board. These grooves and gains, their position, sizes, and shapes, may be easily determined by a study of these details in Fig. 6. Once completed, stiles (B) should be screwed fast to ends (A) at the front, forming the corners into which the quarter columns will be fastened later on.

Frames to hold the drawers and writing board should now be made. Saw out, plane, and square these to the sizes given in the Bill of Material for front rails (G), (H), (I), back rails (O), (P), (Q), and end rails (R), (S), and (T). Lay out and cut mortises into all front and back rails at both ends, and then lay out and cut tenons on all end rails and fit these to their respective mortises. Drill holes for wood screws through the end rails to fasten them to ends (A) when the tenons on the

Fig. 1. Bachelor's Chest. A ROBERT TREATE HOGG REPRODUCTION.

173

ends of the frames are glued to the gains in ends (A).

Get out drawer guides (U) and screw them to the end rails of the two lower frames. Also drill holes into the upper frame for screws to fasten the top.

When the frames have been glued up and carefully sanded, and when corner notches have been carefully checked to make sure the tenons at both ends of the frames will fit, make a trial assembly of all frames and ends (A). When satisfied that members of all joints fit together perfectly, this framework which is to hold the writing board and drawers may be glued together, and the end rails may be screwed fast to the ends of the chest as shown in Fig. 6. Do not fasten the upper frame to the chest at this time, but save it until the top (C) has been screwed fast to it. It may then be fastened to ends (A) with wood screws which can be hidden behind the molding which goes under the top on three sides as shown in Fig. 6.

In passing, it should be noted that the two upper frames are ⅞ inch apart, to give sufficient clearance, so the ¾-inch writing board may be pulled out or pushed in with ease.

Fig. 2. Drawer to Hold Telephone Is Open.

Now get out the two strips (Z-2), to which the telescoping drawer slides are to be fastened, and screw them to ends (A) on the inside, as shown in Fig. 6.

Get out stock and glue it up, to turn the quarter columns. Four ¾-inch-square strips of wood are glued together with heavy brown wrapping paper between them; after turning the column, these may be split apart with a chisel to make four quarter columns. Flutes are cut after turning, and before the four quarters are separated. Glue the quarter columns into the corners that have been prepared for them.

Feet for the chest may now be made. The method used to shape stock for feet like these is shown in Fig. 11, Chapter 32, and also in Fig. 34, Chapter 1. When a sufficient length of foot molding has been sawed, trimmed, and scraped to shape, saw the brackets of the feet to shape on the band saw, as shown in the detail view from which the pattern is made in Fig. 9. Front feet should be reinforced at the glued miter joint with splines, as shown at the bottom of Fig. 6. These feet, when all are cut to shape and the front two assembled, should be fastened to the bottom of the assembled framework with wood screws from the inside. Backing strips (Z-1) should be fastened with glue to them and to the bottom of the lower frame, to help hold the feet securely in place.

Make the drawers next. Details to make one of the two drawers on which there are dovetail joints are shown in Figs. 10 and 11. The remaining lower drawer may be made with the same number of pin members, but make the tails in the middle ⅜ inch wider, and the upper and lower tail ⅛ inch wider when you lay out the dovetail joints.

Lay out dovetails on drawer sides first, and saw these to shape. Then transfer lines from these to drawer fronts and backs. Remove the waste with a dovetail saw and a very sharp thin-bladed chisel. When the joints go together properly, groove the sides and fronts to hold the drawer bottoms. Make trial assemblies, and make sure the drawer fits the opening into which it is to go and that it will slide in and out easily. Glue up the two drawers.

Make the upper drawer. The front of this drawer is divided in the center to simulate two drawer

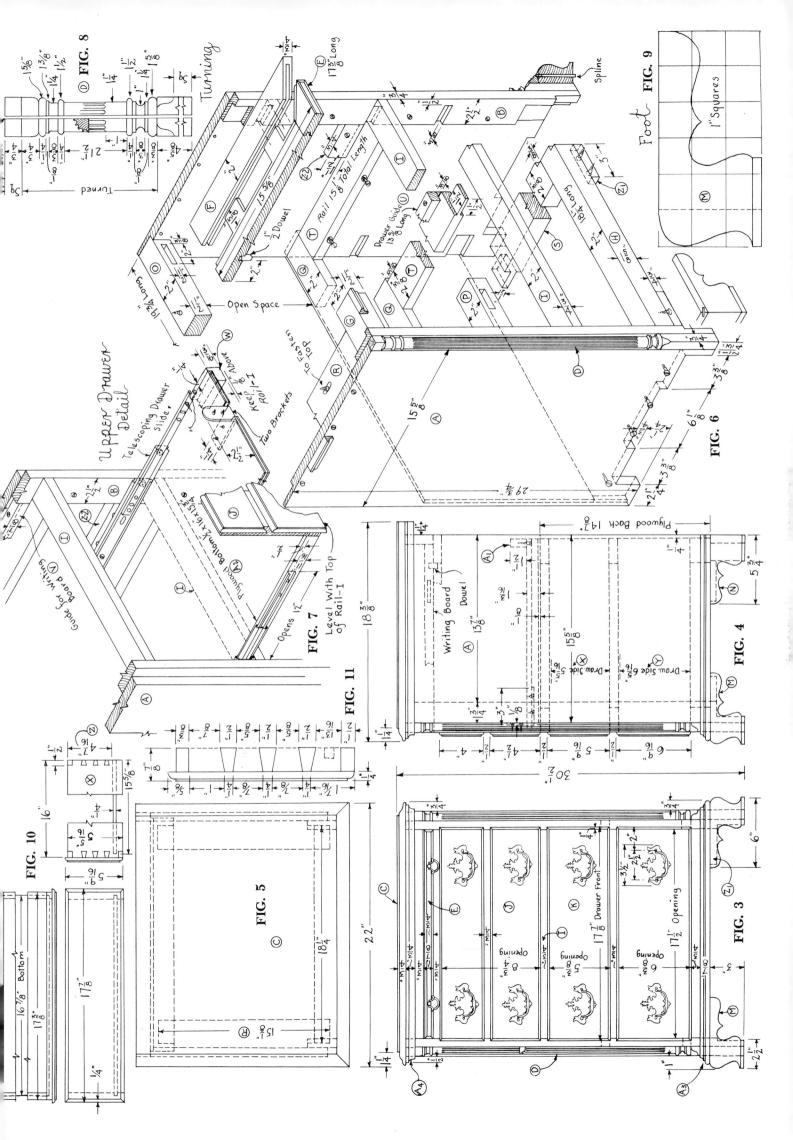

fronts, as shown in Fig. 2. One-half-inch plywood is used for the drawer bottom, but rabbeted strips of wood are glued to both edges on the sides to hide raw edges of the plywood and to make the edges wide enough so the telescoping drawer slides may be fastened to the edges securely. Telescoping slides like these vary in size to support the weight they are supposed to carry. The ones we show in No. 25, Chapter 3, will support 50 pounds, which is adequate for our purposes here. Construction of the drawer is shown quite clearly in Fig. 7. The brackets used to fasten the drawer front to the bottom on this drawer are quite heavy and were hand forged from iron ¼ inch thick.

When the upper drawer has been fastened where it belongs, you may glue up the top (C), and plane and sand it to size. The molding on three edges of the top is cut on the shaper, and the top is fastened to the upper frame with wood screws. Wood screws are then used to fasten the upper frame to the ends of the chest, as shown at the top of Fig. 6. Fasten the molding that covers the screwheads with small brads, but do not glue the molding to the ends of the chest. The molding that goes under the top at the front of the chest may be glued to help hold it in place, since here there will be no unequal shrinkage of it and the wood to which it is glued to tear it loose.

Make the writing board next. Glue up the main piece so it will be only 14 inches wide after planing it to size. The ends may then be rabbeted on both sides on the table saw with a dado head, to make the tongues and tenons, which will later be joined to the cleats on both ends of the writing board. A strip of wood 2 inches wide is then glued to the large piece at the front with a tongue-and-groove joint, which makes it easier to make the tongued-and-grooved miter joints at both corners. Cut the molding on the front of the 2-inch strip after it has been glued to the front of the wide board. Make sure the writing board slides in and out easily, then bore holes for the ½-inch dowels that you will glue into the bottom of the writing board so the writing board cannot be drawn too far out when it is to be used.

Put a good finish on the chest. Then fasten the drawer pulls, and the two smaller pulls to the writing board.

BILL OF MATERIAL

Mahogany

2 Ends (A) ¾" x 15⅝" x 29¾"
2 Stiles (B) ¾" x 2½" x 29¾"
1 Top (C) ¾" x 18⅜" x 22"
2 Quarter columns (D) 1½" x 1½" x 29¾"
1 Writing board (E) ¾" x 15⅝" x 17⅜"
2 Cleats for writing board (F) ¾" x 2" x 15⅝"
1 Front rail (upper frame) (G) 1½" x 2" x 18¼"
1 Front rail (lower frame) (H) 1⅝" x 2" x 18¼"
3 Middle front rails (I) ¾" x 2" x 18¼"
1 Upper drawer front (J) ⅞" x 8¹⁵⁄₁₆" x 17⅞"
1 Middle drawer front (K) ⅞" x 5⁹⁄₁₆" x 17⅞"
1 Lower drawer front (L) ⅞" x 6⁹⁄₁₆" x 17⅞"
4 Feet (M) 1" x 3" x 6"
2 Feet (rear) (N) 1" x 3" x 5¾"
Molding above feet (A-3) ¾" x ⅞" x about 60"
Molding under top (A-4) ½" x ¾" x about 60"

Poplar (Mahogany may be used)

1 Back rail in upper frame (O) 1½" x 2" x 19¾"
1 Back rail in lower frame (P) 1⅝" x 2" x 19¾"
3 Back rails in middle frames (Q) ¾" x 2" x 19¾"
2 End rails in upper frame (R) 1½" x 2⅜" x 15⅛"
2 End rails in lower frame (S) 1⅝" x 2⅜" x 15⅛"

6 End rails in middle frames (T) ¾" x 2⅜" x 15⅛"
4 Drawer guides (for lower two drawers) (U) ¾" x ¾" x 13⅝"
2 Guides for writing board (V) ¾" x ⅞" x 13⅝"
2 Edging strips for upper drawer bottom (W) ¾" x 1³⁄₁₆" x 15¾"
2 Drawer sides for middle drawer (X) ½" x 5⁵⁄₁₆" x 16"
2 Drawer sides for lower drawer (Y) ½" x 6⁵⁄₁₆" x 16"
1 Drawer back for middle drawer (Z) ½" x 4⁷⁄₁₆" x 17⅜"
1 Drawer back for lower drawer ½" x 5⁷⁄₁₆" x 17⅜"
1 Strip for back of upper drawer (A-1) ¾" x 1½" x 16"
2 Backing strips for feet (Z-1) ¾" x ¾" x 3"
2 Strips to which telescoping drawer slides are fastened (Z-2) ¾" x 1½" x 13⅞"

Plywood

1 Upper drawer bottom (A-2) ½" x 16" x 15¾"
2 Drawer bottoms ¼" x 16⅞" x 15⅝"
1 Back for chest ¼" x 14⅞" x 19¾"
1 Pair telescoping drawer slides. Extend one foot and support 50 pounds

THIRTY-TWO

Salem Chest of Drawers

A VERY handsome piece of furniture indeed, this Salem Chest of Drawers. It has the fluted quarter columns and the bracket feet typical of Chippendale-styled pieces of the era.

To build it, first glue up two ends. Plane and sand these to size given in the Bill of Material. Then cut the rabbets on the back edges for the ⅜-inch plywood back, as shown in Figs. 4 and 5.

Glue ¼-inch fill-in strips (H) to the fronts of both ends on the inside. These can be any kind of wood since they will not show.

Next make the two stiles (A). Two-inch gains are cut in these from the inside edges to hold the front rail of each frame which supports the drawers. One side of these stiles extends out from the front edges of the chest ends to make the inside corners into which the quarter columns will be glued after they have been made.

The frames to support the drawers should be made next. Stock for the frames is a full inch thick, making these frames heavy and strong enough to hold heavy loads after they have been put in place. When the rails have all been planed and sanded to the sizes given in the Bill of Material, lay out mortises on the long rails and tenons on both ends of the short rails. Cut and fit these, as shown in Figs. 3, 4, and 5.

Drill holes for screws to fasten the frames to the ends, then glue the frames together. Notice that the front corners of the frames are offset to form the angles that fit around stiles (A). One-half by one-half-inch notches are cut into corners of the front rails to make tenons, which are joined to the gains cut into stiles (A). These notches may be cut out on the band saw after the frames have been glued up, or they may be cut from the front rails with a dado head before the frames are glued together. These gained-in joints, the wood screws through the side rails, and short nails through the plywood back of the chest give the frame of the chest of drawers (sometimes referred to as the "carcass" in furniture terms) sufficient strength and rigidity to support any reasonable load likely to be carried by the drawers. Front rails should be glued into the gains that have been cut into stiles

Fig. 1. Salem Chest of Drawers. A ROBERT TREATE HOGG REPRODUCTION.

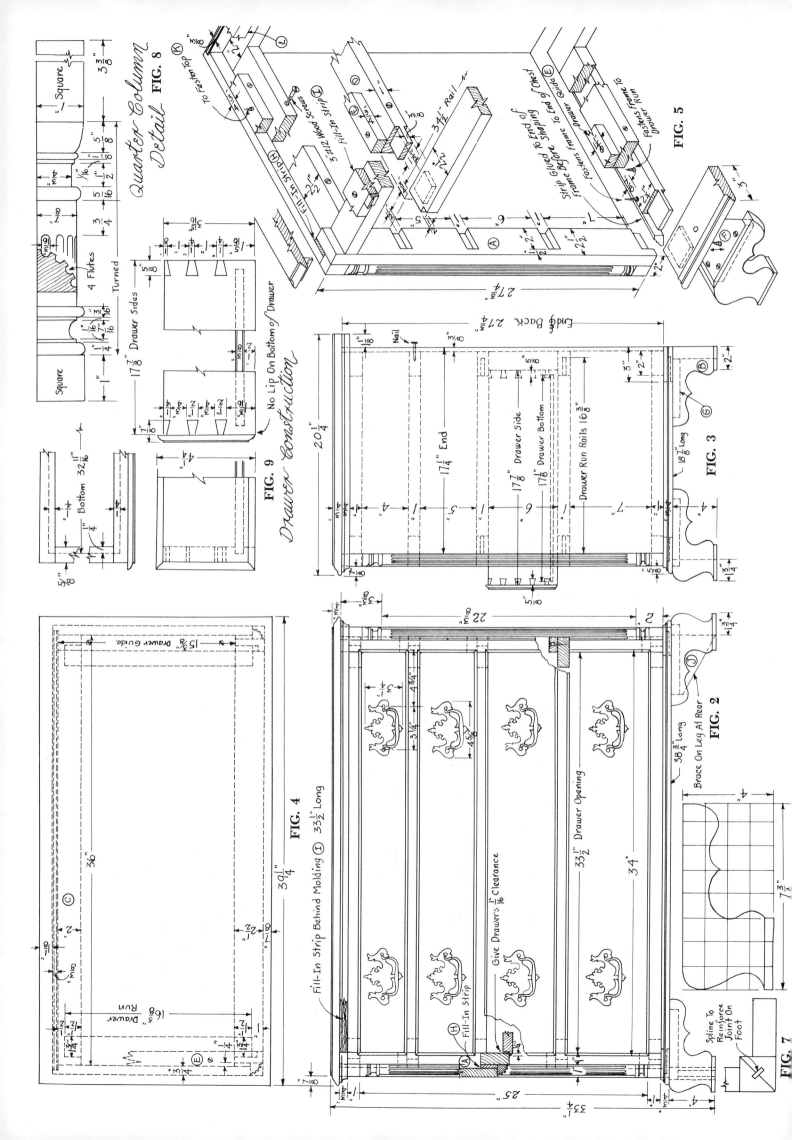

(A), but glue should not be used elsewhere to fasten the frames to the ends and back.

Make the quarter columns next. These are made by gluing together four strips of wood, each an inch square, with heavy brown wrapping paper separating the strips. This glued-up turning square is then put in a lathe and turned, as shown in Fig. 8. After turning, cut the flutes on two of the quarter columns before separating them.

Flutes on columns like this are usually cut on a shaper if one is available. The column is mounted between two centers, fastened to uprights mounted on a narrow board, to make a jig like the one shown in Fig. 10. Use wood screws for centers and divide the end of the column into 22½-degree sectors to separate the flutes evenly.

Columns like this may be made in one piece, as we show it in Fig. 8, but to make cutting of flutes easier, it is better to cut it into three parts, from which lengths measuring 2 inches, 22⅜ inches, and 3⅜ inches may be turned, as shown on the right of Fig. 2. Fig. 10 shows the setup for fluting the longest of these three pieces.

and bottom of the column where the wrapping paper has been glued. Then glue the quarter columns into place.

Make the base next. First cut the four frame rails and plane them to the sizes given in the Bill of Material. On our drawing, in Fig. 5, we show the molding on the front rail cut on the edge of the rail itself, instead of being glued on as are the end moldings. It may, however, be made and then glued on same as the end moldings. It is better to cut the miters on the corners of the front rail, and then miter and glue the end strips to the frame before shaping the molding. Thus the end strips may be glued and clamped to the frame without marring the molded surface. No nails should be used to fasten any of these moldings. Mortises and tenons should be cut on the rails, and the frame should be glued together before shaping any of the molding on the edges.

Stock for the feet should be made next. The four feet may be made from a single piece of stock 1¾" x 4" x 48". This is roughly cut to the approximate shape of the outside of the foot on the table

FIG. 10

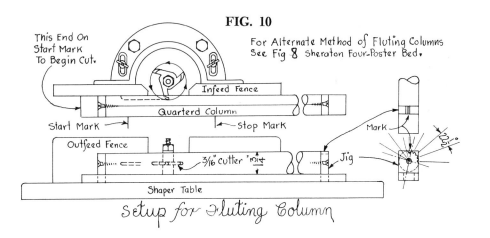

Setup for Fluting Column

If machinery for cutting the flutes is not available, it is not too difficult to cut them by hand with a narrow wood-carving gouge or fluting tool. The author has used this method with good results many times. If this method is used, there is no reason why the column need be cut into three lengths.

When the turning and fluting have been completed, split the column into four parts by carefully hammering a chisel into the joints at the top

saw, as shown in Fig. 11. It is then trimmed to its exact shape with chisels, gouges, and properly sharpened scraper blades, and then sanded down smooth. When shaped, the front feet may be mitered on the corners, using a miter box. Then cut saw kerfs for splines to reinforce the joints as shown in Fig. 7. It is best to clamp the feet to the crosscut fence with the mitered surface flat on the saw table to make these kerfs. Splines run length-

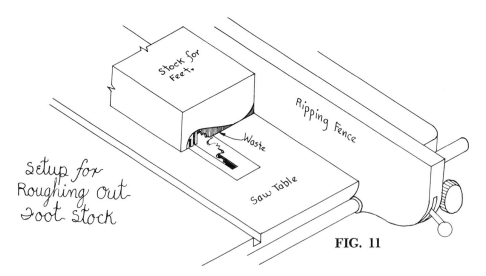

Setup for Roughing out Foot stock

Stock for Feet.

Ripping Fence

Waste

Saw Table

FIG. 11

wise across the miter joint, and thus are 4 inches wide and only 1 inch long. Sometimes corrugated fasteners are used instead of splines to reinforce joints like these.

Before scroll-sawing the feet to shape, cut the recesses on top of the feet where the triangular-shaped bracing blocks (F) and (G) are to be glued and screwed fast to them. Then saw the scrolled edges, using a band saw or a power jigsaw. Sand these edges smooth.

Make bracing blocks (F), (G), and (J). Glue and screw these to the feet. Holes drilled through blocks (F) and (G) hold the screws to fasten the feet to the frame above them. This base frame in turn is screwed fast to the frame that supports the lower drawer.

Drawers should be made next and should be fitted in place before either back or top is put on. By doing this it is easier to correct any binding on any of the drawers, though binding should not occur if dimensions are properly maintained.

Cut stock for drawer fronts; then plane and sand these to size. Cut moldings on four edges of all drawer fronts, then rabbet the fronts on top and at both ends to fit the openings.

Make drawer sides and backs and sand them smooth. Lay out dovetails on drawer sides first. These may be sawed out on a sharp, fine-toothed band saw. Some trimming to the line with a sharp, thin-bladed chisel may be needed, after which the shape of these dovetails can be transferred to the ends of the drawer fronts and the drawer backs,

with a pointed awl, knife blade, or pencil. Dovetail mortise members on the drawer fronts are started by fastening the drawer front vertically in a vise, and then sawing on the waste side of all vertical dovetail lines with a dovetail saw. The saw must be held at a steep angle to the side of the drawer front, so as not to cut into the molded lip. What can't be sawed must be chiseled out. A ½-inch chisel with edges beveled and a thin blade is best for chiseling dovetails, since the beveled edges make it possible to clean out corners with little difficulty. The drawer front should be clamped tightly to the top of a heavy workbench top to hammer the chisel down across the grain where this must be done. More detailed directions for laying out and making dovetail joints is given in Chapter 1, and should be consulted.

When dovetail joints have been made and fitted, cut the grooves for drawer bottoms into drawer sides and fronts. Drawer bottoms are placed in the grooves when sides are glued to the fronts and backs. They need not be glued fast in this case, since the grooves hold them on all edges.

When all drawers have been made and fitted to slide easily in their respective openings, the back of the chest may be cut out, sanded, and nailed on. Then make the top, and cut molding on three of its edges, as shown. Notice how the top extends past the back and sides for a distance of 1⅛ inches to permit the top to be placed tightly against a wall having a baseboard.

Cut the molding, which goes around three sides

under the top, and fasten it in place. At the front this molding may be glued to the chest, but at the ends glue is put only on the mitered corner joints, and brads are used to fasten the molding. Holes left by the brads should be filled in with colored crack filler, or wood, and then sanded so they will not show.

Putting on the drawer pulls completes the building of the chest. These pulls and bails must be removed to do the finishing.

BILL OF MATERIAL

Black Walnut or Mahogany

2 Ends ¾" x 17¼" x 27¾"
1 Top ¾" x 20½" x 39¼"
Upper drawer front ⅞" x 4¼" x 34"
Second drawer front ⅞" x 5¼" x 34"
Third drawer front ⅞" x 6¼" x 34"
Lower drawer front ⅞" x 7¼" x 34"
2 Quarter columns 1" x 1" x 27¾"
2 Stiles (A) 1" x 2½" x 27¾"
4 Pieces for front feet 1¾" x 4" x 7¾" ⎫ Cut from one piece
2 Pieces for rear feet (B) 1¾" x 4" x 7" ⎬ 1¾" x 4" x 48"
5 Front rails for frames holding drawers 1" x 2½" x 34½"
1 Front rail in bottom frame ¾" x 3" x 38¾"
Molding at ends of bottom frame 2 pcs. ⅝" x ¾" x 18⅞"
Molding under top ⅝" x ¾" x length about 80"
1 Fill-in strip behind molding (I) ¾" x 2½" x 33½"

Poplar

2 Drawer sides ⅝" x 3¹⁵⁄₁₆" x 17⅞"
2 Drawer sides ⅝" x 4¹⁵⁄₁₆" x 17⅞"
2 Drawer sides ⅝" x 5¹⁵⁄₁₆" x 17⅞"
2 Drawer sides ⅝" x 6¹⁵⁄₁₆" x 17⅞"
1 Drawer back ⅝" x 3¹⁵⁄₁₆" x 33⅜"
1 Drawer back ⅝" x 4¹⁵⁄₁₆" x 33⅜"
1 Drawer back ⅝" x 5¹⁵⁄₁₆" x 33⅜"
1 Drawer back ⅝" x 6¹⁵⁄₁₆" x 33⅜"
5 Back rails for frames holding drawers (C) 1" x 2" x 36"
10 End rails for frames (D) 1" x 2½" x 16⅜"

1 Back rail for lower frame ¾" x 3" x 37½"
2 End rails for lower frame ¾" x 2¼" x 17"
8 Drawer guides (E) ¾" x 1¼" x 15⅜"
2 Fill-in strips (H) ¼" x 1½" x 27¾"
2 Fill-in strips (K) (under top) ¾" x 1¼" x 15⅜"
1 Fill-in strip (L) ¾" x 1¼" x 33½"
2 Triangular-shaped pieces to hold two parts of front feet together (F) ¾" x 5½" x 5½"
2 Triangular-shaped pieces to hold two parts of rear feet together (G) ¾" x 5" x 5"
2 Braces on leg at rear (J) 1" x 3¼" x 5"

THIRTY-THREE

Chippendale Fretwork Mirror Frame

THE scrolled Chippendale mirror frame, shown in Fig. 1 above the Salem Chest of Drawers in Chapter 32 and in Fig. 1 above the Queen Anne Lowboy in Chapter 9, is a type adapted from what were in many cases more sophisticated models that came from the workshops of Thomas Chippendale and those who emulated his designs. Many English originals were hand carved, gilded, and more highly embellished with ornament. In America the simplification of the original designs resulted in a considerable variety of these charming mirror frames, highly prized as heirlooms by those fortunate enough to own an original. They come in various sizes and shapes, adapted to need. The one shown and described here is probably one of the more popular sizes. The wood used to make it is walnut, but good mahogany would be a perfectly proper substitute.

Mirrors made at the time these frames were originally introduced in America were expensive and had to be imported from England. Small ones were cheaper than large ones, which is one reason small mirror frames are found in greater number than the large expensive originals.

The glass used for these mirrors was usually no more than ⅛ inch thick, and in large sizes there was danger of their being broken in shipping. Today, with mass production methods, good quality plate-glass mirrors usually are ¼ inch thick, and if the frame is heavy enough, as in this instance, a glass of this thickness is stronger than the thinner one. If a ⅛-inch glass is used to make the mirror lighter in weight, the plywood back will be ⅛ inch below the surface of the frame at the back and can be held in place with brads driven into the frame from the inside; or if the metal clips are used, they can be sunk level with the back of the frame.

Our method of bracing and fastening the fret-sawed scrollwork is one of several ways of doing it. On some old mirror frames this scrolled outline was beveled in back and thinned at the edges from the thickness required to bring it even with the back of the molding to which it was glued. This method required considerable carving and trimming by hand, alright in early days when hand labor was not as great an item of expense as the cost of materials that were used. But with today's manufacturing methods, when labor costs far exceed the cost of materials, it is easier and cheaper to use the method shown here. Cutting the scrolls with power machinery is a quick and simple operation, and the method of bracing we show presents no great problems and eliminates the tedious hand trimming of the scrollwork in back to make the edges the proper thickness.

To build the mirror frame, cut a strip of wood long enough to make all the straight molding in one piece. Hand molding planes were, of course, used originally to make moldings like this. Shallower moldings, sometimes used on small mirrors, were often cut with a scratch stock, a kind of scraping tool, and then glued to a white pine base. A molding as deep as this, however, would have required a molding plane. If a shaper with cutters to make the molding is available, it should be used. In a small shop, power equipment or the proper bit for cutting this shape may not be available. In this case the next best thing is either to purchase stock molding resembling our pattern as closely as possible, or better yet to carve the molding by hand with wood-carving chisels, which is what the author would do and often has done. If properly made and carefully sanded, small pieces of molding, like the ones needed here, may quite readily be hand cut to shape.

Before shaping the face of the molding, the inside edge should be rabbeted for the glass, either on the shaper or with an electric hand router or on the dado head. Then the tenons should be cut on the ends of (A) and (B). The lower end has mitered joints, reinforced with ⅛-inch splines. Saw kerfs for feathers may be cut by placing the corner of the glued-up frame in a V-shaped block of the same thickness as the frame, as shown in Fig. 6, and then running the saw kerf on the table saw.

Joints at the top of the frame are made differently. Here an extra block of wood is inserted to make the square corner structurally, and the frame molding is simulated by carving the surface of the

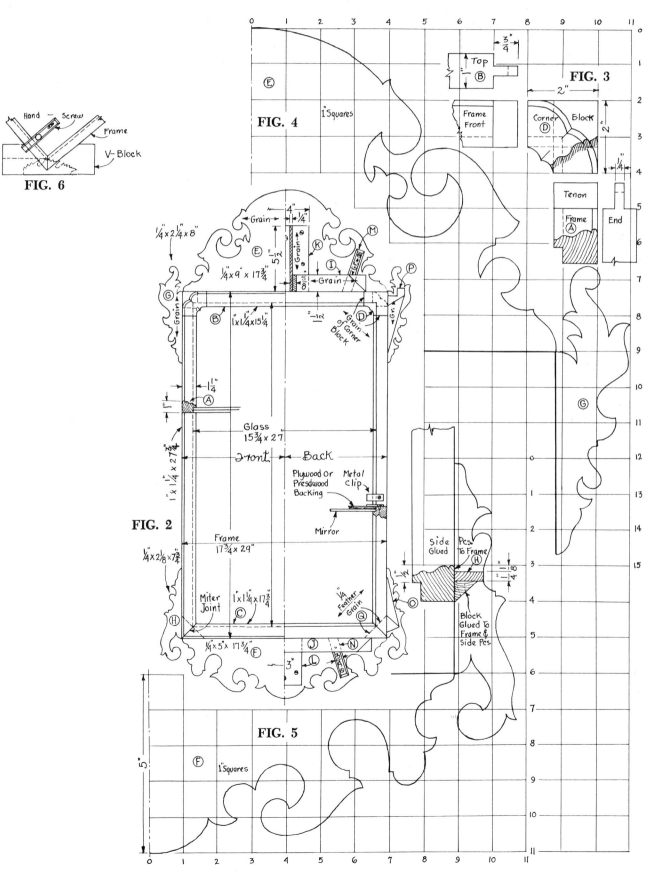

block to get the desired shape. Grooves are cut into blocks (D) to a depth of ¾ inch on the two adjacent edges to which the tenons on the upper ends of moldings (A) are joined.

When the face of the molding on pieces (A), (B), and (C) has been cut to shape, the frame should be glued together. The shape of the molding on the sides and top of the frame should then be carved around corner blocks (D) with woodcarving chisels, being careful to keep the width of this carved element exactly the same as the molding on the face of (A), as shown in Fig. 3.

You are now ready to make full-size patterns of scrolled pieces (E), (F), (G), and (H). Lay out 1-inch squares, as shown in Figs. 4 and 5, and draw the patterns. Use well-seasoned stock for these pieces. Notice the direction of the grain on these members, whose edges are glued to the frame. All bracing members, (I), (J), (K), (L), (M), (N), (O), and (P), should be made and fastened to (E), (F), (G), and (H) before they are glued to the frame. Bracing members (I), (J), (O), and (P) are glued to the backs of (E), (F), (G), and (H). Glue pieces (K) and (M) to (I), and glue pieces (L) and (N) to (J), but do not glue pieces (K), (L), (M), and (N) to (E) or (F). Use thin ⅜-inch wood screws to fasten these to the backs of (E) and (F), since there is less chance that (E) and (F) will split or warp after the frame is assembled by doing it this way. Great care must, however, be taken when driving these screws so they will not split the wood or come through pieces (E) and (F). Holes large enough in diameter for the wood screws to pass through the bracing mem-

bers easily should be drilled and then countersunk for screwheads. Tiny pilot holes should be drilled into (E) and (F), using a depth gauge of some kind to prevent the drill from going through. A good depth gauge for this purpose may be made by drilling through a short length of thin dowel rod and letting the end of the drill stick out only far enough to drill the desired depth.

When all bracing members have been fastened to (E), (F), (G), and (H), glue these to the assembled frame. It is fairly easy to clamp the top and bottom to the frame, since clamps may be fastened from (I) and (J) to the frame. Since brace blocks (O) and (P) are beveled in back to keep them from showing when the frame is hung, clamping blocks, cut on one edge to fit the part of the outline where the clamps are to be applied, should be made. Even with the use of these, pressure should be applied very gently when clamping. If good glue is used and if edges to be glued are square, a great amount of pressure will not be needed to make a good joint. Epoxy glue is good to use here.

When the whole frame has been assembled, the finish should be applied. The mirror and backing should then be put into the frame and fastened. If a ¼-inch plate-glass mirror is used and the backing is ¼ inch thick, they will come level with the back of the frame, and short metal clips cut from thin mending plates with a hacksaw will hold them, as shown in Fig. 2. These may even be sunk into the frame and back if one wants to go to the trouble, but will hardly show after the mirror is hung if fastened as shown.

BILL OF MATERIAL

Black Walnut

2 Pieces frame molding (A) 1″ x 1¼″ x 27¾″
1 Piece frame molding (B) 1″ x 1¼″ x 15¼″
1 Piece frame molding (C) 1″ x 1¼″ x 17¾″
2 Corner molding blocks (D) 1″ x 2″ x 2″
1 Scrolled top (E) ¼″ x 9″ x 17¾″
1 Scrolled bottom (F) ¼″ x 5″ x 17¾″
2 Upper scrolled side pieces (G) ¼″ x 2¼″ x 8″
2 Lower scrolled side pieces (H) ¼″ x 2⅛″ x 7¾″

1 Reinforcing block (I) ⅝″ x 1½″ x 14″
1 Reinforcing block (J) ⅝″ x 1¼″ x 15″
1 Reinforcing block (K) ¼″ x 4″ x 5½″
1 Reinforcing block (L) ¼″ x 3″ x 4″
2 Reinforcing blocks (M) ¼″ x ¾″ x 4″
2 Reinforcing blocks (N) ¼″ x ¾″ x 3½″
2 Reinforcing blocks (O) ⅝″ x 1″ x 4½″
2 Reinforcing blocks (P) ⅝″ x 1½″ x 5½″
2 Feathers (Q) ⅛″ x 1¼″ x 2¾″

THIRTY-FOUR

Hepplewhite Upholstered Armchair

AN upholstered armchair, designed along simple straightforward lines like the Hepplewhite chair shown in Fig. 1, can be useful in almost any room in the house. Fairly easy to build, not too difficult to upholster, and quite attractive too, it will be a worthwhile project for almost any amateur to try his hand at and should improve his skill as a cabinetmaker.

Building a chair is always a challenge, for chairmaking is not easy. The fact that chair members in many instances do not join each other at right angles presents difficulties. In addition to this, members very often have to be fitted together where they curve and where they must be kept slender and light in weight. They also need to be joined together in such a way that the chair will not be weakened structurally to the extent that it would be hazardous for a heavy person to sit in the chair and move about in it freely. Taking these and other requirements we may have neglected to mention into consideration, one can readily see why chairmaking must always be considered a highly specialized branch of the cabinetmaking trade. Add to this the related skills a chairmaker should have to be a finished craftsman, such as a knowledge of upholstering, chair-seat weaving and caning, wood-carving, inlaying, wood finishing, and hand coloring and decorating, they all add up to a formidable array of skills.

To build the armchair shown in Fig. 1, first cut

out two front and two back legs. The front legs have a molding carved on the front and on one side of the chair leg. While still squared to the sizes given in the Bill of Material, mortises to hold seat rails should be laid out and cut into the upper end of both, as shown on the drawings. These mortises should be cut before the side of the front leg is planed to the angle shown in Fig. 4.

When the mortises at the upper end of the front legs have been cut, both legs should be planed on the outside to the angle shown in Fig. 4, making the legs 1⅝ inches wide where the side seat-rails are joined to them. Both legs are then tapered from the bottom of the seat-rails to the floor, where they are only 1 inch wide on three sides and slightly less at the back. The tapering on these is done most easily on the jointer, by laying the upper part of the leg, which is not to be tapered, over the knives upon the outfeed table of the jointer, and then planing the leg from there to the floor end as many times as it takes to cut it to the size desired.

When the tapering has been done, lay out and

Fig. 1. Hepplewhite Upholstered Armchair. BUILT IN THE BERRY COLLEGE SHOPS.

185

cut the mortises near the bottom to hold the tenons on the lower stretchers on the side of the chair. These mortises, like the ones for the seat-rail above them, are cut perpendicular to the sides into which they go.

Draw lines on the two outside faces of the front legs to carve the molding. In furniture factories these are molded on a shaper, and when done in this way the lines do not converge as they reach the bottom of the leg as we show them here. However, if only one chair is to be built, and special cutters to shape them are not available, this molding may be carved by hand with wood-carving chisels with little or no trouble.

Make the back legs next. While it takes a plank 1⅝ inches thick and 5 inches wide to make one leg like this, two can be made from a plank which is only about 2 inches wider. If two or more chairs are to be made, a lot of stock can be saved if wider planks are used from which as many as four legs can be sawed. First plane the plank to the thickness of 1⅝ inches and then from Fig. 3 make a full-sized pattern, using stiff cardboard or thin plywood from which to transfer the shape of the legs to the plank. Then saw the legs to shape on the band saw. After band-sawing them from the plank, taper the lower ends from the seat-rails to the floor, and then smooth all sides thoroughly. Make layouts for all mortises and cut these.

While the approximate angle of the mortise for the side stretcher at the bottom of the back leg may be taken directly from Fig. 3 in the book, it will be a better idea to make a trial assembly of all legs and seat-rails, clamping them together when the joints have been made and fitted. Then, using either the lower stretcher itself or a straight-edged rule, determine the correct layout for this mortise. Use a pencil to make the layout for the mortise on the outside of the leg first. From this pencil layout on the outside of the leg, it will be an easy matter to cut the mortise where it belongs, and at the correct angle. While the seat-rails and legs are clamped together, it will also be easy to measure for shoulder lines and mark these accurately on the stretcher to cut the tenon.

In describing the manner in which the mortise-and-tenon joint for this lower side stretcher, to be joined to the back leg, should be laid out and made, we have gotten a bit ahead of ourselves on normal procedure. To get back on the right track, let us say all seat-rails, chairback rails, and lower stretchers should be cut out, and front and back seat-rails and chairback rails should be made and tenons cut on them, prior to making the trial assembly we have mentioned. There will be little or no trouble cutting tenons on the seat-rail for the front, or for all rails made for the back, and fitting them into the mortises where they belong, because these tenon cheeks are all parallel to the stretcher sides, which is not the case with tenons on side stretchers.

Side rail or stretcher tenons are perpendicular to the top and bottom shoulder angles of these tenons at both ends. These shoulder angles form a 96-degree angle with the outside of the rails and stretchers at the chairback and the same angle with the inside of the rails at the front of the chair. This we show in Fig. 4.

Shoulder angles for medial stretcher A (see Figs. 2 and 3) may be laid out when a trial assembly is made of all parts of the chair we have described up to this point. Notice that the dovetail joint, with which this stretcher is joined to the lower stretchers on the side, does not go all the way to the top of the stretchers, but only a little more than half-way, as shown at the bottom of Fig. 3.

Make the arms and arm supports next. A pattern for the arm support may be made from the dimensions shown for it in Fig. 3. An arm pattern may be made from a full-size layout of Fig. 5. At the bottom the arm support is 1½ inches thick, while at the top it is only 1¼ inches thick. The tenon joining it to the arm is ¾ inch square.

Carve the arm and arm support after sawing them to shape on the band saw and sanding all surfaces except those to be carved. Some care will have to be taken to make a well-fitting joint where the arm goes against the back leg, since this requires cutting the back of the arm to exactly the right angle. The back leg has a shallow notch cut into it to help support the arm, which is also anchored there with glue and a long wood screw, as shown in Fig. 4. The chairmaker must use good judgment at a place like this and not make the notch so deep that it will weaken the chair leg, but

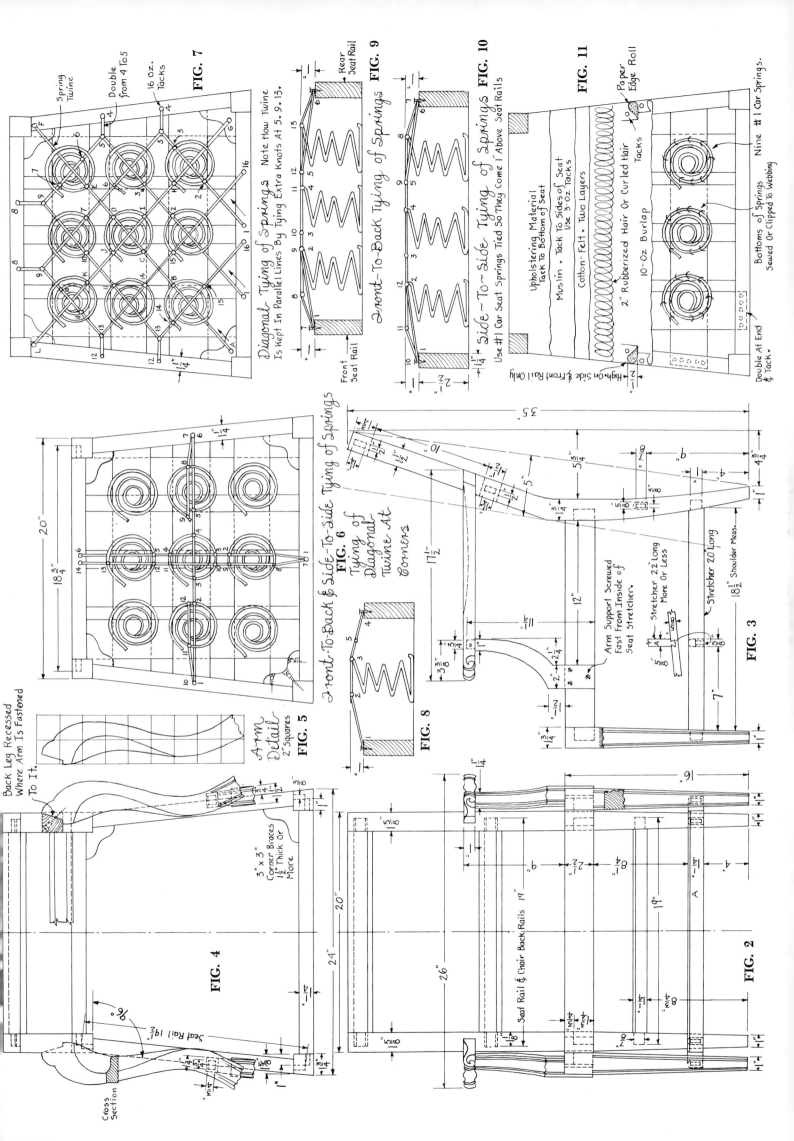

FIG. 7

Spring Twine

Double from 4 To 5

16 Oz. Tacks

1¼"

Diagonal Tying of Springs Note How Twine Is Kept In Parallel Lines By Tying Extra Knots At 5, 9, 13.

Rear Seat Rail **FIG. 9**

Front-To-Back Tying of Springs FIG. 10

Front Seat Rail

Side-To-Side Tying of Springs FIG. 11

Use #1 Car Seat Springs Tied So They Come 1" Above Seat Rails

2½"

1¼"

Paper Edge Roll

Upholstering Material Tack To Bottom of Seat

Muslin • Tack To Sides of Seat Use 3 Oz Tacks

Cotton-Felt • Two Layers

2" Rubberized Hair Or Curled Hair Tacks

10-Oz Burlap

High On Side & Front Rail Only

Bottoms of Springs Sewed Or Clipped To Webbing

Nine #1 Car Springs.

Double At End & Tack.

20"

18¾"

Arm Detail FIG. 5
2" Squares

Front-To-Back & Side-To-Side Tying of Springs FIG. 6

Tying of Diagonal Twine At Corners FIG. 8

1¼"

35"

17½"

10

5¾"

5"

12"

Arm Support Screwed Fast From Inside of Seat Stretcher.

Stretcher 22" Long More Or Less

Stretcher 20" Long

18½" Shoulder Meas.

7"

FIG. 3

Back Leg Recessed Where Arm Is Fastened To It.

3" x 3" Corner Braces 1½" Thick Or More

Seat Rail 19½"

Cross Section

FIG. 4

24"

20"

26"

Seat Rail & Chair Back Rails 19"

19"

8¼"

2½"

9"

16"

FIG. 2

only deep enough to give the arm enough support to keep it in place. In order to make sure that the slant at the back of the arm conforms to the slant of the leg where they are joined, to make a good glue joint, it is best to make this joint before cutting the mortise at the front of the arm for the tenon on the arm support to be joined to it.

When these joints have been made, carve the arms and arm supports. The chair will then be ready to be glued together. Glue front seat-rail to front legs first. Then glue all rails and stretchers in the back to the back legs. These joints may be reinforced with wooden pegs if you wish, though the bottom rail joints in the back are stronger without pegs. Glue the side rails to the assembled front and the assembled back of the chair. Then glue arms to arm supports and screw and glue these fast to seat stretchers and back legs. Glue the medial stretcher to the side stretchers on the bottom of the chair. Then make and glue and screw the corner braces to the seat frame, as shown in Figs. 4 and 6.

Put on a good finish next. To do this consult directions for doing wood finishing in Chapter 2.

Upholstering of the chair may now be started. Use the best jute webbing obtainable to support the springs. Figs. 6, 7, and 11 show how this webbing is interwoven and tacked with webbing tacks to the bottom of the seat stretchers. Some webbing tacks have barbs to give them greater holding power. Double one end of the webbing and tack through the double thickness. At the other end, stretch the webbing with a webbing stretcher, as is shown in Fig. 10 on the directions for upholstering the wing chair in Chapter 40. Then tack the webbing fast with only three tacks at the end where you have stretched it, and double this end back over the three tacks and finish the tacking through the doubled end with five more tacks. Then cut it off the roll. For webbing use 16-ounce tacks.

Now place nine #1 car springs on the stretched and interlaced webbing, as shown in Fig. 6, and with Italian stitching twine sew the bottoms of the springs securely to the webbing as shown in Fig. 11, or, better yet, clip the springs to the webbing with metal clips.

Use the best spring twine obtainable and first tie the springs from front to back and from side to side, as shown in Fig. 6. Begin by tacking the twine securely to the top of the front seat-rail where the figure 1 appears. Start the tack, wrap the twine twice around it, and then hammer the head down on the seat stretcher to hold it. Use 16-ounce tacks to hold the spring twine. Make both ends of the twine long enough when you start it at figure 1 so both ends go all the way across the springs to the back of the chair. Proceed with the twine from 1 to 2 and tie it there with an upholsterer's knot, pulling the top of the spring down when making the knot, so it will be only about an inch higher than the top of the seat stretchers, as we show it in Fig. 9. Use of the upholsterer's knot to hold the springs to the positions shown in Figs. 6 and 7 makes adjusting of the springs easy as you proceed. The sequence shown in Figs. 6 and 9 for tying the springs allows you to pull them down to the proper height and to level their tops, which is a necessary first step in tying springs.

When you tie them from side to side, which is shown in Figs. 6 and 10, you follow the sequence from 1 to 12 in proper order, leaving enough cord when you start at 1 to tie it at 11 and 12 after you have tied the other end to the spring at 8 and 9.

After front-to-back and side-to-side tying, you tie the springs diagonally, as shown in Figs. 7 and 8. Notice the extra knots at 5, 9, and 13 in Fig. 7. These make it possible to line up the cords over each spring to hold it in place properly.

When all seat springs have been tied, cut a piece of 10-ounce burlap to cover them and tack it over them to the top of the seat stretchers. Leave enough to double it over on all four edges as shown in Fig. 11. Use 3-ounce tacks to fasten the burlap and begin tacking at the center of each side, working from there to each corner.

Paper edge-roll should now be tacked to the top of the front and side seat stretchers, as shown in Fig. 11. This may be bought already made up and is used to round the sharp edges of the chair seat, shape it up better, and help keep the filling material in place more easily. None is put on the back seat-rail. On top of the burlap a 2-inch layer of curled hair—or rubberized hair, a newer material used for the purpose of making a soft, well-padded seat—is spread as evenly as possible over the seat. Sew long loops of twine all over the burlap and work some of the curled hair into these loops to prevent it from sliding about. If rubberized hair is used, no loops of twine need be sewed to the burlap to hold it. Rubberized hair is glued to the burlap with rubberized spray glue to hold it firmly in place.

To smooth the surface of this padding, two layers of cotton felt are spread over it, and all of this is held in place by stretching a sheet of unbleached muslin over the top and tacking it to the sides of the chair rails a little higher up than where the row of nails shown in Fig. 1 will go. Be sure to begin tacking at the middle of every side and tack from there to the corners.

When muslin has been tacked fast, cut the upholstering material. Good fabrics to use on a chair of this style are the cut velvets made of nylon, brocades, or tapestry. The material shown on the chair in Fig. 1 is not especially well suited to the chair we show, but would be better on an oak or maple chair of an earlier period. An upholstering material with a finer figure and a somewhat smoother background would do much better.

At the arm support, the covering material must be carefully cut and fitted around it, as shown in Fig. 14, which also gives directions for doing the job. First cut this cloth, going from the edge of the material at the side of the chair up to the slanted lines. Then make the angle cuts at both sides. Flap Z may then be tacked and glued to the inside and top of the seat-rail under the arm support, and the flaps at each side may be doubled back under the cloth on both sides of the arm sup-

port, and tacked to the seat-rail with gimp tacks. No covering material over the springs should be fastened to the inside of the seat-rail at the arm support until all have been fitted and placed there. This includes burlap, muslin, and upholstering material.

Where the cloth fits around the back chair leg, it is cut on the bias from the corner, but not quite to the inside corner of the back leg. This allows the corners to be tucked under. When the cloth is pulled down to tack it to the sides and back of the chair, a portion of cloth beyond the cut you made from the corner will be pulled down below the surface that still shows.

At the front of the chair some of the cloth should be trimmed off so it will not be too thick to tuck the side under the front, as shown in Fig. 1. Do this the way we show it in Fig. 13 in the drawings for the Chippendale Ladder-Back Side Chair in Chapter 37. Such corners should be blindstitched before the banding, which partially covers it, is put on.

All that now remains to finish the upholstering of the seat is putting on the banding. To make and put this on, follow the directions given in steps 1 to 5 inclusive in Fig. 13 in Chapter 37. A piece of black cambric should be tacked to the bottom of the seat-rails to close it and keep out the dust and dirt.

To upholster the back of the chair, stretch and weave webbing strips up and down and from side

FIG. 12

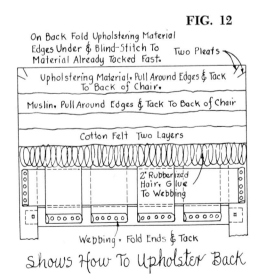

Shows How To Upholster Back

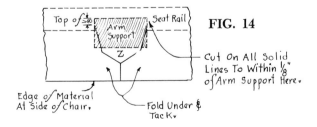

FIG. 14

Cut On All Solid Lines To Within 1/8" of Arm Support Here.

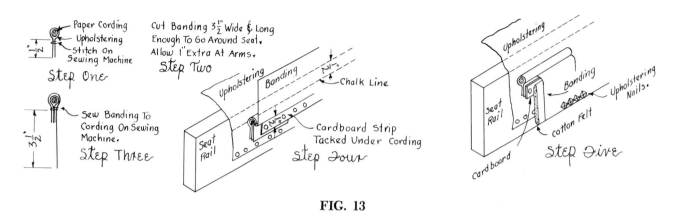

FIG. 13

to side over the area to be upholstered, as shown in Fig. 12. No springs are put on the back, but a 2-inch layer of rubberized hair is glued to the webbing, the strips of which have been interwoven so they come close together. Over the curled hair put two layers of cotton felt, and over this stretch unbleached muslin which is tacked to the back of the chair. As on the seat, begin tacking at the middle of each side and tack to the corner. Then fit a piece of upholstering material over the muslin and make two pleats at the upper corners, as shown in Fig. 12. Tack this to the back, and then cut a piece of material having an extra inch on each side to fold under, and blindstitch it to the cloth on back of the chair. This is the final step in building the chair.

BILL OF MATERIAL

Mahogany

2 Front legs 1¾" x 1¾" x 16"
2 Back legs 1⅝" x 5" x 35¼"
2 Arm supports 1½" x 4¼" x 11¼"
2 Arms 1" x 4" x 17½"
2 Side stretchers ⅝" x 1¼" x 20"
1 Medial stretcher (A) ⅝" x 1¼" x 22"
1 Back stretcher ⅝" x 1¼" x 19"

Poplar or Pine

1 Front seat-rail 1¼" x 2½" x 22½"
2 Side seat-rails 1¼" x 2½" x 19½"
1 Rear seat-rail 1¼" x 2½" x 18¾"
1 Chairback rail 1½" x 1½" x 18¾"
1 Chairback rail 1½" x 1¾" x 18¾"
4 Corner braces for seat 1½" x 3" x 3"

THIRTY-FIVE

Windsor Side Chair

I N spite of the best efforts by contemporary designers, no chair more handsome than a good American Windsor has yet been created. Most of these American Windsors are very comfortable to sit in, because of the carefully shaped and scooped-out seats and the comfortably curved, slanted, and resilient backs. They are the very essence of grace and charm and constitute one of the major contributions bequeathed to us by early Colonial craftsmen in the furniture field.

English Windsors, from which our own early ones were adapted, had a solid or a scroll-sawed splat in the center of the chairback. They were in most instances heavier and not nearly so graceful as their American counterparts. They do not begin to compare in beauty and style with good American Windsors which were made in a great variety of graceful designs.

This Wallace Nutting reproduction of an early pattern is particularly nice and a good one to copy.

The two greatest deterrents to building a Windsor chair, from the amateur cabinetmaker's standpoint, are that certain parts must be steamed and bent, and that some turned spindles are so thin that they cannot be turned on ordinary wood-turning lathes usually available to home craftsmen. Nor is it possible to purchase or procure these parts from craft supply houses to which the amateur cabinetmaker has access. This is due to the expensive equipment needed for their manufacture and the special skills required to produce them, so that no manufacturer can afford to sell these items in small quantities at retail prices. Furthermore, tastes differ, and too few craftsmen would wish to select the same items to make it a paying venture, if the service were offered.

It is, however, possible to build a chair like this in the home workshop if the craftsman has the determination and ingenuity to attempt it, and if he is willing to go to the little extra trouble it takes. Thin spindles, like the ones needed for this chair, can be first turned at both ends in the lathe, to make the dowel-shaped tenons. To do this, cut the strips of wood 1 inch square and about 23 inches long. Mount them in the lathe and turn these parts.

Fig. 1. Windsor Side Chair. A WALLACE NUTTING REPRODUCTION.

Then make a full-sized pattern from the drawing shown in Fig. 7, trace this on one side of the stock, and band-saw it to that shape. Trace it next on the adjacent side, and saw to this shape on the band saw. You now have a squared version of the shape you want. Carefully round the spindle with a spokeshave, scraper blade, file, and sandpaper, and few can tell it was not turned on the lathe.

As to bending the top of the chair, it requires the means for steaming the wood for the period of 6 to 8 hours, and then the cauls and clamps for bending it. Any vessel of metal, large enough to hold it, and which can be covered with a lid, and to the bottom of which heat can be applied, will do to prepare it for bending. Such a device is shown in Fig. 13. Once it has been steamed for a long enough period of time, remove it from the steam bath and place it in the caul. Apply pressure with clamps and keep it there until dry. You will need to wear gloves to do this. Heating the cauls beforehand will help.

Once the piece of wood has been removed from the steam bath, the sooner it can be clamped into the cauls and bent, the better. A minute should be all the time it takes for a piece like this, so everything should be in readiness before the piece is taken out of the steam bath. This will include having the cauls warm, having the clamps adjusted properly, and having a helper at hand to expedite the job. Use C-clamps, as shown in Fig. 14, since they may be adjusted and screwed tight more quickly than wooden hand screws. Be sure to have enough clamps ready to do the job right.

Once the piece of wood has been steamed and clamped into the cauls, it is best to get the moisture out of it as soon as possible, since the sooner you can get it dry, the better it will hold its shape. It is for this reason the ventilating grooves are cut into the cauls crosswise. Place the cauls over a radiator, or some other good place where you may dry it quickly.

It is also a good idea to apply a sealer to the ends of the piece of wood before steaming it. This prevents a greater amount of moisture from entering the wood at the ends, and it helps prevent checking during the drying process.

Air-dried stock is best for bending, and it should be straight grained and free of knots and checks. No shaping or carving is done before bending. This is done only after the piece has been bent, dried, and holes drilled in it to hold the spindle ends.

To build the chair, first cut out stock for the turnings and spindles. Turn the legs from stock 2″ x 2″ x 19″. The bottoms of the legs should be trimmed to the proper length and angles after the chair has been assembled. Note the sharp and crisp turnings and the beauty of the curved elements on these legs, stretchers, and outside spindles on the back. The convex sections are bulbous, the curves changing direction sharply rather than with a gradual sweep. Cusps and fillets are sharp and crisp, and curves join fillets at, or near, right angles. The turnings should be sanded very carefully to preserve the crispness to which attention has been called, for these features distinguish good from shoddy turnings.

When all spindles and turnings have been made, get out stock to make the seat. Well-seasoned, kiln-dried stock should be used for all legs and stretchers, but seats, bent tops, and bows in Windsor chairs should be air dried instead of kiln dried, and preferably be kept just a little on the green side. Then as drying proceeds after the chair has been put together, these air-dried members will shrink, and in doing so will lock themselves tightly around the kiln-dried legs and spindles, and stay tight even after years of service.

At Wallace Nutting's Framingham Studio, when the author was employed there, these seats were carefully and painstakingly formed. First they were roughly scooped out on a special machine, and then they were finished by hand with wide shallow gouges, scraped, shaped, and checked frequently with templates to make each one of its kind alike. Then they were finished off by hand with garnet papers, ranging from coarse to very fine.

Chairmaking is never a simple task. As a matter of fact only the most skillful and experienced cabinetmakers are usually chosen for this kind of work, and they usually become specialists. One of the more exacting tasks in making Windsor chairs is to determine boring angles and to make the setups for doing them properly. When chairs are mass produced, a sample chair is first built,

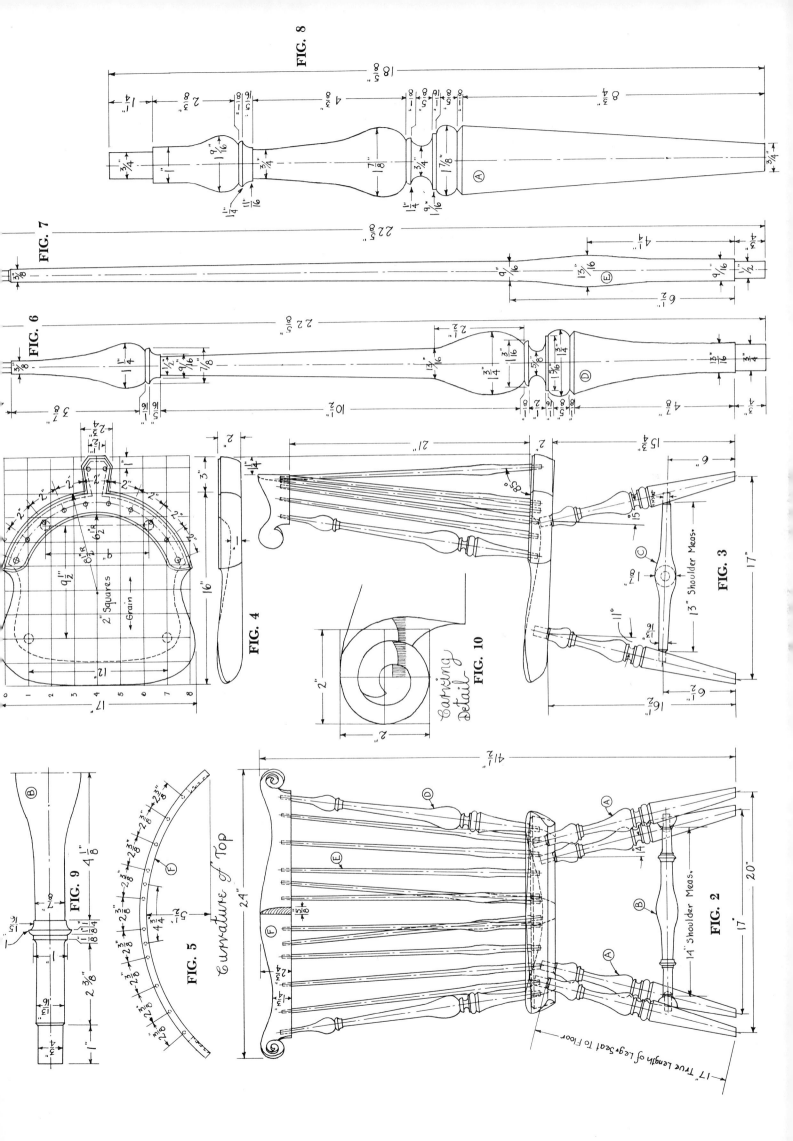

FIG. 8

FIG. 7

FIG. 6

FIG. 4

FIG. 10
Carving Detail

FIG. 3
13" Shoulder Meas.

FIG. 5
Curvature of Top
2 Squares
Grain

FIG. 9

FIG. 2
14" Shoulder Meas.
17" True Length of Leg-Seat To Floor

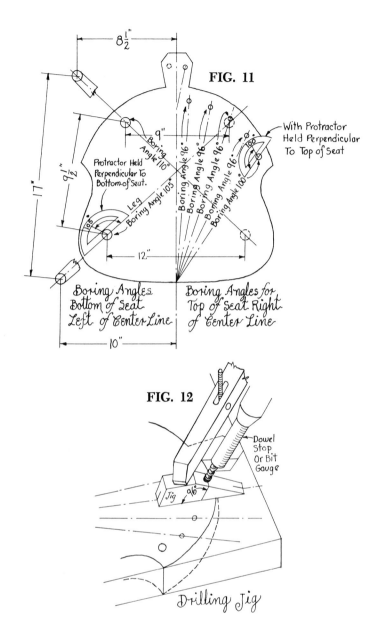

FIG. 11

With Protractor Held Perpendicular To Top of Seat

Boring Angles Bottom of Seat Left of Center Line

Boring Angles for Top of Seat Right of Center Line

FIG. 12

Dowel Stop Or Bit Gauge

Drilling Jig

layout has been made on the stock from which it is to be cut, the jig may be lined up and clamped fast to bore each hole at the proper angle.

When the holes on top of the seat have been bored, the spindles may be stuck into them. Then by arranging them in their proper order against the front of the chair top, the boring angle for each spindle, where it goes into the top, may be marked for drilling. All drilling into the top should be done before the top is shaped or carved. Spindle holes for all spindles (D) and (E), with the exception of the two bracing spindles in the middle of the back, are drilled to be parallel to the sides of the chair top. The holes for the two bracing spindles must be drilled at a slight angle, and this must be carefully done to prevent the drill from coming

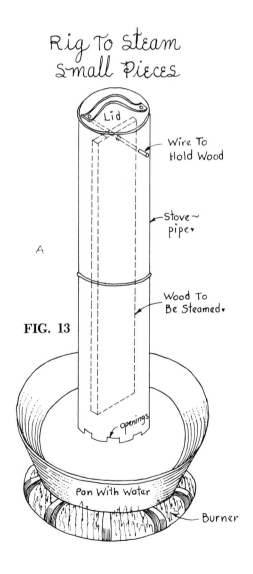

Rig To Steam Small Pieces

Lid

Wire To Hold Wood

Stove-pipe

Wood To Be Steamed

Openings

FIG. 13

Pan With Water

Burner

from which model such things as the angle of each hole has been carefully calculated. With these calculations made, jigs can be made to hold the seat at proper angles, so drilling and boring machines can be adjusted to bore holes at the correct angles.

Since, in most instances, the amateur chairmaker's sample chair is the only one of its kind he may wish to build, simple jigs and setups to do the job are best. Fig. 12 shows such a jig and setup for drilling or boring holes. It will be better to bore these holes on the top and on the bottom of the seat before scooping it out, or even before sawing it to shape, as we show in Fig. 12. Once the seat through the wood on the front side of the top. (See Fig. 3.)

When spindles and top have been fitted, shape and carve the top. Make a full-sized pattern of the carved, spiraled scroll, sometimes referred to as an "ear," shown in Fig. 10, and carve it by first outlining the scroll with a V tool and then trimming the background with an extraflat carver's gouge.

Saw the upper edge to shape and thin it out as shown in the cross-section in Fig. 2.

Glue stretchers (B) and (C) to legs (A) first, when assembling the chair. Then glue the legs to the holes which have been bored into the seat. If clamps are needed to pull the joints tightly together, small blocks of soft white pine should be fitted halfway around the legs to go under the clamps to prevent clamps from marring the turnings. Since bottoms of the legs have not yet been trimmed to rest flat on the floor, the assembled parts, consisting of members (A), (B), and (C), may be hammered into the holes in the bottom of the chair seat with a rubber mallet, though in doing this one must be careful not to split the leg. If the hole is tight for the leg tenon, some care must be taken not to put too much glue into the hole, or it may prevent the tenon from entering the hole all the way. A precaution to prevent this may be taken if a narrow groove is cut lengthwise on the tenon on the inside so the glue may be forced out of the hole when the legs are hammered in.

When the bottom of the chair has been assembled, spindles (D) and (E) for the back may be glued to the holes on top of the seat. The chair top may then be glued to the tops of the spindles. This will complete the building of the chair.

Most Windsor chairs are finished with a yellow brown transparent stain, which may be made with burnt umber mixed with turpentine. Sometimes Vandyke brown, a much darker stain, is substituted.

Wallace Nutting chairs were always finished with six coats of shellac. Every coat was put on thin enough so it could be brushed on easily. When completely dry, each coat was thoroughly rubbed down with fine steel wool. The final coat was hand rubbed with powdered pumice stone and water, and the chair was then given a good polishing and burnishing with beeswax that had been dissolved to a paste with turpentine. A good durable finish may be had with fewer coats of a good floor varnish.

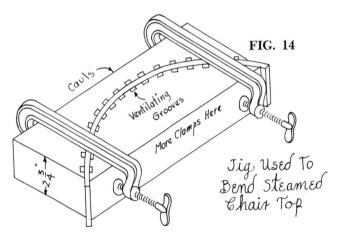

FIG. 14

Jig Used To Bend Steamed Chair Top

BILL OF MATERIAL

Hard Rock Maple

4 Legs (A) 1⅞" diam. x 18⅝"
1 Stretcher (B) 1⅞" diam. x 16"
2 Stretchers (C) 1⅞" diam. x 15"
2 Spindles (D) 1¾" diam. x 22⅝"
10 Spindles (E) 1³⁄₁₆" diam. x 22⅝"

Clear White Pine

1 Seat 2" x 17" x 19"

Hickory or Ash

1 Top ⅝" x 2¾" x 28"

THIRTY-SIX

Queen Anne Side Chair

C HAIRMAKING at its best is exemplified by the walnut Queen Anne Side Chair, shown in Fig. 1. Black walnut is of course the only proper wood to use in building a chair of the Queen Anne period. Both the weight of the wood (for good black walnut is a heavy material) and the way in which the seat frame of this chair is constructed make the chair quite heavy, though its graceful lines belie this fact until one attempts to lift or move it. One could say of it that it is a "solid" piece of furniture as chairs go, because black walnut is a dense, heavy wood, and because the seat-rails are bulkier than they usually are on most modern versions of such chairs. This is good. Otherwise, because of the flamboyant curvature of most of its members, there is a possibility one might feel insecure when using the chair. One need only heft one of these chairs to make sure that it furnishes adequate support, even though the graceful curve of the back may belie this fact.

To build the chair, start by making the front legs. The legs are made of stock 3" x 3" x 16½". Two blocks of wood measuring 1¾" x 2" x 2⅜", or longer, are glued fast to two adjacent sides of these legs near the top, as shown in Figs. 3 and 8. While these blocks of wood (E) may be glued to the leg before any sawing to shape is done, most chairmakers find it easier to glue them to the leg after most of the major part of the leg has been sawed to shape. It is easier to glue the blocks to the legs before any sawing or shaping is done, since all

parts are still square, which makes clamping a simple matter. There are, however, disadvantages we will note below. The blocks should be glued to the legs before any rounding, carving, or final shaping of the leg is done.

Frequently additions like leg blocks (E) are fastened to the leg with one or more short dowels to reinforce the glue joint. Quarter-inch dowels about 1 inch long would suffice if two are used on each block, and they would make the joint stronger. The author has never felt it necessary to use dowels to reinforce joints of this kind, and so far has had none of them come apart. If good glue is used and if the chair is given enough protective coats of finish, such as a high grade of floor varnish will provide, there is little likelihood that the glue joints will fail to hold.

Make a full-sized pattern of the leg from the one we show in Fig. 11. If the blocks (E) have not been fastened to the leg, the pattern may be laid upon the outside of the leg to trace, and two op-

Fig. 1. Queen Anne Side Chair. A ROBERT TREATE HOGG REPRODUCTION.

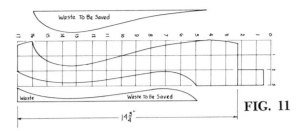

Waste To Be Saved

Waste

Waste To Be Saved

FIG. 11

$14\frac{3}{4}''$

posite sides of the leg may then be sawed to shape on the band saw. When you do this, carefully save the waste, in order that you may tack it back on the leg to help in sawing off the remaining two sides. Brads to fasten this waste must be placed where they will fasten the waste pieces to waste not yet cut off the leg, so the nails will not interfere with the remaining saw cuts to be made or leave holes in the good part of the leg.

When all four sides of the legs have been sawed to shape, you should have the leg outline shaped pretty nearly the way you want it except that it will be square instead of rounded as you want it when it has been completely formed. The dowel on top of the legs, used to fasten the legs to the seat-rails, must be formed. Since this is made on a corner of the main piece it is not practical to turn it on the lathe. It is best to saw off the waste around it, leaving it at least 1 inch square when doing this, and then rounding it with a wood file to fit the 1-inch hole in the front seat-rail, as shown in Fig. 4. To make sure the dowel will fit the hole, bore a 1-inch hole into a block of wood to see if it fits.

Having to shape these dowels by hand is one reason why it is better to glue blocks (E) to the legs after band-sawing the legs to shape rather than before this is done. These blocks should now be glued to the legs, with the grain going in the same direction as the grain of the leg, as shown in Fig. 8. The blocks should be sawed to shape after they have been glued to the leg, so clamps may be applied in making the glue joint. With the pattern of the block drawn on the back of (E) it may then be sawed to shape on the band saw.

The rounding and shaping of the leg should now be begun. Chisels, a spokeshave, scraper blades, and a good wood file may all be used to shape the legs. Shaping, on a leg like this, may be done by mounting the leg on the lathe between lathe centers, which permits turning it as the work pro-

gresses. A block of wood, with an arc to fit the back of the leg cut out of its upper edge, will permit the workman to fasten the leg to the workbench top with a clamp at the middle of the leg while shaping and carving it.

The upper part of the leg should be shaped as nearly right as possible before the shell is carved on its knee. Make a full-sized pattern from Fig. 9. If fillet sections (1-inch-long areas between the lines drawn closest together on the pattern) are cut out with a sharp knife, it will make a stencil by means of which the design may be transferred to the leg. The broken lines may then be filled in or corrected as need be to carve the shell.

Fillet lines between the beads and flutes may be started by outlining the beads, or convex areas, of the shell, first with a wood-carver's V tool, and then flattening the area between the beads with a skew chisel, or a macaroni (square U-shaped tool). Flutes are cut last. Depth of carving on these shells does not vary more than $\frac{1}{8}$ inch between these members at their highest and lowest parts, as can be seen in Fig. 1.

To shape the foot, a full-sized pattern made from the drawing shown at the top of Fig. 8 will be useful, but most of the lines for carving the foot must be drawn freehand and trued up and corrected as the carving proceeds. One thing you must be careful of when shaping the feet is to make them as nearly alike as possible. Too much variation in size or shape will show up badly, because the legs on the chair are close enough together to make comparison easy.

Back legs, top rail in the chairback, and rear seat-rail should be made next. By using full-sized patterns made from the two drawings shown in

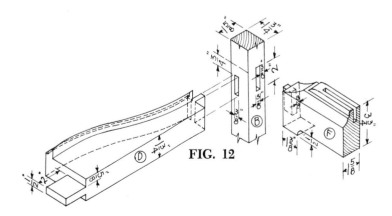

FIG. 12

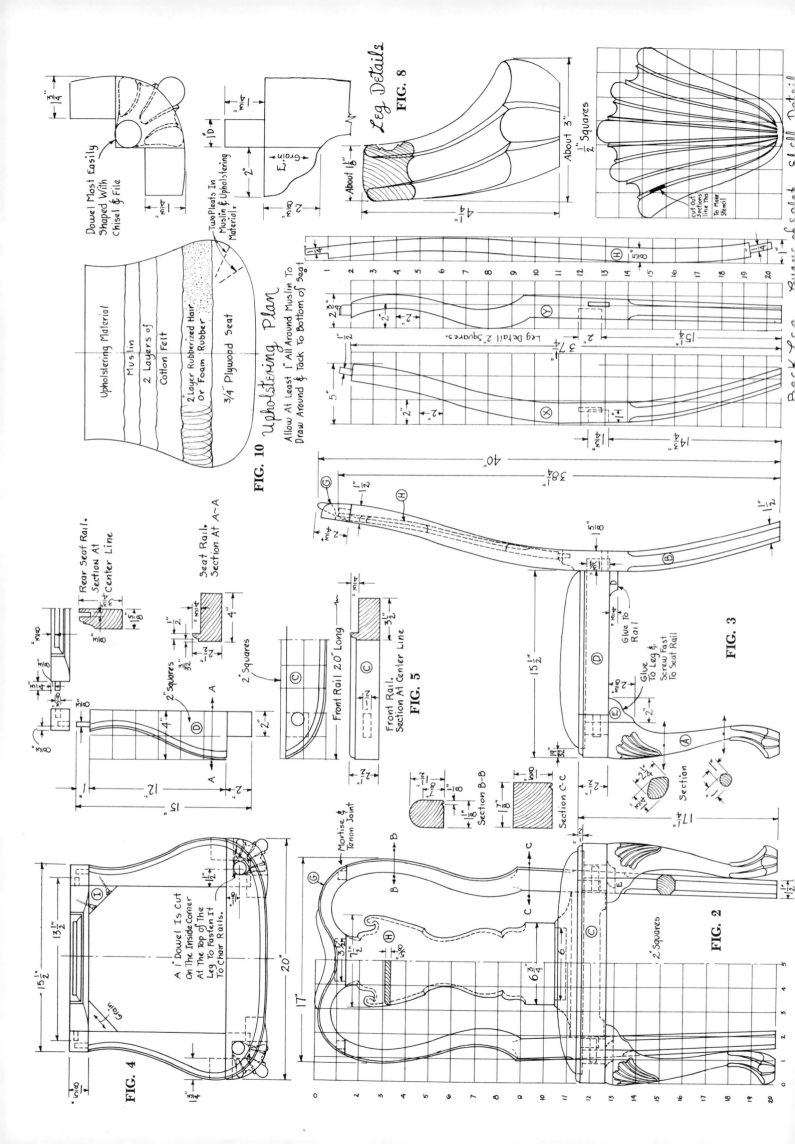

Fig. 6, the back legs may be cut to shape on the band saw. Thick stock is needed to make legs like these, and though pieces could be glued together to get the thickness needed, the use of solid stock of the required thickness is recommended, since this is the correct way of doing it. Although it takes a plank 5 inches wide to make one of these legs, as shown in pattern (X) in Fig. 6, four or five may be cut from a plank only twelve inches wide. Pattern (Y) on the right side of Fig. 6 is correct only if drawn on the plank before the leg has been shaped to pattern (X). If it is to be used as we show it, the waste from the sawing to pattern (X) must be tacked back on after sawing to this pattern. Actually, only the waste on the left side of (X) needs to be tacked back on to saw the leg to the shape of pattern (Y), and if it is done this way, an elongated pattern of (Y) should be made to lay out the shape on the leg so the last two sides may be sawed to shape. A stretchout of (Y) may be made by laying a piece of flexible cardboard like Bristol board on the hollow side of the leg, cut to pattern (X), to find the true length of a pattern to fit this curve. Having measured this on the chair, we find the difference in length to be only about $\frac{5}{8}$ inch. If graph squares are used to plot a stretchout pattern, the squares would need to be lengthened only about $\frac{1}{32}$ inch vertically, and remain the same 2-inch width across to plot the stretchout.

The bottom of both legs should first have all four sides squared to each other, and these surfaces smoothed up to where the S curve begins. A pattern for the top rail should now be made, and its lower curves should be sawed to shape on the band saw. Do not saw it to shape on top, but keep the top straight so clamps may be used to glue up the chairback.

Draw patterns to make the splat and cut this to shape. If your band saw is large enough the saw guard may be raised high enough to saw the splat to the shape of the pattern in Fig. 7. If not, then this curvature must be arrived at by using gouges, chisels, and scrapers. In any event this part of the shaping of the splat should be done before it is cut to the shape shown in Fig. 2.

Now make the back seat-rail except the tenons. Do not shape the top of the rail until the mortising and fitting of the joints has been completed. Make all mortises on legs and rails before cutting and fitting the tenons, since it is easier and better to do it this way.

Make a full-sized octagon pattern measuring $1\frac{1}{2}$ inches across the flats, like the one shown in cross-section on Fig. 2. Trace this on the bottom of the back leg to start cutting this part of the leg to the octagon shape. Since the leg is smaller at the bottom than it is where the stretchers are joined to it, the flat sides of this octagon-shaped part will become wider as the top is reached.

When the lower part of the back legs has been shaped, lay out and cut the mortises for the rear seat-rail. These are $\frac{3}{8}$ inch thick, 2 inches wide, and $\frac{3}{4}$ inch deep. As may be seen by looking at Fig. 2, the back legs come closer together at the floor than at the seat. This makes it necessary to cut the shoulders of the tenons on the rear seat-rail at an angle of about 92 degrees instead of 90 degrees as they would be if the two legs were parallel. Before laying out this angle, you may check for accuracy by drawing a center line on a clean floor or large piece of plywood. Draw a base line perpendicular to the bottom of the center line, and above this base line lay pattern (Y), so the inside of the pattern at the base is $5\frac{1}{2}$ inches from the center line, and the outside of its greatest width at the top is $8\frac{1}{2}$ inches from the center line. Lay a full-sized pattern of the rear seat stretcher under (Y) with its center lined up with the center line of the chairback layout. This will give you the exact angle for the shoulders of these tenons. When doing chair work, it is a good idea to check all angles for joints that are not square in this manner, using full-size layouts to ensure accuracy.

When the rear seat-rail has been fitted to the back legs, cut the mortise into the top for the joint with the bottom of the curved splat. Then complete this joint. The joints at the top of the chair should now be made, and here, if one is not too experienced at chair joinery, leave a little extra wood on top of the shoulders of the tenons on both back legs and splat, when fitting the joints. This is trimmed down after a trial assembly of the back of the chair has been made. Corrections can then still be made to ensure well-fitting joints.

Once these joints have all been properly fitted, you will be ready to shape the top of the rear seat-rail and to bevel the edges of the splat at the back, if you have not already done so. Also lay out and cut mortises into the back legs for holding the seat-rails (D), which go on each side of the chair. Then glue the chairback together. (See Fig. 12.)

Shaping, on the upper part of the back legs and on the top rail, which has been held in abeyance up to now so clamping and gluing could be done more easily, should now be undertaken and completed.

Now cut out stock for the front seat-rail (C) and side rails (D). Saw side rails to shape immediately, and hollow out at the top of these for the seat. Some of this may be done with a dado head on a table saw; the work may then be completed with a portable electric hand router if the two rails are clamped with the insides together. The quarter-round molding around the outside may be shaped with the same machine or on a regular shaper. If such machinery is not available, molding and hollowing out may be done with wood-carving chisels and other hand tools.

It is best to shape the front rail of the seat after mortise-and-tenon joints, and holes for fastening the front legs, have been made and fitted. When all this has been done, and the front rail has been sawed and shaped up, the chair may be glued together. For chair work of this kind, special clamps with flexible bands to fit around the curved parts are often used in furniture factories. For the amateur who has no such equipment, the waste sawed off of the front seat-rail may be used under the clamps in front of the chair to pull the joints together when gluing up the chair.

Once the chair is glued up, all necessary sanding and cleaning up of glue joints should be done to get the chair ready to put on the finish. To put on a good finish read the directions given in Chapter 2.

Fig. 10 gives some directions for upholstering the chair seat, which is made by sawing a ¾-inch plywood panel to shape. Use a fairly good grade of plywood with no hollow places on the inside layers around the edges. If pine or some other soft solid wood is used for the seat, the grain will have to run across the seat from side to side. Corner bracing blocks (I) are needed only at the back of the chair to brace it at the seat; these are shown in Fig. 4. This kind of seat is known as a slip seat. It may be screwed fast to the bracing blocks to hold it in the chair after it has been upholstered. About ⅛-inch clearance should be left all around the edge to pull the covers around and tack them fast under the seat.

First fit a 2-inch layer of rubberized hair or foam rubber to the seat board. If foam rubber is used, taper the edges on the underside by trimming at an angle with large shears all around the edges, thus leaving the edges flat and square with the top for only about half the thickness of the foam rubber. Over the foam rubber put two layers of cotton felt, and then over this stretch a sheet of strong muslin. This is pulled tight around the edges of the seat, and tacked underneath with 3- or 4-ounce tacks. Tacking should be started in the middle on every side first, and tacking goes from there to each corner. Do not draw the muslin down too tight, and try to avoid wrinkles like those on the corner of the chair in Fig. 1, where it was evidently done hurriedly and improperly. It will need to be done over before the upholstery material can properly be put on top of it. Cuts with scissors should be made into corners like this to permit drawing it smoothly around the corners without wrinkling. Over a good smooth surface draw the upholstery material around the edges and tack it fast below the seat to complete the chair.

BILL OF MATERIAL

Walnut

2 Front legs (A) 3″ x 3″ x 16½″
2 Back legs (B) 2¾″ x 5″ x 38¼″ *
1 Front seat-rail (C) 2½″ x 3½″ x 20″
2 Side seat-rails (D) 2½″ x 4″ x 15″
2 Small blocks (D₁) ¾″ x 1¾″ x 2¼″

* Each additional 1⅞ inches added to the width of this plank will permit the cutting of another leg.

4 Blocks (E) 1¾″ x 2″ x 2⅜″
1 Back seat-rail (F) 1⅝″ x 4⅜″ x 13½″
1 Chairback top rail (G) 1½″ x 2¾″ x 16″
1 Curved splat (H) 1″ x 7½″ x 20¼″
2 Brace blocks for seat (I) 1½″ x 1¾″ x 3½″

Birch Plywood

1 Seat ¾″ x 15″ x 19″ (Width and length approximate sizes)

THIRTY-SEVEN

Chippendale Ladder-Back Side Chair

THIS ladder-back Chippendale chair is one of a set of dining chairs, designed by the author and built by students in the workshops of the Berry Schools, for the Georgian Colonial Dining Room in Oak Hill. Oak Hill is the ancestral home of Martha Berry, Founder of the Berry Schools, just outside of Rome, Georgia; it is one of the few great pre-Civil War mansions in that section of Georgia to have escaped the torch and the looting on Sherman's March to the Sea.

This great mansion was restored, refurbished, and to a great extent refurnished during Martha Berry's lifetime, a work in which the author was privileged to have a hand. It remained her home until her death in 1942. Since then it has been preserved as a shrine and school museum in her honor.

The set, consisting of eight side chairs and two armchairs, is built of Honduras mahogany and is upholstered in a brocade fabric.

To build the side chair, first cut out two back legs. As indicated in our Bill of Material, two of these legs may be cut from a plank about six inches wide. These must be properly shaped and mortised to make a pair—one left and one right leg, as shown in Fig. 2. A pattern for these legs is shown in Fig. 8 for the Chippendale Ladder-Back Armchair in Chapter 38, except that on the side chairs no mortises are cut into the legs to join arms to them. In all other respects the back legs for both chairs are alike.

Shape the legs as shown in the pattern (armchair, Fig. 8 in Chapter 38) and in Fig. 2, but do no carving on the two outside edges until the entire chairback has been assembled.

Cut out, plane, and shape the front legs. Lay out and cut mortises into these, and chamfer the inside corner of the leg as shown in Figs. 2, 3, and 4. The bead molding on the opposite outside corner may also be carved, or shaped, at this time. Cut away the offsets at the top of these legs so the upholstering fabric will come flush with the surface of the chair leg after it has been put on.

Layouts from which full-size patterns of the rails in the chairback may be made are shown in Fig. 10 of Chapter 38 for the armchair. Lay these out full size on lumber 2⅛ inches thick for the top rail, and on stock 1¼ inches thick for the three bottom rails. These rails are first sawed to the curvatures shown in the drawing at the top for the upper rail, and near the middle of the chairback in Fig. 2 for

Fig. 1. Chippendale Ladder-Back Side Chair. BUILT IN THE BERRY COLLEGE SHOPS.

201

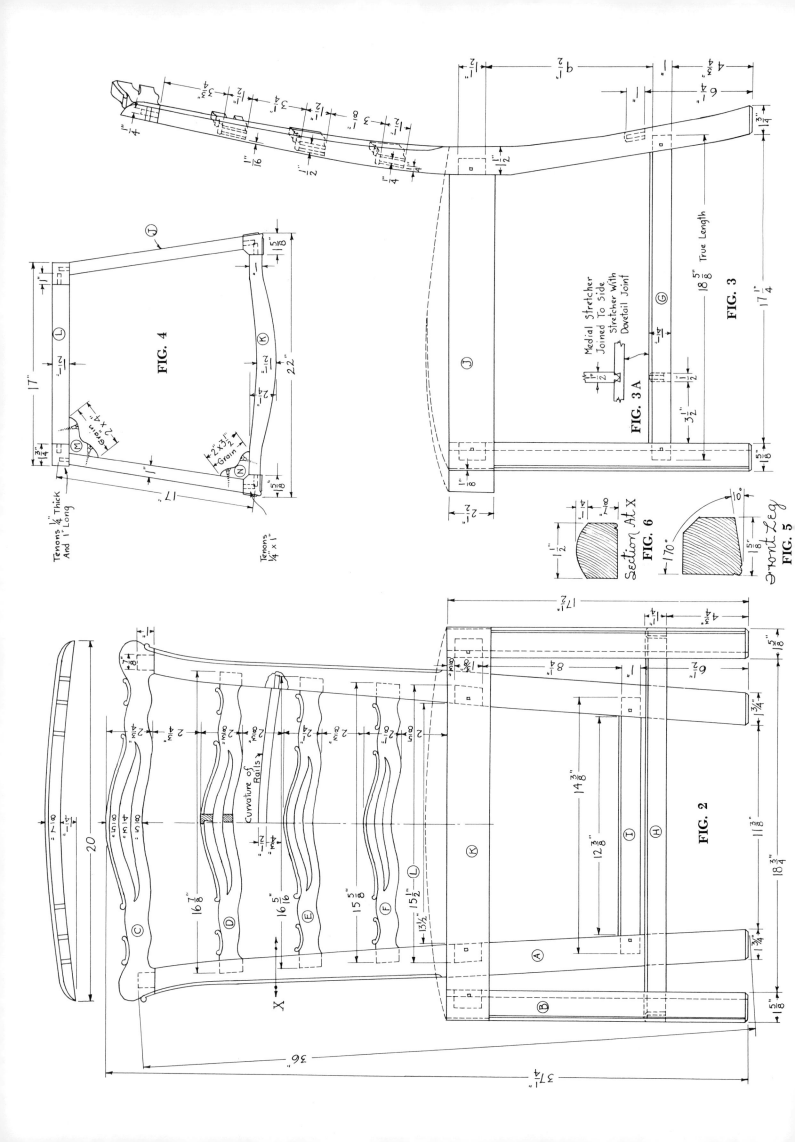

FIG. 4

FIG. 3

FIG. 3 A

Medial Stretcher
Joined To Side
Stretcher With
Dovetail Joint

18 5/8" True Length

Section At X
FIG. 6

Front Leg
FIG. 5

Tenons 1/4 Thick
And 1" Long

Tenons 1/4" × 1"

Curvature of Rails

FIG. 2

the three lower rails. This is done on the band saw. Surfaces are then smoothed and sanded. If one is available, an adjustable curved-bottom plane is ideal for doing this work. If not, sanding drums fastened in a drill-press chuck may be used, or hand trimming, filing, and sanding will do the job.

Before cutting the rails to shape, as we show them in Fig. 10 for the armchair in Chapter 38, cut mortises for joining the back legs into rail (C), and lay out and cut tenons on both ends of rails (D), (E), and (F). Fit these to the back legs, lining them up very carefully so both back legs are joined to them at the proper angle, which must be the same on both sides. Then cut the rails to shape at the top and bottom, and cut the opening in the middle. Do not carve the molding on top of these rails until the chairback has been assembled and glued together.

Cut out stock for the lower stretcher (I) and seat-rail (L). Make a trial assembly of the back and, when you have it properly fitted together, glue it up. Make seat-rails (J) and (K) and bottom rails (G) and (H). Cut tenons on both ends of these, and shape them as shown in the drawings. Glue seat-rail (K) to the front legs; then make a trial assembly of seat-rails (J) and lower side rails (G) with the glued-up front and back. Check the trial assembly carefully to be sure both sides of the chair are joined to the front and back of the chair at the same angle. This is very important, to avoid having a lopsided chair once it has been glued up. Proper shaping of bracing blocks (M) and (N) will also help prevent this. While the trial assembly is being made, the dovetails on both ends of medial stretcher (H) may be cut, and layouts for mortise members of these dovetail joints may be laid out on side stretchers (G). Remove side stretchers (G) from the chair to make the dovetail joints, as shown in Figs. 3 and 3-A.

Before gluing the chair front and the side and medial stretchers to the chairback, carve the back of the chair as shown in Figs. 1 and 2. See cross-section on rail (D) in Fig. 2.

Now glue the side rails to the back and front of the chair, and then glue the medial stretcher to side rails (G). When glue has been cleaned from the joints and the chair has been carefully sanded, you will be ready to put on a good finish. We recom-

mend this be done in the same manner as putting the finish on the Pierced Splat-Back Chippendale Chair in Chapter 39; before starting, read the instructions given for doing that chair.

The upholstering on these chairs is done differently, however, since springs, which the splat-back chair did not have, are put into the seats of these chairs. Three rows of the highest grade 3½-inch webbing are tacked to the bottom of the chair seat, going from front to back, and three more are interwoven with these going from side to side, as shown in Figs. 7, 8, and 9. First double over the end of the webbing and tack it with five 16-ounce tacks to the bottom of the rear seat-rail. With a webbing stretcher, pull it over the bottom of the front seat-rail and hold it there with three tacks, and then double back the end and tack it with five more tacks. Do the same thing with the webbing going from side to side.

Use nine #1 car-seat springs for each seat, placing them upon the webbing on the inside of the seat frame, as shown in Fig. 7. Clip the bottoms of these springs to the webbing to hold them securely in place, as shown in Fig. 9.

Using the best grade spring twine obtainable, tie the springs first front to back, and then side to side, as shown in Figs. 7, 10, and 11. Drive a 16-ounce tack partway into the front seat stretcher at 1, Fig. 7. To this tack tie the middle of a long piece of twine, and then tie it with an upholsterer's knot to the top of the spring at 2. An upholsterer's knot is a square knot made by passing the twine over the top of the coiled spring, then looping it around the upper coil and back toward you under the wire. From here loop it over the spring, then back under the string, thus forming a square knot. Pull this knot tight, being sure to keep the loops of the knot on top of the wire. Keeping the knot on top of the wire makes the twine wear much longer, since the top of the knot will stand greater wear than the bottom. See Fig. 14.

Proceed from 2 to 3, from 3 to 4, and so on to the rear seat rung where you drive another 16-ounce tack partly into the wood and tie the end of the twine to it. Then drive the tacks into the wood completely. Starting at 7 on the front seat stretcher with the other half of the twine, tie it from front to 14 in the back, in the same manner as you did the first half. Tie the two other rows of springs from front to back in the same way you did the middle row. When tying the knot at 2 and 5, compress the spring so its top will be about 1 inch higher than the tops of the seat stretchers. Then when the spring is tied at 8, and from there back

to 14, the upper coils of the springs can be pulled down so they too will be only an inch higher than the top of the seat frame.

Now tie the springs from side to side, as shown in Figs. 7 and 11. Start at 1 on the left seat-rail. Go from 1 to 6, where you tack it as you did the front-to-back twine. Then tie from 7 to 9, compressing the springs until they are 1 inch above the seat frame. Then tie the twine from 10 to 12 in the same manner.

Next tie the springs diagonally, as shown in Figs. 8 and 12. Rows of twine should be kept parallel as shown in Fig. 8, or it may be done as shown in Fig. 7 in drawings in Chapter 34 on the uphol-stered Hepplewhite Armchair.

When the springs have been tied as described above, tack a piece of 10-ounce burlap over them as shown in Fig. 9. When tacking burlap, muslin, upholstering material, or any other cloth to a seat, start tacking in the middle and tack from there to the ends on either side. First slip-tack; that is, drive the tacks only part of the way into the wood so they can be moved if necessary to adjust the cloth until it is correctly fitted. Then drive the tacks home.

On top of the front and side rails tack strips of 1-inch paper edge-roll, as shown in Fig. 9. This helps keep the filling material in place and prevents wear on the upholstering material at sharp corners.

To fill and pad the seat you have a choice of several different kinds of filling material. Curled hair, which for years was considered the best filling material, is now in many instances being replaced by rubberized hair, and by foam rubber, or by both. Certain advantages to using rubberized hair and foam rubber should be noted here: the cost

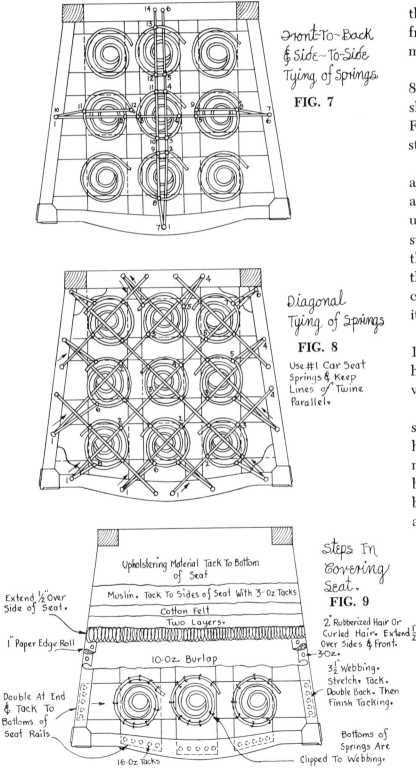

Front-To-Back & Side-To-Side Tying of Springs

FIG. 7

Diagonal Tying of Springs

FIG. 8

Use #1 Car Seat Springs & Keep Lines of Twine Parallel.

Steps In Covering Seat.

FIG. 9

Upholstering Material Tack To Bottom of Seat

Extend ½" Over Side of Seat.

Muslin. Tack To Sides of Seat With 3-Oz Tacks

Cotton Felt

Two Layers.

1" Paper Edge Roll

2" Rubberized Hair Or Curled Hair. Extend ½" Over Sides & Front.

3-Oz.

3½" Webbing. Stretch. Tack. Double Back. Then Finish Tacking.

10-Oz. Burlap

Double At End & Tack To Bottoms of Seat Rails.

16-Oz Tacks

Bottoms of Springs Are Clipped To Webbing.

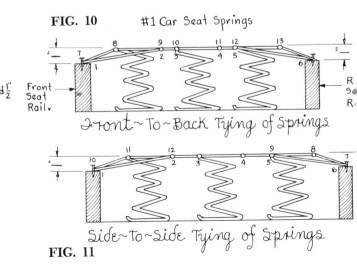

FIG. 10   #1 Car Seat Springs

Front Seat Rail.

Front-To-Back Tying of Springs

Side-To-Side Tying of Springs

FIG. 11

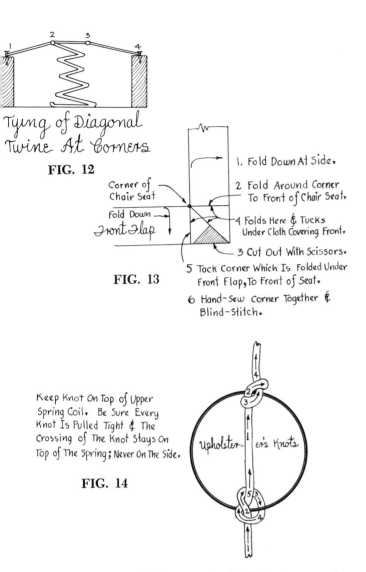

Tying of Diagonal Twine At Corners

FIG. 12

Corner of Chair Seat

Fold Down
Front Flap

FIG. 13

1. Fold Down At Side.

2 Fold Around Corner To Front of Chair Seat.

4 Folds Here & Tucks Under Cloth Covering Front.

3 Cut Out With Scissors.

5 Tack Corner Which Is Folded Under Front Flap, To Front of Seat.

6 Hand-Sew Corner Together & Blind-Stitch.

Keep Knot On Top of Upper Spring Coil. Be Sure Every Knot Is Pulled Tight & The Crossing of The Knot Stays On Top of The Spring; Never On The Side.

FIG. 14

Upholsterer's Knots

no holes or sunken areas will be left to be filled in with cotton, as would be the case were the filling material to be held in place with loops of twine.

If rubberized hair is chosen as the filling material for this seat, use a 2-inch layer and extend it at least ½ inch over the front and sides of the seat frame, to form a well-rounded contour at the sharp edges of the seat. Over the hair put two layers of cotton felt and hold this in place with a sheet of good grade muslin tacked to the sides of the seat with 3-ounce tacks, as shown in Fig. 9.

Now fit and cut the upholstering material. There are a number of materials to choose from for Chippendale chairs. The chair shown in Fig. 1 was upholstered in brocade, but tapestry may be used, and is an appropriate material and should wear well. Recently very high grade cut velvets of nylon have appeared on the market, and they are excellent both in quality and pattern for chairs of this style.

Slip-tack the cover until corners are cut and fitted. Enough cloth must be left on all sides to tack it fast to the bottoms of the seat stretchers, and tacking is started at the center on each side. Where the cloth is to be fitted around the back chair leg, cut the cloth on the bias from the corner to the inside corner of the chair leg exactly. Then fold both corners under and tack it with gimp tacks or small-headed upholstering nails to the sides and back of the seat-rails.

To make the front corner, fold the cloth down over the chair rail at the side, then follow the steps in their proper order, as shown in Fig. 13, to complete the corner. Tack the chair cover to the bottom of the chair rails. Then cover the bottom of the chair seat with a piece of black cambric.

is usually less, and they may be held in place easily by gluing them to the burlap, wood, or other materials with rubberized spray glue which holds them firmly. Afterward, edges of the filling material may be trimmed to shape, and corners may be trimmed to get good contour around the edges. Furthermore, since the filling material is glued fast,

BILL OF MATERIAL

Mahogany

2 Back legs (A) 1¾" x 4" x 36" *

2 Front legs (B) 1⅝" x 1⅝" x 17½"

1 Top rail (C) 2⅛" x 2¾" x 20"

1 Rail (D) 1¼" x 2⅜" x 16⅞"

1 Rail (E) 1¼" x 2¼" x 16⁵⁄₁₆"

1 Rail (F) 1¼" x 2⅛" x 15⅝"

2 Side stretchers (G) ½" x 1¼" x 18⅝"

* Make one left and one right leg. Two legs may be cut from a single plank 6 inches wide.

1 Medial Stretcher (H) ½" x 1¼" x 20"

1 Back Stretcher (I) ½" x 1¼" x 14⅜"

Soft-textured Hardwood
(yellow pine, soft maple, or other)

2 Side seat-rails (J) 1" x 2½" x 17"

1 Front seat-rail (K) 2¼" x 2½" x 20¾"

1 Back seat-rail (L) 1½" x 2½" x 15½"

2 Corner braces (M) 1¼" x 2" x 4"

2 Corner braces (N) 1¼" x 2" x 3½"

THIRTY-EIGHT

Chippendale Ladder-Back Armchair

THE only difference between the ladder-back armchair and the ladder-back side chair just described in Chapter 37 is the arms which have been added. The sizes of other elements of the chairs are exactly alike.

In many instances when a set of chairs consisting of one or more armchairs and a number of side chairs is made, armchairs are made somewhat wider than the side chairs in the set. Since the side chairs in this set are generous in width, the armchairs were made no wider. On a long table like the one shown and described in Chapter 15, having legs which do not interfere with placing chairs like this close to the table and close together as well, wide chairs such as these are not only acceptable but desirable. Most dining chairs are not made as wide as these, especially side chairs, in order that enough of them may be placed along the sides of a table to fit between table legs that are not very far apart.

Chippendale chairs of good design quite generally are built with wide seats, because at the time they were originally conceived the skirts worn by ladies were voluminous, making wide chair seats not only desirable but necessary.

Because the parts of the chair, with the exception of the arms and arm supports are all alike, no description of the parts or construction described for the side chair will be repeated here, except as

it applies to the differences made by the addition of the arms and the arm supports.

So, to build the armchair, proceed as you would were you building a side chair. When making the two back legs, the mortises to which the back ends of the arms are joined will have to be added, as shown in Figs. 4 and 5. Arms and arm supports will have to be cut out, shaped, fitted together, and to the chair, and then carved. Please note that in doing this the chair itself may be completely assembled and glued up, just as were the side chairs, before the arms need be fitted to it. Carving on the arms and arm supports should, however, be done before they are glued to the chair.

The mortise-and-tenon joints used to join the arm supports to the arms should be made and fitted before shaping the bottom of the arm, since leaving the bottom of the arm flat from front to back will make the doing of this easier and minimize the risk of splitting off a section under the arm where the support is joined to it. Full-sized patterns for the arms and supports may be made from the patterns shown in Fig. 9. A careful ex-

Fig. 1. Chippendale Ladder-Back Armchair. BUILT IN THE BERRY COLLEGE SHOPS.

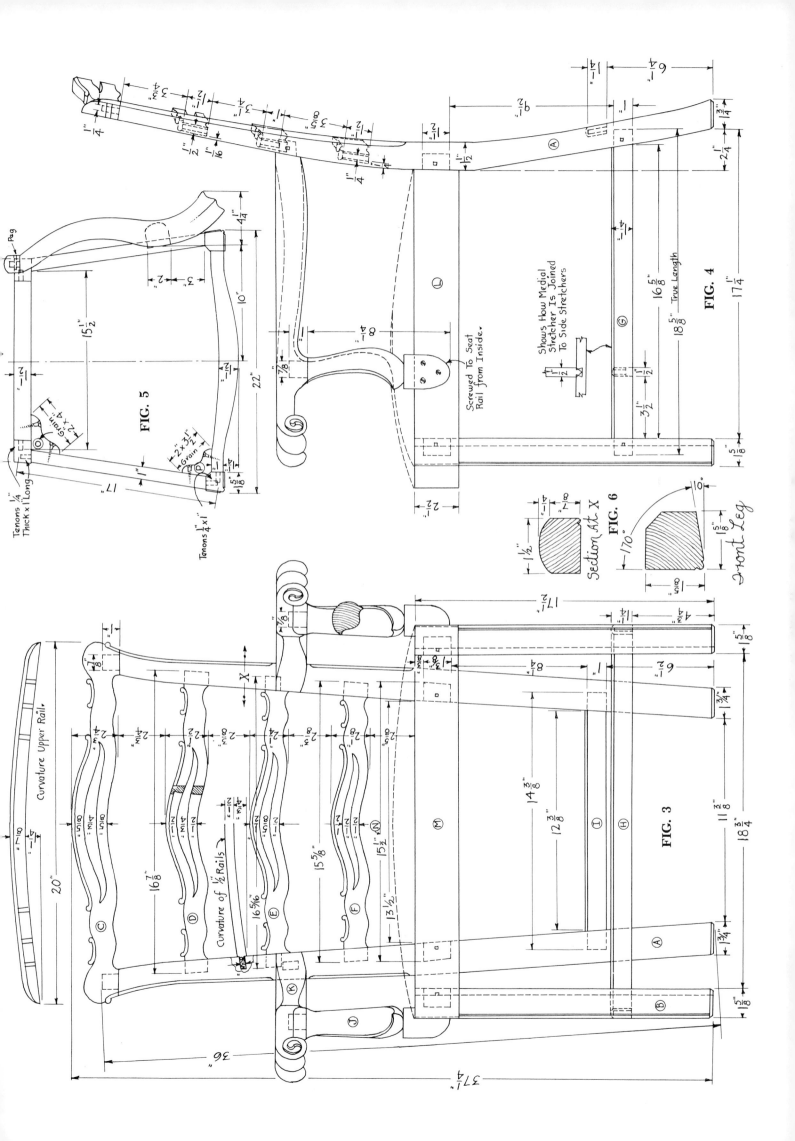

FIG. 5

FIG. 4

FIG. 6

Section At X

Front Leg

FIG. 3

Curvature Upper Rail.

Curvature of ½ Rails

Shows How Medial Stretcher Is Joined To Side Stretchers

Screwed To Seat Rail from Inside.

Peg

Tenons ¼" Thick × 1" Long

Tenons ¼ × 1

Grain

of the arm supports. Arms and supports should be sawed to shape before assembling, but parts of the shaping, such as the place where the arm and support join each other, may be completed after the two have been glued together.

Wooden pegs are used to strengthen many of the mortise-and-tenon joints on these chairs.

Since the arm supports are fastened to the seat of the armchair at both sides, it should be noted that the chair-seat covering materials must be fitted around them. We show how to do this in Fig. 11. First cut the cloth from the edge of the material at the side of the chair up to the slanted lines. Then make the angled cuts at both sides, following the directions given in Fig. 11 carefully. Flap Z

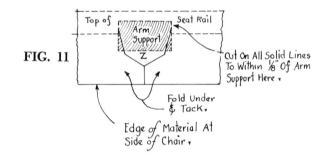

FIG. 11

may then be tacked or glued to the inside and top of the seat-rail under the arm support, and the flaps at each side may be doubled back under the cloth on both sides of the arm support and tacked to the seat-rail with gimp tacks. No covering material over the springs can be fastened to the inside of the seat-rail at the arm support until all have been fitted and placed there. This includes burlap, muslin, and upholstering material.

Fig. 2.   Side View.

amination of Figs. 1, 2, 3, 4, and 5 will show how the arm and its support should be shaped and carved. The cross-section view of the arm support in Fig. 3 shows the 45-degree angle of the shaping

BILL OF MATERIAL

Mahogany

2 Back legs (A) 1¾" x 4" x 36" *
2 Front legs (B) 1⅝" x 1⅝" x 17½"
1 Top rail (C) 2⅛" x 2¾" x 20"
1 Rail (D) 1¼" x 2⅜" x 16⅞"
1 Rail (E) 1¼" x 2¼" x 16⁵⁄₁₆"
1 Rail (F) 1¼" x 2⅛" x 15⅝"
2 Side stretchers (G) ½" x 1¼" x 18⅝"

* Make one left and one right leg. Two legs may be cut from a single plank 6 inches wide.

1 Medial stretcher (H) ½" x 1¼" x 20"
1 Back stretcher (I) ½" x 1¼" x 14⅜"
2 Arm supports (J) 2" x 2¼" x 9¼"
2 Arms (K) 1¾" x 4" x 19½"

Soft-textured Hardwood

2 Side seat-rails (L) 1" x 2½" x 17"
1 Front seat-rail (M) 2¼" x 2½" x 20¾"
1 Back seat-rail (N) 1½" x 2½" x 15½"
2 Corner braces (O) 1¼" x 2" x 4"
2 Corner braces (P) 1¼" x 2" x 3½"

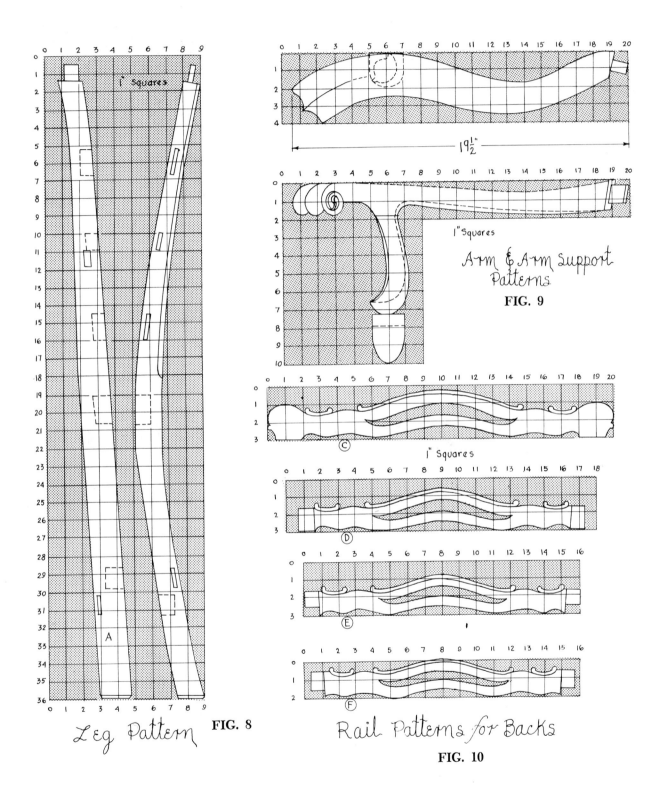

1" Squares

Leg Pattern   **FIG. 8**

19½"

1" Squares

Arm & Arm Support Patterns

FIG. 9

1" Squares

C

D

E

F

Rail Patterns for Backs

FIG. 10

THIRTY-NINE

Chippendale Pierced Splat-Back Chair

THE beautifully carved pierced splat and top rail give this chairback a lacelike aspect. Some Chippendale chairbacks are aesthetically disappointing in appearance. Those with a Gothic motif seem better fitted to an institution than a home. The elaborately scrolled ribbon backs often appear weak or frivolous. The designs of backs with a Chinese motif, the structural elements of which are made to simulate bamboo, seem "arty" and never quite appear to belong in schemes of furnishing meant for our Western ways.

There is just a touch of the Gothic in the cutouts on the bottom of the splat on this chair, and the intertwining of the curved elements of the chairback may very well have been adapted from the ribbon backs that in Chippendale's books of elaborate furniture designs gave the impression of being structurally unsound, uncomfortable, and impractical.

Regardless of the origin from which this motif may have been adapted, it is sturdy enough and does credit to the great style of furniture whose name it bears.

Only genuine mahogany should be used to build such a chair. High-grade South American mahogany, which is heavy and quite dense in structure, should be used.

To build the chair, first make two front legs (A). These are squared on three sides, but the fourth side, at the sides of the chair, is slanted to conform to the angle of the chair seat from front to back. The legs are cut away at the top to a depth of about ⅛ inch at the front and sides, to keep the upholstering material even with these surfaces of the chair legs. See Fig. 16. When this has been done, make layouts and cut the mortises. While side rails are fastened to these and to the back legs at an angle, the mortises are cut into the legs perpendicular to the sides against which the shoulders of the tenons are joined. Tenons on the rails and stretchers are cut at an angle to make them perpendicular to the shoulders of the tenons fitted to the legs.

After making all mortises in the front legs, shape the molding on the outside corner. This may be done with a spindle shaper, or with a portable hand-shaper.

From our drawings in Fig. 12, make a full-sized pattern of the back leg. As we have indicated in our Bill of Material, two legs may be cut from a plank only a few inches wider than the one which is wide enough to make one leg. Remember, though, to make the layouts for one right and one left leg, to make the pair. Lay out and cut the mortises on these two legs, and then lay out and cut tenons at the top.

Now make full-sized patterns of the chair rail at the top and of the pierced splat. On a piece of

Fig. 1. Chippendale Pierced Splat-Back Chair. BUILT IN THE BERRY COLLEGE SHOPS.

stock cut to the proper size, as given in the Bill of Material, lay out the design of chair rail (D). This should include the design for carving it. A sheet of carbon paper, placed under the pattern, can be used to transfer the design to the wood, but a better way is to cut a stencil on a full-sized pattern made of Bristol board. This is the method used by professional wood-carvers, and we show how such a pattern may be made in Fig. 17. (Also see Fig. 52, page 22.) Carvers cut these stencils with carving chisels.

When building this type of chair, the carving should be done only after the entire chairback has been assembled and glued up. Doing it this way permits the wood-carver to make small adjustments and corrections after the pattern has been transferred to the wood. Drawing the elements to be carved on the wood before the chairback has been assembled does make it easier to check proper placement of areas to be cut out, including mortises and tenons.

Make the rear seat-rail (H) and lower stretcher (G). The five pieces: legs (B), rails (D), (H), and (G) should be made and the joints fitted together before cutting the openings in rail (D) and before sawing the outline of rail (D) to shape. Doing it this way permits the use of clamps while this part of the work is in progress, without danger of badly marring ornamentation. The same rule should be observed when fitting the splat to these members. Joints should be made and trued up before making the cutouts or doing the carving.

Some chairmakers prefer to fit the splat before fitting the top rail. The author has always done it the other way, and the one who tries it both ways will find advantages and disadvantages to whichever sequence he uses.

Once all joints on the pieces comprising the back of the chair have been made to fit together, you will then be ready to make the cutouts on the splat and top, and to cut the outlines to shape on the band saw. Smooth all edges which have been cut to shape very carefully with files and open-coat garnet paper. Then true up your designs which are to be carved, and proceed with this most interesting part of the work. Figs. 2, 13, and 15 should show all you will need to know to accomplish this.

After the chairback has been carved and carefully sanded get out stock to make stretchers (E) and (F) and seat-rails (I) and (J). Cut tenons on the rails and stretchers, where they are to be joined to the legs, and fit all of these joints. The dovetails on medial stretcher (F) may be cut and shaped as soon as it is determined the stretcher is cut to the proper length. The dovetail mortises on the side stretchers (E) are best laid out while a trial assembly of the chair is being made to check the other joints. Note that this dovetail does not go much more than halfway across stretchers (E) and (F).

Once the trial assembly has been made and all joints checked out, glue the front seat-rail to the two front legs and peg the mortise-and-tenon joints as shown in Fig. 16. The mortise-and-tenon joints at the bottom of the chair can also be made stronger by reinforcing them with wooden pegs about ⅛-inch to ³⁄₁₆-inch square.

Glue side rails and stretchers to the front and back. Then glue the medial stretcher to the side stretchers. Clean up all glued joints and do what sanding remains to be done, finishing up with #6/0 or #8/0 open-coat garnet paper.

You are now ready to put on a suitable finish. One of the most beautiful of these results from the chemical action of quicklime dissolved in water applied to mahogany wood to color it. This treatment turns the mahogany to a rich red color that to our way of thinking cannot be matched by using any other method of coloring on mahogany. After whitewashing the chair with this ingredient, it should be cleaned off with soft burlap or other cloth, and then washed off thoroughly with boiled linseed oil thinned with turpentine. This must be allowed to soak into the wood and dry thoroughly before filler and the coats that come after it are applied. Chapter 2 on wood finishing will tell you how to proceed from here.

No springs are used to upholster this chair. Fig. 16 shows how the upholstering is put on. To do the upholstering proceed as follows: first stretch a good grade of 3½-inch webbing from one side of the chair to the other, tacking one end to the top of the left side with two 16-ounce tacks, and then doubling the webbing back over the tacks and

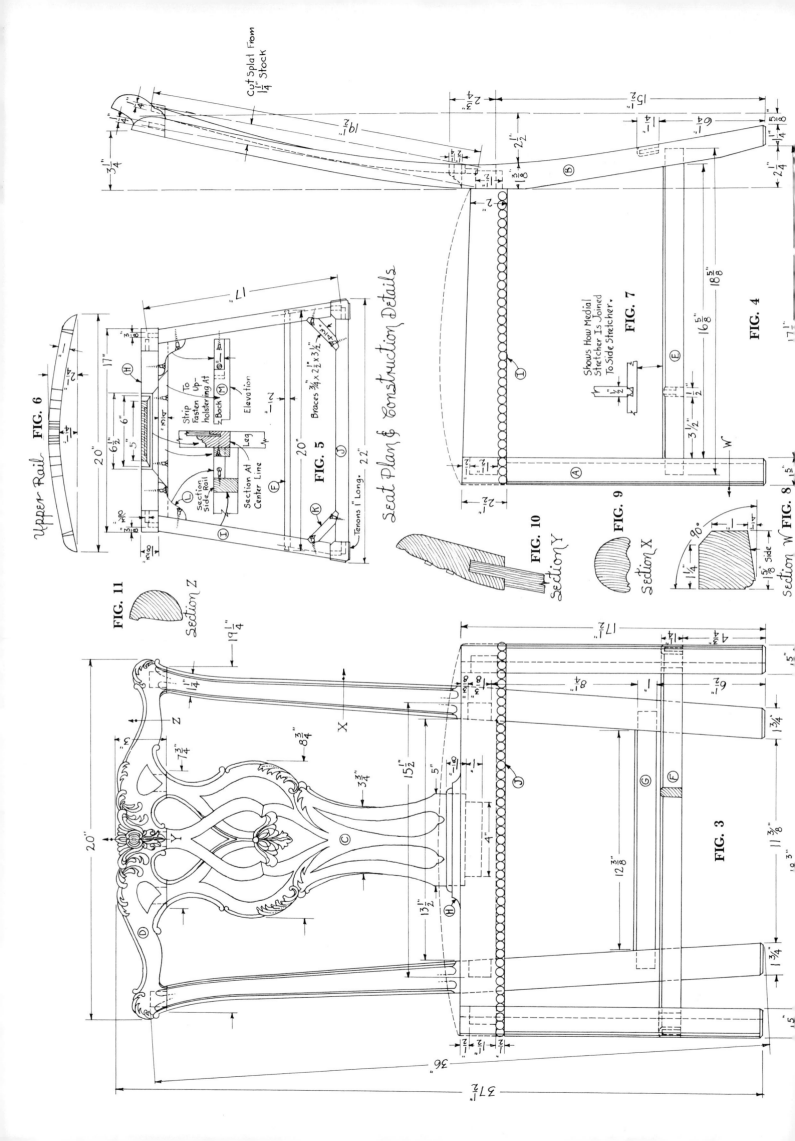

Cut Splat From 1 1/4" Stock

FIG. 6 Upper Rail

Seat Plan & Construction Details

FIG. 11

Section Z

FIG. 5

FIG. 7 Shows How Medial Stretcher Is Joined To Side Stretcher.

FIG. 4

FIG. 10 Section Y

FIG. 9 Section X

FIG. 8 Section W

Section At Side Rail

Section At Center Line

Braces 3/4 x 2 1/2 x 3 1/2"

Tenons 1" Long

Strip To Fasten Upholstering At Back

Leg

Elevation

FIG. 3

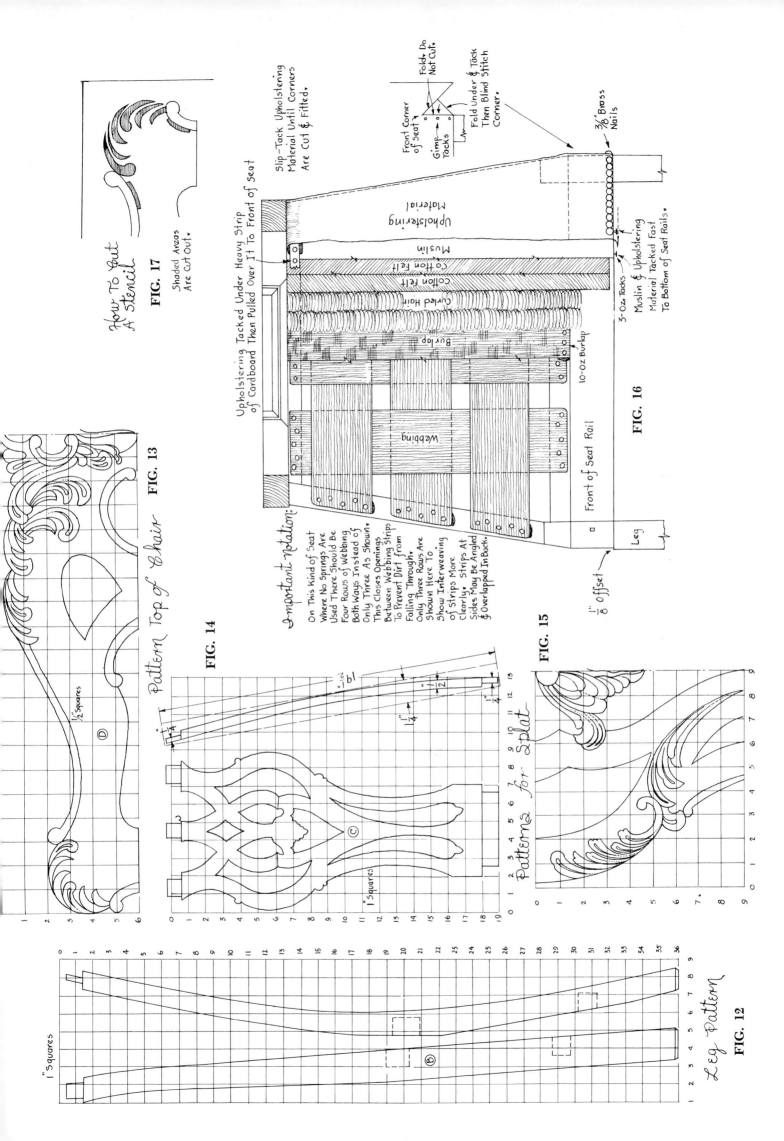

How To Cut A Stencil — **FIG. 17**

Shaded Areas Are Cut Out.

Pattern Top of Chair — **FIG. 13**

½ Squares

Pattern For Chair — **FIG. 14**

1" Squares

Patterns for Splat — **FIG. 15**

Leg Pattern — **FIG. 12**

1" Squares

FIG. 16

Slip-Tack Upholstering Material Until Corners Are Cut & Fitted.

Front Corner of Seat

Gimp Tacks

Fold Do Not Cut.

Fold Under & Tack Then Blind Stitch Corner.

Upholstering Tacked Under Heavy Strip of Cardboard Then Pulled Over It To Front of Seat

Upholstering Material

Muslin

Cotton Felt

Curled Hair

Burlap

Webbing

10-Oz Burlap

Front of Seat Rail

Leg

1⅛" Offset

⅜" Brass Nails

5-Oz. Tacks

Muslin & Upholstering Material Tacked Fast To Bottom of Seat Rails.

Important Notation:

On This Kind of Seat Where No Springs Are Used There Should Be Four Rows of Webbing Both Ways Instead of Only Three As Shown. This Closes Openings Between Webbing Strips To Prevent Dirt from Falling Through. Only Three Rows Are Shown Here To Show Interweaving of Strips More Clearly. Strips At Sides May Be Angled & Overlapped In Back.

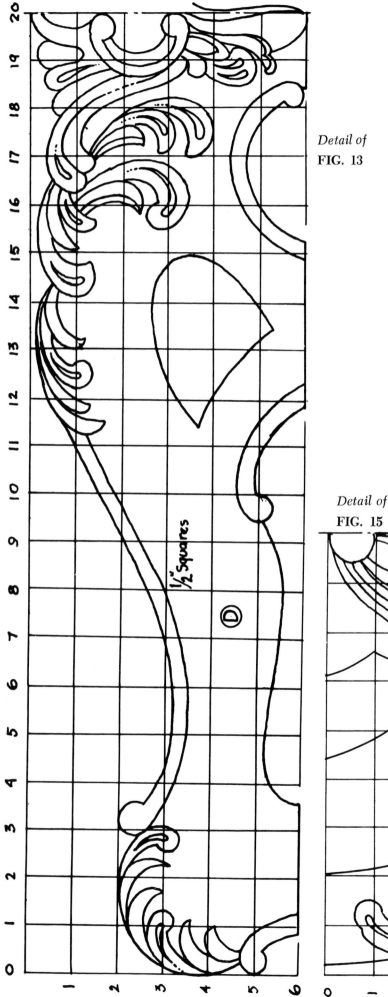

1/2 Squares

Ⓓ

Detail of
FIG. 13

adding five additional tacks to hold it. Stretch the webbing at the other end by using a webbing stretcher (shown being used in Fig. 10 in Chapter 40 on the Chippendale Wing Chair) and drive in three tacks. Then double back the end and put in five more tacks to hold it securely.

Weave four strips of webbing through the four strips already in place, tacking the webbing at the back to the top of strip (M), and bracing members (L), which have been glued to strip (M) and to the chair seat-rails. Stretch the webbing so it is taut at the front of the chair, and tack it as you did the webbing going from one side of the chair to the other.

On top of the webbing tack a sheet of good burlap. Sew the burlap to the webbing with thin strong twine. The seat may then be filled with curled hair. A less expensive filling material is sometimes substituted, like a good grade of moss or a thin layer of foam rubber. If curled hair or moss is used, it must be evenly distributed over the whole seat, and should be allowed to hang over the edges to pad the sharp corners at the top of the seat. A few loops of twine, sewing the filling material to the burlap, will help hold it in place.

A substitute for curled hair is the very good new

Detail of
FIG. 15

material, rubberized hair. On a chair seat of this kind, a very well-padded and smooth base may be made by putting a 2-inch layer of foam rubber on top of a 1-inch layer of rubberized hair, or even a 3-inch piece of foam rubber. If the seat is to be filled with these, they should be glued to the webbing. Burlap may be used, but can be dispensed with. A rubberized glue in a spray can is good for this, and the hair and foam rubber may be trimmed around the edges to give shape to the seat.

Over the filling material place two layers of 10- or 12-ounce cotton felt. This need be used only if curled hair or rubberized hair is used! It is not needed over foam rubber. On seats like this, one should use cushion cotton because it is heavier. This helps make the surface softer and smoother and helps keep dust, which may form on the inside of the seat, from coming through the cloth. Over the cotton felt stretch a sheet of first-quality muslin. The muslin is slip-tacked. Begin tacking at the centers of the seat-rails and tack toward the ends, not driving the tacks all the way into the wood until the muslin has been properly fitted over the entire seat. Three-ounce tacks may be used to tack both burlap and muslin to the chair seat. The muslin, as well as the cloth used to cover the chair, should be carefully fitted at the corners. There will be a pleat at the front corners, the cloth being folded under to keep from having a raw edge, and this edge is also blindstitched to close the corner.

While muslin, burlap, and webbing are all tacked to the top of strip (M) with tacks showing, the seat cover cannot be tacked this way, of course. In order to hide tacks with which the cover is held in place at the back of the chair, a strip of stiff cardboard is tacked over the wrong side of the cover

Fig. 2.   Enlarged View of Back.

at its rear edge, and the cover is then pulled over this to the front of the chair, as shown in Fig. 16. There must be enough cloth to be pulled into place and tacked to the bottoms of the seat-rails at the sides and front of the chair.

At the back legs the cloth is already folded under to make the finished edges where it goes around seat-rails (I) from tacking it in the manner shown. After tacking the cover to the bottoms of the seat-rails, cover the underside of the seat with a piece of black cambric to keep out the dust and to hide the bottom layers of the upholstering. The bottom edges of the seat at the sides and the front are then finished off with a neat row of ⅜-inch brass-headed upholstering nails, as shown in Fig. 1. This completes the chair.

BILL OF MATERIAL

Honduras Mahogany

2 Front legs (A) 1⅝" x 1⅝" x 17½"
2 Back legs (B) 1¾" x 3¾" x 36" *
1 Splat (C) 1¼" x 8¾" x 19½"
1 Top rail (D) ⅞" x 3" x 20" †
2 Side stretchers (E) ½" x 1¼" x 18⅝"

* Make one left and one right leg. Two legs may be cut from a single plank 6 inches wide.
† Takes stock 2⅛" x 3" x 20".

1 Medial stretcher (F) ½" x 1¼" x 20"
1 Back stretcher (G) ½" x 1¼" x 14⅜"
1 Rear seat-rail (H) 1⅜" x 2¾" x 15½"

Soft-textured Hardwood

2 Side seat-rails (I) 1¼" x 2½" x 17"
1 Front seat-rail (J) 1¼" x 2½" x 20¾"
2 Corner braces (K) ¾" x 2½" x 3½"
2 Corner braces (L) 1¼" x 2" x 4"
1 Strip inside rear seat-rail (M) ¾" x 1" x 14½"

FORTY

Chippendale Upholstered Wing Chair

A WING chair like the one shown in Fig. 1 is cozy, comfortable, and beautiful. The price of a good reproduction is high if you buy it. An authentic antique chair of the type we show here would bring a fantastic sum. The design of this chair, inspired by the finest Chippendale types, has vigorous, free-flowing curves on the wings, arms, and cabriole legs; beautifully carved feet and knees; and a generously proportioned seat and back.

The front legs are carved from heavy solid mahogany, 3 inches square, with the two extra blocks glued to the top on two sides, as shown in Fig. 4, to extend the width of the beautifully carved knees. The back legs are from a single piece of mahogany from top to bottom, and not joined to a less expensive wood under the upholstery as is sometimes the case with cheap versions or imitations of chairs of good quality. Mortise-and-tenon joints securely unite the various members, and adequate braces of iron and wood strengthen the frame. For the parts of the frame which are to be covered with upholstering materials, birch, gum, soft maple, or some other wood which is neither too soft nor too hard—so it will hold tacks well without splitting—may be used. The cloth used on the chair shown in Fig. 1 is a yellow cotton and rayon damask.

To build the chair, first get out stock for the front legs. For these use solid stock 3 inches square and 14½ inches long. Make layouts for the mortises

you must cut at the top of the leg on two adjacent sides to hold the seat stretchers, and cut these mortises. Then glue two blocks of mahogany, 2¾" x 3" x 3¼" to the same sides of the leg on which you have made the mortises, 2½ inches from the top of the leg, as shown in Fig. 4. From Fig. 5, make a full-sized pattern, and draw the outline of this pattern on one inside surface of the leg to saw it to shape on the band saw. Save the waste from sawing it the first time to tack back on the leg, so you can mark the outline and then saw the remaining two sides to shape. The leg has now been cut to shape, but being still square in section it must be shaped and rounded with a spokeshave, chisel, file, scraper blades, and sandpaper. When doing this leave the foot square at first, and round its parts only as you do the carving. In carving the foot, outline the toes and complete them after most of the ball has been formed. Horizontal lines should be drawn around

Fig. 1. Chippendale Upholstered Wing Chair. DE-SIGNED AND BUILT BY THE AUTHOR.

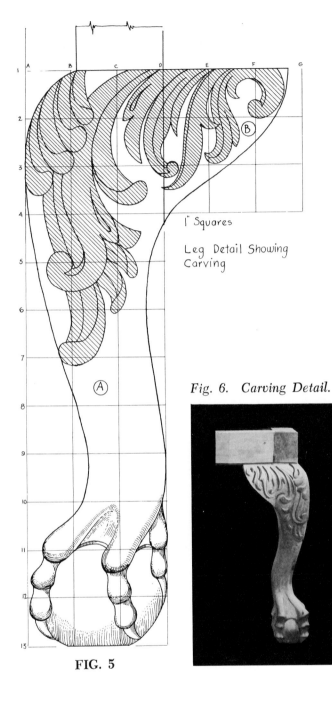

1" Squares

Leg Detail Showing
Carving

Fig. 6.   Carving Detail.

FIG. 5

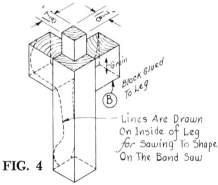

FIG. 4

the foot where toe joints are to be, before actually
shaping them. The carving on the knee requires
time and care, but it is not as difficult to carve as
the foot. Outline each leaf with a V tool, then cut
away the background, and finally model the leaves
which are shown in greater detail in Fig. 6. Fig. 5
shows a pattern which may be enlarged to carve
the knee.

Make the back legs next. Make a full-sized pattern for the side of the legs from Fig. 7. Cut two
legs from a plank of the size specified in the Bill of
Material, which can be done if the legs are marked
off side by side. After the legs have been sawed and
dressed to the proper shape, lay out and cut all
mortises. Make all stretchers for the back, these
being (D), (G), (H), and (I). Then make vertical
strips (J). Cut mortises on rails (H) and (I) to
fasten vertical strips (J) to them. Notice that the
shoulders of the tenons at the upper ends of (J)
are square, while the shoulders at the bottom must
be cut at an angle. The tenon at the bottom of (J)
is then cut perpendicular to the shoulder of the
tenon, as shown in Figs. 3 and 9. Strips (J) must be
put into the chairback in order to draw the upholstering material around them so it may be fastened to the back of the chair. When these two
vertical strips have been glued to rails (H) and
(I), the chairback consisting of legs (C), rails
(D), (G), (H), (I), and strips (J) may be glued
up.

Make the front seat-rail and glue it to the front
legs. Then make the side rails (F) and glue them
to the front and back of the chair.

Turn the arms (K) and the vertically placed,
cone-shaped cylinders fastened near the front of
the seat. Saw the arm support first to the shape
shown in Fig. 3, then to the shape shown in Fig. 2.
Save the waste from the first sawing and tack it
back on, and the second sawing will be easy to do.
Assemble, fit, and fasten the three-piece arms to
the chair.

Make and assemble the wings. Lay out full-sized
patterns for the various parts from Fig. 8. The construction of the entire frame should be easily under-
stood after studying Fig. 9.

When all the above parts have been made and
glued together, procure, fit, and fasten the metal
braces and angle irons. Mending plates, bent

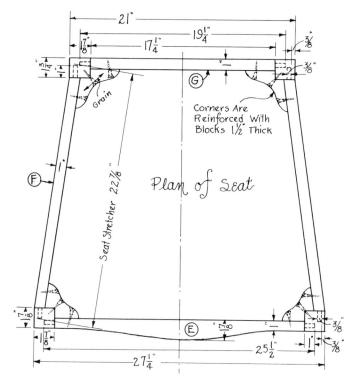

FIG. 1

corner irons, and **T** plates, which may be bought at any hardware store, may be used for this purpose, except under the arm and arm support. Here a longer piece of band iron will be needed, and it should be ¼ inch thick and an inch wide, and should be heated on a forge to shape it, as shown in Fig. 9. This brace needs to be quite strong because when a chair as heavy as this one is moved about, it is held near the front of the arms to be lifted about.

Apply all finishing materials to the lower parts of the chair before starting the upholstering. Furniture finishing is discussed in Chapter 2.

To upholster the chair, proceed as follows: tack good webbing to the bottom of the seat frame, stretching it tight with a webbing stretcher as shown in Fig. 10. Also tack webbing to the inside of the back (Fig. 13), to the inside of the arms

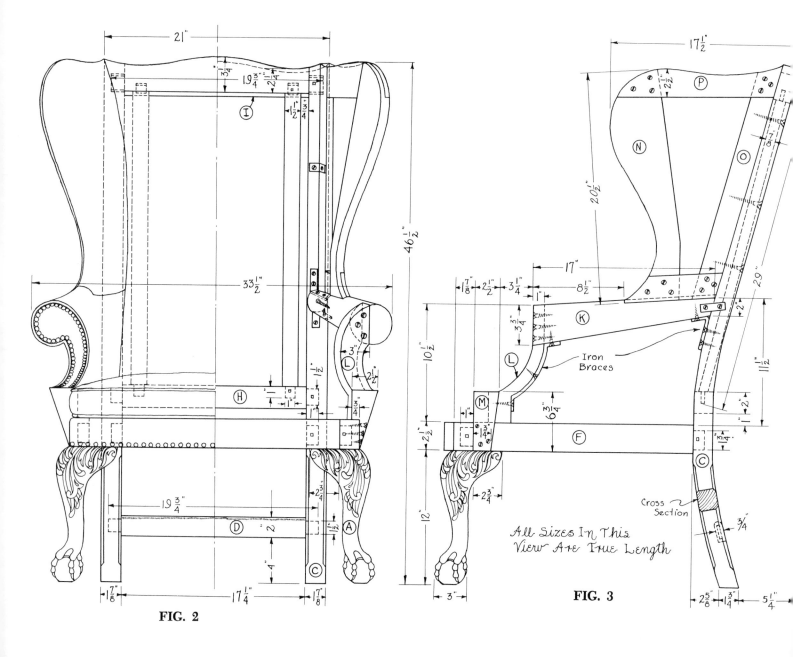

FIG. 2

FIG. 3

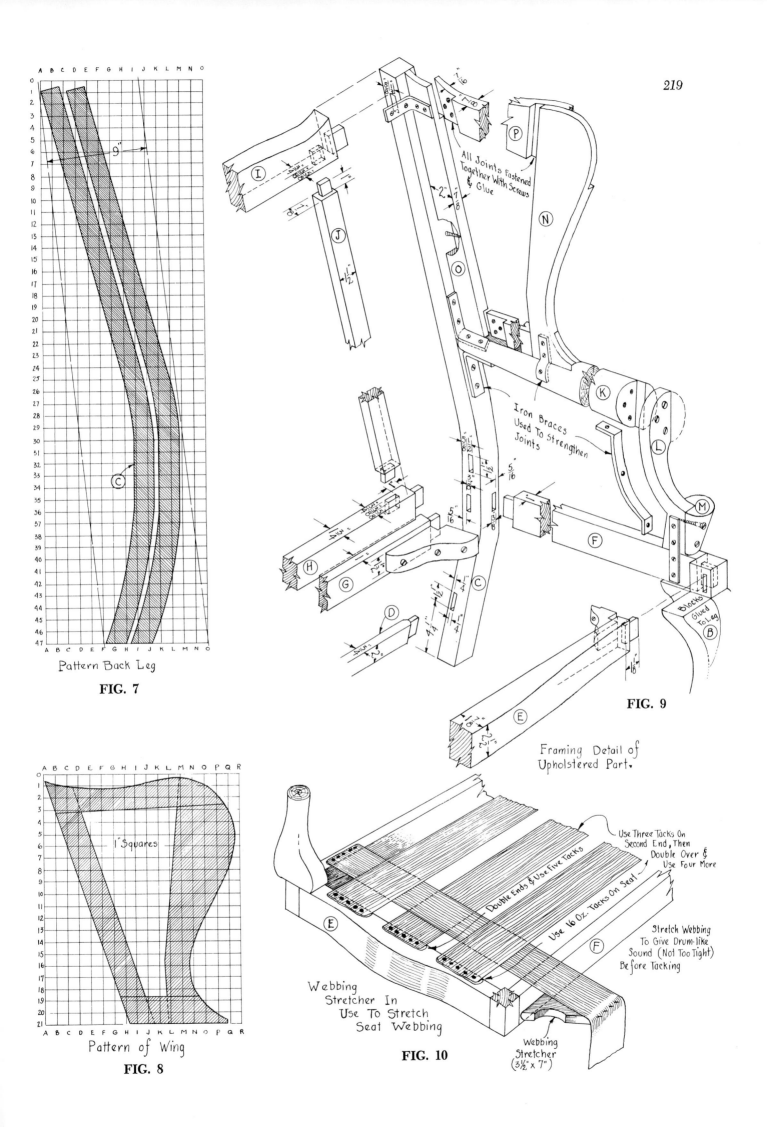

Pattern Back Leg

FIG. 7

Pattern of Wing

FIG. 8

1" Squares

All Joints Fastened Together With Screws & Glue

Iron Braces Used To Strengthen Joints

Blocks Glued To Leg

FIG. 9

Framing Detail of Upholstered Part.

Use Three Tacks On Second End, Then Double Over & Use Four More

Double Ends & Use Five Tacks

Use 16 Oz. Tacks On Seat

Stretch Webbing To Give Drum-like Sound (Not Too Tight) Before Tacking

Webbing Stretcher In Use To Stretch Seat Webbing

Webbing Stretcher (3½" x 7")

FIG. 10

(Fig. 12), and the inside of the wings. The webbing must be interwoven, stretched, and tacked as shown in the drawings. When starting, double the ends of the webbing and tack through the double thickness. Tack only one piece of webbing to the inside of the arm. Draw a piece of burlap over the arm, and a piece of webbing over the burlap. When all of the upholstering material has been placed over the inside of the arm, pull the material down over the outside of the seat stretcher and tack it (Fig. 12).

By fastening the upholstering material, muslin, and webbing to the outside of the seat stretcher, the tops of the seat stretchers are left free to tack the burlap and other covering material over the springs of the seat.

For the back of the chair, sew or staple nine 4-inch pillow springs to the webbing where the strips intersect. Sew twelve #2 broad-block coil springs to the seat webbing. Tie all seat springs eight times, as shown in Fig. 12, with upholsterer's knots. The method of tying these knots is shown in Fig. 14 in Chapter 37 on the Ladder-Back Chippendale Side Chair. In the chapters describing the other upholstered chairs in the book, the tying of springs is described more fully, and a study of the drawings and text in these chapters will be of considerable help in doing the upholstering on this chair.

Tack the twine where it says "start" in Fig. 12, leaving the short end to tie to the spring later. Proceed from the tack through the spring to the top of the far side, and from there to the second spring where it is knotted to both sides. Proceed in this manner to the spring on the opposite side of the chair, tie a knot to the inside wire, and then go through the spring to the bottom edge of the seat stretcher and tack it fast. From there go to the top of the spring, tying the twine to the part of the coil closest to the last tacking. Then tie the short end, left at "start," to the top of the spring on the opposite side from the first tie. Use this method to tie all the seat springs, pulling them down about level with the tops of the seat stretchers. The short pieces of twine on the corner springs, which are tacked to the bottoms of the seat stretchers, are put on after the long pieces are in place. Tie them to both sides of the coils on top of the springs.

The springs in the chairback are tied only two ways, to keep them from being too stiff (Fig. 13).

Cover the tied springs with about three yards of heavy burlap. Pull the burlap through the opening between the back legs and vertical strips (J) and tack it with 6-ounce tacks to the backs of the strips. Lay the filling material on the back, cover it with muslin and the remaining upholstering material, and draw these materials through the opening and tack in a similar manner. At the bottom of the back, draw the materials through the opening between the seat-rail and rail (H) and tack to the latter. Draw the upholstery materials tight at the top and tack them to the back. Cover the webbing on the arms and wings with burlap, and sew the filling to it.

After the burlap has been tacked in place, lay the chair on its back and evenly distribute a 5- or 6-inch-thick layer of moss over it. This thickness will be reduced considerably once the muslin has been stretched over the filling material. Sew long loops of twine all over the burlap. Work some of the moss into these loops to prevent it from sliding out of place. The moss is first picked (pulled apart) to form a springy mass. Do not pull all of the moss through the loops, only enough to hold the rest of the moss in place.

Pad the insides of the wings and arms in the same manner, varying the thickness of the filling from about 1 inch, or a little more, around the tops of the arms to greater thicknesses where needed. Take great care to keep the filling springy and uniform. Stretch the muslin over the filling, one surface at a time. Now stuff the seat. A stuffing regulator can be used to shift the moss after the muslin has been stretched, if this is necessary to get a smoother surface. All surfaces will be improved considerably by placing a layer of 10- or 12-ounce cotton felt over the muslin. The cotton felt helps keep dust, which may form on the inside of the chair, from coming through the cloth.

On the wing chair as in other upholstered chairs described in the book, rubberized hair and foam rubber may be used as filling material in place of curled hair or moss. If these substitutions are made, glue them to the burlap and trim them to shape as you were instructed to do on the upholstered chairs in Chapters 34 and 39.

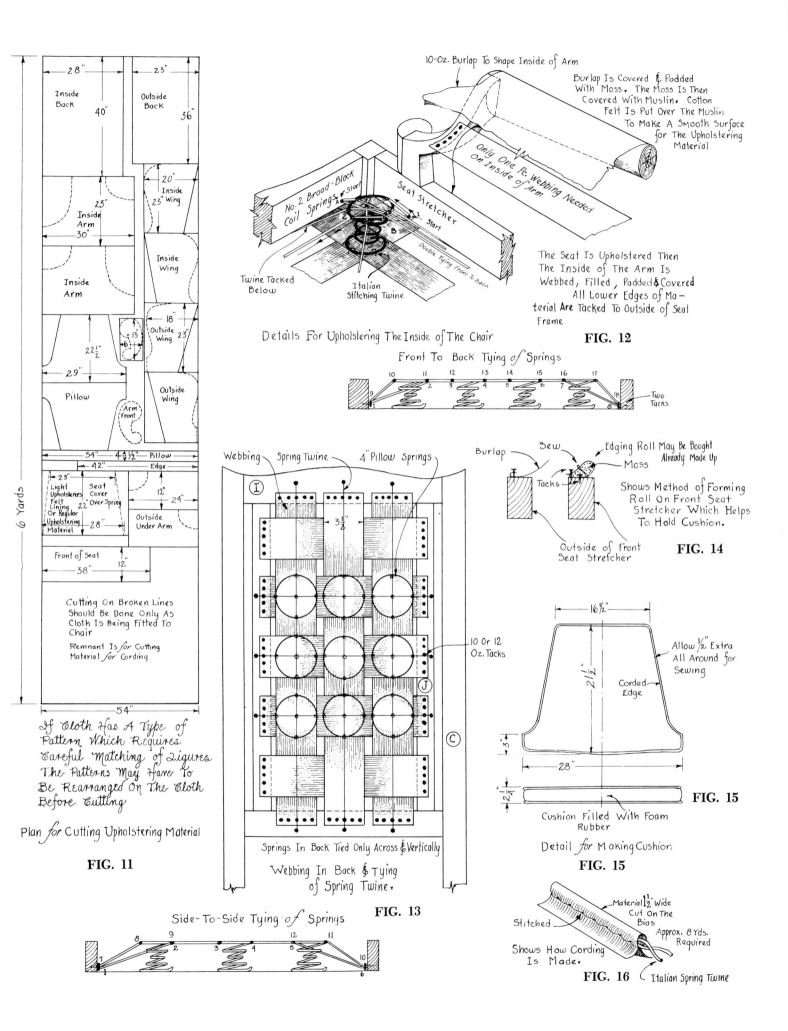

Plan for Cutting Upholstering Material

FIG. 11

Details For Upholstering The Inside of The Chair

FIG. 12

Front To Back Tying of Springs

Webbing In Back & Tying of Spring Twine

FIG. 13

Side-To-Side Tying of Springs

Shows Method of Forming Roll On Front Seat Stretcher Which Helps To Hold Cushion.

FIG. 14

Detail for Making Cushion

FIG. 15

Shows How Cording Is Made.

FIG. 16

The seat at the front has a built-up roll edge, consisting of a roll of moss encased in burlap and tacked to the top of the seat stretchers (Fig. 14). Make this roll fairly hard by sewing a running stitch along its entire length after it has been tacked in place. Since these rolls can be bought at a low cost already made up, it is hardly worth the trouble of making them yourself.

The outside of the frame, the back of the chair, the outsides of the wing frames, and the places below the arms are filled and then covered with muslin. Now the chair is ready for the upholstering material.

As shown in the diagram, Fig. 11, about six yards of 54-inch material are needed. All patterns in Fig. 11 are large enough to provide for the seams and for turning under at the edges. It will be simpler to cut all edges straight at first, leaving each piece sufficiently large to put it in its place on the chair and then mark it for cutting. With the machine, sew the inside wing piece to the piece on the inside of the arm before tacking it to the chair. Slip-tack the material to the chair; that is, do not completely drive in the tacks at first. Allow for their removal and the restretching of the cloth as the fitting progresses. Use 3-ounce tacks, and always tack from the center of the cloth toward the ends. Draw the inside wing cloth around and tack it to the outside of the wings.

Draw down and tack the material covering the inside arms to the outside of the seat stretcher. Do the same to the webbing and other covering material. Tack the material under the arms on the outside below the arm roll, then sew it to the material above it with a curved needle using the blindstitch. Fasten the cloth for the inside back to the rear of the vertical strips (J).

The cording, or piping, is made by covering Italian spring twine with upholstering material (Fig. 16). The cording starts under the arm, goes around the front outside edge of the wing, around the upper edge of the top rail at the back of the chair, down the edge of the other wing, and then on below the arm. To this cording is sewn the outside wing covering and the top edge of the material used for the outside back of the chair. Sew the blindstitch with a small curved needle. Sew the verticle edges of the cloth on the back of the chair to the outside wing material and to the other material that was drawn around from the side. Sew these seams, which are also blindstitched, as close to the edges as possible. Cord the top and bottom edges of the seat cushion (Fig. 16). Fill the seat cushion with one or two layers of foam rubber cut to the proper shape and size.

Next cut and then sew the material to the fronts of the arms. This material is folded under around its edges and blindstitched to the other material. Finish the chair with large-headed brass upholstery nails. A row of nails around the bottom of the upholstered part puts a nice finishing touch to this part of the chair.

BILL OF MATERIAL

Mahogany

2 Front legs (A) 3″ x 3″ x 14½″
4 Blocks glued to front legs (B) 2¾″ x 3″ x 3¼″
2 Back legs (C) 1⅞″ x 9″ x 48″ *
1 Rear stretcher near floor (D) ¾″ x 2″ x 19¾″

Birch, Gum, or Soft Maple

1 Front seat stretcher (E) 1⅞″ x 2½″ x 25½″
2 Side seat stretchers (F) 1″ x 2½″ x 22⅞″
1 Back seat stretcher (G) 1″ x 2½″ x 19¼″

* Both legs are cut from a single plank this size.

1 Bottom rail in back (above seat-rail) (H) 1¾″ x 2″ x 19¼″
1 Upper rail in back (I) 1¾″ x 3¼″ x 19¾″
2 Vertical strips in back (J) ⅞″ x 1½″ x 29″
2 Arms (K) 3¾″ diam. x 17″
2 Arm fronts (L) 3″ x 4¾″ x 10½″
2 Turned vertical cylinders, lower part of arms (M) 2½″ diam. x 6¾″
2 Wing fronts (N) ⅞″ x 5¼″ x 20½″
2 Wing backs (O) ⅞″ x 2″ x 22½″
2 Wing tops (P) ⅞″ x 2¾″ x 15″

Glossary

ACANTHUS LEAF. A naturalistic form of ornament of Classic derivation. Any leaf with an irregular edge. For furniture it is used in various conventionalized forms.

ADHESIVE. A substance used to attach one surface to another, such as glue or cement.

ANTIQUES. A term loosely applied to all old furniture, or to objects more than a hundred years old. So far as furniture is concerned, those pieces most worthy of being so designated are confined to periods ending with Sheraton's style in Europe and with Duncan Phyfe's in America.

APRON. A narrow strip of wood, or shaped element, such as the horizontal cross member under a tabletop, chair seat, or lowboy.

ARBOR SAW. A circular saw mounted on a revolving spindle or shaft, powered by an electric motor.

ARM SUPPORT. The member supporting the front of a chair arm.

BACKSAW. A saw used for doing fine cabinetwork, whose teeth are sharpened like the teeth of a crosscut saw but are finer (14 points to the inch). Its blade is thin, and the back of the blade is reinforced with a heavy metal strip.

BALL-AND-CLAW. A carved foot found mostly on Chippendale designs. It is a form of ornament said to have originated in China and is supposed to represent a bird's claw grasping an egg.

BAMBOO TURNING. A type of turning formed to simulate bamboo, used by Chippendale for chairs and tables. It is also sometimes found on early American Windsors.

BAND SAW. A powered sawing machine whose saw is in the form of an endless belt and is mounted on two large wheels.

BANDING. A narrow band of veneer applied around the edges of drawer fronts, doors, etc.

BAR CLAMP. A clamp whose squeezing elements are mounted on a long shaft.

BEADING, BEADS. In cabinetwork, usually a molding having a projecting convex rim.

BED BOLT. An iron bolt used to fasten the long horizontal rails to the posts of a four-poster bed.

BED BOLT COVER. A small brass ornament used to cover the head of a bed bolt.

BELT SANDER. A sanding machine on which the abrasive coating is on an endless belt running over pulleys or drums; at one point it runs over a platen with which pressure may be exerted to the surface to be worn smooth. Belt sanders, both stationary and portable types, are powered by electric motors.

BEVEL. A 45-degree angle, planed or chiseled on the edge of any surface.

BIT. Usually an auger bit used to bore holes into wood. Bits have one or more cutting lips and a screw which pulls them into the wood. A helix on the shaft removes shavings from the hole.

BIT GAUGE. A device which may be clamped to the shaft of a bit to regulate the depth of the hole being bored.

BLEACHING. Lightening the color of wood by chemical or other means.

BLIND STITCH. A stitch used in upholstering so the stitching will not show. The stitch first goes into the cloth underneath the overlapping layer whose edge, when stitched fast to it, is pulled over the top of the place where the stitch first went into the cloth, thus hiding the stitch.

BLOCKFRONT. A term applied to the unique type of construction for fronts of early American chests of drawers, chest-on-chests, highboys, and secretaries. It consists of a concave, but flattened, recession at the center and two convex, but flattened, swells on the ends. It is a type of construction supposed to have originated with John Goddard, a famous cabinetmaker of Newport, Rhode Island.

BRACE. 1. A crank-shaped tool into which an auger bit may be fastened to bore a hole. 2. A connecting member of wood or some other material used to support weight or resist pressure.

BRACKET. A supporting member found at the junction of legs and stretchers on chairs, tables, etc.

These may be plain, carved, or pierced.

BREAD-MIXING TABLE. A Pennsylvania-German type used to knead dough and hold it while rising.

BROCADE. A type of woven upholstering material in which the design is raised and resembles fine Chinese embroidery.

BURLAP. A material used in upholstering to hold the filling. It is woven from jute yarn and produced mostly in India.

BURNISHING TOOL. A short oval-shaped rod of case-hardened steel, mounted on a handle and used to turn the sharpened edge of a steel wood-scraper blade.

BUTT JOINT. The term refers to a joint on which the squared end of one member is butted against the side or end of another member.

CABINET. A piece of furniture having compartments such as drawers, shelves, or other divisions built into a case.

CABRIOLE LEG. A cyma-curved leg that swells outward at the knee, and turns inward at the ankle. It is found principally on Chippendale, Queen Anne, and Louis XV furniture.

CALIPERS. A measuring instrument with two jaws which are used to measure diameters, or distances between two surfaces. There are two kinds: outside and inside calipers.

CAMBRIC. For upholstering, an inexpensive cotton fabric which resembles a fine linen fabric of higher quality.

CANOPY. The frame or tester over a high four-poster bedstead, with or without its covering material.

CANTED. Set at an angle.

CARCASS. The frame or body of a piece of cabinet furniture.

CARRIAGE BOLT. A bolt with a thin dome-shaped head.

CARVE. To sculpture, shape, or form by cutting with chisels or knife.

CARVING IN THE ROUND. Carving freestanding forms or objects on all sides.

CAUL. A form made of wood or metal, used with clamps to hold veneers in place on shaped surfaces while the glue sets.

C-CLAMP. A metal clamp shaped like the letter C.

CHEEK OF TENON. The wide side of a tenon.

CHEST OF DRAWERS. A piece of cabinet furniture in which the compartments are composed of drawers.

CHEST-ON-CHEST. A chest of drawers divided into two sections by a prominent horizontal molding. In most instances the upper section may be lifted off the lower section if the piece of furniture needs moving.

CHESTS. Boxlike receptacles of wood with hinged lids.

CHINESE CHIPPENDALE. A type of furniture in which the structural members were made to simulate bamboo, or with fret-carved stretchers, or with members having other Chinese characteristics.

CHIPPENDALE STYLE. Refers to the style originated by Thomas Chippendale, an English cabinet-maker, and one of the four most famous designers of furniture of the eighteenth century.

CHUCK. 1. An attachment for a machine, used to hold the piece being worked. Adjustable metal chucks may hold drills or pieces of metal. 2. For wood turning, a wheellike disk of almost any thickness, mounted on a faceplate and having a recess cut into its center on one side. Work to be turned is held in this recessed area by a friction fit.

CIRCULAR SAW. 1. A circular disk of steel having saw-teeth around its perimeter. 2. A machine on which such a saw is mounted.

CLAW-AND-BALL. Same as ball-and-claw.

CLEAT. A narrow strip of wood joined to another piece to provide added strength or finish to the member.

CLOCK DIAL. The face of a clock on which time is measured by graduations and a pointer.

CLOSED COAT, OR "CLOSEDKOTE." Backings of paper or cloth on which abrasives are packed closely together.

COCK BEAD. A narrow, raised beading surrounding the edge of a veneered surface as a form of protection and finish.

COLONNETTE. A column in miniature.

COLUMN. A round shaft or pillar, usually having a capital and a base.

COMPASS. An instrument for describing or drawing a circle.

CONTACT CEMENT. An adhesive with a neoprene rubber base that bonds two surfaces, to which it is applied, together on contact, without the use of pressure to accomplish this.

COPED JOINT. One in which the end of a wood molding is shaped so it will conform to and fit over the molded shape of another molding to which it is to be joined.

COPING SAW. A saw having a thin and narrow blade, held in a U-shaped frame under tension to cut intricate patterns in wood.

CORDING. A cord around which upholstering material is stitched. It is used as trim, or to round sharp edges on upholstered chairs.

CORE STOCK. The center of a plywood panel, or base to which veneer is glued.

CORNER CUPBOARD. A cupboard which is triangular in plan, so made to be placed in the corner of a room.

CORRUGATED FASTENER. A small piece of sheet steel used to fasten two pieces of wood together. Its sides have been shaped into equally spaced curved ridges and hollows, and one end of these ground to a chisellike edge so it may be hammered into the wood.

COVE. The concave section of a molding or some other object.

CROSSCUT FENCE. The adjustable metal bar or strip mounted on a table saw to hold and guide a board or other piece of wood while it is being pushed across the saw to cut it to various lengths.

CROSSCUT SAW. A saw used to cut wood across the grain. Its teeth are filed at an angle in front and back and to a point at the top.

CROSS-SECTION. A cutting off at right angles to an axis of an object in order to give a more comprehensive idea of its shape, or the representation of such a cutting. Cross-sections also can be made to show two or more constituents and their relations to each other more clearly. In many instances the constituents in the representations are shaded with lines going in different directions, or with other identifying markings, to distinguish one from the other.

CROWN MOLDING. The molding found on top of a cabinet. Its shaped front is fastened at an angle to the top and sides of the cabinet.

CROW'S NEST. Two square boards joined together with four colonnettes to form the support for a piecrust or tilting tabletop.

CUP CENTER. The dead center of the lathe held in the tailstock.

CURLED HAIR. A high-grade filling material for upholstered furniture. It is manufactured for this purpose from horsetails and manes, cattle switches, and hog bristles.

CURLY MAPLE. Maple having a grain that, when finished, produces the effect of rippling water.

CURVED-BOTTOM PLANE. A hand plane having a flexible steel shoe which may be adjusted to conform to the curvature of the work being planed.

CUSPS. Those parts of a wood turning on which the curves being turned reverse their direction; sharp edges formed by exact reversal of direction in a turning.

DADO. A square groove cut across the grain of the wood.

DADO HEAD. A combination of dado saw blades, or of two dado saw blades and one or more chippers, sometimes called spacer blades. Two dado saws used alone will cut a groove $\frac{1}{4}$ inch wide. Chippers are made to cut thicknesses of $\frac{1}{16}$, $\frac{1}{8}$, $\frac{1}{4}$ inches. When chippers are used they must be placed between two saws. Grooves varying in width of $\frac{1}{8}$ inch to $1\frac{3}{16}$ inch may be cut with a dado head.

DADO SAW. A circular saw blade having both rip and crosscut teeth, designed to cut grooves $\frac{1}{8}$ inch wide. These saws vary in diameter from 6, 8, to 10 inches.

DIAMOND POINT. A wood-turning chisel having a flat blade on which the cutting end is ground at an angle of from 30° to 40° from both edges to a sharp point in the center.

DISH TOP. A round tabletop having a raised rim.

DIVIDERS. An instrument having two legs with sharp points, used for measuring or laying off distances between two points.

DOUGH TABLE. See bread-mixing table.

DOVETAIL. Part of a joint used in woodworking which resembles a dove's tail. It is in the shape of a flaring tenon, which fits into a mortise of like shape, making an interlocking joint.

DOVETAIL JOINT. A joint composed of mortises and tenons resembling a dove's tail.

DOVETAIL SAW. A small, fine-toothed, thin-bladed saw used to cut dovetail joints. The blade is about two inches wide and is reinforced on the back with a stiff metal strip.

DOWEL. A round wooden pin fitting into a hole in an adjoining piece to prevent slipping, or a long rod from which such pins are made.

DRAKE FOOT. A three-toed foot found on Queen Anne furniture.

DRAWER. A boxlike receptacle which slides in or out of a piece of furniture.

DRAWER GUIDE. A strip of wood fastened to the top or bottom of a drawer run to keep the drawer straight in its track.

DRAWER RUN. The track or support upon which a drawer rests or moves.

DRESSER. A structure having open shelves set upon a closed cupboard.

DROP FINIAL. A turned ornament fastened to the bottom edge of a lowboy or highboy apron.

DUNCAN PHYFE. See Phyfe, Duncan.

EARLY GEORGIAN. The name given to furniture design and styles of ornament developed in England from 1702, when Queen Anne came to the throne, until about 1750 in the reign of George II. The furniture is distinguished by its use of curvilinear line and contour, particularly as exemplified by the cabriole leg. Ornament, especially wood carving, was a distinguishing feature. At first mostly walnut was used, but toward the end of the period mahogany replaced it.

EARS. A term applied to the enrichment found at the ends of the upper rail on a comb-back Windsor chair.

EDGE ROLL. Made by wrapping a roll of stuffing material in a strip of burlap, muslin, or tough paper. Stitching holds the stuffing material in place. Edge roll is tacked to edges of frames to keep loose stuffing materials from working thin or coming out of place.

FACE BOARD. A board prominently exposed to view on the front of cabinetwork.

FACE SIDE. Front side.

FASCIA BOARD. A flat horizontal member, formed like a flat band or broad fillet on a building or piece of furniture. It is usually fairly broad and well defined.

FEATHERED. Describing figured grain, resembling a feather, on mahogany or other valuable wood.

FEATHEREDGE. A term applied to the edges of panels where they are thinned for joining to stiles or rails.

FILLER. A paste used to fill pores of open-grained cabinet woods. It is composed of a powdered quartz base mixed with linseed oil, turpentine, and a drying agent.

FILLET. A flat narrow band used as a connecting member for curves of moldings and turnings.

FINGER JOINT. A joint used to connect the swinging bracket, or apron, to a table frame. It is a wooden hinge resembling the fingers of both hands when they are interlocked, hence the name.

FINIAL. A turned or carved decoration used at the tops of chair posts, in the break of pediments, and similar terminations.

FLATWORK. Designs carved in wood in which the surface of the carving remains flat.

FLOCKING. Fibers made of shredded cloth or felt, applied to a surface and held there by a special adhesive to imitate a feltlike finish. It is forcefully blown on the adhesive with a flocking gun.

FLOCKING GUN. A tool used to blow shredded felt upon a surface over which a special adhesive has first been spread to hold it. A piston in a cylinder forces it from the gun with air.

FLUTING. Parallel U-shaped grooves cut into wood to secure a decorative effect.

FOAM RUBBER. A spongy, fine-textured rubber made of latex, used as a stuffing material in upholstered furniture.

FRAMING SQUARE. A measuring tool of steel, having a "blade" or "body" $1/8''$ x $2''$ x $24''$ joined at right angles to a "tongue" $1/8''$ x $1\frac{1}{2}''$ x $16''$. It gets its name from having tables of measurement stamped on its sides; they are used for laying out angles and distances on structural elements of a building like rafters, braces, etc., often referred to as "framing."

GADROON. A carved molding also known as nulling. The short flutes or reeds are sloped.

GAIN. A square U-shaped groove, like a dado, except that it does not go all the way across a board.

GAUGE. See marking gauge.

GIMP. A woven ribbon used in upholstering to cover the heads of tacks on a piece of furniture.

GIMP TACKS. Tacks having small oval-shaped heads, used to nail gimp to a frame.

GODDARD, JOHN, 1723–85. An early American cabinetmaker of Newport, Rhode Island, credited with originating the blockfront motif in American furniture design. This motif is one of the few innovations in furniture design that had not been used on European models. A grandson, John II, also became a well-known cabinetmaker 1789–1843.

GOTHIC. Furniture motifs or entire pieces derived from the Gothic style of architecture.

GOUGE. A chisel having a blade the cutting edge of which is U-shaped or in the form of a semicircle.

GRAIN. The stratification of wood fibers in a piece of wood due to annular formation of fibers and seasonal growth factors.

GRAIN LINES. Well-defined lines formed by annual growth rings in the wood.

GRANDFATHER CLOCK. A tall-case clock, the timing works of which are powered by weights.

GRANDMOTHER CLOCK. A smaller version of a grandfather clock.

GROOVE. A long narrow channel. In furniture making a square U-shaped channel running parallel to the grain is known as a groove.

GUSSET BLOCKS. Triangular-shaped blocks or pieces of wood used as braces to strengthen joints.

H, AND H-AND-L HINGES. Hardware, the members of which are in the form of those letters in the alphabet.

HALF-LAP MULTIPLE DOVETAIL JOINT. A dovetail joint in which the members do not extend all the way through the joint. Because of this they do not show on one side, for instance, in drawer construction, where they are often used.

HANDKERCHIEF TABLE. A drop-leaf table with a triangular-shaped top resembling a handkerchief folded on the bias.

HANDSCREWS. Clamps used in woodworking having two jaws of hard, tough wood. The jaws are adjusted with two threaded spindles, one at the rear end of the jaws and the other at the middle. The jaws are opened or closed by grasping the handles of the spindles in each hand and revolving the clamp.

HARDWOOD. The wood of broad-leaved trees as distinguished from that of cone-bearing trees.

HEADSTOCK. The motor and live spindle on the left end of a lathe.

HEEL OF SKEW. The part of the cutting edge on a chisel where it forms an obtuse angle with the edge of the blade.

HEPPLEWHITE STYLE. A style of furniture design attributed to George Hepplewhite, one of the four greatest English cabinetmaker-designers of the eighteenth century.

HIDE GLUE. Glue made from hides and other by-products of slaughterhouses.

HIGHBOY. A tall chest of drawers supported on high legs, or on a frame. It has a lower section wider and deeper than the upper section, and the two are separated by a fairly prominent horizontal molding which helps hold the upper section in place.

HOGARTH, WILLIAM. An English painter 1697–1764, who in his writings referred to the cyma curve, a distinguishing feature of the cabriole leg, as "the line of beauty."

INDEX HEAD. A circular disk mounted on a lathe, or the spindle of a machine, into which holes or notches are cut to indicate degrees found in a circle, and a mechanism for locking the spindle to certain positions on the disk.

INFEED TABLE. The table on the jointer, in front of the knives.

ISOMETRIC DRAWING. The representation of an object in isometric projection. Isometric drawings are built upon a framework of three lines and consist of three isometric axes. The lines form three isometric (equal measure) angles of 120° each, one line being vertical and the other two 30° above or below a horizontal line. On isometric drawings, actual lengths may be measured only on isometric lines.

JACK PLANE. The most useful all-purpose hand plane in the woodworker's kit, having a bed 14 or 15 inches long, and the means for holding a plane iron and adjusting it.

JAPAN DRIER. A drying agent for paint and other finishing materials.

JOINTER. A machine powered by an electric motor for planing lumber. It consists of a cutter head between two tables which may be adjusted up or down to regulate depth of cuts made by the cutter head.

JOINTER PLANE. A hand plane with a bed 22 to 24 inches long. It is used for leveling large surfaces and for straightening edges of boards to make a glue joint.

KEEPERS. A clasp of brass or iron used to hold two sections of a large dining table together.

KERF. The width of cut made by a saw.

KNEADING TROUGH. See bread-mixing table.

KNEE. The upper part of a cabriole leg which swells outward from the frame.

LACQUER. A synthetic organic finishing material that dries by evaporation of volatile constituents.

LADDER-BACK CHAIR. A chair on which the back consists of a number of horizontal slats resembling a ladder.

LATHE. A machine for turning wood, metal, or other materials.

LIP MOLD. A quarter-round molding surrounding the edges of drawer fronts and used to prevent dust from entering the drawer opening.

LOW RELIEF. Modeled carving on which the background is lowered not more than ⅛ inch.

LOWBOY. A term of American derivation, designating a dressing table or a side table resembling the lower section of a highboy, but not made as tall. Lowboys were made in the William-and-Mary, Queen Anne, and Chippendale styles. They were rectangular in form. Distinguishing features were the valanced apron and unique arrangement of the drawers. In most cases there was a long drawer over three smaller drawers, of which the two on the outside were deeper.

MACARONI. A term sometimes applied to wood-carving chisels whose cutting edges are formed into a square U-shape.

MAHOGANY. A tropical wood having a richly figured, somewhat open grain. It is orange red in color. It is the king of cabinet woods, medium hard; when once correctly dried, it holds its shape remarkably well. The fine grain is easily worked with edge tools and is neither too hard, too soft, nor too brittle.

MALLET. A hammer of wood or hard rubber or some other material. It has a barrel-shaped head and is used for driving some other tool, like a chisel, into wood. It is also used for striking a surface without marring it.

MAPLE. A light-colored, close-grained wood. The wood is hard and dense, and widely used in making high-grade furniture.

MARKING GAUGE. A tool that consists of a square wooden bar, or steel beam, usually about eight inches long, on which a wooden or cast-iron head or block slides. The bar is graduated in inches and fractions thereof and has a steel point or spur on one end. This is used to mark lines on a board parallel to the edge or side along which the block or head is made to slide.

MASONITE. A fiberboard made from steam-exploded wood fiber.

MEDIAL STRETCHER. A stretcher joining two other stretchers at or near the centers as a brace.

MITER. An angle cut on the end of a molding or other member, to form a joint with an intersecting member.

MITER BOX. A tool or instrument for sawing miters, especially those needed to join moldings together. In bygone years these were made of three boards nailed together in the form of a trough, into which saw cuts were made to guide the saw so it would cut several of the angles most often needed, like 90°, 45°, and perhaps a few more. Miter boxes today are made of metal and the saw may be adjusted to cut a greater variety of angles than was possible on the old wooden miter boxes.

MODELED SURFACE. Shaped or carved surface.

MORTISE. The rectangular cavity cut into a piece of lumber into which a tenon is joined.

MORTISE-AND-TENON. A joint commonly used in woodworking, consisting of a mortise, or rectangular cavity, cut into one piece of wood, and the end protruding from the shoulder near the end of another piece of wood, made to fit into the mortise.

MOSS. A stuffing material for upholstered furniture, made from hanging moss which grows on trees in Southern states. It is an air plant, and must be prepared especially for the purpose. It is a cheaper substitute for curled hair.

MUNTIN. The molding or wooden divisions between panes of glass in a door or window.

NESTED TABLES. Small light tables that can be stacked to fit below the largest one of the set. There are usually four, but, sometimes as few as two. Tops of the smaller tables are made to slide in runners fitted under the tops of the larger tables.

OAK. A hardwood extensively used in furniture making in England and America during the seventeenth century and earlier. It was to a great extent replaced by other woods, mostly because of a reduction in the scale in which furniture was built later on. Prominent grain markings characteristic of this wood make it unsuited to fine-scaled delicately detailed work. In recent years there has been some revival of its use, but its principal use in furniture making is still for inside structural elements requiring strength but which do not show on the outside.

OCCASIONAL TABLE. Tables designed for general use as the occasion arises; one suited to more than one purpose.

OFFSET SCREWDRIVER. A screwdriver designed to work in close places, having the handle at right angles to the bit which turns the screw.

OGEE. A molding with an S-shaped profile.

OIL STAIN. Stain made by dissolving oil aniline colors in turpentine, benzine, naphtha, or similar solvents. Aniline and benzine are made from coal tar, naphtha is derived from petroleum. Turpentine is an oil produced from the sap of long-leaf pines. The coloring matter in oil stains comes from a wide variety of sources.

OPEN COAT OR "OPENKOTE." Abrasive paper on which about 70 percent of the surface is covered with abrasive material.

OUTFEED TABLE. The table on the jointer over which

the wood slides after having passed over the cutter head.

PANEL. A board set in a frame. The board's surface is usually not level with the surface of the frame, though this is not always the case.

PARING CHISEL. Usually a tang chisel with a thin blade. The tang is the long, thin point at the back end of the blade by which the blade is joined to the handle.

PARTING TOOL. A double-ground-edge chisel used for cutting-off work and for making cuts to size on the lathe. The long edges on both sides of the blade are thinner than the riblike middle of the blade to reduce friction.

PATINA. A unique tinge resulting from aging, polishing, or seasoning of the surface or finish on a piece of wood. Ordinarily a natural process as the result of age.

PEDIMENT. The triangular-shaped top of a classic building. It is a motif adapted for the tops of important cabinets and secretaries. The bonnet top is also spoken of as a pediment, it being a variant of this type of superstructure.

PEMBROKE TABLE. A small light table with drop leaves. It got its name from the Countess of Pembroke who is said to have had one made to her specifications.

PERIOD FURNITURE. That which belongs to a definite style.

PHYFE, DUNCAN. The best-known early American cabinetmaker. He did outstanding work in the Sheraton and Empire styles at the beginning of the nineteenth century. His shop was in New York.

PILASTER. A flat architectural column fastened to a wall or cabinet.

PIN MEMBERS. The projecting members on the end of a board in a dovetail joint.

PINE. A widely used softwood gotten from cone-bearing evergreen trees. White pine lumber is soft, fine-textured wood, white in color when freshly planed. It fades with time to a warm yellow color, and it was and still is greatly favored as building lumber for houses and for inexpensive furniture. Because it was plentiful and easily worked, it was one of the principal woods used in early Colonial work. Yellow pine, which grows in Southern forests, has more distinct grain lines and is harder. It was not widely used as lumber for furniture.

PIPING. See cording.

PLANER. A machine for planing rough lumber smooth and flat and to exact thickness.

PLUMB. Vertical.

POLYVINYL RESIN EMULSION GLUE. A white glue that hardens when its moisture content is absorbed into the wood. It has elastic qualities which are beneficial to joints subject to dimensional changes.

POPLAR. A semihardwood used in furniture making extensively. Heartwood is olive green to pale brown; sapwood, grayish white. Easily worked with machine or hand tools, and when properly seasoned it resists warping. It is widely used for inexpensive furniture, for drawer sides and other hidden structural elements, more expensive woods being used on exposed surfaces.

PORTABLE BELT SANDER. See belt sander.

PROPORTION. The comparative relation of one element to another, such as the ratio of the length to the width of an object.

PROTRACTOR. A semicircular instrument having gradations marked on one side for measuring the number of degrees in an angle.

PUMICE STONE. A volcanic glass, ground into fine powders for rubbing down furniture finishes. It comes in grades F, FF, FFF, and FFFF. FFF is best for most rubbing jobs.

QUARTER COLUMN. The fourth of a column split lengthwise so its top and bottom are quadrants.

QUEEN ANNE STYLE. A style named after Queen Anne of England who reigned from 1702 to 1714. It followed the William and Mary Style. Distinguishing features were slender cyma-curved cabriole legs, chairbacks generously curved to fit the human back, and walnut wood used to the exclusion of almost all other kinds, especially during the beginning of the period.

RABBET. A groove or step cut on the edge of a board.

RADIAL ARM SAW. An electrically powered circular saw mounted on an arm that can be rotated on an axis to make angle cuts. The motor and saw are mounted on a yoke, so it can be tilted for angle cuts. A big advantage in using this machine is that with it large pieces of work can be held stationary while the saw blade is moved through the work.

RAIL. Narrow horizontal members of a frame; a structural member or support extending from one vertical member to another.

RATTAIL HINGE. A hinge made of iron which has a tail resembling a rat's.

REEDING. A carved ornament found on chair legs, stretchers, or columns, composed of convex molds resembling a bunch of reeds tied together.

RELIEF CARVING. A form of ornament in which the figure is put in relief by lowering the background and also shaping the design itself.

RETURN MOLDING. A molding running from the front to the rear of a cabinet.

REVERSE CURVE. A cyma curve—one which turns in the opposite direction from its beginning.

RIP FENCE. The guiding member on a circular saw, used to regulate the width of cut when ripping lumber lengthwise. It is a straight bar, usually several inches high and usually about as long as the table of the machine on which it is used.

RIPSAW. The saw used to cut a piece of lumber lengthwise. Ripsaw teeth are filed straight across, so that each tooth chisels or planes the wood to remove it.

ROLL EDGE. A method of upholstering the front of a chair seat to form a large roll which prevents the cushion from slipping forward.

ROSETTE. A medallion carved with a flower ornament.

ROUNDNOSE. A chisel with a flat blade, the sharpened end of which is ground to a semicircular shape. Roundnose chisels are used mostly for wood turning.

ROUTER PLANE. A two-handled hand plane used for removing wood between two sawed or chiseled edges to make dadoes or grooves. The cutting edge of the blade is set at an angle to the stem clamped to the adjusting screw which raises or lowers it. Blades are ¼ inch and ⅜ inch wide.

RUBBERIZED HAIR. A spongy rubber furniture stuffing material made from latex. It has a rough surface and when used is usually covered with cotton felt before the covering material is put on.

RUBBING OIL. A paraffin oil used with powdered pumice stone for rubbing down final coats of furniture finishes.

RULE JOINT. The joint on table leaves in which a cove molding on one leaf slips over a quarter-round molding on the other. This construction prevents an open space when the leaf is dropped.

SADDLE SEAT. A dipped seat, or in other words one that is hollowed in the center.

SAW KERF. See kerf.

SAWHORSE. A rack on which wood is laid for sawing by hand.

SCALE DRAWING. A working drawing on which a fraction of an inch represents an inch or a foot.

SCALE MODEL. A small replica of a larger object on which each part is reduced in size in the same proportion as the whole.

SCRATCH CARVING. Carving in which the figure is formed by lightly incised lines.

SCRATCH STOCK. A tool resembling a marking gauge, but on which the spur is sharpened to a chisel point and used to scrape out narrow grooves in wood.

SCRIBER. A small tempered-steel shaft, ground to a fine point at one end and fitted to a handle. It is used to mark off fine lines on wood or metal. A scratch awl.

SCROLL. A spiral or convoluted form in ornamental design resembling the rolled end of a parchment scroll.

SCROLLWORK. Fancy designs in wood in which interrelated curves are an important element.

SEALER. Wood-finishing materials thinned with solvents so they penetrate the wood and harden the surface to resist penetration of succeeding coats of finishing material. Sealers also "tie down" stains and fillers and prevent them from being absorbed into subsequently applied finishing coats.

SHAPER. A machine for cutting moldings to shape.

SHELL ORNAMENT. Carved ornament resembling various seashells, found especially on Queen Anne, Chippendale, Louis XIV, and Louis XV furniture.

SHELL TOP. Refers to the ceiling of china cabinets which were carved to resemble cockleshells.

SHELLAC. A finishing material made from processed lac mixed with alcohol. Lac is a resinous substance secreted by a scale insect to cover its eggs on twigs of trees in India.

SHERATON, THOMAS. The last of the great English furniture designers. Many authorities consider him the greatest of them all.

SHOULDER OF TENON. The rear end wall of one or more sides of a tenon, and perpendicular to its sides.

SIDE CHAIR. A chair without arms.

SILEX WOOD FILLER. A powder ground from crushed flint or quartz and mixed with an oil-base thinner for filling pores of open-grained wood.

SKEW CHISEL. A chisel on which the cutting edge is ground to an angle to the edges of the blade.

SLIDING BOLT. A door fastener consisting of a metal

housing from the end of which a rod may be slid into the socket of an adjoining member to hold the door in place.

SLIDING T-BEVEL. A steel blade held in a handle with a thumbscrew, so it may be rotated to lay out angle lines on wood.

SLIP FEATHER. A triangular-shaped spline used to reinforce the miter joint of a picture or mirror frame.

SLIP SEAT. An upholstered seat slipped into a rabbet in the chair-seat frame.

SLIP TACK. The temporary tacking fast of upholstering material by driving tacks only partway into the wood, so they may be moved in order better to adjust the position of the cloth.

SLOYD KNIFE. A thin-bladed knife with a short fixed blade in the handle, used for carving.

SNAKE FOOT. Properly a snakehead foot, from its resemblance to the head of a serpent.

SOCKET FIRMER CHISEL. One in which the handle is fastened into the cone-shaped socket of the blade.

SOFT-TEXTURED CABINET WOOD. Wood, the fibers of which are soft enough to offer little resistance to the cutting action of a plane or other edge tools.

SPACER. The chipper blade of a dado head, so called because its thickness is a factor in determining the width of the cut.

SPINDLE. 1. A horizontal or vertical axle revolving on pin or pivot ends in a machine. It holds cutting tools and transfers motion from the power source to the tool. 2. A light shaftlike turning, or other long, thin stick of wood, used in chair construction or on other pieces of furniture.

SPINDLE SHAPER. A machine in which the cutter or shaping tool is fastened to a spindle revolving at high speed.

SPLAT. The vertical central member in a chairback, so called if it is a single piece.

SPLAT BACK. A chair having a splat in its back.

SPLINE. A thin piece of wood glued into grooves for joining two members together and to strengthen the joint, especially the ends of a mitered joint.

SPLINED MITER JOINT. A joint reinforced with a spline.

SPOKESHAVE. A two-handled tool used to plane sticks of wood to cylindrical shape, or to round sharp corners. It usually has an iron body and its bottom, from which the blade protrudes, is very short so it may smooth curves too small for a circular plane.

SPRING SEAT. The seat of a chair or sofa in which the stuffing and upholstering material is supported on a network of springs fastened to a frame.

SPRING TWINE. A strong twine usually made from twisted jute fiber and used for tying springs on upholstered furniture.

SPUR CENTER. The short tapered shaft fitted into a tapered socket in the headstock of a lathe to hold spindles for turning. Sharp spurs on the end of the spur center are hammered into the stock to spin it when the motor turns.

SPUR OF GAUGE. The steel pin fastened to the beam of a gauge to do the marking.

STAIN. A coloring agent that penetrates wood fiber to color it.

STEAMING. Exposure of lumber to steam for a certain length of time so that it may be bent.

STENCIL. A pattern, usually made of cardboard or similar material, sections of which are cut out so the lines of the pattern may be transferred to the wood with a pencil.

STILE. The vertical member of a frame enclosing panels in a door, or the vertical member of some other type of furniture framework.

STRAIGHT-EDGE. A thin, flat rod or bar of steel, wood, or plastic material, one of the long edges of which is perfectly straight. It is used to lay out straight lines on wood, to test surfaces for flatness, and to line up two or more members when assembling them.

STRAPWORK. Carved ornament resembling interlaced straps.

STRETCHER. Any turned, straight, or curved horizontal bracing member on a chair, table, or cabinet frame.

SURFACE PLANER. See planer.

TABLE SAW. A power saw having a heavy cast-iron base to which an iron table with a smooth level surface is fastened. An electric motor with an arbor on which saws can be mounted is affixed to the base under the table. The saw protrudes through a slot in a removable plate set into the tabletop. The saw may be raised or lowered, and either the saw or the table may be tilted to saw at an angle. The tabletop is fitted with movable bars of wood or iron, known as fences. These hold or regulate the wood in its proper position to be cut.

"TACK RAG." A rag for wiping dust-free a surface about to receive another coat of finish. It is usually made of cheesecloth saturated with water, turpentine, and varnish, to make it just sticky enough to pick up dust or lint from a surface over which it is wiped. It is not wet enough to deposit moisture.

TAIL MEMBER. In dovetailing, the angled tenon that fits into the socket of like shape and size cut into another piece of wood to which it is to be joined.

TAILSTOCK. The movable casting which may be clamped to a lathe bed by means of a lever any place between the headstock and the end of the lathe. It holds the dead center, which is a short tapered shaft fitted into a socket in the end of the hollow spindle moved back and forth by a handwheel fastened to an adjusting screw, to hold one end of the piece to be turned.

TALL CLOCK. See grandfather clock.

TANG CHISEL. A chisel whose blade is fastened to the chisel handle with a naillike tapered shaft.

TAPESTRY. A woven upholstery material.

TEAK. A hardwood native to India and the islands of the East Indies. It resembles walnut in color and grain, though it has more of a tawny yellowish tinge. Silicates and minerals drawn into the wood dull ordinary edge tools very quickly, and knives tipped with carbide must be used to work it. It is a very durable wood because of its oily composition.

TENON. The male member of a mortise-and-tenon joint.

THROUGH DOVETAIL. A dovetail joint in which the ends of the tails and the ends of the pins are exposed after the joint has been assembled, because their length equals the thickness of the board to which they are joined.

THUMBNAIL MOLDING. A molding whose shape resembles the end of a thumb. A refinement of the quarter round.

TILT-TOP TABLE. A small round table, the top of which may be tilted to a vertical position.

TOE OF SKEW. The acute-angled point of a chisel.

TONGUE AND GROOVE. A joint cut on edges of boards, consisting of a channel or groove on the edge of one board and a rib on the edge of another, which fits into the groove.

TOWNSEND. The surname of a family of famous New England cabinetmakers who worked in New-

port, Rhode Island. They were related to the Goddards by marriage and carried on their work in the same tradition.

TRACERY. Decorative openwork of Gothic architecture, or carving which bears some resemblance to it.

TRIAL ASSEMBLY. Assembly of structural elements in cabinetwork for the purpose of determining how well the pieces fit together.

TRIFID. The three-toed carved animal foot with two weblike clefts between them carved on some Queen Anne furniture.

TRIGLYPH. A block or tablet used as a decorative element on the frieze of the Doric order. It had three vertical angular-shaped grooves cut into it. On furniture, ornament incised or carved in relief and arranged in groups of three as decorations on early chests, cabinets, etc.

TRY SQUARE. A small square consisting of a handle fastened to a blade at right angles. The blade is 6, 8, or 10 inches long. It is used for testing squareness of lumber or squareness of work being assembled.

TRY-AND-MITER SQUARE. A try square on which the handle, where it is fastened to the blade, is slanted to an angle of 45°, so it may be used to lay out or test 45° angles.

TURNING SQUARE. A piece of stock, square in section crossways, used for making spindle turnings, such as legs, stretchers, etc.

UPHOLSTERY. The work of the upholsterer, or the materials used to do the work.

VARNISH. A liquid preparation, or transparent coating, that dries when spread over the surface of wood and forms a hard lustrous surface. Varnish is made from copal gum dissolved in linseed oil. A good varnish suitable for furniture should be transparent, dry hard, resist heat and moisture. It should be tough enough to withstand a great deal of wear over a long period of time.

V-CUTS. Incising cuts made with a V-shaped carving chisel. In spindle turning, incising cuts made with the toe of a skew chisel.

VENEER. Usually made of a thin layer of beautifully grained wood, applied with glue to a core stock of softwood or laminated stock. Veneer of extra fine quality runs from a thickness of $\frac{1}{28}$ of an inch to thicker sizes. It is generally cut in sheets from the outside of a log by rotating the log, which has first been soaked in water, in a giant lathe. Various figured effects are secured by slicing it from the butt end of a log, or from the sides of the log.

VIBRATING SANDER. A lightweight finish-sanding machine. On the bottom is an orbital or an oscillating shoe to which abrasive paper may be clamped. When the motor is turned on the sander is moved back and forth over the surface in the direction of the grain of the wood. Mostly fine-grit papers are used in these machines. The oscillating type may also be fitted with felt pads for rubbing down furniture with pumice stone.

VISE. A device having jaws to hold stock which is to be worked on, and a screw and lever for tightening or loosening the jaws. The vise is usually attached to the left end on one side of the workbench.

V-TOOL. A wood-carving chisel having a blade with two sides, joined together in the form of a V.

WALNUT. A hard cabinet wood, chocolate brown in color. It is tough, dense, durable, and very strong in comparison to its weight. It is used to make furniture of the highest quality.

WARP. Curved as opposed to being flat; bent out of shape.

"WASH COAT." A greatly "watered"-down sealer or surface coating, diluted with a thinning agent. The purpose of using a wash coat is usually to hold down stain or coloring matter and prevent it from bleeding through into subsequent finish coats.

WATER STAIN. Made by mixing dry powders with water. They come in a variety of colors and are inexpensive, but tend to raise the grain, especially when brushed on.

WEBBED FOOT. A foot used in the Queen Anne style on the bottom of cabriole legs. It has three toes with simulated webs carved in the grooves separating the toes.

WEBBING. A tough banding made of jute fiber used to support coil springs in upholstered furniture.

WEBBING STRETCHER. A short piece of wood about 3 inches wide and 6 inches long, into one end of which nails with pointed ends have been driven. The pointed ends of the nails are hooked into the webbing and, when used as a lever with the opposite end placed against the seat frame, it can be made to stretch the webbing prior to tacking it to the frame.

WIND. The warping of a board on an angle from corner to opposite corner.

WINDSOR CHAIR. A light chair composed of slender turned spindles.

WING CHAIR. An upholstered armchair with wings on each side. These were originally intended to ward off drafts of cold air.

WIRE EDGE. The turned up, paper-thin edge of a plane blade, turned up as a result of whetting it on the oilstone.

WROUGHT IRON. The iron from which early American hardware was made. It is a malleable iron, easily worked on the forge.

Index

INDEX